THANK GOD IT'S WEDNESDAY:

An American Family in Saudi Arabia

Maralyn G. Doyle

DEDICATION

To family and friends who saved all my letters,
Aldene Gordon, Kendra Gordon Cooper,
Dale Gordon, John and Alice Doyle, and especially my
old friend and teacher, Dr. Edward A. Hacker, whose
encouragement and hard work made this book possible.

TABLE OF CONTENTS

FOREWORD

What is it like for an American family to live in a country where the possession of a Bible can result in a prison term, where women are not allowed to drive or even to ride a bicycle, where the weekend starts on Thursday and tomorrow starts at sunset, where men with long hair can be seized by religious police and given a haircut? It is a country where there are sea snakes a hundred times more deadly than a king cobra, where the bite of a fly can cause a life long illness, where cockroaches are three inches long, and where the temperature can be as low as 12°F and as high as 125°F.

Over four years, Maralyn and John (Jack) Doyle and their son Alex became intimately acquainted with that experience. The country is the Kingdom of Saudi Arabia, and this book is a record of their daily life in this Islamic culture. It is told by the letters Maralyn wrote to her family and friends over a period of four years: 1973 to 1977.

That was thirty years ago, and the kingdom has changed, but the change has been physical, not cultural. Now there are four-lane highways where there had been dirt roads or no roads at all. And now there are Holiday Inns, shopping centers, and high-rise apartment complexes, where there had been quaint market places, small shops, and scattered mud-brick houses. However, the culture has not changed. Women still can't drive, work with men, or travel without the express approval of a male guardian. They still must cover their heads and wear floor length cloaks that shroud their bodies. Bibles and all Christian symbols are still forbidden, as well as alcohol, pork, and gambling. Hands are still cut off for stealing, and people are still beheaded for more serious crimes. The face of the kingdom has changed, but not its heart. It is still the Saudi Arabia of thirty years ago: conservative, puritanical, and completely bereft of civil liberties.

What is it like to live in such a country, especially for a woman? This book tells you. It describes incidents that are humorous and those that are frustrating—incidents that are joyful and others that are sad. Above all it describes the everyday difficulties of living in a land that is alien in both climate and culture.

My relation to this book is that of editor. I gathered the letters together, deleted the repetitious and irrelevant passages, arranged them in chronological order, and wrote the glossaries and footnotes. A quick read of the glossaries before one starts the main text is recommended, as they give a context to the places and people mentioned in Maralyn's letters. If there are any factual errors in the glossaries or footnotes, I alone am responsible for them. And I should also add that I am not an expert on Saudi Arabia or the Middle East.

I included in this book a number of Maralyn's favorite recipes, about half of them from the *Al Hasa Cookbook*, which was compiled by the wives of the American, European, and Muslim expatriates living in eastern Saudi Arabia. This cookbook was published in 1976.

Edward A. Hacker
Professor Emeritus
Northeastern University

INTRODUCTION

In August 1973 my husband Jack and I flew out of Boston's Logan Airport with Alex, our three-year-old son, a few suitcases, and three hundred pounds of airfreight. I was twenty-six and Jack was thirty-one. We were bound for Saudi Arabia.

Jack had just completed his master's degree in teaching English as a foreign language at Indiana University. At the end of his studies, he received only one job offer. It was from the College of Petroleum and Minerals in Dhahran, Saudi Arabia. Since Jack had an interest in Arab culture from his Peace Corps experiences in Libya (1966–1968), he accepted the offer.

The college, founded in the mid sixties to nurture and develop Saudi technical talent, was regarded as the MIT of the kingdom. The curriculum included a preparatory year during which the English Language Institute of the college was expected to achieve a uniform proficiency in English among the Saudi students. After successful completion of this year, the students would begin their four-year studies in engineering or business. All courses were taught in English.

Jack accepted a two-year contract at the college to teach in the English Language Institute. Our arrival just preceded the first wave of Americans and Europeans who flocked to the Middle East following the oil embargo caused by the Arab Israeli War of 1973. As oil revenues skyrocketed, the Saudi government began spending huge amounts of money on modernizing their kingdom. Inflation increased, as did the number of construction companies, like Fluor and Bechtel and later defense contractors like General Dynamics, Lockheed, Northrop, and Raytheon. However, all of these companies stood in the shadow of the Arabian American Oil Company (Aramco), which dominated the Saudi economy.

The wealth of Saudi Arabia depends on its oil, and Aramco had been in the kingdom since the 1940s. They had provided the impetus to found the College of Petroleum and Minerals (CPM), which was built a mile from Aramco's headquarters and main compound located in Dhahran.

Jack grew up in Boston and graduated from Northeastern University with an English teaching degree. I met Jack at Northeastern University, where I graduated as a philosophy major. We married in 1968, following his return from Libya. I worked as a newspaper reporter and a social worker before we moved to the Indiana University. Except for this year in Indiana, I had never lived outside of New England.

In the four years we lived in Dhahran, I wrote many letters to friends and family back home. I knew it was unlikely any of them would ever visit me, so I tried to provide a complete picture of life there. I also wanted to share Alex's growing up, as well as things that happened to him that his grandparents and aunts would miss because we lived so far away. Many of these letters were saved and, in rereading, do paint a panorama of day-to-day life in a foreign culture in a rapidly developing country. They show culture differences, culture shock, and culture clash. They portray the artificial world of living in a compound and the problems of daily living in the Saudi Arabia. They give snapshots of a preschooler growing up there, his adventures in the expatriate world of the college, and in the larger world as well.

This manuscript has been assembled from letters saved by several friends and family members. They have been edited to remove redundancies or family references, and in some places, brief explanatory text was added. Some names and identifying details have been changed.

THE FIRST YEAR

September 1973 to June 1974

Richard M. Nixon: President of the United States.

Oct. 6, 1973: Arab-Israeli war, Egyptian and Syria forces attack Israel.

Oct. 17, 1973: Saudi Arabia stops shipment of oil to US for six months.

Oct. 26, 1973: The Arab-Israeli war ends.

Nov. 1, 1973: Watergate scandal starts. Leon Jaworski appointed as the new Watergate Special Prosecutor.

Nov. 11, 1973: Egypt and Israel sign a US sponsored cease-fire accord.

Dec. 17, 1973: Attack by terrorists on two planes: Pan American and Lufthansa at Rome airport. Thirty-two passengers killed, among them Americans flying to Dhahran to be with their families for Christmas.

Apr. 5, 1974: The then tallest building, World Trade Center opens in NYC (110 stories).

Aug. 9, 1974: Richard Nixon resigns presidency, Gerald Ford becomes 38th president.

CHAPTER 1

Thobes and veils, Wednesday is Friday, banned items,
religious police, ladies undergarments and Saudi students

September 10, 1973

We arrived in Saudi Arabia the evening of the eighth. Stepping off the flight in Dhahran was like walking into warm water. The humidity was unbelievable. The nights are very humid and the days dry and hot. The temperature has been over a hundred the last two days. We had no problem getting through customs, but one Britisher had all his newspapers confiscated. He looked a little steamed. They even took his *London Times*, which is sold here.

A driver asked the people who were waiting for their bags if they were going to the college. We said yes and piled into the car. The driver kept giving us funny looks and addressing Jack as "Doctor." Soon he realized that he had picked up the wrong party. He was at the airport to pick up a Dr. Hamad, and now poor Dr. Hamad was back at the airport with no one to meet him. So they made a few calls, roused a few deans, and sent somebody else after the doctor. I think Dr. Hamad was single, hence the funny looks we got.

Our two-bedroom house resides in a walled compound on the college grounds. To be admitted to the compound, you have to pass through a gatehouse checkpoint. We have in the kitchen a gas stove, a big refrigerator, and more cupboard and closet space than I can use. And it is completely outfitted with dishes, pots and pans, silverware, and utensils. The college had bread, milk, eggs, butter, and cheese in the refrigerator for us. It turned out that they expected us the following day. The living room is furnished in attractive Danish modern with an imitation Persian rug on the floor. We have two closets in our bedroom and a queen size bed, with a table and lamp on each side of it. All bedding is supplied. We are supposed to get a washing machine, a desk, and more furniture for Alex's room.

The hot water is hot, and the cold water is warm. Our toilet has the world's laziest flush, and the water leaves rust spots on the bowl. We can't drink the tap water because it is brackish, and a truck comes around in the morning to fill a five-gallon jerry can with "sweet" water. Also a truck comes around every morning to collect garbage. There are sanitation standards here.

We have a telephone, but calls must go through the college switchboard. There is a yard and I may do some gardening after I get settled. I have a wire clothesline, but no dryer. Lots of construction is going on at the college. Jack's office and classrooms are a short walk from the main campus. A small apartment is attached to our house, and a couple from Oregon, the Blairs, lives there. He is with the English Department. We just met his wife tonight. She said she could hear us through the walls, which are paper-thin.

The first night in our house, Alex told me that there was a bee on the floor. I looked and saw a two-pound cockroach.[1] I think he was rearranging the furniture. I slammed a garbage pail on top of it and screamed for Jack. He stepped on the cockroach and nearly got carried away, and then replaced the garbage can over the squashed insect. The next morning I removed the garbage pail and discovered the body covered with ants. Jack said if I left it there long enough the body would have disappeared. We haven't seen one that size since. Tonight Jack killed a small one in another part of the house. There also seem to be lots of small ants. The other day I went out, and Alex told me to close the door because I was "letting all the little buggers in." Haven't seen lizards, spiders, or anything really terrible yet.

We are trying to figure out ways to beat the high cost of groceries. Food prices are at least 50 percent over what they are in the States. I keep finding things that go crunch in the local bread. And milk is a problem. There is a dairy plant here which reconstitutes powdered milk. Their milk seems to be more palatable than the other brands, but

---

1   A slight exaggeration, but it was big—about three inches long.

that isn't saying much. They do make good yogurt. The butter is frozen and comes from Denmark.

We have to buy more food. Anyone without a car can take the morning shopping bus, which leaves the compound at 9:00 a.m. for the nearby town of Al-Khobar,[2] it returns at 11:00 a.m. There is also a bus to the souk (market) in town, two nights a week. At the other side of the souk is the Arabian Gulf.[3]

September 11, 1973

This country is hard to describe. *Real* desert—for miles and miles and miles. Little spots of green here and there where there is an embassy compound or a college housing compound. Lots of old machinery lying around. Lots of building going on. Many recently paved roads.

Al-Khobar has fabulous jewelry stores, and one can find Waterford crystal, any kind of camera, a Mercedes, Volkswagens, Christian Dior glasses frames, French perfume, underthings a la Fredericks of Hollywood, prescription drugs sold over the counter (no regulations on the sale of drugs, except for narcotics and mood drugs). There are many fabric stores and many tailors too. Most of the Arab men here wear flowing robes called thobes,[4] and they wear red-checkered cloth wrapped around their heads called gutras.[5] Heavily veiled women walk in groups on the street, where there are many beggars. In the main shopping street, a man kneels on a rug praying. The heat is indescribable. It is another world.

The temperature has been 104 to 106 degrees, but got down to ninety-eight the other day.[6] The humidity at night reaches 100 percent,

---

2   See "Al-Khobar" in glossary A.

3   More commonly called the Persian Gulf in the Western world.

4   These thobes cover the whole body down to the ankle. In the summer they are white, but in cooler weather wool thobes in dark colors may be worn. Under the thobes loose white pants called Sirwai (Sarwai) are worn.

5   The double black cord that Arab men wear around their heads to hold down the gutra is called the igal.

6   For mean temperatures and mean rainfall throughout the year in Dhahran, see "Dhahran" in glossary A.

which produces a very, very heavy fog. The condensation rolls off the roof like rain. But the days are dry. The growing season is about to begin and I will plant flowers outside. Periwinkles are said to do well here.[7]

Jack might not be teaching for a couple of weeks. They have twenty-one English teachers instead of thirty. Some textbooks haven't arrived, and they have four hundred and fifty students in the English language courses instead of four hundred as they expected. I think Jack may be putting in overtime. Nine new buildings are being erected on the jebel (hill) near here. They are all huge, and by next September the Language Institute will occupy all of the present college and the remainder of the college will move to the jebel. It's very impressive.

So far I like it. We have Alex in a nursery school two days a week. A bus comes and takes him to Aramco, about a mile away. The woman teacher has a good reputation. I am going with him for a while to get him use to riding the bus, and I want to check out the Aramco library.

The weekend here is Thursday and Friday. The Arab workweek is Saturday through Wednesday. Jack and I took a bus into Al-Khobar this morning to do some shopping in the market. I dressed in a long dark skirt and long-sleeved blouse and still got a few stares. It seems that as long as one does not dress loudly or display great amounts of skin one is safe. The women from Aramco seem to be more prone to miniskirts and sleeveless tops and jeans, which the college people say is "asking for it."

The other night we took the college taxi into town. They have a taxi service. We had to take a local taxi back. The local taxi driver had fake fur covering his dashboard. Halfway out of town, he pulled over, got out of the car, and started to walk out into the desert. He kicked off his sandals, faced west, and began to pray. Ten minutes later he came back to the car and saying nothing drove on.[8]

---

7   Periwinkles like hot, dry weather.

8   Muslims are required to pray five times a day.

The driving here must be seen to be believed. The other night our bus was behind an asphalt truck. Since our driver wanted to make a turn about five hundred yards up the road, he stayed behind the truck. A car was approaching in the distance. Just then two cars behind our bus both began to pass us. One passed on the left and one on the right. They had to get past the bus, the asphalt truck in front of us, and back into the lane, while also avoiding the oncoming car. Somehow they did it.[9]

I haven't tried going alone to the market yet, and I'm a little nervous about attempting it. Many shopkeepers speak English. Today, thinking the meat might be less expensive, I went to a local butcher shop; the butcher didn't speak English. I ended up buying about seven pounds of lamb. He hacked at it with a cleaver. I got splattered with bone and blood and when I got home spent an hour picking over the lamb to remove the bone splinters. The butcher shops leave the meat hanging out all day in the hot sun, so it's best to get there in the morning. The egg and chicken man also speaks no English. I bought an Arabic phrase book this morning so I could at least deal with the basics of shopping.

There may be Arabic classes starting this fall, taught by a woman here who is getting her doctorate in Arab studies. I plan to take the class. There is also a possibility of working part-time in the college library. Most of the secretaries at the college are male Pakistanis.

We have a post office box at the college. It took about five days for an airmail letter from Jack's mother to reach us from New Hampshire. I still haven't found out anything about packages.

September 15, 1973

Strangely enough Jack met someone here who knows three of Jack's friends back in the States. I met a woman today who only a few weeks ago was in the same part of New Hampshire as we were.

I wish I could describe the land. It is so faded. All beige white and pale blue. The sky is quite pale. Almost never any clouds. The sand is everywhere and very fine. The plants and bushes in the compound

---

9   The driving hasn't improved much. "Saudi Arabia Has the Highest Road Accident Death Toll in the World," http://www.greenprophet.com/2010/03/saudi-arabia-death-toll-driving/.

are mostly jimson, frangipani, and oleander. There are a few palms. Even the leaves on the trees seem faded. The vastness and the emptiness are almost overwhelming. Such a feeling of solitude! The hot, dry wind whistles eerily through the electrical wires on the roadside. The faculty compound being built on the jebel is only partially landscaped and is very exposed to the elements. It is surprisingly windy here. Two-wheeled carts pulled by donkeys are everywhere. Camels are few and far between. There is a date plantation nearby. The water is full of minerals and leaves clothes feeling stiff and dirty. I bought an iron, not steam, because of the minerals in the water.

We bought a Hitachi shortwave with AM, FM, and three shortwave bands. It runs on 220 or 115 volts. We are very pleased with it. I can get classical music, news, BBC, rock from Radio Kuwait,[10] and the Voice of America.

September 16, 1973

I found out about packages. The Saudi post office is mostly concerned about packages containing alcohol, so vanilla extract, which is 12 percent alcohol, is impossible to get here. No problem with books, unless they are religiously offensive or blatantly obscene. The college picks up packages at the airport, takes care of the duty, and brings them to the college post office where the recipient who pays the duty picks them up. The best way to ship is air. Sea freight can take up to six months. It arrives about ten miles away at the port of Dammam where the recipient must go to claim his mail. Magazines by subscription aren't censored as much as the newsstand copies. When they censor they use a magic marker, and it ruins the other side of the offensive page as well.

The advantages here are good housing and free maintenance service. The phone is free, medical costs are low ($2.50 for a first visit to a gynecologist),[11] drugs are cheap, and the college pays 25 percent. The college provides bus service to nursery schools, mar-

---

10   Kuwait City, Kuwait, is about 234 miles from Dhahran.

11   In 2012 dollars, about $13.

ket, and to the beach once a week, which really makes a car unnecessary. There are no utility bills. The big disadvantage is the high cost of everything. Our food budget is half our income. And we pay income tax to the Saudi government, which equals what we pay to the American government. Double taxation! Another disadvantage is that I may not be able to work. Saudis frown on women working. If that's the case then there will be very little for me to do here. Perhaps I can do some typing for Jack's department or work part-time in the library typing cards.

Went to the market alone for the first time today, armed with a few key Arabic phrases like, "How much?" "Give me — kilos of —," "Good morning do you have any —?" At a vegetable stand I asked for one kilo of oranges. I had to repeat it. Then I not only got the oranges but a bag of about six eggplants as well. I kept saying "La!" (No!) Pointing to the eggplants. They were put back. Then I went to the Arabic speaking butcher to ask for ground lamb. He began mincing it with his knife, and I kept saying "La!" and pointing to the grinder. He said something in Arabic and ground it up for me. The trouble is when I say something to them in Arabic I don't understand their answers. I can count to ten in Arabic, but the lamb came to thirteen riyals. I'm learning Arabic numbers so I can write them down in case I don't understand what they say.

Finally I got some very lean, excellent, ground lamb. The trouble with local lamb is that it must be ground before it can be chewed. Otherwise you need a set of choppers set in concrete to bite through it. We had a roast leg the other night, and you should have seen Alex chomping down on it and yanking at the other end with both hands trying to pull it apart. All I can say about the sheep here is that surviving in this land makes them tough.

September 19, 1973

We have been very busy setting up housekeeping. I am learning to cook all over again, using the seasonal vegetables one finds at the stands. The growing season here starts about now. Farmers plant and harvest all winter. We have seen sheep and goats grazing on God-knows-what on the other side of the road from the compound. I don't know how they survive on that sandpit. This whole country is one big sandpit. Yes, I know how they survive, very poorly. There is also an oil well (#21) right across from the compound gate. Who knows, we may be living on a million dollars worth of oil.

The rice here is a little gamey. I have to wash the rice to remove husks, unidentified items, and occasional bugs. It has a flavor that the sterile packaging process must remove back in the States. It takes getting used to.

The Aramco library is quite extensive. It has all kinds of magazines, even the *New York Sunday Times*, although it's about a week late.

Alex loves nursery school. He has been there two days now. The teacher, Mrs. Leggett, has been running it for seven years and has quite a yard full of gear: a wooden train, a climbing tower, a playhouse, lots of tricycles, an outdoor drinking fountain, a tree-shaded yard, and a herd of seven rocking horses.

Jack has been saying "Thank God it's Wednesday" all day. The weekend starts tonight.[12] Tomorrow we are going to take the bus to the market, and then in the afternoon we are going to take the bus to the college beach at Half Moon Bay. On Friday the head of Jack's department is giving a shish kebab party for the whole department. On Sunday I have been invited to a faculty wives tea party by the dean's wife. He is dean of the entire college. I am uncertain what to wear, possibly a long green nylon shirtdress I have been saving for cooler weather. It is only ninety-eight today. It has been 104 to 106.

Long distance phone calls are very complicated to make and receive. Someone advised placing them from the post office in Dammam, ten miles away. If one is expecting a call here at home, it should be arranged in advance by the party calling so that the person here will be at home. We are seven hours ahead of Boston. One o'clock in the afternoon here is six in the morning in Boston.

I am taking conversational Arabic, which started today. The class meets twice a week for forty-five minutes and consists mostly of women who have married Arabs. The second forty-five minute class is written Arabic, but I didn't want to get involved in that yet. The Arabic is Levantine (spoken in Lebanon and Palestine). It is spoken a little differently

---

12   As I wrote earlier, in Saudi Arabia Thursday and Friday is the weekend.

here. It is very difficult to get material on Saudi Arabic. For Levantine Arabic we are using Defense Department manuals, which had been duplicated so many times that the "e" comes out "o." Miriam, the instructor, is getting a doctorate in Arabic. All I want to do right now is deal with the butcher and avoid getting eggplant when I want oranges.

We haven't found a bank yet. Think we will use the British Bank of the Middle East. And think also that we will keep our money in riyals. Jack says keeping it in dollars is a gamble. His salary went from $9,600 to $10,140 just since he signed his contract, because the riyal was revalued upward.[13]

I made Jack's cousin Ellie's oatmeal bread, and it came out beautifully.[14] Jack likes it.

Something is cheap here—seafood. Shrimp are large and very inexpensive. So are fish. And as you might expect, gas is cheap—twenty-five cents a gallon.[15] They don't allow diesel-powered cars into the country for some reason.

Jack has discovered the format of Arab radio programs, four to five minutes of world news, three minutes of temperatures in Europe and the Middle East in centigrade, then for two minutes they name all the pharmacies that are open twenty-four hours a day. There must be a rush on something in the middle of the night. He says it's not just Saudi Arabia, but Iraq, Kuwait, and other Arab countries.

September 23, 1973

Reports from people living here indicate that correspondence is usually not checked, that they are mainly interested in alcohol, pro-Zionist propaganda, and pornography. Someone here gets a copy of *Ms.* every month and it isn't touched.[16]

---

13   In 2012 dollars, $10,140 is about $52,485.

14   For recipe see "Ellie's Oatmeal Bread" in appendix 1.

15   In 1973 gas in the United States was about forty cents a gallon (roughly $2.07 in 2012 dollars).

16   The first issue of *MS.* magazine came out in the summer of 1972. It was founded by Gloria Steinem, a famous feminist, lecturer, and journalist of the seventies.

Days begin at sunset instead of just past midnight. So at six thirty tonight it will be tomorrow—Wednesday and not Tuesday. Our time zone is Greenwich plus three.[17] It gets dark at 6:00 p.m. on the dot, and light at what seems like 5:00 a.m. When the temperature drops down to ninety-eight, it seems positively balmy.

Jack just told me it would cost as much to mail an aerogram to the States as a letter in an envelope, since the local mail person charges the same for everything, postcard, envelope, and air letter.

September 25, 1973

My Arabic class began today. The alphabet has twenty-nine letters and about six or eight are sounds never heard in English, and a few only found in Arabic.[18] Wish we had brought our tape recorder.

A British woman married to an Iraqi told me his correspondence is monitored. In fact, the post office has become so nonchalant about it that they joke with him about it and hand him all his letters in a large manila envelope. Apparently the Saudis are concerned about agitation from other, less conservative Arab nations.[19] The previous college dean has been in jail for having too many opinions about the government. Anyway, the woman said her mail from Britain was hardly bothered at all. She thought maybe spot checks were employed once in a while.

Ramadan starts this week.[20] It is the year's biggest Moslem religious observance. It lasts a month and Jack only teaches until one instead of five p.m. and then gets a two-week vacation. We won't be travelling then because we can't really afford it. Bahrain is our nearest vacation destination, but it is relatively expensive.[21] Iran, up the Gulf, is inexpensive and has some good crafts and is a more varied land than here.

---

17   It is Greenwich minus 5 in the US (Eastern Standard Time), an eight hour difference.

18   Some say twenty-eight letters, because, since the letters of Alif and Hamze sound the same, they regard them as one. However, since they have different functions they may be distinguished.

19   The vast majority of Muslims in Saudi Arabia are Wahhabis, a very conservative Islamic sect. It is the official religion of the kingdom. See glossary B.

20   See "Ramadan" in glossary B.

21   A small island in the Persian Gulf, about sixteen miles due east of Al Khobar, which is on the eastern shore of Saudi Arabia.

This week's European edition of *Time* has Ann Margaret's cleavage modestly filled in and pages thirty-seven through forty-one are missing.[22] Piques my curiosity. I went shopping alone last night and didn't have any problems with the locals, as some other women here have had. The downtown area is known for its "rubbers." This is the slang term for men who deliberately brush or rub against women as they walk by them. Some of the new wives here weren't too well prepared for the culture. Eye contact means flirting. It invites rubbers, stares, and comments, which sometimes happen anyway. A woman must walk without looking at anyone. The Saudi women wear all black, with heavy veils. Once in a while I spot the latest high-heeled shoes under all the black. Begging is allowed in the market place, and the beggars can be very persistent. Giving of alms is part of the Moslem religion, so it is tolerated. I don't give.[23]

Jack understood he was to be paid today, so he went to the accounting office. "No, No, not today," he was told, "maybe tomorrow." Jack says it's like when somebody greets you and says, "How are you?" It is usually meaningless, and that's how "maybe tomorrow" is too.

I was promised that Jack's desk would be delivered yesterday, but it still hasn't come. Am awaiting delivery of my washer also.

September 28, 1973

Went swimming in the Arabian Gulf yesterday at the college beach at Half Moon Bay. Desert right up to the water. The Gulf is so salty it burns the eyes. Floating is effortless. Across the bay we could see the palms and lights at Aramco's beach. There were little starfish floating in the water and a few sea horses. The water was clean and about eighty degrees. The beach road passed dunes and anthill like mounds that were fifty to seventy-five feet high, a peculiar land formation that seems to typify the area. A few palms were here and there, and two camels grazed on scrubby plants in the middle of nowhere. The pipeline paralleled the road most of the way. We got

---

22   Swedish born singer and performer, born 1941. Discovered by George Burns.

23   Alms giving is one of The Five Pillars of Faith. See "Islam" glossary B.

stuck in the sand when the people we were with pulled off the road to take a picture of the camels. They were only the second and third camels I have seen since we arrived. This beach is the first thing we've come across that argues for having a car.

One day our neighbor was driving his Volkswagen bus along the road. A taxi appeared zooming across the desert towards him. It was loaded with Arabs. The neighbor figured that the taxi driver saw him. But the taxi plowed right into the back of his Volkswagen bus, causing considerable damage. Fortunately, there were no injuries. Since a policeman was standing on the corner, the Volkswagen owner thought he had an open-and-shut case. After all, he WAS on the road and the taxi driver wasn't. That is, until the taxi driver got out and went over to the policeman. They kissed and embraced like long-lost brothers united after twenty-five years. The Volkswagen driver decided his goose was cooked. As it turned out, he paid for all his own repairs. Wonder if they have no-fault insurance here.

Rumor has it if anyone is involved in an accident here both parties are jailed until one gets tired and confesses. To get a driver's license, there are no rules of the road to learn, but one has to come up with twelve signatures before a license is granted. That is the hard part.

I have been finding what may be floor sweepings in the local bread. I asked somebody to recommend a good bakery. The loaf I purchased there had black spots in it. I examined one spot and discovered what *Consumer's Report* terms an "insect part." Well, that did it for me. I am now buying frozen Pepperidge Farm Bread at one dollar a loaf.[24] The local bread is about twenty cents a loaf.

A cockroach outwitted Jack the other night. He spotted one in the fruit bowl and whopped it with his slipper. It rolled over, played dead, and as soon as Jack turned around it got up and scurried into a crack.

October 1, 1973

Jack is in town shopping tonight at 10:30 p.m., because the market bus leaves three hours later than usual due to Ramadan. I made shish kebab tonight. Marinated Australian mutton in lemon juice, olive oil,

---

24   In 2012 dollars, about $5.18.

onion, and oregano and put under the broiler with peppers, tomatoes, and onions. It was delicious. The Australian mutton has it over tough Saudi lamb.

I bought some good feta cheese at Omar's market where we buy most of our food, also some black olives and some green olives from big buckets. Fresh olives like that have a texture the canned ones lack. I am convinced I am going to be poisoned to death by some of the canned goods sold here. The tins are rusty, dented, and discolored. I try to buy as much fresh food as I can.

We are still awaiting the arrival of a desk for Jack and for our washing machine. Also promised to us are drain baskets for the kitchen sinks (big stainless steel twin sinks) and a toilet brush, which is supposed to come with the house. The toilet flushes with about as much movement as a puddle after a rainstorm. We have to fill up the wastebasket and pour it down. This is known as flushing by hand.

The cockroaches turn up in the oddest places. Found one nestled in Jack's athletic socks.

A Greek-American math professor here, Neville Dmitrios, is married to a woman from Bolivia, Serafina. They have a little girl, Alegria, who is Alex's age and is trilingual: English, Spanish, and Greek. Anyway, they are all American now. He is quite funny in a strange way. We had a wild-eyed bus driver one night who was taking the curbs quite literally and driving over them. This was greeted with jeers from the passengers who found that the bus didn't have any springs. On the way back from the market, the driver went first to the South Compound, where he rounded a bend next to the housing, stopped the bus, and backed up in order to take the curve properly. The Greek announced, "He decided not to run over the house," which was quite plausible at the time since he had already run over about everything else.

All our bus drivers are Saudi—that is the law here—and they speak practically no English. Yesterday the nursery school bus to Aramco broke down. It was backfiring at first, and the driver kept looking around like someone was shooting at him. Then the bus acted like the gas wasn't getting through. Finally, in the South Compound, it stopped forever. All the kids, including two other mothers beside myself, had to climb into a Land Rover and ride back to the North Compound. I had an awful headache by the time I got home.

October 4, 1973

I finally got hold of a list of banned items. The Saudi consulate in New York City denied the existence of such a list. The typewriter I am using, a Hermes 3000 portable, is on it. How we got it into the country, I will never know. If it gets confiscated my correspondence will come to an abrupt end. Also banned: Lord & Taylor, Corvette, Zenith, Sears, Columbia Records, anything by Frank Sinatra, Converse tennis shoes, Whirlpool, Willys-Overland, Kaiser products, RCA, and lots of others I can't recall, since I returned the list.

Another thing is giving me a headache. I have been after Housing for a week now to get a desk here for Jack. We're supposed to have one. They promised me one last Thursday, and Tuesday I called again. They said they were going to get a truck. Our neighbors, Ben and Alice Benjabril (Moroccan and American), who have two small kids and a smaller housing unit than ours have been bugging housing about their cramped quarters. Last week they wrote a letter stating, "Our house is so small that there isn't even room for a desk!" Well, yesterday a truck full of Arabs and furniture appeared and *two* desks were delivered to their home. They claim their house is now wall-to-wall furniture. I took the opportunity to warn them of the dangers of using hyperbole around here. It appears that saying, "...there isn't even room for a desk" arouses the "We'll show'em" instinct at the Housing Office.

Somebody told me that a telephone call from here to the States costs twenty-eight dollars for the first three minutes.[25] Rumor has it that censors listen to all calls from overseas. One person here complained that her Christmas call from her parents included a censor who was listening to Arab music on his radio!

The moon is quarter to half now, the nights are lovely and jewel like. The sky isn't black but a dark blue, and the stars and moon seem a delicate cream color against it. I heard a donkey braying this afternoon. What a ridiculous sound!

---

25   This would be about $145 in 2012 dollars.

Yesterday one of Jack's worst student came up to his desk after class and asked, "What does it mean when somebody say 'OH CHIT,' sir?" Everybody who hadn't left the room delayed their departure to see what he would say. Jack said, "Oh, you mean, 'Oh Shit!' That's like when you walk a mile to bring a paper to somebody, and when you get there you realize you've forgotten it, then you say, 'Oh Shit!'" Then he explained 'shit' in relation to the bathroom. He can usually smell (excuse me) when they are trying to put him on. He probably wouldn't have bothered if this fellow had been one of the better students. They tried to get him to explain what wine was the other day. He said, "Come on, you guys know what wine is!" Alcohol is forbidden here. They wanted to put him on the spot.

I opened the front door tonight and looked straight into the fleshy underbelly of a lizard clinging to the screen at eye level. Nasty shock. The outside light attracts bugs, which in turn attract lizards. God knows what lizards attract, but I hope I never meet it. Made the mistake of lifting up a corner of the carpet last night. Living there were two cockroaches, one odd black bug, and lots of ant-like things, but with big hips.

We went shopping today, and Jack spent the first hour trying to cash his paycheck. Nobody queues here. Just a mass of humanity pressed against the teller's cage, all trying to be first. Since that took an hour, we didn't get a chance to look for a watch or a birthday present for me.

Took some material to a thobe maker last Saturday. For two dollars and fifty cents he will make an ankle-length shirt-like dress with open collar and long sleeves.[26] I'll pick it up this Saturday.

October 5, 1973

We went to Ras Tanura today, the site of the biggest oil refinery in Saudi Arabia.[27] The department chairman, Harvy Woolrich, invited us and took his two children. It is about an hour from the college. We passed corrugated tin and wood villages, oases, camel herds, and a few crude two-wheeled carts pulled by donkeys. We also passed several date plantations. There seemed to be more vegetation than on

---

26   About $13 in 2012 dollars.

27   See "Ras Tanura" in glossary A.

the road to Half Moon Bay and none of the dramatic sand dunes or huge anthills. The beach was much nicer, the water a soft clear green, and warm. There were a few nine-inch waves. A row of almost perfect shells marked the high water point. They were mostly whole. It seems they don't get as battered as shells on the Atlantic coast. Along the beach were oval pieces of cuttlebone. The bone is actually the whole fish, which just fossilizes upon being washed ashore. It provides grit for birds.

On the way there we saw increasing lines of pipe heading to the refinery. They were of varying widths, but very exposed. They didn't seem to be patrolled either and seemed so vulnerable. The man we were with told us that in the vicinity there are ground-to-air missile bases and radar stations for protection.

In the distance from where we were on the beach, we could see the gray shapes of tankers loading. Took a few pictures but I doubt if the photos will show the ships, since we could barely see them. They were right on the horizon's edge.

In the distance we could see burn-offs or flares from the refinery. They just ignite the gas left over from the refining process. The oil from Saudi Arabia is "sour" (from hydrogen sulfide, I think). It has to be made "sweet" before it can leave the country. Libyan oil, on the other hand, is not sour. It has low sulfur content and is considered superior to most of the oil found in the world.

We saw a nine-inch, prehistoric looking, horned, desert lizard. He was a pale color, and his skin texture—very rough and bumpy— matched the salt-stiffened sand so well that we could only see him when he moved.

We played bridge last night with Ben and Alice, our neighbors with the cramped apartment and two desks. They have two children: Nora and Nadia. They just put money down on a Datsun sedan. They are about thirty-fifth on a waiting list for the new shipment, which is due just after Ramadan—end of October. No color choice.

Bought some pulverized Turkish coffee at Bayounis—the local coffee merchant.[28] Arab coffee is a very light roast heavily flavored with car-

---

28 The grind is very fine, finer even than espresso.

damom. The Turkish is darker (no cardamom) and is made in a long handled brass pitcher, which is held over the flame. A heaping teaspoon of the coffee added to the water with a teaspoon of sugar is brought to a foaming boil three times. The grounds settle to the bottom of the cup and are not consumed; the result is thick, turgid, and mocha brown. But with the Arab coffee the effect is like drinking a hot medicinal tea, as the coffee flavor is hardly noticeable and the cardamom is overpowering.

October 8, 1973 [Letter by Jack]

Yesterday we learned that war began between Egypt and Israel.[29] We've been listening to war reports from BBC and the Voice of America, plus our neighbors have been listening to the broadcasts in Arabic. Otherwise things here are very calm, quiet, and normal.

Sunday (a workday here) is a big day for mail. We seem to get what people in the US have mailed over the weekend or on Monday a week or so ago. Today was a beautiful dry sunny day (low seventy-three, high one hundred), and I went jogging tonight.

I took my students through the chapter on clothes, including makeup and women's underwear. It's been a trying day, and I still have a lot of work to do.

October 9, 1973

Learned that there have been two Saudi Air Force jet crashes in the vicinity, one about a kilometer from the compound. People have to stop talking when jets pass overhead. Makes me a wreck. There is no basement to run to.

Went to a meeting of the Arab Culture group a couple nights back. Saudi Arabia is the only Moslem country to have Mutawa or religious police.[30] Any Saudi Moslem caught violating the fast during Ramadan is subject to fine and/or imprisonment. There is a law that Saudi Mos-

---

29   The war was between Israel and the countries of Egypt and Syria. Israel mobilized the reserves on October 6 (morning of Yom Kippur). It is called the Ramadan War, the Yom Kippur War, and the October War. Later, when the Soviet Union threatened to enter the conflict, the UN ordered a cease-fire.

30   See "Saudi Arabia" in glossary A.

lem men must go to the mosque (if possible) to pray five times a day and that Saudi women must be veiled. The veiling is going out in most other Arab countries. Saudi women wear heavy veils and long black shawls called abayas. Some Arab men wear Western-style dress but the majority of Jack's students wear thobes. The king sets the example, and the government employees follow.

We don't know what to believe on the news concerning the war in the Middle East. The Israelis won't allow correspondents, and the Arab news reports have a history of being highly exaggerated. Every now and again we find the BBC on short wave, and they admit it is difficult to tell what's happening. I called the consulate today to inquire about registering in case of evacuation, and they sent a card to be completed. Any airlifting of Americans would be either to Iran or to Greece where the US has bases. Then the individual may decide to return or go farther away. Actually I was hoping for a trip home.

Jack had to do a chapter on ladies' clothing today in his class. Including bras, panties, nylons, and girdles. Last night as he was preparing for today he kept moaning, "Where is the censor when I need him?" He moved them through it fast, but some of the other teachers here who had to cover the same chapter got so bogged down in the ensuing uproar that they abandoned the lesson mid chapter. (One has to be here to appreciate how sensitive such a topic can be.) Jack explained everything to them, but didn't let it get out of hand. The key was apparently not to indicate that you felt that this was a particularly uncomfortable area and not to appear self-conscious.

October 10, 1973

I took the nursery school bus to Aramco with Alex and then got off and walked to the library. I spent about two hours there and then walked back to the nursery school, which is in a home. I passed lush tropical shrubs and vines, palm trees, and flowers, whose names I did not know.

Unfortunately all the good things like a beauty salon, taxi service, barbershop, commissary, ceramics shop, dark room, women's exchange, etc., are within the Aramco compound, and they have a huge central air-conditioning plant that air-conditions the homes of the employees. We can use their two libraries, their beauty salon, their dining hall with a surcharge, but not their crafts shops, their commissary, or their movie theaters. They even have their own mortician and cemetery, but if Aramco leaves Saudi Arabia, then all the bodies will have to be moved to the States, because the Saudis believe that an infidel buried in their country desecrates the ground. The bodies are placed in cement vaults and can be moved by cranes.

My Arabic is still nowhere near the point where I can even basically communicate. I can't say things like, "I will be back later" or "Close the door" or "What time is it?" I can say, "Stop," "Yes," "No." There isn't any "Hello" or "Good-bye." I can say, "I want paper" (one of those useless things I learned in Arabic class). Also "How's the family?" I can count from one to twenty, but do not always understand the numbers above ten when they are spoken to me. I can ask for various kinds of vegetables, meats, and their price, and say, "That's too much." To some extent the attempt to speak Arabic is appreciated, since so few Americans bother to try. However, it is frustrating to be answered in English.

I find my art ability, what small amount I possess, is coming to my aid in communicating. I drew a needle the other day for a shopkeeper who knew no English. It also helps in communicating with maintenance. I didn't know Arabic for "drain basket" and didn't even know if that's what they call it here in English, so I drew a picture of one and added an aerial view of a sink with an arrow indicating the drain. Also drew a toilet brush for their edification, since we were supposed to get one and didn't. Today Jack's desk finally came. Still awaiting the washing machine.

Couldn't find BBC on shortwave today, so I don't what's happening in the war.[31] I may start work next week at the library.

We went to a neighbor's house last night and had homemade beer. It was twice as strong as US beer, and though I had only three glasses, I felt sick this morning.

---

31   Arab-Israeli war.

Alex was building an airplane with his blocks. He pointed out the cockpit, the galley, the aisle, the seats, and the wings. When I inquired where the toilets were, he said, "There aren't any. They'll just have to hold it."

October 13, 1973

Last night at half past eleven we went out with a map of the heavens and tried to locate constellations, but the moon was too bright to make out anything but the brightest stars. Betelgeuse is one. And we saw the constellations of Scorpios, Sirius, Andromeda, and Pegasus. Oh yes, a neighbor, very sensible English woman, told me how she and her husband were out one night looking for constellations and noticed something whizzing across the sky towards the horizon accompanied by another similarly bright fast object. They assumed it was two satellites until they abruptly stopped and whizzed back across the horizon where they had come from. She said they suddenly began believing in flying saucers.

Did you know that Betelgeuse means in Arabic "Armpit of Orion" and the star Rigel in Orion is translated as "leg" in Arabic?

The weather is improving, and Jack is taking up tennis. I may start running again in a week or two. This lifestyle is conducive to gaining weight. Nothing to do but eat and cook. Still waiting for our washing machine to be delivered. Listening to war news on BBC, Voice of America, and Radio Kuwait. No English language newspapers available at the local bookstore and no *Time* magazine at all. The latest *Newsweek* was October 8 and had no war news.

There have been a few incidents in town against American women, but it is difficult to tell whether these are connected with the war or were just freaky occurrences. When my neighbor, a slight, attractive girl, was shopping downtown in Al-Khobar the other night, she was pinched three times on the thigh and other places (and has a bruise from it). Today two fellows on bikes hit the back and head of a teacher at the American Consulate School as she walked down the street.

I was told that in the '67 war, students rioted and marched to Aramco where they did some damage, and also visited the American Consulate. The college locked the compound gates for three days and let no one in or out. There were no attempts to bother the faculty, which consists of mixed nationalities, at least one-third being Arab. Lots of British here too.

When we returned from stargazing last night there were two fleshy-colored lizards on the wall of the house up near the eaves where the front door light shone. They were snacking on the bugs drawn by the light. It made me nervous passing under them to go into the house. I was afraid that they might fall on me.

You cannot imagine the production it is doing business with a bank here. It takes an hour to open a savings account, twenty-five to thirty minutes to cash a traveler's check, almost an hour to cash a paycheck, especially if it is a Thursday morning—the first day of the weekend—which is a busy time.

October 15, 1973 [Letter by Jack]

I went running tonight with Frank Harris, and he took me over a route through the desert that several runners here use. It's an unpaved road. Anyway, you can't beat the desert for solitude at dusk. I figure it must be some kind of class to be able to say that I jogged over the sands of Arabia. We had quite a wind here this afternoon. It is often strong, but this time it was a minor sandstorm. The local Aramco paper, which has radio and television listings, had an article on the stars. So for two nights now I have been out looking at the sky trying to make out the constellations. One problem is the compound streetlights, but a bigger problem is the full moon we've had the last few nights. Since the sky is always clear here at night, I thought it would be a good opportunity to study astronomy.

October 19, 1973

We have Radio Kuwait on right now and who knows what to believe about the war. Dean Smith is warden for US passport holders, whatever that means. We got a notice a day or two ago asking that we register with the US Consulate immediately. This is in case we have to be evacuated in a hurry. We have already registered.

The Egyptians and Syrians now claim to have shot down forty more planes than the prewar Israeli Air Force was reliably reported to have had.

The Royal Saudi Air Force is based about two miles from here. Terrific. Ras Tanura, the big oil port, is forty miles to the north, and the air force headquarters two miles to the south. I was told that in World War II that the Italian Air Force bombed Dhahran by mistake. Dhahran had about twenty people living here then. The Italians thought they were someplace else.[32]

Spent the afternoon at Half Moon Bay, swimming and picnicking. Water temperature was eighty-six degrees. Alex had a good time. A huge dune had rolled right up to the water, and we stood on the top of it making sand slides with our toes. There was a school of small silvery fish a hundred yards out. They were flinging themselves out of the water like a handful of silver coins in the sun. The dune provided the only soft sand. The rest of the beach area was a salt-encrusted flat peppered with bits of litter, flotsam, and jetsam. The shell selection was quite poor.

When we first picked a spot to put our blankets down, the guy we were with drove his Land Rover to the top of the first dune I mentioned. It overlooked the water. Below was a fiberglass boat beached against the dune and a couple embracing in the nude. I felt like a voyeur. Jack said he could imagine the guy saying to the girl, "Oh shit, don't look now but there is a Land Rover above us." They later appeared with suits on. Usually at the beach one does not see a soul for two miles in either direction. I am sure the couple from the boat chose the dune part of the beach because it offered a shield against the view from the flats area.

On the way home, we stopped at the base of a huge thirty-foot dune. It was quite steep, but we managed to climb to the top on all fours, Alex included. It was fun running down.

The food here is so flavorful. The tomatoes taste better, and the potatoes too. Produce also tends to be less perfect than produce in the States, more bad spots and bugs. I bought Danish salami yesterday and some English water biscuits, which are like round saltines without the

---

32   It was 1940. The intended target was British installations on Bahrain.

salt. Fresh shrimp are cheap and delicious. The ginger biscuits are very spicy. One can buy Devon cream (clotted cream) frozen. And all kinds of cheese.

October 22, 1973

All Alex's matchbox toys were stolen from our garden. I have been replacing them. They're cheaper here than they are in England or the States. However, here they are priced according to size, not wholesale cost.

Had Ramadan sweets at my teacher's house last night, a sweet pancake folded in half and stuffed with cheese filling, then soaked in sweet syrup. She made baklava, caramel custard (not Arab), and some Arab sugar cookies. Served Arab coffee with cardamom flavoring—black, sweet with the grounds on the bottom.

Somebody's Arab beetle collection was on exhibit at Aramco. One the size of a postcard appears to weigh about two pounds and has a rhino-like horn up front. Dreadful looking. The locusts in Saudi Arabia resemble large grasshoppers and are eaten roasted by the Bedouins. Spiders here are also quite large. Some varieties of cockroach are two to three inches with four-inch antennae. Monster movie material.

Have been cooking shrimp ninety-seven different ways since it is the cheapest form of protein in Saudi Arabia, along with eggs. So far I like my shrimp broiled best, but it is also very good sautéed in garlic butter, with parsley and lemon juice.[33]

Am about to give up on wearing contacts, because it's agony. There is almost always a dust haze, and I am taking my lenses out and washing them two and three times an hour even in the house. Microscopic particles of sand wedge under the lenses. Feels like sandpaper. There are stories about people getting corneal scratches from wearing them. Sandstorm season is May to June. Last summer a sandstorm lasted one month, the longest ever. Like a month long blizzard. People described finding little sand dunes by the crack in the doorsill, every morning.

Alex's nursery school has a Halloween party planned, and the teacher suggested that they come in costume. Imagination and mate-

---

33   For recipe see "Shrimp Marinated" in appendix 1.

rials being in short supply, I think I will send him as a sack of potatoes I will pull a pillowcase over his head and write the label on it with a magic marker.

October 23, 1973

Things are quiet here, still. Students on vacation.[34] There is an on-again-off-again cease-fire in the Middle East.

We are going to Aramco's library and dining hall tomorrow. They serve breakfast with *bacon* for a reasonable sum. Bacon is not generally imported here due to religious beliefs. Aramco has a commissary for its own employees.

October 30, 1973

Alex is outside in a ghost costume I made him (he didn't want to go as a sack of potatoes), even though it is only about 1:30 p.m. I'm sure the Arabs don't know what to make of Halloween.

I am reading a travel folder: *Introduction to Bahrain*. Bahrain is a little island nation sixteen miles off the Saudi coast in the Arabian Gulf. There's some oil there, but no way near what there is elsewhere in the area. Bahrain was called "Dilmun" in ancient times. It has a king, a desert, a mountain, and a plurality of springs, pearl diving, and a shrimp fishing industry. Their fishing boats, called dhows, are heavy looking wooden vessels with hand woven cloth sails. All over Bahrain are ruins and artifacts dating back to the Bronze and Copper Ages. The island has fallen prey to one invading force after another over the course of history, but it is now independent. It is more liberal than Saudi Arabia. They serve liquor to non-Moslems, although one must possess a license to buy a bottle. Bahrain also has a gambling casino. We plan to go there after Christmas for four or five days.

Jack found a book on the archaeology of southern Arabia, and one called *Looking for Dilmun*, by Geoffrey Bibby.

There are several restaurants in town. The Chinese restaurant is supposed to be good, but the Chinese who run it look like Filipinos.

---

34   End of Ramadan.

There is a "Turkish" restaurant, which serves Lebanese food. Passed an outdoor cafe Monday and saw two men sitting in folding chairs with five-foot-high water pipes beside them. Jack thought it smelled a lot like grass, but it was probably a local tobacco he wasn't familiar with.[35]

October 30, 1973 [Letter by Jack]

When we were leaving the States, many people thought Alex would come home speaking Arabic. He has yet to learn any or to play with any of the Arab kids (none of whom are his age). He has been playing with Neal, whose family comes from a part of England near Scotland. The other day while I'm sleeping he and Neal came into the house and the bedroom door flew open and Alex announces to Neal, "Me dod's 'ome!" Looks like he's going to get, of all things, a Scottish brogue.

November 3, 1973

There are no Christmas decorations sold here or displayed in the stores.[36] I may get a fake tree. People in the compound have decorated their trees with starfish or seashells.

It is almost midnight and the Voice of America is coming on, broadcast is from Rhodes.[37]

---

35   Grass, slang for marijuana.

36   The importation of Christmas decorations is banned in Saudi Arabia.

37   A Greek island between the Greek mainland and the island of Cyprus.

CHAPTER 2

Guy Fawkes Day—the burning man, sleeping with a mouse,
classroom cheating, Thanksgiving, the Aramco Christmas
pageant: sheep, camels, and angels, obscene phone calls

November 5, 1973

It is Jack's birthday today, and I made him a cake. He didn't want any presents, but I got a can of cashews for Alex to give to him. Birthdays are big deals for Alex. Jack just came in from running on the desert, and I have to get supper. The only way I know it is November is that it gets dark early now, about 5:00 p.m. The daily low is sixty and the high eighty. It is cooler out and I needed a sweater today. The evenings here are like Boston in mid-September.

There was a small sandstorm all day today. Sand and snowstorms are similar except that sand does not go away. It drifts and, like snow, is almost the same to drive through. Today the blowing sand obscures the jebel, and the sun is a dim disk in the sky. My glasses and face are filmed with fine dust. This is not a contact lens day. I walked out of the compound with its eight-foot walls to the administration building. It whipped my skirt about my ankles and stung my skin. The sandstorms are much worse in June. They are called shamals.[38] The wind blows out of the northwest from the inland desert towards the Gulf. They were much worse than usual this year, lasting nearly a month. People couldn't go outside, and consequently they became house-bound and depressed. It was compared to living in Alaska in the winter.

The mornings are much more pleasant. The next five months are supposed to provide the best weather Saudi Arabia has. Today Jack told

---

38   The word "shamal" means north. It often creates sandstorms and is stronger during the day than the night.

me the director of the language lab commented, "Today is quite windy and cool," to which a Saudi replied, "Yes, Saudi Arabia has the most changeable weather in the world." The director recalled that it rained four times last year with only ten overcast days. We all had a good laugh.

We get *Time* and *Newsweek* here. My November *Newsweek* was censored. One whole page in the middle of the war news was torn out and the last page removed. I discovered by reading the summary in the table of contents that the last article, which was about Princess Anne's forthcoming wedding, had some antimonarchist comments on the second page.[39] Probably censored because they don't want anyone in the kingdom to get ideas. Anything dealing with internal politics in the US is never censored. What seems to be censored is anything to do with sex or religion in which a claim is made for Jesus-Son-of-God (this just gets magic-markered to death), an Arab having an alcoholic drink, and anything to do with Saudi Arabia that is even slightly derogatory. Also of course, cleavages, anybody kissing, or sitting on someone's lap. All of this is objectionable.

The wind is still blowing hard, and I can hear the oleander scraping against the walls, the leaves rustling, and the vents on the kitchen exhaust rattling. Tomorrow night the college is showing *Pete and Tillie* for their weekly movie.[40] We are going with another couple here and pooling our kids with a sitter. This movie will be a refreshing change from Doris Day and Rock Hudson.

November 8, 1973 [Letter by Jack]

The water is ruining our clothes, so we are going to try a different soap and/or a water softener. Maralyn is fed up with having no washing machine (understatement of the year). Tomorrow night there will be a Guy Fawkes bonfire at the beach party.[41]

---

39   On November 14, 1973, Princess Anne married Mark Phillips, an officer in the Queen's Dragoon Guards.

40   A drama/comedy, starring Walter Matthau and Carol Burnett.

41   Guy Fawkes' Night (Bonfire Night, Fireworks Night) is celebrated the fifth of November in the United Kingdom and New Zealand. It is not a public holiday. It celebrates the failure of the Gunpowder Plot. Guy Fawkes is the name of the conspiracy of a group of Catholics to blow up the House of Parliament and the Protestant King James on November 5, 1605. Guy Fawkes played a principal part in this conspiracy.

November 9, 1973

I am waiting for a chocolate cake to cool so I can frost it. Today Guy Fawkes Day was belatedly celebrated by the British contingent. They had a bonfire at the beach. I wasn't going until Alex came yelling, "Can I go to the bonfire with Neal?" I called Neal's mother and asked her if she had invited him. She said no, but she had asked him if he was going. I hadn't told him about it since I didn't intend to go. Jack was too tired, and I am basically inert. The bus was to leave at 5:00 p.m. and it was already quarter to. I decided to go, since Alex wouldn't be fun to live with knowing that all his friends were going.

They had made a huge pyre of scrap wood with a dummy tied to a stake at the top of the pyre. The boys had firecrackers. People brought picnic suppers, toasted marshmallows in the embers, drank hot coffee and cold drinks, while the kids ran around. Alex sponged sandwiches from three different people. The beach was beautiful at night. The moon was full and made a path of light from the water's edge to the horizon. There were two sailboats with wooden masts bobbing in the path. It would have been a lovely photograph. Alex was concerned about the dummy. Why he was up there? Why he was being burned? What did that person do to people? He wanted to take his clothes off and go swimming. But it was quite cold because of the wind chill factor. It couldn't have been more than fifty-eight degrees. I wore a jersey, a sweater, and an unlined wool jacket and was still chilled to the bone. There has been a stiff wind here for several days.

I am reading a short history of the Middle East, and I think memorizing a chemistry manual would be easier. The names are unfamiliar. They changed dynasties every century or so. From the time of Muhammad on, there seemed to be a war every other generation, and each time a new Islamic sect was formed. There was endless plotting and scheming going on. I would like to LEARN it, but without a photographic memory, it is impossible. I have been doing more reading here than any other time in the last five years.

He and the others were caught, tried for treason, and executed. Guy Fawkes is burned in effigy on a bonfire.

November 13, 1973

We are sharing Thanksgiving with Myra and Barry Anderson, Janet and Alan Harkness, Miriam and Marwan Khalifa. The Harknesses are an older couple, in their late fifties, and he's in chemistry along with Barry Anderson. Marwan is Palestinian and in physics. Miriam, his wife, is teaching school here and running Arabic classes, plus the Arab culture group one night a month. Myra is supplying the turkey, Miriam the vegetables, Janet the drinks, and I'm bringing the pies and bread. The weather is much nicer now, though it still can't be compared to anything in the States. Practically no clouds and it seldom rains. The weather can be described as follows: it is windy, very windy, or not windy; and it is cool, warm, hot, very hot, or unbearably hot. When it is cool and very windy, it is actually cold.

I am making Boston baked beans. The navy beans are soaking tonight and will be boiled, baked, and browned tomorrow. Can't find any canned beans here. Anyway can't get salt pork either so I went to Aramco's dining hall this morning while Alex was at nursery school, had breakfast, and saved my bacon for the beans.

Because alcohol is banned in Saudi Arabia, wine making is quite a passion here. Some of the British specialize in beer. We've even had mead, which is made from fermented honey.[42] It tastes better than the homemade beer and wine, maybe because I have fewer expectations.

Jack will have to work Christmas day. We have a week's vacation after Christmas. Another Islamic holiday—the Eid Al Adha.[43]

November 15, 1973 [Letter by Jack]

Maralyn got another call from the library here this week, and the guy apologized profusely for not getting back to her sooner. After

---

42   Mead is easier to make than beer. Basically it is honey, water, and yeast. There are many varieties, which are created by adding fruit, fruit juices, grapes, grape juice, or malt.

43   This is the Festival of Sacrifice. See "Eid Al Adha" in glossary B.

applying for the job, she had decided against it. She had called personnel three or four weeks ago to say she wasn't interested. Upshot is that she decided not to argue and to give it a try. She starts this Saturday and will be working mornings. We're trying to get our shopping down to one trip a week. We went in town last night, and it was a hectic two hours of running around.

Only six weeks to the next vacation, when we hope to go to Bahrain. We've scheduled to have supper at Ben and Alice's (our neighbors) tonight and then go to the movies here to see Robert Redford in *The Candidate*.[44] Afterwards it's back to their house for bridge and tea. We have a compound picnic scheduled tomorrow, and Saturday night we are to play bridge at the Woolriches . So all in all, we never had it so good!

November 17, 1973

Thirty ships were backed up waiting to be unloaded at Dammam harbor. The school needs books, the faculty who had shipped by sea needs household goods, and the stores have been out of things like flour for nearly a month. Some Staffordshire[45] mugs came in this past week. We bought two, and now I would like a couple more that match. Housing gave a horrendous set of plastic dishes to everyone here in the compound: gray Wedgwood design on white, with shallow little cups. At least the mugs are china.

Tonight we will play bridge with the Woolriches. Ben and Alice have been invited. I think they'll have two tables. The last time we played bridge, Kerry Woolrich served delicious oatmeal cake with a topping like that on German chocolate cakes.[46]

Yesterday I went to a picnic at a neighbor's. Everyone brought a covered dish, and the hostess, Erma Britton, had prepared barbecued beef, which was delicious. It's interesting that if someone holds a social event, everyone invited shows. I am so used to apathetic gath-

---

44   Redford plays a young idealist who runs for the Senate.

45   There are a number of companies in Staffordshire, England, that produce china and pottery.

46   For recipe see "Oatmeal Cake" in appendix 1.

erings in the States that this is a real change. There is nothing else to do, so people socialize. I find myself going to things I would have ignored in the States. The young couples mix with the middle-age couples. The divisions here seem to be more along the lines of longevity at the college. There are those who came this year, those who have been here two or three years, and those who've been here longer, the real old timers.

We are still awaiting a washing machine.

A neighbor on the other side of the compound found a five-inch scorpion on her back step. Has it in a jar. Not that common, however.

November 18, 1973

All the phones on campus are dead today.

Friday we discovered a gray mouse in the house. Jack tried to chase it out of the kitchen with a broom, but it did a U-turn, darted under the crack in the kitchen door, and disappeared into the rest of the house. That night about 1:15 a.m. Jack rose out of bed with a yell, turned on the light, and screamed, "There's a mouse in the bed!!" I said, "You're having a nightmare." Then I saw the mouse streak across the floor. Jack had been asleep, but something was tickling him. He kept brushing at it, thinking it was an ant. But when he felt something furry go into the sleeve of his pajamas, he yelled and threw off the blankets. The mouse then ran the length of his body and jumped onto the floor. He spent the next hour standing in front of the bedroom door—the crack of which was lined with shoes—holding a broom, saucer-eyed, saying, "I've found something better than coffee!" We couldn't find the mouse. It disappeared. And Jack had to take a tranquilizer to get to sleep again. We have a mousetrap, but apparently the mouse dislikes cheddar cheese because he hasn't been caught yet.

Did you know nobody can come to Saudi Arabia without a sponsor? They prohibit tourism.[47]

---

47   Even to this day, Saudi Arabia does not issue individual tourist visas, but if circumstances warrant it, visitor's visas, residence visas, and transit visas are given. Some visas are issued for group tours that must follow prefiled itineraries.

Thanksgiving, November 22, 1973, 9:00 p.m.

The article on King Faisal, from the November 19 issue of *TIME*, arrived from the States.[48] They had deleted the lines from our newsstand copy which said he smokes only in private, that certain members of the royal family might want to reconsider the choice of Prince Khalid as his successor if Faisal should die, and that he was advised by a small council. As you can see the deletions are curious.

We spent Thanksgiving with the Andersons next door. They had mead, white wine, and a locally made distilled product, sidiqui, which is like a mild whiskey or scotch (mild in flavor not strength).[49] Smuggled scotch goes for about twenty dollars a bottle here.[50] I had mead, red wine, white wine, and a mixed drink with the local product in it. The first three are homemade, and I don't know where the sidiqui is made. Probably Aramco. We had turkey, mashed potatoes, candied sweet potatoes, creamed onions and peas, vegetables in a relish tray, gravy, rolls, pumpkin, and mince pie. I made the rolls and pies.

Myra Anderson (our neighbor) has been invited to go on an archaeological expedition to Bahrain for the month of December with a "noted" British archaeologist named Oates, whom she worked with in southern Turkey last summer.[51] The Bahraini government has rented them an air-conditioned flat in a high-rise building in the capital, hired three cars and three drivers, and generally made their life luxurious. She invited us to stay there when we go to Bahrain the end of December. Moderately priced hotels are about thirty dollars a night for a double.[52] The capital has a big paperback bookstore, a jewelry souk (sort of a jewelry district), a small archaeological museum displaying some of the artifacts uncovered by a Danish expedition (described in

---

48   The title of the article was "The Life and Times of the Cautious King of Araby." At this time King Faisal (Feisal) was sixty-seven.

49   "Sidiqui" means "my friend."

50   This would be about $104 in 2012 dollars.

51   This is Professor David Oates (1927–2004), a famous archeologist, Fellow of the British Academy, and president of the British School of Archeology in Iraq.

52   Equivalent to about $155 in 2012 dollars.

the book, *Looking for Dilmun*, by T. G. Bibby),[53] a hundred thousand burial mounds, an old Portuguese fort on top of an Arab fort on top of a pre-Islamic village, and a freer, more tolerant atmosphere than here. And alcoholic drinks are available there, especially Carlsberg beer.[54]

From what I've gathered by talking to people here, women living in the college go through highs and lows. Very bad depression seems to hit almost everyone at one time or another, having little to do with one's psychological makeup. The only factor I can find that determines whether one hits a bad low or not is how much one has to do and how meaningful it is. The depressions haven't hit the level of suicide, because (I imagine) the option of going home exists even if it means breaking a contract. For some people the month-long shamal, or sandstorm, that hits in June can set them off. For others it can be the death of someone at home or a crisis with children left in the States. Or it can be some problem with the housing or just culture shock or some personality conflict within the compound. I would love to do a study on the personality types that make it here and those that don't. There are several teachers living in the bachelor's compound whose wives and families were originally here with them, but packed up and left.

The feeling of frustration can be intense at times. The phone lines—all four hundred of them—were accidentally dug up and cut about four days ago by a backhoe digging holes for planting palm trees. I think this is the only place in the world where men use jackhammers and power shovels to plant trees. Today the cable arrived to replace the wire unearthed, along with a splicing machine, but now they have to wait for an operator to run the splicing machine.

We went to Al-Khobar last night. There is a local version of a fast-food stand, little shwerma shops where a rotating spit grills lamb against a gas flame.[55] As the meat cooks, the man shaves off the cooked pieces with a knife, puts them into Arab bread with pickled turnip, chopped tomatoes, mint, tahini, and a very fiery hot sauce. He then rolls them up and wraps a piece of paper around them. The result is

53   Published by Alfred A. Knopf: New York, 1969.

54   A beer made in Denmark.

55   The rotating spit is vertical.

a shwerma. Usually the shwerma man also sells fried chickpea balls (falafel). The smells are delicious, and it is usually about suppertime when we are shopping, and each time my resolve not to take a chance by eating "off the street" fades a little more.

I was trying to think of all the time-consuming things I have to do in Saudi Arabia that I didn't have to do in the States. I rinse all my vegetables in bleach water, to be safe. All the meat is frozen so it must thaw before being cooked. There are no places to run to for a pizza or submarine sandwich; so all cooking has to be done at home. Imported convenience foods are exorbitantly priced. Everything has to be ironed here because there are no dryers, and perma-press fabrics come out wrinkled. I have to hang wash out on the line. Drinking water comes from a jerry can, because tap water is salty. I don't have a vacuum yet, so I have to sweep the rug and floors with a broom.

A neighbor complained that a Yemen gardener planted potatoes on his front lawn and then harvested them without even offering him one! Two other neighbors both told me, "Many people here have tomato plants, but no one has ever seen a tomato on them." The Yemeni gardeners are suspected of harvesting the crops, and unless one has a taste for green tomatoes, one never gets any. I just planted tomatoes, flowers, parsley, and some salad vegetable, the Arabic name of which neither Jack nor I can translate.

November 23, 1973

Jack had an invitation from two of his students to come to a party Thanksgiving evening, and they arrived for him about a quarter after seven. They had even hired a cab to take him from the compound to the student housing. Jack played a game of chess with one of them and got beaten in a close match. This student had been to England, and his English is quite good. His father used to be Minister of Commerce for the Saudi government and was quite friendly with the king. They served tea and cake and brought him back about 12:15 a.m., by which time I had convinced myself Jack was in some kind of trouble with the government and I would never see him again. He told me he thanked all of them except the one he played chess with and said to this student, "that he wasn't a good host, beating his guest at chess." They all laughed.

Yesterday when we had Thanksgiving dinner at the Andersons', most of the men there who are in the Chemistry Department were swapping stories about the students. During exams there is a big cheating problem—craning necks—much more than in the States. Two students who were good friends got their chemistry grades. One got a D and the other a B. Both of them went to the instructor, and the one who got the B said, "This is my friend. He got a D. I got a B and we both want a C."

Cheating here doesn't carry the moral overtones it does in the States. It seems to be a game of trying to outsmart the instructor. One member of the chemistry department said, "The only way you can try to prevent cheating here is to have one naked, circumcised student in a room with one instructor. And then there *might* not be any cheating."

Last year Barry Anderson was proctoring another teacher's exam. He wrote a big red zero on the paper of a student he caught cheating. Later this student went to his own instructor and said, "Sir, my exam was not marked." The instructor looked and it wasn't marked! So the instructor went to the chairman of the department who seemed to recall someone saying a student had been caught cheating and had gotten a zero marked on his paper. They put the paper under a microscope and found traces of red ink. When the student showed up the next day, they told him he had been flunked for cheating and made him look through the microscope. The student then faked a heart attack, almost swooning on the floor, scaring the instructor out of his wits.

Another student in physical education had cut so many classes that the instructor gave him an F. The student asked why. The instructor explained that the student had cut classes on such and such dates and the student said, "Oh, no, sir. You are mistaken. I was there those days." They argued some more, and finally the instructor was beginning to believe he had indeed been mistaken when it occurred to him to ask the student what the class had done on a certain day. "Played soccer," the student replied. "No," said the instructor taking a chance, since he didn't remember himself, "We went to the pool." The student shrugged and said, "Well, you caught me," and walked away.

Ben, our Moroccan neighbor, proctored an exam and caught a student cheating. The student came up after class and said, "Sir, are you a Moslem?" Ben said, "Yes." Then the student said, "Well, then we should help each other!" Ben disagreed and took twenty points off the student's exam.

We still don't have a washing machine, and Jack went to see the director of housing about it. Other people's machines are ruining all our clothing. For example, Janet Harkness's machine tears the clothes apart on anything but "gentle." Alice's machine spits grease and doesn't wring the clothes out. Consequently they dry like boards. Kerry Woolrich's machine only fills up halfway, so half the amount of soap is necessary. Myra Anderson's machine takes an hour and a half to do seven pounds. One of the machines in the bachelors' compound fills up and stops. Calgon should be added with each wash to prevent the clothes from drying stiff enough to walk around by themselves. All our clothes are turning gray, and most of our underwear was new when we left the States. I hate asking people if I can borrow their machines. The fact that the phones were out for six days made it worse, since I couldn't call first. Jack thinks there will be some action now, since he complained to Purchasing and a dean about our lack of a washing machine.

I am working twenty hours a week at the library. For the first six weeks I am filling in for the Pakistani secretary who has gone on vacation with his family. He handles the correspondence for the library director and also the job of periodicals librarian until a librarian can be hired from the States. After that, rumor has it, I will be writing a monthly library bulletin, but so far I have heard nothing specific about it, such as what it is supposed to accomplish. They hired me because of the journalism background on my resume. There is a lot of tension between the women and Saudi men employed there. The women are doing a lot of typing and card filing. One is a trained British midwife, one has her master's in social work, and another has a master's in library science. Most of them have bachelor's degrees. They work all day typing cards; it would drive an imbecile crazy. What I'm doing is more interesting.

The library here has no money problems. They just order or subscribe to anything they want. One bimonthly magazine *Chemical*

Abstracts costs $2,500 a year to get.[56] They hope to move into their new library in June, and to build their book collection up to two million and their periodicals list up to five thousand. This won't be done overnight but over a period of years. The new college buildings are very impressive.

[Letter continued by Jack]

I don't think being invited to the student compound is run-of-the-mill procedure, so I feel quite honored. They have a lounge or common room, which is a simple room with wall-to-wall carpeting, a few chairs, and a couple of couches, a television, and air-conditioning for the real hot weather. The students in each "line"—rows of rooms that are in actuality arranged in the form of a horseshoe—each chip in 50 SR for their common room, and the college pays the balance.[57] Here in Saudi Arabia students of any age, six to thirty, are paid to go to school by the government. The reason for this is to make it less likely that their families will keep them home to work in the family business or elsewhere for their income.

November 26, 1973

We will be in Bahrain between Christmas and New Year's. We haven't made any reservations yet, but Jack's ten-day vacation starts the twenty-seventh.

In the slip of the tongue department: I went into the dairy store in Al-Khobar and asked for yogurt. The man looked at me, and I finally said it in English. When I went home I had Jack check the Arabic dictionary for the word I used. It meant breast.

Jack just finished ripping up about five pounds, literally, of uncorrected language lab quizzes, but he's had a devil of a time trying to decide what to do with the pieces. (The students cheat like mad, so he doesn't mark them, just goes over the answers in class while the test is still fresh.)

---

56   Adjusted to the 2012 dollar, this would be about $12,940.

57   SR = Saudi Riyals. The official abbreviation is SAR. The exchange rate at this time was about $1.00 = 3.60 SR, so 50 SR would be about $14. In 2012 dollars about $259.

Jack has no spare time at all, despite the fact that we have no car and no television, unlike most of the people here. He has an abundance of bridge players, tennis partners, and people to go running with. He has no time to work on his Arabic, since he is teaching an extra five hours—a total of twenty-five a week. There seems to be more to do here than other places we've lived. Anyway I think Jack is pretty happy here.

It has gotten down to a daily low of about fifty-two degrees. The wind is fifteen to twenty-five knots[58] and that lowers the temperature even more.

November 28, 1973

We just got back from a shopping trip to Al-Khobar where we picked up a clockwork train set for Alex. It has a circle of track and a windup steam engine that pulls a red boxcar and a yellow tank car. Jack had it out on the floor and all set up, "to make sure it worked." We also found a yellow bike for Alex for Christmas.

I don't think the local merchants quite understand Christmas. They have paper lanterns strung around the stores and a bigger selection of masks than I saw at Halloween. The colors are pink and orange and yellow, among others. It looks like Chinese New Year.

My sweet peas are coming up. They look so strange when they sprout. Long and stringy. The tomato plants that were put in are turning yellow around the lower leaves. The calendula is doing okay.[59] It seems all the seedlings from the gardeners are not doing too well, but the things I planted from seed directly in the ground are doing fine.

[Letter continued by Jack]

The stores in Al-Khobar are becoming more and more filled with goods, and we're finding more things we didn't think we could get. The train set is really nicely made for a relatively cheap windup toy. Also, after looking all over town for a bike for him without being able to find

---

58   Twenty-five knots is about 28.8 miles per hour.

59   Marigolds.

one, we looked for the third time in a bike store and found a bike that is better than I had hoped for and cost less than I expected. I got paid yesterday and will be going alone into town tomorrow to cash my check and pick up the bike and sneak it home.

I joined a tennis tournament—The American Consulate Tennis Tournament Doubles—and I'm scheduled to play tomorrow afternoon with an Englishman, Joe Fahey, as my doubles partner. He is on the same rung of the tennis ladder as I am.

December 1, 1973

A neighbor has lent us a plastic Christmas tree. It is made out of the same kind of plastic as is found in fake flowers. It looks more realistic than most artificial trees. It is table size, about one and a half foot high.

Jack is going to sneak Alex's bike from his office in the administration complex to a closet in our house. We have to get a bell or horn for it. If there isn't a horn on a car or bike, it might as well be missing a wheel. Someone here told us that anyone caught driving drunk was in terrible trouble. I observed that no one could tell because they all drive as if they were drunk. We are still not planning on getting a car, if it is at all possible to avoid it.

One of Jack's students wrote in a composition that he "Enjoyed washing girls." Don't they all.

December 5, 1973

We are going to a consulate party tomorrow night for all the people participating in the tennis doubles tournament. It cost two dollars and fifty cents per person,[60] but rumor has it that real drinks will be served. We are going with Jack's tennis partner, Joe Fahey, who has a car.

After a few visits to a few administrators for a few weeks, Jack finally succeeded in getting us a washing machine. It is a used Frigidaire that does a twelve-pound load, top loading, and has several settings. Unfortunately when they tried to get the twenty-seven inch wide machine into the bathroom, they found that the bathroom door was twenty-seven inches wide. Taking off the door was a job they decided

---

60   By the 2012 dollar, this would be $12.94.

to do the next morning, so they left it there in the hall, leaving me with a six-inch passageway. Meanwhile the power went out at 8:00 p.m. In the dark I banged into that washer twenty-seven times trying to get from the kitchen to anyplace else in the house.

When the power went out, I went to neighbor's to borrow candles. I found they had made an occasion of it and had another couple over. They were sitting around eating shrimp, cheese, and crackers, and drinking mead. They invited me to stay. Ten minutes later the phone rang and it was Jack, who had groped his way to the phone with a terrified Alex clinging to one leg. He wanted to know where I was. I brought a candle home and returned to the scene of the party. Jack joined us after Alex had gone asleep. About 9:30 p.m. we saw a flash in the western sky. Another short circuit. It turned out that Al-Khobar, part of Dammam, most of the college, both compounds, and the jebel were out of power. The power didn't come on again until half past eleven the next morning, five minutes before I returned from Al-Khobar with two dozen candles that I was buying for myself and two of my neighbors. I also had to miss work in order to get the bus into town.

The blackout covered about a fifteen-mile stretch of the coast and was caused by a short circuit that spread to four other transformers. They don't use the same wiring specs as Western countries; nothing is built into the electrical system to prevent short circuits from spreading. Also the current here varies, which is quite bad for television sets, air conditioners, and refrigerators. It is allegedly one hundred twenty volts, but this fluctuates from ninety to one hundred and fifty. Several families have lost their high-voltage regulators in their television sets due to these current fluctuations.

The morning after the power failure, the delegation for installing the washing machine showed up at 8:00 a.m. They looked and then left to consult with the master planner. Then ten painters arrived with ladders and buckets and tarpaulins and were swarming around the house and walking on the roof. One door into our house was completely blocked by a ladder and two Saudis. I couldn't look out of a window without staring one in the face. I left at 8:45. When I got back at 11:15 a.m., the washing machine was in the bathroom, and two tiles had been replaced in the floor. They had it connected up but it leaked.

They came back several times, and by five o'clock, I had two washes out of it. The only problem is that it must drain into the tub until a leak in its drain tube can be plugged—the drain pipe leaks all over the bathroom floor—and the machine shimmies when it goes into a spin cycle. It was "used" but it is a big machine and washes okay. It is wiser, however, to set it on "gentle" because one of Jack's new socks got chewed on "normal." But it's mine and I love it.

Neal is having a birthday party next Monday. Alex has been invited, along with sixteen others.

December 6, 1973

Last night Jack, Joe Fahey, and I went to the United States Consulate, which had a party for all the players in a tennis doubles tournament. The players were from Aramco, Northrop, the college, and the United States military. The consul's house was quite large and lovely. There was carpeting on all the floors, even the bathroom. The furniture was Chippendale. The consul and his wife, who had been stationed in India, brought their own personal Indian decorations for the walls and tabletops. The dining room table could seat at least twenty. Another room had a sliding glass wall through which could be seen a patio area where tables and chairs had been placed. Music was piped out onto the patio. There were at least fifty people there. They had three houseboys: two circulated with drinks, and one manned the open bar. The open bar served: Beefeaters gin, Johnny Walker, Jim Beam, and rum. An endless supply. The dining room table had been set up buffet style with platters of sliced ham, sliced turkey, rolls, two kinds of dip, chips, Fritos, olives, pickles, cucumber and carrot spears, mayonnaise, two kinds of mustard. The ham was delicious, not too salty.

The consul was from either Texas or the southwest. His wife was carefully coifed and wore a long green shirtdress with gold buttons. It was a nylon material. Unfortunately I wore a long green shirtdress with covered buttons. Mine was a brighter green, and hers more of a yellow-green. It was a lovely party. Jack had seven gin and tonics and I had four. I think Joe had seven. Nobody was visibly drunk. Jack said embassy parties in Libya were like that. Jack smiled a lot at the party. This morning he had a headache over one eye and had the heating pad over his face. I had jangled nerves, since I'm unaccustomed to drinking.

Jack and Joe played two guys in their first doubles match today. They lost. Neither Joe nor Jack was in much shape to play after last night. The only thing I can't understand is that their opponents were at the same party that we were and yet they played well. They must be used to heavy drinking.

December 9, 1973

Greetings from toasty warm Saudi Arabia! Jack just turned off the air-conditioning as he came through the door. I took a pumpkin pie out of the oven, and I'm now roasting a chicken from France—French Hen, as Alex likes to call them. I have begun hanging Christmas cards around the living room, and tomorrow Jack will buy lights for the plastic Christmas tree. It is hard to feel any Christmas spirit when it is seventy-five degrees outside and there are flowers and leaves everywhere. There is a variety of pine here, sort of what weeping willow is to a maple, this tree is to an evergreen. Anyway, be that as it may, I was thinking about cutting some pieces and making a door swag.

Alex's buddy Neal is having a birthday tomorrow. We bought a Matchbox Daimler 1911, which is larger than the usual Matchbox toy. There are going to be about eighteen kids at this party. Saints preserve us! Fortunately I will be at an Arabic class. Neal's mother is borrowing Sally, Alex's sitter, to help with the proceedings. The British seem to make a very big deal out of birthdays what with delivering little printed invitations to each child, and giving out door prizes, and having games and refreshments. When Alex went to Matthew's birthday party next door, he brought a three-riyal package of modeling clay as a present. He came back with prizes that included assorted candies, a windup chicken in a plastic egg, a Donald Duck squirt gun, a little blow-up balloon, etc. Jack said the only thing worse would have been if we had sent the Donald Duck squirt gun instead of the clay.

There are one hundred and thirty kids in this compound, and I figured if we spend ten riyals on presents for each one whose party Alex got invited to we'd never save a cent. Neal's mother told me that a small gift is all that is considered necessary, so I didn't feel cheap about the clay until Alex brought all his loot home. It was like Christmas here.

The other day while I was next door visiting, workmen were in our yard repairing a leaking outdoor faucet. Jack called me at Myra's to tell me to be careful coming home. One of the workmen sprayed himself in repairing the plumbing. He then removed his pants, hung them on my clothesline, and was finishing the job in his undershorts!

As of now we are leaving for Bahrain on the twenty-ninth of December for four days or until our money runs out. Jack is giving me money for a Christmas present, and I would like to buy a pair of Bahraini pearl earrings. This is the Hajj season in Saudi Arabia,[61] so they are super strict about inoculations, because pilgrims are coming from all over the Moslem world. We have to have another cholera shot and must take six tetracycline tablets before coming back into the country.

I think everyone will have to work Christmas day since the Saudis don't recognize the holiday.

The library work is okay but not exciting. I am making about $2.56 an hour, which is not very much.[62] Believe it or not, the college is having budget problems. So they are cutting back on supplies like chalk! Jack's chairman told him to carry his chalk and erasers around in a plastic bag.

December 11, 1973 [Letter by Jack]

We now have lights for our tree. Also I bought Alex a bell for his bike and made arrangements to go to Bahrain.

Three months into a new culture is a classic time for a good bout of cultural shock, and the prospect of not being home for Christmas is start-

---

61   The month each year when there is a pilgrimage to Mecca. See "Hajj" in glossary B.

62   About $13.25 in 2012 dollars.

ing to get to people. Even to us a little. Alex has a cold once again. Expect the mails will be slow or fouled up until after the twelfth of the month.

December 15, 1973

Got some red felt and made Alex a Christmas stocking. Trimmed it with green and white ball fringe.

The new and old are often intermixed here. Once in a while a Saudi man will wear a thobe *and* a suit jacket. And it is not unusual to see an Arab in a thobe on a motor scooter.

The Arabs love ornamentation. Their trucks and cars have elaborate grillwork, along with their roof racks. License plates are hand decorated, each number a different color.

Red and white gutras or head cloths are common here. Some people at the college use them for tablecloths. The Saudis must cringe. The head cloths are surprisingly expensive (ten dollars),[63] because they are machine embroidered, not printed.

When I wore a brightly striped thobe to work, a Saudi informed me, "Here in my country men wear these, not women!" I repeated this to Maggie, a former British social worker who is now working in the library for her second year. She's bitter towards the Saudis, because of their view of women, as most of the non-Arab women who live here a while become. She said, "Well, you tell him we wouldn't have to wear the bloody things if it wasn't for their attitudes towards women!"

[Letter continued by Jack]

We're starting to get Christmas cards as of today's mail and we're hanging them above our small tree. My driver's license came in the mail. Now, I can rent a car, if I need to. These first three months have been tough, but there is great promise for change. Having a washing machine helps a lot. Our Bahrain vacation is just two weeks away, and of course Christmas is even closer. Aramco radio plays a lot of Christmas music, which is nice, but one Bing Crosby album—which they play over and over again—has "White Christmas" and "I'll be Home for

---

63   About $52 in 2012 dollars.

Christmas" on it.[64] We're going to have some people over for Christmas dinner. Weather still in the mid seventies. Also as I've said before, I'm looking forward to the end of this year and a new teaching schedule and hopefully time for more exercise, bridge, etc.

December 15, 1973

I plan to return from Bahrain with at least three pounds of bacon and a canned ham. One of the English teachers tells Jack over and over again that "you can buy pornography there," as if Jack's interested.

Thursday, the local religious police were seizing any male with long hair and publicly scissoring off the excess. Every now and then there is a crackdown on how the foreign females appear in public, too much skin exposed, etc. Last year rumor had it that trousers too wide at the bottom were slashed by the zealous who feared the corrupting influence of hippie styles.

P.S. If they play "I'll Be Home for Christmas" once more on the Aramco station, I think I'll cry.

December 18, 1973 [Letter by Jack]

Our house shows the Christmas spirit as our tree is very colorful and we decorated our walls with Christmas cards. We're planning to have Christmas dinner at 6:00 p.m. and have invited two married couples and three bachelors. The two bachelors I called tonight sounded very grateful to get an invitation. I plan to cut my first class on Tuesday, so that I can get pictures of Alex and his presents.

[Letter continued by Maralyn]

Alex had a Christmas party at nursery school today. His teacher made him a felt stocking, filled it with candy, a Matchbox toy, and a little Christmas tree ornament with a picture of him in the center. She

---

64   Crosby's "White Christmas" sold over thirty million copies. He recorded it as a single in May 1941. The also popular "I'll Be Home for Christmas" was recorded by Crosby, October 1943.

evidently told him to smile for he has this awful grimace that makes him look like the nursery school heavy.

December 21, 1973

Last night we went to the Aramco Christmas pageant with Joe Fahey. Aramco has money! A crane erected the pageant stage set in their stadium. The lighting would have done justice to any theater in the States. They used real donkeys, sheep, and camels. The announcer read the Christmas story from the Bible as it was acted out on the set. The Arabs in the pageant wore tennis shoes beneath their biblical robes. A host of fourteen sheeted angels appeared on the second story of the stable over the manger as the Christ Child was born. The camels behaved quite well, but the sheep ran in circles. Naturally they didn't show the birth, but judiciously switched to the shepherds in the fields. Saudi sheep are peculiar looking, like a cross between a cocker spaniel and a goat. An organ and a small brass ensemble accompanied the choir of fifty voices. It was nicely done.

It was freezing in the stands with that stiff desert wind. We brought a blanket, the Juraib blanket, which weighs twenty pounds and has the binding Alex is so fond of. Alex was happy to finger the blanket edge and suck his thumb during most of it, punctuated by an occasional, "Where are the camels?" or "I want to go home!" or "When is this going to be over?" At the end, as we were leaving he said, "That was really great, Daddy!"

On the Juraib blanket: The blanket has been christened after the director of housing, Mr. Al-Juraib, who bought a flock of them to cover everything from baby cribs to queen size beds (for the former TOO BIG; for the latter TOO SMALL). It gets down to fifty-eight degrees in the morning because we don't leave the heat on when we go to bed, and the blanket is just enough to keep us warm. In the same vein, the plastic, pseudo-Wedgwood, gray and white, standard issue dishes are referred to as "Juraib-ware."

Aramco had a special chartered Christmas flight to bring family from the States to Dhahran for Christmas. One of my co-workers persuaded her reluctant mother—whom she hadn't seen in two years—to come to the college for Christmas. She even sent her half the fare. Her mother thought it wasn't safe but finally decided to come. She was due in Monday night. The flight stopped in Rome, and the Aramco group for the remainder of the trip switched to a Pan Am plane. Before the plane could leave it was firebombed by Arab terrorists. Thirty people were killed.[65] The girl got a call that evening from the US Consul telling her that her mother was listed among the missing. The next morning her father called and said her mother was dead, but that the charred body was difficult to identify. Two hours after she got the call, Aramco chartered a flight to Rome and then to the States for relatives here who had lost family on the plane. The librarian at the Consulate School was told her niece was killed and her daughter was in critical condition in a Rome hospital.

Most of the losses were at Aramco. There were eighteen Americans killed. Many of the staff here who had planned to have relatives come on this flight had changed their plans at the last minute, or couldn't raise the money in time, or couldn't get reservations. This kind of community is like a hothouse for emotions. It is hard to be isolated from the intensity of people's feelings. Everyone discusses it over and over again. It accomplishes nothing really except to raise feelings to a fever pitch with no release in sight except hysterics.

December 26, 1973

It didn't seem like Christmas because the weather was so mild. It was somewhere in the sixties. We spent Christmas Eve at Joe Fahey's. Joe and his Arab roommate share the cost of a Sudanese chef. They had a buffet of some Arab and some English food. We brought Alex because we couldn't get a sitter for Christmas Eve. He didn't want to go to sleep at Joe's because "Joe doesn't have a Christmas tree, and Santa doesn't come where there isn't a tree, and Joe isn't going to get any presents." I suppose Alex didn't want to be considered an associate of Joe's under those cir-

---

65   On December 17, 1973, terrorists attacked a Pan Am and Lufthansa plane at Rome airport. The Pan Am plane was destroyed at the airport; then the Lufthansa plane was hijacked with thirteen hostages on board. The terrorists were caught and found guilty.

cumstances. I told Alex I would discuss the matter with Daddy, but he fell asleep at Joe's.

We are still recovering from Christmas. We had eight over for dinner, and they left at half past midnight. I had to go to work this morning, and Jack had to teach, though all the students had left unofficially yesterday or the day before. He came back when nobody showed and went to bed. It has been cloudy for the past three days, a first since we've been here. It also rained briefly, the only time since we arrived.

Alex is absolutely entranced by his bike. He tried to take it to bed with him last night. I think he put four miles on it yesterday just riding it round the block. He ate supper last night with one hand on his fork and the other on the handlebars.

I gave Jack a 450-piece jigsaw puzzle of a Renaissance painting, a flashlight, a can of tennis balls, and a can of popcorn. I had some cashews for him, but he unloaded the grocery bag the night I bought them and ate them all before Christmas.

We played a little bridge last night and one of the non-players started in on Jack's puzzle. The turkey was excellent. The stuffing was a box of Bell's stuffing mix, but I didn't tell anyone. The mix was cheaper than the sum total of the ingredients needed at local prices. I had sweet potato and pineapple casserole, peas, cranberry jelly, rice, gravy, relish tray, stuffing, and turkey. The Andersons brought mead to drink and Christmas cookies on a tray. (Alex bit off the foot, head, and arms of every single gingerbread man.) I also made lemon meringue and pumpkin pie. According to Jack, one of the bachelors who came had four pieces of lemon pie. I am boiling up the remains of the turkey for soup. The turkey was Danish, weighed twelve pounds, and cost about $16.50.[66] I am glad we have time to recuperate from Christmas before leaving for Bahrain.

December 27, 1973

Yesterday the Andersons gave me a ride into town to shop. As we went in, we passed three uniformed Saudis standing in the middle of the

---

66   About $85 in 2012 dollars.

intersection (a risky occupation under the best of circumstances). I said, "What's this?" Barry replied, "It's the police—a form of vagrancy here."

At this same intersection there is a round metal police booth in the northeast corner of the roads, well off the tarmac. A policeman sits in it all the time. Behind it, lying on its side is another metal booth, bashed in on one side. I asked once why the booth was located in the northeast corner instead of in the middle of the intersection as is the usual case. The bashed-in booth was pointed out to me, accompanied by, "THAT'S why!"

December 31, 1973

It was a cloudy and rainy the day before we left for Bahrain, but the twenty-ninth dawned bright, clear, and crisp. It took us forty minutes in the baggage check line to get out of Saudi Arabia, but only ten minutes to fly to Bahrain.

Our cheap hotel in Bahrain was made of concrete and ceramic tile. Jack said that we were safe from fire because there was nothing that could burn except the mattresses and furniture. However, the concrete and tile made voices carry all over the place, and anyone talking on the central staircase might as well have been standing next to your bed. Our room—a concrete bunker—was ten by twelve feet with a bathroom, which was a "closet" with toilet, sink, and shower. There was a bureau and a wardrobe with no hangers and a path about four to five feet wide between a double and single bed. A window let in air but no light, as it looked out on a concrete wall two feet away. The room was damp and cold, and smelled vaguely musty. The toilet had to be flushed with a wastebasket full of water. The mattress was not well supported. Pressing down on it with one finger caused it to sag to the floor. A muezzin in a minaret,[67] not two hundred yards from our side of the hotel, broadcast the call to prayer over a loudspeaker at three in the morning, bringing me two feet off my bed.

We had lunch at the Moon Plaza Hotel restaurant, recommended by Myra Anderson. The check came to twenty-four dollars![68] We each had two gin and tonics, appetizers, and shish kebab. They served *canned*

---

67   A minaret is a tower, which is a traditional part of a mosque and from which a muzzein (muezzin) calls the faithful to prayer five times a day.

68   About $124 by the 2012 dollar.

peas, *minute rice,* and gave us five pieces of meat, which they flamed by pouring a ladle of brandy over them, which then soaked the rice and the peas. Alex's hamburger was so heavily seasoned he ate very little of it. Our hotel restaurant's meal was much nicer at a quarter of the price.

We did some shopping, bought eight or so books in the great bookstores there, some kitchen utensils I couldn't find in Saudi Arabia, and a pair of pearl earring with money Jack gave me for Christmas. The earrings are set in twenty-two karat gold. Bahraini pearls once were quite famous. Their pearl divers go seventeen fathoms deep without diving gear to collect oysters.[69] It is no longer so lucrative, since the Japanese began producing the larger *cultured* pearls. Pollution from the oil industry has been destroying the oysters.

The atmosphere was quite different from Saudi Arabia. Rather like the contrast between Puritan New England and French New Orleans. The British influence has something to do with it also. Bahrain had been a British colony and benefited from the British gift for establishing bureaucracy and a measure of organization and efficiency. Bahrainis are more tolerant. Allowance is made for other religions. Periodicals are not censored before being sold. December 16 and 17 are a national holiday. Women participate in the businesses and for the most part are not veiled. The medical facilities are more comprehensive, the airport quite modern and attractive.

Alex went crazy from lack of room to play, and this drove us crazy. So we cut short our visit, figuring we weren't getting our money's worth in Alex's company. The trip was worth it though.

January 4, 1974

When we got back from Bahrain early on the morning of the thirty-first, I made some coffee using the sweet water in the jerry can (tap water is salty). Later Alex wanted some water, and I poured him a cup. There was an ant floating on the top. I looked in the jerry can and there must have been one hundred ants floating in the water. Apparently the cap had been left off when we departed, and they all climbed

---

69   A fathom is six feet, so seventeen fathoms is 102 feet.

52

in and drowned. I then checked the remains of the coffee and found an ant in that. Who knows what we drank.

Did you know that any Bible coming into the country has to be officially registered?[70] Everything is checked.

January 13, 1974

Jack is giving his students a test this morning. He got up at quarter to seven to teach the extra class he was given, which happened to be a language lab session with the seven worst students in the whole first-year class. None of them showed up, and as he was leaving, he ran into three of them. He said, "Hi," and they said, "Hello." He asked, "Did you enjoy your vacation? Did you go far?" The students didn't understand Jack. Then one of them had the nerve to ask, "You no mark absent?" Jack was steamed. I suggested he should have rounded them up and dragged them off to lab. He said he wasn't killing himself for students with attitudes like that.

There have been problems here with anonymous phone calls. Usually no one speaks; you just hear the sound of heavy machinery in the background. Sometimes the caller says something in Arabic. Myra Anderson got five calls of the first variety in an hour. She got so mad she called Juraib, the director of housing. He came right over, dialed a number, motioned her over to the phone, and asked, "Is this what you hear?" She said, "Yes." He remarked, "Oh, we know who's doing it. He's crazy." And he pointed to his forehead. Another wife, Kandra Arsenault, was getting obscene phone calls in broken English. The caller would say, "I want make love you." Here women are so physically hidden from the world that just to see an unveiled woman on the street has the same effect as a see-through mini dress in a small town in New England. As one of the English teachers here said, "These guys could fall in love with a woman's footprint in the sand."

---

70   Even to this day, the possession of a unregistered Bible may result in a heavy fine, beating, or deportation (if the person is a foreigner). If the person is a Muslim, then the punishment may be even greater.

CHAPTER 3

Obscene Arabic, on the Day of the Apricots, secret police and
Arabian prisons, exploding mead, catching a Saluki
with tuna fish, the tale of the mad Scotsman

January 16, 1974

I think I have been going through a post holiday let down. Last night we talked about going home this summer. Airfare would cost between three thousand and four thousand dollars.[71] We would have no car when we got back to the States. And we would have living costs for three months, which would come out of our savings. I suggested, "What about one of us going back?" and Jack said, "Nothing doing!"

Summers are hot here. Sandstorms occur in June. In July and August the temperature reaches 116 degrees. Almost everybody is gone. For those who stay, there aren't that many summer school teaching jobs available. Jack would prefer being here teaching to just being here. So I guess we're all in this together.

After Tuesday Jack has another ten days off. He teaches about thirty weeks out of fifty-two. His hours will go from twenty-five to fifteen this coming semester.

The college has a weekly movie. The students see it one night and the faculty the next. This week they have an Italian western. A few weeks ago they had *Pete and Tillie*. In it someone asks Tillie why she stays married to Pete, she replies, "Because he's a *pistol*." One of the students asked Jack what it meant when a girl says, "He's a puzzle." The student added, "Does it mean he's sexy?" Jack thought and thought

---

71   For round-trip tickets, in 2012 dollars, about $13,985 and $18,646 respectively.

and then remembered the line in the movie, but decided he didn't have the energy to tackle it at the end of a long, hard day. So he told the student he didn't know.

A name that is quite commonly used here is "Isa," which means Jesus in Arabic. It predates Jesus Christ of course.

This is a nice place to raise kids. The compound is large and shady. There are over a hundred kids here. Alex has plenty of people to play with and can go outside without anyone worrying about where he is. Jack's first attempt to brew mead was okay if you wanted something to drink, but it was not very potent. After sampling the first two bottles, I advised him to try root beer. It would be the same procedure with the same lack of kick. The second two batches are going to be better. I can tell by the smell.

We've been buying a lot of Austrian and Swiss apple juice for its prized glass bottle, which has a wire clamp and porcelain stopper. They're great for bottling the wine. I'll bet the store owner wonders why such costly apple juice is so popular. A variety of grape juice comes in the same type of bottle but costs two dollars a bottle. All are slightly carbonated but say on the label in German "alcohol free."

The girl whose mother died on the Pan Am flight in Rome came back Friday. Pan Am offered to settle for $17,000 damages and is discouraging lawsuits by claiming "act of war," which is not covered by the Warsaw convention.[72] The girl is heavily sedated and hasn't been to work at the library or to Arabic class. But she did come back.

Want to cure incipient alcoholism? How about latent heterosexuality? I have just the place! Tired of looking at scantily clad women in magazines? The place I have in mind eliminates it. A partially bared breast or LEGS will never again offend your eyes!!! That's because HERE IT DOESN'T EXIST!

January 17, 1974

Yesterday Alex went to a birthday party in the afternoon. He has one dress shirt, so I usually have to iron it for him. I overheard him telling Neal's mother that I was ironing his sweatshirt for the party.

---

72   About $79,247 in 2012 dollars.

Have to police the nursery school bus to Aramco again tomorrow. My turn comes up every two weeks for one morning. Between the pre-schoolers and the wild-eyed Saudi bus driver, I may find myself taking a tranquilizer for the return home. They aren't really awake on the way over, but on the way back all hell breaks loose. Two kids were spitting on the windows. Three were at the back holding onto the next-to-last seats and springing up and down on the back seats. Three were trying to see how many sentences they could make up with "poops" as the noun. And then two English boys began chanting, "WE HATE ARABS!" WE HATE ARABS!" (being what the bus driver and his assistant were). Shortly after that they turned to a little boy whose father was Saudi and mother American and demanded to know "Is your daddy an Arab?" The little boy said, "Yes, he is, but when he gets older, he's going to be an English-man." Then the boys began to chant again, but broke into a disagreement and began kicking each other, at which point I risked my life and limb by going down the aisle while the bus was in motion to separate them before homicide occurred. All this time the bus driver was driving like he was in the Monte Carlo Grand Prix, over roads that aren't suited for a logging operation or a half-track, let alone a beat-up school bus. By the time I saw that crew off the bus, I was ready for a nursing home.

I made "Mom's Sugar Cookies" tonight.[73] They are good. Every-body likes them.

January 18, 1974

There is a terrible wind today. It looks like a blizzard in the com-pound. The trees are being whipped and tossed, garden gates are swinging and banging. There is a fine film of dust on the stovetop where it has blown in through the louvers in the exhaust fan. The rubber tree outside the back door has a dusty film on its dark green leaves. The floor feels sandy near the crack under the door. The curtains are moving inside even though the windows are closed. Jack's tennis partner just called off the game scheduled for this morning. He lives in the other compound where there are no trees yet and he couldn't see his car fifty feet away.

---

73   For recipe, see "Mom's sugar Cookies," appendix 1.

I have already described the shwerma vendors in Al-Khobar who have a little table and a revolving spit with a huge chunk of lamb. I started eating them cautiously. First with just meat and bread. Then I succumbed to the tahini, pickles, and a little sauce. Since I always rinse vegetables bought in town in a weak bleach solution, I was afraid to eat the tomatoes and mint leaves in the shwerma. Occasionally I'd threaten Jack with suicide by threatening to eat a shwerma with everything on it. Wednesday night Jack went in town and brought two shwermas back with him. He persuaded me to try one with everything. Unfortunately I always ask for one with "shway hot sauce" (a little hot sauce), and Jack neglected this detail. The hot sauce certainly killed any organism lingering on the tomato or mint. It nearly killed me. Jack ran around the house panting through his mouth like a fire-breathing dragon. Water does nothing to alleviate the burning sensation. It has to wear off. Suspect the shwerma man would find this all very amusing.

January 18, 1974

There is a phrase in Arabic, "fil mishmish", which means, loosely, a kind of vague nonspecific "eventually." Literally it means, "on the day of the apricots."[74] Apricots here have a very short season, like two weeks out of the year. This saying is used a lot. The Arabs especially like "Inshallah," which means "God willing."[75] Instead of promising to do something—like delivering a washing machine tomorrow morning—they simply say, "Inshallah."

I have dust in my nose. Maybe this very dust comes from an ancient Assyrian civilization or from Mesopotamia. But I think the wind is in the wrong direction for Mesopotamia, which would be north. The wind is northwesterly and off the desert. "Shamal" means north in Arabic.

January 22, 1974

There is a fairly extensive secret police organization here. There are no questions asked or charges made. People are just jailed. One man

---

74   Or "tomorrow when the apricots bloom."

75   Perhaps closer to Arabic thought is "If Allah wills it."

I work with spent three years in jail and never knew why. The previous dean of the college had the same misfortune, which is why he isn't the dean now. He also had the misfortune to be married to a woman whose family was busy intriguing against the king. Here if the wife commits an offense, the husband is locked up or deported, depending on whether he is native or foreign. One American woman used to drive from Aramco to a hospital in town to visit her sick husband. She'd dress up in the traditional (male) robes and got away with it for three weeks. Then one day they were waiting for her. The sick husband was immediately deported. I suppose she went with him.

Anyway, one can't be too careful. Larry Black, a member of Jack's department, was incarcerated for three days over Christmas. No charges were brought, though he did attack a Saudi guard outside our compound. He thought the guard was stealing a watch from another teacher who was yelling for help. The prisons do not provide food. It is up to the family or sponsor. The department chairman got a note saying, "Dear Harvy[76] (1) I am in jail, (2) please feed my cat, and (3) bring me some food!" and that's how poor Harvy found out. Now Larry is back teaching, like nothing ever happened.

January 22, 1974

Seven guys just came to repair my washing machine. What a circus. It's a quarter to eight. I decided to go to work a little late this morning.

We had a little lesson on Arabic words to avoid using the other day. The words to avoid saying are "nick" and "zip." "Nick" means fuck. "Zib" means penis (Britishers call zippers "zips." There is no "p" in Arabic and Arabs hear and say a "b" instead, so when a British woman goes into a notions store and asks for a "twelve-inch zip" it's usually causes a laugh. And "fuss" means cunt. So our Arabic teacher warned us not to use the term "zip" or "fuss" or "fussy" or the word "nick." While on the subject a woman in the class whose husband is Iraqi asked what a word that sounded like "unique" meant since her husband was always yelling it at taxi drivers. He was yelling, "Eunuch."

---

76   Harv Woolrich, the chairman.

Would you believe that the library and the college are having budget problems? The college just got a 20 percent across-the-board increase for this fiscal year. They needed much more since new buildings have been opened on the jebel. Almost every department is broke until July. No paper clips. No fluid for the duplicating machines. No money for spare parts for the broken washing machine. The library has $60,000 left in its account for this fiscal year. They are going to have to stop ordering and stop payment on invoices. Saudi Arabia can only spend 40 percent of its annual income because it doesn't have enough of an economy to absorb the revenue. And the library goes begging.

January 25, 1974

I was making gingersnap cookies and left Alex long enough to answer the phone.[77] When I got back to the cookies, I found Alex had the dough out on the counter and had shaped it into a house.

Discovered two small worms in the pizza dough I just rolled out. Funny how inured one becomes to such things. Unfortunately if everything were thrown out because it had bugs in it, we would starve. A neighbor bought Yemeni honey to make mead. It still had bees in it, dead of course. The bottle of maple syrup I bought recently had mold growing on the surface. I strained and boiled it. I am now taking my life in my hands and buying shwermas with everything on them. I have become addicted to them. They also sell falafels—deep-fat fried chickpea balls. You can get five, the size of slightly flattened golf balls, for fifteen cents.[78] They are flavored with garlic and cumin.

Bought a Moulinex coffee grinder and blender yesterday. Jack likes hummus, and it is almost impossible to mash chickpeas without a blender.[79] Of course most people here use canned chickpeas, but *that* offends my sense of purity.

---

77   For recipe see "Gingersnap Cookies," appendix 1.

78   About 70¢ in 2012 dollars.

79   For recipe see "Humus," appendix 1.

I am afraid that the mead Jack is brewing might create enough internal pressure to shatter the bottles. I keep wondering how we would explain glass-in-the-ceiling to Juraib, the director of housing.

January 26, 1974

The job in the library is monotonous. I have to go through more than a thousand periodicals, making a list of which ones are on the shelves and how many issues are present for each year. It's a lousy job and excruciatingly boring. Plus the fact that I am in the middle of the periodical room where the students study, and a woman in the periodicals, or anywhere else for that matter, is quite a novelty. Here if you look a male in the eye, it's considered a pass. So I can't look at anyone, which is difficult in a room full of people.

Jack doesn't have attendance problems with his regular class. But he does have with the seven flunkies he was given as an extra class. They should have dropped out, but didn't. They don't do a thing, are at the bottom of the orientation class, and have very poor English. The chairman had hopes that they would quietly leave the college, but they are apparently getting something out of it they can't get at home. All Saudi students go tuition free, plus they collect a salary of about one hundred dollars a month from the government.

January 29, 1974 [Letter by Jack]

Today some visiting dignitaries came to the library, and all the women working there were ordered to lie low until the men left. They usually shut them all up in a little room like they don't exist. It is against the law for women to work in Saudi Arabia. And to ride bicycles. And to take cabs. And to drive.[80]

---

80   All of this is still true. There is now some talk of letting married women drive—under restricted circumstances—so that their husbands will not have to interrupt their workday to drive their children or wife to the doctor, dentist, or other such places.

February 1, 1974, 9:30 a.m.

We bought a little Sanyo canister vacuum cleaner. The two sand-storms we had made me realize that I couldn't get along without one.

The college budget is so empty that the Maintenance Department cannot afford spare parts for anything that breaks down from now to July. And my washing machine is in the repair shop for the second time.

Talib, the Bedouin husband of Alexandra, the American librarian I work with, came in looking for his wife today. Somebody said, "She's upstairs in the director's office. She's been there all morning." Pretending to be jealous, he said, "I'm getting my sword! Did you ever see a Bedouin fight? In Yemen my tribe fought Egyptian tanks in pickup trucks!" I said, "That might explain the driving around here." But he didn't think that was very funny.

At that time, his tribe was fighting the Egyptians in 1962 as part of the Royalist faction. He had the misfortune to travel to Egypt in the middle of all this and was jailed because his name on the passport was the tribe's name. They thought he might be planning to assassinate Nasser.[81] He has since changed his name. He is here for his PhD dissertation, which will be about the college. He is getting his doctorate in education from the University of Arizona.

Bedouin women have the custom of piercing one nostril and inserting a jewel. The mother-in-law of Alexandra has a turquoise and gold jewel. Alexandra's husband had to go to Kuwait for a while, and who should appear on the doorstep to chaperone the American daughter-in-law each evening while the husband was away, but his mother. Alexandra was insulted. She also cannot smoke in front of her mother-in-law, which made the evenings rather long. The mother-in-law also prays over her four-year-old grandson a lot, which frightens him. Alexandra has been married ten years, and this is her first time in Saudi Arabia. Her husband didn't prepare her very well. For example, he never told her that in this country women couldn't legally drive.

---

81   Gamal Abdel Nasser was president of Egypt from 1956–1970.

I asked Alexandra how her mother-in-law viewed her and Hamid the four-year-old son. She said, "They think Hamid is quaint, but they think I am old enough to know their customs better." She refuses to wear the abaya (black satin shroud) and veil, and they are shocked.

I visited Alexandra last night. The mother-in-law was there and she seemed pleasant enough, but there wasn't much conversation. Alexandra's Arabic is the Cairo variety, and the mother's is a Bedouin dialect. As I was leaving, I turned to the mother-in-law and said, "Tsharafna," which means, "We are honored." She said it back so I think we communicated briefly.

There is an Arab proverb to the effect that "to its mother, the baby donkey is a gazelle."

February 1, 1974 [Letter by Jack]

Maralyn is moping around the house because she's without her washing machine, and is in a general bad mood because she has heard rumors that there is no money for spare parts until next year. Now first of all we don't know that the machine needs a spare part, and secondly as a rumor mill this place is fantastic. Not only do the rumors not hold water, but most of them wouldn't serve as sieve. Take for instance the rumor that started when Maralyn missed one of her Arabic classes. The rumor was that Maralyn quit the class since she had a Saudi to teach her while she gave him English lessons.

Saturday five men showed up here at 8:00 a.m. with our washing machine in working condition. It's once again in our bathroom.

February 2, 1974

We had a little explosion the other day. We were at Aramco and came home to an odd yeasty smell. The mead that Jack was trying to brew turned out to be more powerful than we had even imagined. The cupboard door had been blown open. There were gouges in the paint inside the kitchen cabinet and a zillion pieces of glass. A sticky mess had spilled out onto the linoleum.

Any shortages in the States hit here about six months later. It's called freighter-lag.

Everyone here goes to Shiraz, Isfahan, and Teheran for vacations.[82] They're cheap to get to and cheap to stay there. Joe Fahey is there right now. He should have come back yesterday. No sign of him. The last time he went someplace (Kuwait) he lost his passport and was delayed ten days while he got a new one.

Jack is listening to a quiz show in Arabic where the host asks people in the studio audience questions about the Koran. If the answer is right, the man gets twenty or forty riyals, about five to ten dollars.

February 3, 1974

I looked at the moon tonight. It's two-thirds or three-quarters full. The last few nights it's been wild and sinister looking with great bruises of black clouds sweeping across its face. A scene for Edgar Allan Poe.

There's been a rabies case near here. A wild fox bit a horse that went into a writhing foaming fit. The horse's teeth grazed a Saudi who tried to get near him. The man had to have the series of required shots. Anyway, no animal here is inoculated against rabies. Animals from outside get into the compound all the time; people go out on the desert and bring back animals. Sheep and camels are exposed to the carriers. Being exposed to rabies is a real and frightening possibility.

Met a Saudi today whose father was beheaded. His father had killed a man who cheated him. The father of the dead man had a choice between collecting blood money from him or having his head.[83] He chose the latter. He fled to Kuwait but was extradited and executed.

The Bedouin husband of Alexandra, the American librarian, is looking for a dog, a good Saluki.[84] His family's neighbors in Thugba, a town a few miles from here, had spotted a fine looking Saluki stray scrounging through garbage. Talib saw the dog and decided he wanted him. He spent the last two days in Thugba chasing after the Saluki with an open can of tuna fish under cars and over walls. Apparently Salukis adore tuna fish. It's like catnip to cats. Knowing that Arabs

---

82   These cities are in Iran.

83   This is still the case.

84   The Saluki is an ancient breed of dog that originally came from the Middle East. The Bedouins used them for hunting gazelle and hare.

think dogs are lower than cockroaches, I can imagine his stock plummeting around the village as the neighbors look out and see him pursuing a dog with an open can of tuna fish. They probably think he was in the States too long.

February 8, 1974

We had the couple next door over for supper. I baked a turkey and stuffed it with a packaged stuffing mix. Darned if Jack didn't find a piece of glass in it. Buying stuffing mix is more economical than buying Pepperidge Farm bread and using it for stuffing. In this case it wasn't. Although the local bread has all kinds of insects in it, I've never found glass.

And now for the tale of the mad Scotsman. A few days ago, a bleeding, bruised, starving, and thirsty man, clothed in rags, was apprehended as he attempted to break into the student dormitories. He was brought to Juraib, director of housing, who is also alleged to be an officer in the Saudi secret police. He questioned the man who claimed to have been wandering the desert for four days, "eluding the CIA." The Scotsman said he had all the secrets to the defense of Saudi Arabia and the CIA was going to kill him. He added that he would only tell these secrets to a fellow Scotsman because the English were the same thing as the Americans. So the director of housing, who apparently takes everything literally, called in two Scotsmen on the faculty, Graham Donald and a fellow named Mitchell, and told the man, "Here are your Scotsmen. Now tell them the secrets." Well, as things turned out he didn't know anything or what he told turned out to be so utterly fantastic that Juraib decided that he had no secrets. At any rate he did say that he had been working at Avco and, before that, was ten years at Aramco.[85] The Avco personnel officer told them the man was bonkers and that Avco had tried to send him back to London a week ago. The plane was scheduled to stop in Cairo on the way. When the Scotsman learned that, he bolted across the airfield and into the desert. They couldn't find him. He later explained that the CIA was waiting for him in Cairo and he would only return to England on a direct flight. So

85   Probably Avco is AVCO Aviation.

the two Scotsmen from the faculty accompanied him to the airport on Wednesday and saw him onto the plane to London.

As you can imagine, stories like that travel fast. This, as far as I can determine, is pretty close to what happened.

I tried sidiqui, the local equivalent of bathtub gin, the other night. I had an inch in the bottom of a tumbler of coke, twice. It felt lovely. Oblivion, or at least a deep shade of rose, is a refreshing change now and then. But I was bitterly repentant the following morning. I awoke with a headache that would do justice to a concussion. The stuff, being somewhat impure and very strong, makes it risky drinking. That's just two glasses! My neighbor has been drinking it straight and taking Alka Seltzer and Rolaids like mad all the following day. It's quite expensive, and they had a gallon of the stuff. It's practically straight alcohol. Never again. I have never had a hangover to equal that.

A woman whose husband had a bleeding from drinking sidiqui told me that the doctors said they never touch the stuff.

I went shopping in town with Alexandra, the librarian, and Talib, her Saudi husband. He bargained in Arabic with the local vegetable man:

Talib: How much is the grapefruit?
Shopkeeper: Three and a half riyals a kilo. (That was
   about a dollar for two pounds.)
Talib: What? That's too much!
Shopkeeper: Three and a half riyals!
Talib: That's outrageous!
Shopkeeper: Three and a half riyals.
Talib: Okay, I'll go to Dammam (a city twenty miles away.)
Shopkeeper: Two and a half riyals.

I got them for two and a half riyals. On the way home, he drove to his parents' home in Thugba. There are twenty-six people living in the house. The uncle has two wives, and they apparently get along. Most of the kids are from those unions. I stretched my mind trying to find Arabic to cope with the situation. Under pressure my mind shuts down. Each family member who is married has a room in the house. Cows, goats, and sheep are kept out back. Alexandra had three years of literary Arabic and one year of Egyptian colloquial conversational Arabic at university. She met her husband because she needed a tutor. She claims that all the courses did for her was to make her realize how much Arabic she didn't know.

The American who has been with the college the longest, Dr. Robert King Hall, and who is one of the founders, got a long entry in *Who's Who*. Anyway, the British here think he is a member of the CIA. All non-Americans believe that the CIA is lurking under every bush and tree, and that the CIA is a bunch of fabulously equipped James Bond clones. They are also given credit for training their Saudi counterparts.

February 11, 1974

Jack and Joe Fahey lost their semifinals game against the US Consul and the director of the British bank here. Jack is mad at himself. They played on the Consulate courts. The Consul had a line judge, a fresh can of tennis balls opened for each game, and a rooting section. The elastic gave out in Jack's tennis shorts while he played. They stayed up, barely. I tried to comfort him in his misery with, "Well, who could concentrate on his serve with THAT on his mind?"

February 13, 1974

It's been raining. It started late in the afternoon and continued into the evening. It makes Saudi Arabia seem like a normal place. The wind was from the southwest today, and the moist warm air brought the temperature up into the seventies and made it seem like spring.

I have been having a problem with my garden. Three gorgeous, healthy, robust tomato plants about a foot high just disappeared. I came home and noticed a bare spot in my garden and three new holes sloppily filled in. I was mad! I went around complaining to everyone. I told Ben, who also grows tomatoes, about it. He told a gardener in Arabic, and the gardener observed, "They are all savages. Only a savage would do that." Some new people are paying the gardeners extra to work on their garden. Technically the gardeners receive a salary from the college. I am afraid my neighbors may have made it worthwhile for the gardeners to steal my tomato plants. Today I came back and noticed three different, smaller tomato plants in the holes occupied by the first three. Someone is playing musical tomato plants. Rumor here is that everybody has tomato plants but nobody ever has a tomato. That's because the gardeners harvest them first. Well, harvesting the very plants just takes the cake.

I blame the pollution from the Aramco refineries for a lot of the sickness here. You would not believe the sulfur smell when the wind shifts. It's a wonder there is paint still on the house. The first time some newcomers smelled it they went around their house covering their drains because they thought it was sewer gas.

February 15, 1974, Friday [Letter by Jack]

This is contract renewal time, and the future outlook changes from day to day as one learns who's staying and who's going, and who has changed their minds. Also under discussion at this time is summer school, which looks to be a real bare bones project. If they asked me, I would teach.

[Letter continued by Maralyn]

There's been a shortage of the kinds of frozen meat I usually buy in the stores here. The rest of the selection is pretty grim. Australian meat is stringy and tough and the freezing job has usually been done at least twice from the looks of things. The lamb is not so bad, but the beef is horrendous. The Danish beef is just as bad. So last week I bought a turkey. This week the situation was the same, so Jack went to the Saudi fish market and bought an eight-kilo hamur (like haddock, about twenty pounds).[86] It was the smallest one they had. After trimming, cleaning, etc., I am going to get five meals out of it. We had the first meal tonight. It's lovely, fresh, firm-fleshed meat. I put seasoned breadcrumbs, butter, and lemon juice on top and put it in the oven.

---

86   A Gulf grouper.

Even Alex ate it. I also bought another tin of Australian corned beef, which looks like a canned ham. We've had New England boiled dinner so often that I'll never get homesick—only sick of corned beef. If the situation doesn't improve by the time I go shopping next week, I will have to send Jack out after half a camel. Or maybe we'll eat omelets all next week.

Jack has promised to take me to the Aramco dining hall for our anniversary, if I can find a babysitter. That's like trying to find my original three tomato plants.

There was a huge black beetle on our front steps the other day. They're about the size of a half dollar. The neighborhood kids had a stoning party that lasted all afternoon. Nobody had the nerve to step on it. It's a wonder there are any shingles left on the house.

Jack's students from last semester asked him if the group he has now is better than they were. Jack replied, "Of course. They don't have physical education just before English."

My washing machine is out of commission again.

February 16, 1974

Our weekly mail allotment arrived today. I think they hold our mail and present it to us all at once.

Couple of interesting things going on here. One of my neighbors, Alice, dialed a friend and got connected directly into a conversation between Jen and another man. It was a passionate exchange, arranging trysts around an absent husband, and such phrases as "undressing me with your eyes." Alice kept expecting that her friend would pick up the phone and she would be disconnected from the call she was over-hearing. She finally hung up and dialed again. She got her friend this time. Anyway, Alice is sure the switchboard operator was listening in on that conversation, so the line was open and her call got circuited in. The "other man" is Arab but not Saudi. Alice wanted to tell Jen to be careful about what she said on the phone. I said it was too late. The administration already knew what was going on, and it would just give Jen anxiety attacks. Since this compound is so small, things get out.

I'm hoping Jen's husband is not a violent man. He's never home anyway, so he probably has no idea what's happening.

It's funny what you notice when you know what to look for. Jen disappears from women's group meeting halfway through the session. She gets up at seven in the morning and is walking around the compound in time to meet her friend in the truck. Then she comes to work in the library about eight. Her husband isn't up till eight thirty or nine, so he doesn't know.

At any rate, Jen's husband is incredibly immature and wrapped up in himself. This is a terrible place to bring a woman. She has no family nearby, she can't drive, she can't go to school or take courses, she can't go out alone, and when she arrived here she had no friends. The first thing Jen's husband did was to go out and buy himself a motorcycle. Women can't ride them. He spends all day in the English Language Institute lounge shooting the breeze, so by the time he gets home, he doesn't feel like talking to her. She's working in the library and bored out of her mind. So she found something to make her life interesting and someone who will pay attention to her. This someone is a single Lebanese air-conditioning technician working for the Maintenance Department. I think she's being used. Maybe they're using each other.

They had a party last night. Today she asked me if their stereo bothered me. I told her I didn't hear it. However, there were some people sitting right next to our kitchen wall, which is their living room. I heard one woman's voice very clearly telling a joke: "Why does the coyote howl? Because there are no fire hydrants in the desert, only cactus." I told Jack what I heard. He said I should have told her, "No, your stereo didn't bother me but the coyote joke I heard did." I said, "All she needs to know when her affair gets out is that I could hear conversation through the wall. She would be certain I was the one who told on her."

Well, so much for the compound gossip.

A few years ago one of the men here went off on a vacation, found a hooker, and brought her back here as his "wife." He did pretty well peddling her to the bachelors until the administration found out, and now he's not here anymore and neither is his "wife."

According to the Aramco calendar on the desk in front of me, May is NEVER SMOKE IN BED month.

February 17, 1974

Read in the local paper that the Concorde is going to begin flying to the Gulf area.[87] Super. Nothing like living near an airport. The sonic booms from the Concorde ought to clear my sinuses.

It is against the law here for men to urinate standing up. They must squat.[88] Or get a flogging.

February 23, 1974

Some women were fired at the library. They were told the library had been reorganized and their jobs were abolished. It is known that director thought one talked too much (the one who lost her mother on that flight in Rome) and the other was "working against him." She wasn't any more than anyone else there. It made everyone uneasy. The administration has also become touchy about women being seen by the students. Officially it's against the law for women to work in Saudi Arabia. There is a snack bar where we have been buying coffee to bring upstairs. Now we have to get an "office boy" to do it for us. Whenever visiting dignitaries come through on tour, all the women are told to remain in their offices until they've gone.

Made the initial corrections on Jack's students' compositions. One of them said that after class he went to the "snake park." I wondered if there was a zoo for snakes near here. Then I recalled the typical Arab/English confusion over the letter "p" (there is none in Arabic) and concluded he meant "snack bar." There *is* a snack bar here.

The Woolriches invited us to a party. I look forward to it.

February 25, 1974

---

87   Commercial flights of the Concorde began on January, 1976, but operations and test flights began in 1974, and test and demonstration flights were made as early as 1971.

88   The reason for this is that a man might get urine on his pants and this would make him unclean and negate his prayers.

Woolriches' party went well. The department is divided into groups of people who have something in common. Britishers, couples with no children, bachelors, and couples with children. Harv Woolrich had red, white, and rose wine, all homemade of course. It wasn't bad. Unfortunately we had just eaten before we came so I couldn't enjoy the food.

I opened a Betty Crocker chocolate fudge cake mix to make the oatmeal chocolate chip recipe on the box. It was loaded with little white worms and mahogany-colored beetles a quarter inch long. I threw it out. I couldn't bring myself to sift it and use the mix anyway.

March 5, 1974

Nothing much new here. Rumors about who's going, who's staying, who's leaving her husband, when school's going to start, when graduation's going to be, etc.

Joyce lent me a pile of British Women's Weeklies. They are like a combination *True Romance*, *True Confessions*, *Women's Day*, and *Better Homes and Gardens*. With Dear Abby and Dear Doctor thrown in. Knitting directions are included in every issue, so I concluded that the British women do more knitting than American women do. The magazines even printed some recipes from World War II rationing booklets. They use much less meat than American recipes, and some of the main dishes had no meat at all. They had odd items like herring kabobs, steak and kidney pie, scrambled egg suppers, etc.

March 9, 1974

Three of the college wives are leaving, two to get divorced. One was married eight years, the other ten. The latter can't get her husband to sign for her to leave. The Saudi government won't issue an exit visa to a wife unless her husband gives written permission. It absolutely infuriates me. Rumor has it that if one goes to the US Consulate, the Consul can help. The husband is probably hoping that if he withholds permission, she'll get over it and change her mind. The first wife has a kid and was having an affair with someone here. Her husband knew about it and would just arrange to be out of the house for the evening when the other party was coming.

CBS film crews were at the college last week, filming classes that will be shown on *60 Minutes*.

We had the loan of a small portable television Saturday for two days. There is a break in broadcasting about 6:45 p.m. for fifteen minutes so all Moslems can go through their evening prayers without missing anything. They broadcast a few hours each evening. We mostly watched the English language station. They have several series from the States, plus kid shows and old movies.

I think we are definitely coming home this summer. Jack is working out flights on Flying Carpet Airlines—our nickname for Syrian Arab Airlines. I keep listening apprehensively to the news about fighting on the Golan Heights. Americans aren't exactly loved in Damascus. At least I've never heard of a Syrian Arab plane being hijacked by Arab terrorists (all their flights stop in Damascus).

March 12, 1974

We are having Joe Fahey over to supper. I am baking fish in foil with vegetables. The fish is excellent here. The things I am going to miss when I move back to the States are the fish, the coffee, and the shrimp.

Last night the mice in the walls kept Jack awake most of the night. At noon today he came home and began banging on the bedroom walls screaming, "GET UP! WAKE UP! YOU CAN'T SLEEP WHEN YOU KEEP ME AWAKE AT NIGHT!" I suggested he call maintenance and tell them to come and get rid of the mice for us. The way they operate, they'd probably send eleven guys with little nets and one guillotine. Each time my washer has been taken to the repair shop, they have sent seven men. It's impossible to get anything done without a crowd. One man will come to repair the toilet and two come to watch.

March 14, 1974

Locally spices are sold loose in the spice souk and weighed out by the Arab shop owners. Imported American spices are sold (McCormick's, French's) in the supermarket. I was thinking about what was cheap here that I could bring home to people and I thought of "the spices of Arabia." But I KNOW nobody would use them, because they'd think they were contaminated with a variety of foreign bodies. They probably are, so I am thinking of other things. Everything is so expensive.

There was a yard sale on the central green area of the compound yesterday. Everybody sold unwanted items. I bought Alex some toys, cheap. One of my neighbors, an American, had a pair of boy's sandals someone bought in England for her. They were too big and had not been worn. The Americans and British would inquire about the price. They would not bargain. But the Arabs would try to beat her down, saying, "Well, if you want to get rid of them why not sell them for less than you paid?" She would explain that they had never been worn, were brand new, and that sandals here would be at least half again more. And they'd try to beat her down anyway. She said she'd rather give them away than lower the price anymore. Haggling is part of the Arab society. It's a game. But Americans don't play it and don't understand it. They feel it is demeaning to haggle over a few cents. If a price is too high, they just walk away. Or they pay it if they want it badly enough. But they don't haggle.

Some friends here were sent some games for Christmas. One game was missing. They complained. The college's customs broker told them that the packages contained contraband—three pairs of dice—and only because he (the customs broker) assured the customs officials that they were fine, upstanding citizens whom he knew personally did the game with the dice get through without being confiscated.[89] Probably at that moment, the customs broker was feeling guilty about stealing the missing game.

March 17, 1974

Jack, two guys from his department, and I went out to eat at the airport restaurant tonight and then to a Woody Allen movie, *Play it Again Sam*, at the British Air Works outdoor theater.[90] At the restaurant I had hummus, broiled shrimp with French beans, and French fries, and it

---

89   Items used for gambling or games of chance are banned in Saudi Arabia.

90   Released in 1972, starring Woody Allen and Diane Keaton.

was pretty good. I watched the Saudi's night fighters land and take off on practice runs from the airport. Alex was left with a sitter.

Tonight one of the lines in the movie was "I'd sell my own mother to the Arabs if I could go to bed with her." Everyone roared. The projectionist screwed up changing reels, putting on one that had already been shown, and then putting on another that was ahead of the one they should have run. Somebody yelled, "The Saudis are getting in on everything!"

There is actually a lot of that among the foreigners here. According to them, the Saudis never do anything right, etc. Nobody wants to give them credit for anything.

The sun is now warm and gentle. One can go out in the evening without a coat. The wind is from the south, and the cold winds from the north have ceased. People are spending weekends at the beach, though it is still too cold to swim.

Came across a dead two-pound Saudi beetle today, like the one the kids were stoning on my front doorstep a month back. Was tempted to box it up and send it home. But I decided against it because I didn't want to touch it. Also there might be some regulations against sending bugs across international borders, and it might give some customs inspector a nasty shock.

The bus driver of the nursery school bus almost drove over a curb Wednesday when he spotted a dachshund on the sidewalk at Aramco. Arabs cannot understand why Americans like dogs. They consider them unclean animals. Taxi drivers will refuse fares that are accompanied by dogs, though they have been known to allow goats in their cabs. Anyway, you have to admit that a dachshund is pretty strange even to someone accustomed to dogs. The driver giggled and called in Arabic to his buddy who sits up front to share the sight. And then he hit the curb.

We borrowed a television the other night. *The Collector* was the movie for the evening.[91] Before it came on they showed *Green Acres*.[92] If there is something Arabs appreciate even less than dogs, it's pigs.

---

91   Based on John Fowles' novel. Released in 1965, starring Terence Stamp and Samantha Eggar.

92   A TV series that ran from 1965 to 1971, starring Eddie Albert and Eva Gabor.

They are so superstitious about pork that most of them won't even handle it, let alone consume it. So it's not even imported here. I would also bet there isn't a pig in the country, unless they have wild boars someplace in the hinterlands. Can't imagine what the Saudis think of a television program where a glamorous rich woman has a pet pig on a leash.

Peter Jennings of the ABC news was here at the college yesterday, filming.[93]

Today Jack caught a fly out of the air in front of his English class and slammed it against the wall, knocking it out, while continuing to lecture. From the back of the room came a "Yasallaaam!" the local equivalent of WOW! or COOL MAN!

Actually he does that a lot here. The flies are not as fast as they are in the States. A girl who has been here three years told me her husband does the same thing to flies, and when they went back to the States last summer, he went bananas because he kept trying the move on US flies but they were too quick for him.

March 19, 1974

There is going to be a Tennis Awards Ball at the Consulate at the end of April. All the participants in the tennis tournament get invited and have a sit down dinner with open bar and dancing afterwards. For this social event of the season, Jack is supposed to wear a white shirt, bow tie, dinner jacket, and black shoes. All he has is a pair of brown shoes that a heel came off of a while back, and there are no cobblers in Saudi Arabia. Leaving him with a pair of white leather tennis shoes. Well, it IS a tennis awards ball.

---

93   Peter Jennings (1938–2005) was the anchor and senior editor of ABC program: "World News Tonight." Film taken of the college was shown on the ABC Evening News on March 27, 1974.

CHAPTER 4

Public beheadings, zip code humor, Turkish toilets, Saudi Brushers, the DDT man—death, destruction, terror, Arabic soap operas, graduation

March 20, 1974

There was a thundershower on the way back from town tonight. Lightning is very dramatic on a desert landscape. There was thunder and huge drops briefly splattered on the dusty bus and sidewalks. Almost like a normal place.

We had shwermas and sanbusi for supper. The meat sanbusi was better than vegetable sanbusi. They used fresh coriander in the vegetable mixture. It looks like parsley and tastes like soap. I've bought it by mistake, thinking it was parsley, and ruined several dishes with it.

A man in the Math Department now has his daughters—two little girls, ages six and seven—living with him. His wife, in the States, ran off and joined a commune shortly after he came. He flew back at Christmas time to get the girls. They were on the bus tonight. Nice kids.

March 21, 1974

The temperature is in the high eighties to low nineties and, in effect, it is summer. The lizards are coming out again. I saw a very odd looking one on the walk today. It was lead-pipe gray and about nine inches long and looked like a snake with legs. The only other kind I have seen here are fleshy pink and rubbery; they are called geckos. They have a tendency to cling to the front door screen at eye level so that when the front door gets opened, you are eyeball to eyeball with a gecko. A little unnerving. But the worst thing in the warm weather is the huge three-inch-in-diameter, black cockroach type beetle with nine-inch antenna. They tend to be attracted to the front door light, along with the geckos and moths. I came up the steps one night and spotted the long antennae waving and just the tip of the head. I feared for my life. I am afraid to kick at them in case they'd eat my foot.

I think I will throw an early birthday party for Alex so he can be the center of attention for an afternoon. Probably in June before everyone leaves. As I have written, birthday parties are very organized here: hand deliver invitations, cake and ice cream and games, and give out nice favors.

March 25, 1974

Nothing much has changed here. Jack and I were in simultaneously bad moods the other night and had an argument over living here. The tensions are awful and the same in the compound. Everybody is fighting with everybody. We need to go someplace the first week in April to get away, but can't afford to if we are going home this summer. People say this happens every spring.

Recently Ben and Alice invited a Moroccan couple and a Saudi couple to supper. They all came into the house except the Saudi wife. After a few minutes the Saudi, Ali, said, "My wife is outside on the steps." So Alice had to let her in through the kitchen door. She was veiled and refused to enter the room with the others, being mixed company. Alice showed her into the bedroom. She spoke no English and Alice no Arabic. The Moroccan's wife went into the bedroom to keep her company. The Saudi said to the Moroccan, "It is in the Koran that this should be so." The Moroccan was incensed and, since he considers himself an authority on the Koran, replied, "Let's settle this once and for all. Where in the Koran is it that women should be treated this way?" And Ali, the Saudi, backed down, conceding that while maybe it wasn't in the Koran, it was "custom." The Moroccan allowed that. The Saudi wife refused to be served dinner until the men had eaten. And she ate in the bedroom. Alice said it was a tense uncomfortable evening all around. And this Saudi got his doctorate at Vanderbilt

University in Nashville, Tennessee. One would have hoped that his stateside experiences might have had some liberalizing influence.

The college has begun putting bachelors together, three to a house. The aforementioned tensions mentioned have hit the bachelors as well, and one teacher in the English Institute finally moved out on his two Arab roommates. The last straw was when he discovered a pot of beans baking in the oven covered with aluminum foil. He took the foil off the beans and the tear matched his roll of aluminum foil. He threw a fit and went to personnel to complain and deliver an ultimatum. He had complained before. It seems Arabs have a custom of inviting family, relatives, and friends to come stay for a while, "My house is your house." American roommates have problems accepting the presence of some guy sleeping in the hall for two weeks and helping himself to communal food.

In the March 10 *New York Times* Sunday Magazine, there is a good article about Aramco and their scheming and plotting in Saudi Arabia.[94] However, Aramco actually does some good things here: maintaining a trachoma clinic, publishing Arabic newspapers for their Arab employees, holding English classes for them, providing medical care for all employees, funding home financing programs for Saudi employees, etc.

March 26, 1974 [Letter by Jack]

It's near vacation time so not only are the students and teachers tired, but also teaching restless students is twice the work.[95] Finally I couldn't keep up, so I canceled my first two classes this morning in the hope that we would all get some sleep. The weather here is now quite warm and summery and the trees are starting to lose their leaves (the sun is *too* much). Alex and Neal are now very much into *Batman* as they have capes. Alex's is a pillowcase that hangs down his back. He runs all over the neighborhood chasing bad guys.

---

94   The title is "The Richest Oil Company in the World," by Leonard Mosley.

95   The vacation is Eid al Adha.

[Letter continued by Maralyn]

I am making a halter-top gown out of slippery nylon knit for the Consulate ball.

The job in the library is awful. Personalities clashing. Alexandra, the librarian, is trying to bring changes in operations and being fought like grim death by the director, an Iraqi. Both of them spend most of their time recruiting foot soldiers, and I am spending all my time trying to avoid the conflict and not being tricked into taking sides. All this static in the air makes for a bad working atmosphere and a ripe one for rumors, which both of the combatants seem to be spreading. Some of them were, "There is a spy in the library," "Four girls in the library are going to be sacked," and "The director says the Americans are better workers than the British," etc. I plan to resign before the trip home. Maybe the personnel director can come up with a better job. If not, no job is better than one in an atmosphere of tension and intrigue.

It's like summer now. My parsley is the only thing that could be described as flourishing in my garden. Petunia plants are springing up unbidden. The former tenant must have grown them. I need fertilizer for the calendula. The tomatoes need to be tied to stakes, though no fruit has formed yet. And Ben's garden looks lush and tropical, making ours look anemic and causing Jack to apologize to all who come to our house, and have to pass Ben's first, by saying, "We really haven't spent any time on ours."

March 28, 1974

It is still the law here that men and women are stoned to death for adultery. However the government claims that in the history of Islam this has only been done fourteen times. It requires four witnesses who actually saw the act. Then it becomes the "public nature of the act," that is, doing it in front of four witnesses that is punishable, not so much the crime between two people. If one man kills another man, the family of the victim can chose between having the man's life or collecting a huge sum of money from him. For the former, it is usually a public execution, and the man is beheaded by sword. These events are not announced beforehand. One could come upon a public beheading by just happening to be in the area. I have not heard of that occurring here, but there are stories of people witnessing it in Jeddah.

We have been invited to a big anniversary party one of my coworkers is holding, but I haven't been able to locate a sitter. They have two gallons of sidiqui, the local bathtub gin of which on two glasses I once got nauseatingly hung over all the next day and have sworn off forever. I am not drinking again until the Consulate party. Malt has finally turned up on the grocers' shelves after a long absence, and everybody is starting to make beer again. As for the winemakers, whenever you spot someone buying ten pounds of sugar and five pounds of raisins at a crack, and maybe a can of yeast as well, you know what they're up to.

Last year one of the professors in the General Studies Department was asked to leave because he had had affairs with his students. His field was poetry, and everyone says he had gorgeous clothes and dressed immaculately. This is an ideal country to work in if you are gay. No pressure to date. Plenty of men, no women to even look at. This must be an awful spot for a straight bachelor with a high sex drive. Oh well, there are plenty of sheep here, as the students like to joke.

I am smuggling the Sunday *New York Times* out of the library and reading it thoroughly in the evenings. The latest one is about a month old. Finally found a *Time* and *Newsweek* in town last night.

As I wrote a while ago, the Arabic for penis is "zib." There is no *p* in Arabic, so *p* sounds like *b* to an Arab. Yesterday an American came into the library and asked me where the ZIP code directory was. I didn't know where reference material of that nature was stored, so I asked Omar the Saudi employee, whose English is pretty limited, where the ZIP code directory was. He looked like he was fighting back a laugh and obviously had no idea what a ZIP code directory was. The more I explained the more Omar looked like he was going to choke. Finally I asked the library director, who told me where it was.

March 30, 1974

We had a wild thunderstorm today with rain pouring down for an hour. Hailstones bounced down for ten minutes during the rain. My garden is flooded. There are no storm drains here, so when it rains it really floods. There have been weather predictions for more of the same tonight, but I think the clouds passed by north of Dhahran. Everyone's roof leaks. They seldom have rain here, and this winter has been unusually wet. Since leaky roofs are not usually a problem, they don't bother to fix them when they do leak because they figure it won't rain again for a long time. My neighbor has a bad leak over her bed. We discovered one here, but it was conveniently over the sink. It has been an unusually rainy year so far. I was stranded at my Arabic class and the poor girl with the leak over the bed was there as well. Her husband was at class, and all she could do was moan over the drenched bed she was going to have to use tonight.

Had a tour of the new library on the jebel today. Architects must design in a vacuum. The front of the building had a star-shaped pool, which is connected by tiled trenches to a series of other pools. Right in front of the main door to the building is a one-foot wide moat so that anyone entering has to step over it. I can visualize any number of people breaking a leg in it. The director told the architects that it was unacceptable. The new library is expected to open by this summer.

April 6, 1974

The phones have been out of order since last week when we had that bad rainstorm. The wiring insulation comes from the El Cheapo Cable Company and tastes delicious to rats. The rain soaked the cable, and the rats have been chewing on it. The peace is wonderful, but I keep thinking that if anyone from the States is trying to call, they're out of luck.

Neal's granDAHD from England is here. On the way to the compound from the airport, he casually mentioned to Neal's father that he had a quart of Jim Beam whiskey in his shopping bag. Neal's father screamed, "Jesus Christ, don't you know they put you in jail for that here? It's against the law! How did you get through customs?" It turned out that they just glanced at his shopping bag, but didn't search it. Someone in England told him he ought to bring his son a bottle, and he thought that was a good idea. I had a glass of Jim Beam yesterday, about an inch and a half in a drinking glass, and felt lovely for about an hour.

Nigel was christened at Aramco, where there is a priest.[96] They also had a christening cake, which was a dark cake loaded with raisins, with marzipan covering and a boiled icing on top of that.

The Consulate Tennis Awards Ball is in two weeks and we are both looking forward to unlimited gin and tonics and a bountiful buffet. My gown has a halter front and no back. Jack's not sure it's decent. About twice since I've been here I've gotten the desire to get roaring drunk. Not lately, but I would like to get slightly uninhibited.

April 7, 1974

Joe Fahey, Jack, and I got back from a trip to the oasis of Al Hasa and Hofuf.[97] It is a two-and-a-half hour drive away. Most of the dates in Saudi Arabia come from this region, which has two million date trees. The rock formations reminded me of the Grand Canyon and Bryce Canyon in the States. We went around the oasis, climbed a rocky jebel where Jack took some pictures, and then went to visit a series of caves. Alex didn't want to go in because he said that dragons lived in them. We talked him into it. Walking through the narrow passageways with teetering boulders perched above made me feel like I was tempting the gods. I kept thinking, "What if there is an earthquake while I'm in here?" However, it was at least twenty degrees cooler in the caves than it was in the afternoon sun outside. After we left the caves, Alex wanted to go back. When he got home he ran straight up to Neal's to tell him he'd been in a cave that had dragons hiding in it. And HE wasn't scared!

We took some pictures outside of the caves. I took pictures of the old walls of the fortified town, made of mud and crumbling now. I also took pictures of the two-wheeled donkey carts and one hennaed donkey. On Thursdays there is a camel market in town. We went in the middle of the week, which was a beautiful time, because we were the

---

96   Priests are very rare in Saudi Arabia.

97   The Hofuf Oasis is near Dammam. It is the world's greatest producer of dates and is a well-known camel market.

only Westerners there. Shopkeepers were willing to bargain and come down on their prices.

The town of Hofuf was a very interesting place—quite different than Al-Khobar or Dhahran—with hallways of little stalls and everything at least half the price of what it costs in Al-Khobar. They had rows of small shops with brass pans of pumpkin seeds, watermelon seeds, squash seeds, sunflower seeds, and several kinds for which I only know the Arabic name.

The spice souk displayed brass pans of cardamom, cumin, coriander, henna, peppercorns, saffron, and spices I couldn't identify, plus a balance scale to weigh them on. There was a gold souk, but at the price of gold these days, I didn't bother to find it. Bedouin women sat in little stalls selling masks, veils, and abayas, the long black shrouds Saudi women wear. There were rows of mattress shops selling foam rubber rectangles with bright cotton covers. We looked at some Bedouin rugs, but everything seemed to be from Iran. People here say you can do better on oriental rugs in the States when they're having a clearance sale. It was a fascinating town. Anyway it was a real change from Al-Khobar and Dhahran. I felt like I was more in contact with the true Saudi Arabia, not this boomtown amalgam of the worst of the East and the worst of the West, which is found in Al-Khobar.

One of the stall keepers asked Jack which one of them (Jack or Joe) was married to me and whose son Alex was. He did not speak English so the conversation took place in Arabic. I told Jack that he should have told the stall keeper that they were both my husbands and we didn't know who the kid belonged to.

Little Arab kids kept following us around. Alex couldn't tell them apart, so everywhere he went, he thought he was seeing the same kids and would say, "There are those Arab kids again." Jack observed, "Those Arab kids sure get around." Then, Alex would yell at them, "Ashra, sitta, humsa!!" (ten, six, five, in Arabic). I don't know where he learned that.

On the road to the oasis of Hofuf we passed two dead camels, a dead goat, two dead cats, and one dead dog. All traffic casualties. Can you imagine hitting a camel? What must be left of the car?

We ate lunch yesterday at a hotel in Hofuf, because it was the only place I could think of where there would be a bathroom I could use. They had a Western toilet with no flush handle and a Turkish toilet, which has a hole in the floor to be squatted over that did flush. And no toilet paper any place. Naturally Alex had to "do poops." I knew it was more than I could cope with, so I handed the job to Jack, along with a box of Kleenex. When Jack came back he asked, "How did you flush the Western toilet?" I figured he would show Alex how to use the flushable Turkish toilet, which is why I gave him the job, old Middle East hand that he was.[98] In retrospect I recalled a large can beside the Western toilet, which was probably used for flushing. I don't want to know about the mess that got left in there. At the time, I didn't have a clue how to use the Turkish toilet. I asked Joe later and he said that you face front with feet on either side of the hole. I would have faced the wall. And Alex would have fallen in.

All overseas phone calls are monitored. A German woman got a call from her daughter, and they began talking in German. The censor cut in and told them they had to speak in English or Arabic.

April 13, 1974

Alex went to the beach with Neal today. They couldn't go swimming because of the jellyfish, apparently a problem in the spring. So they spent the afternoon throwing mud balls at the jellyfish marooned on the beach. I asked Neal if his mother made them "peanut butter and jellyfish sandwiches" and killed myself laughing while he looked at me as if I had rocks in my head. My mind's going.

In the Arabian Gulf there is a species of poisonous sea snake. They come out from the coral reefs this time of year to lay eggs near the shore. Their small jaws can't bite onto legs or arms but can bite fingers or toes. Supposedly there is no antidote for their venom.[99]

---

98   Jack was in the Peace Corps in Libya before he was married.

99   More than one species of poisonous sea snakes live in the Persian Gulf. The deadliest is the beaked sea snake, whose venom is a hundred times more deadly than a king cobra.

A Saudi at the library gave me a postcard with a photo of the sand dunes in the Empty Quarter.[100] In the very center are five tiny buildings—a seismological station. Jack sent the postcard to his friend George in the States and wrote on the back, "You thought we lived in the middle of nowhere—behold! Our house is the third from the left."

I made a southern pecan pie yesterday.[101] It is so rich I can't eat more than a small piece. The next pie will be a "Black Bottom Pie," chocolate on the bottom and vanilla on the top.

In the Arabian world, hair is considered very seductive. That's why men cover it with head cloths. Unveiled Arab women, even if they are not Saudi, usually wear a head covering of some sort. The Saudi women wear all black with a heavy veil on the face. Only Bedouin women wear the facemask, covering everything but the eyes.

April 15, 1974

Arabian cockroaches fly! I opened a cupboard, and this four-inch cockroach streaked across the shelf and flew down to the counter. I screamed and got Jack out of bed to kill it. He couldn't find it. Later that evening I opened the door again, armed with a flyswatter, and discovered the cockroach sitting there. I beat the bejesus out of him. He was only one inch long. When the creatures move, they look longer than they do lying bashed and beaten on the linoleum.

The sandstorm season starts in another month. It's just incredible how the sand gets through the slightest crack. I made Jack a mask out of white cotton jersey, with two holes for the eyes. He looks weird in it.

I went to town tonight, alone, to do some shopping, and the same Saudi "brushed" me twice! I was ready to go for his throat if he went by me again. Actually, I've had very few problems with brushers. I think

---

100   In Arabic, Rub' al Khali, a vast desert six hundred miles long and three hundred wide in the southern part of Saudi Arabia. In summer the temperature at noon is about 140° F., at night below freezing. It has sand dunes as high as one thousand feet. It is abundantly rich in oil.

101   For recipe see "Pecan Pie," appendix 1.

it's because of my imposing five-feet, ten-inch height. Other women here have been rubbed, pinched, brushed, which is the back of the hand against one's thigh, and patted, etc. It happens more at night than any other time.

In the April 8 issue of *Newsweek*, in the "Newsmakers Section" is an item about the Duchess of Bedford.[102] The Saudis were greatly offended by it and obliterated the whole thing. I got a copy somebody brought back from Iran, uncensored, and it described her three days in bed in a hotel with a stranger who forced his way into her room. They also ripped out the page in "The Sexes" section where a British journalist described his sex change from male to female. Well, *they're* the ones who go around holding hands all the time.[103] I was finally getting used to seeing the men kiss and hold hands (they kiss as a greeting) when I saw two Saudi women walking around the compound the other day holding hands, and I got culture shock all over again.

Do you know that "fanny" in British English means very specifically a woman's sexual organs? It's considered quite crude, in contrast to its connotations in American English, which is a rather genteel reference to the buttocks. Also "bangs" in British English means breasts, and "fringe" means what Americans call "bangs." A "pouf" is a homosexual and a "loo" a bathroom. This information comes from the British contingent in the library. They went into convulsions after somebody used the term "bangs" to describe a haircut. Alex picked up some of these expressions, the more polite ones, and corrects me when I say "tomato," but pronouncing it "to MAH to." He also says "LEEver" for "lever." He calls training wheels "stabilizers."

The British have been supervising the training of the Saudi National Guard. The local National Guard unit has a parade every

---

102   The Duchess of Bedford was Nicole Charlotte Pierette Schneider (French born) who married the Thirteenth Duke of Bedford (John Ian Robert Russell) on September 1960. She was a TV producer and author. The *Newsweek* article recounts an incident she wrote about in her autobiography *Nicole Nobody*, which happened in Manchester in 1946.

103   It is quite common for Saudi males who are friends to hold hands while they are walking.

morning across from the library. They all wear baggy brown wool one-size-fits-all uniforms and, I suspect from the size of them, have to be five feet or under to join. They drill to the accompaniment of bagpipes and drums. You have to listen to it to believe it. The only instrument that sounds like it's supposed to sound like is the drum. And when you can tell that a bagpipe isn't being played properly, then you *know* there's a problem.

However, the Americans are about to take over the training and equipping of the Saudi National Guard. It's part of a huge arms-and-technology-for-oil deal. The Saudis want to modernize their National Guard because they guard the oil fields. Last year there were two cases of sabotage at Ras Tanura, Aramco's huge refinery. The Saudis fear the Palestinians are trying to sabotage the oil fields.

It looks like there will be a big demand for English language teachers. Personally, I'd like to get out before the big war that's going to ensue after everybody gets jet fighters, Skyhawk missiles, atomic submarines, tanks, radar systems, and modern armies. There has always been tension between Iran and Saudi Arabia over sundry islands in the Gulf. Iran is sending arms to the Sultan of Oman, where there is an insurrection in the mountains. Every now and again, the local paper shows a picture of a bombed camel train, hit because it was suspected of bringing supplies to the liberation front in the mountains. The Yemenis are aiding the rebels. The Shah of Iran is aiding the Kurds in their disagreement with the Iraqis. And there have been border clashes between Iran and Iraq recently. The unpleasantness on the Golan Heights is getting a little hot now, threatening our planned trip back via Syrian Arab Airlines. But you ain't seen nothing yet. Wait till they all get armed.

Did you know that the population of Saudi Arabia is between three and eleven million? How's that for specificity? Nobody's ever taken a census. It's a UN estimate.

An Egyptian I work with told me that his brother is in the missile corps in Egypt and was given a medal by Sadat for shooting down fifteen Israeli jets (as with all Egyptian war statistics, divide by five). This man catalogs the Arabic books for the library. He came here because his wife was offered a job teaching physics at the Saudi girls' high school. He said he was lucky to find a job too.

Egypt is like India. They have an overdeveloped educational system and no economy to absorb their college graduates.[104] So they export them all over the Arab world. Lots of them are working in Saudi Arabia, and Jack said Libya was loaded with them.[105] There are also Indians (from India) here, but the Saudis are suspicious of anyone who believes in more than one God.[106] So most of these Indians are either Muslims or Christians. We had shwermas for supper tonight. It's nice not to cook supper once in a while. Our phone is still out of order. Jack has been getting upset with Joe Fahey because he comes over and stays until all hours, and is always trying to involve Jack in this or that activity, then dumps on him for sleeping as much as he does and not doing anything. I think Joe is okay but I agree that he doesn't know when to leave. I feel caught in the middle. I am not as sensitive to Joe as Jack is and find him interesting.

April 20, 1974

I skipped work today and went in town shopping. I didn't get to go over the weekend because we went to the Consulate party Wednesday night.

The party was sort of a bust—Jack threw up afterwards. He wasn't feeling well before he went. We went with Joe Fahey, who had been Jack's doubles partner. All the Brits brought their tuxedos to Saudi Arabia and what Joe calls "dickie bow ties." The Americans weren't anticipating such formality. Jack attended wearing a sports jacket, slacks, and tennis shoes. My dress was rather slinky looking but not tacky. The colors in the print were flattering. As for the rest of it, tables were set up in the garden outside. The Consul's wife had hung Japanese lanterns on wires running from the house to the wall around the edge of the garden. Food was served buffet style at a table just outside

---

104   In recent times this is also true of Saudi Arabia, but few find jobs outside of the kingdom.

105   Jack was in the Peace Corps in Libya before he was married.

106   The official religion of Saudi Arabia is Wahhabism, which is strictly monotheistic and is strongly opposed to polytheism. Hinduism, which has many major gods, is condemned and considered worse than Christianity, which too is regarded as polytheistic since Christians regard Jesus as divine.

the door, and a bar was next to it so anyone could go up and ask for a drink from the bartender. Everyone took liberal advantage of *that* feature. The night was lovely and clear and balmy, like a New England evening in the middle of July. We were chatting with crazy Larry Black, a former Green Beret and EFL teacher in Jack's department,[107] when a stunning blonde wearing a gown, backless down to the limits of the law, sauntered by. Larry stopped midsentence and announced, "Excuse me, I never could pass up a bare back," and he took off after her. Although it was a very nice party, it couldn't match the first one, which was such a refreshing *American* change from the life we had been leading.

I picked up a Bahraini English language newspaper that was about a week old. There was a rather unusual murder in Bahrain. Not the clichéd Arab-with-curved-dagger-and-flowing-robes-stabs-man-in-back routine. Seems that this electrician thought a neighboring cab driver had the hots for his wife. Wearing insulated gloves, he connected up a wire garrote to 250 volts. He waited all Friday night for the cab driver. The electrician had put sand in the lock to the cab driver's garage to occupy him while he crept up behind him with the "live" garrote. He electrocuted and strangled the man simultaneously. Then he buried the corpse in the garden. Apparently not being able to stand the suspense, the electrician initiated the inquiry by calling the police to complain that a neighbor, the cab driver, had insulted and assaulted him and then escaped. The police went to the neighbor's home, and his family promptly reported him missing. Then the electrician confessed and showed investigators where the body was. This was done voluntarily, before the police had any idea that a murder had been committed. At the end of the article, the police department spokesman was quoted as saying, "We have worked day and night to solve this crime and our findings will shortly be presented to the court"—taking credit for acts of God. So much for gore in the Gulf.

My phone is still out of order. I figure service here is about on a par with service in the States. Except to us it's free and worth every penny.

---

107   EFL, **E**nglish as a **F**oreign **L**anguage (studying English in a non-English-speaking country).

April 21, 1974

The college art show was held, and there were two paintings I wanted. One cost forty dollars and the other almost one hundred dollars.[108] Art is high priced here, like everything else. There was one super realistic painting of a Saudi street scene from an old village, like a mixture of Andrew Wyeth for detail, Salvador Dali for tone, and Georgia O'Keefe for subject matter. Pretty gloomy, all in all. But the Saudis went wild for it. The artist didn't price it but took bids from people. As of today the highest bid was one thousand dollars.[109] I asked the Saudi I worked with why it was so popular. He replied to the effect that it *was* Saudi Arabia. Speaking of which, I saw a one-foot-long rat that had been killed by a car on a street downtown.

A very good book about Saudi Arabia is *Passing Brave* by William Polk and William Mares.[110] They traveled by camel across the Nafud,[111] a desert to the north which was crossed by Lawrence of Arabia.[112] Lawrence had successfully attacked the Turkish stronghold of Aqaba (because they never expected an attack from the desert, all the Turkish guns were cemented into place facing the water). Polk and Mares talk about the transition of Saudi Arabia from desert kingdom to twentieth century. They couldn't locate a decent camel, camel saddles were almost impossible to locate, and the old wells hadn't been tended in years because the Bedouin were gradually settling down. It's fascinating.

---

108   By the 2012 dollar, $40 is about $186, and $100 about $466.

109   By the 2012 dollar, $1,000 in 1974 is now about $4,662.

110   Published by Macrae Smith Co., 1945.

111   An-Nafud, in Arabic "The Desert." It is twenty-five thousand square miles, has frequent sandstorms, and large sand dunes.

112   Thomas Edward Lawrence (1888–1935). He graduated from Oxford and did postgraduate work in medieval pottery. Later became a field archaeologist for the British Museum in the Middle East. Studied Arabic. Enlisted in British army in 1914, worked for British Military Intelligence. He fought with the Arabs against the Turks with considerable success.

April 24, 1974

I have harvested my first tomato out of my garden. It was a little pink and slightly misshapen. It wouldn't win any prizes in a garden show, but I beat the gardeners to it and the neighborhood kids as well.

The high so far has been 104 degrees. It's the humidity that's killing us. The sandstorms are due to begin in another month or less. I can't imagine a sand blizzard with temperatures of 110 and high humidity. I just can't imagine it. Washes have to be hung inside the house or they will be encrusted with sand. It blows in everywhere.

April 27, 1974

We went swimming yesterday at Half Moon Bay. The water was a little cool, and I just lay about in the sun. Joe went in swimming and Alex followed. He had Alex's shovel and plastic bucket. They were catching jellyfish, very strange, light blue cellular masses. One was so large it completely filled Alex's bucket. Alex was very excited, dancing around yelling, "Chop them up! Throw sand on them!" Joe dug holes in the sand and threw them in, while Alex pranced about cackling the equivalent of Count Dracula's "MBAHAHAHAHA!"

A lithe, tanned beauty in a bikini was sunning herself on a sailboat a hundred yards off shore. Joe and Jack were cursing themselves for not bringing field glasses, when a motorboat with three Saudis in it zoomed past, cut the motor, came to a stop, and cruised idly around the sailboat—not once, but twice—gunned the motor and zoomed back into the bay. Twenty minutes later they were back again, stopped about two hundred yards from the sailboat, drifted until they were about the same distance past her, gunned the engine again, and raced off.

This fascination with anything female is an aspect of Arab culture here which is amusing at first and then wears thin. They'll stare as if you had two heads. The female college dietitian, who is well past fifty, was approached by a Saudi kitchen worker who put his hand down the pocket of her thobe, which is about twelve inches deep from hip to near the knee, and announced, "What deep pockets you have!" It's when you realize that you could be ninety and in a wheelchair and they'd still stare that it becomes strange. I suppose if you're over the hill, it's marvelous balm for the ego, but the dietitian was pretty steamed.

May 5, 1974

The college is now going bananas trying to get enough teachers for the summer. They dallied around for so long that all the people who might have stayed decided that the college budget problems meant there would be so few teaching positions that they had better make other plans. So some decided to go to Europe and some decided to go home.

I went to a beautiful beach in Jubail about an hour and fifteen minutes north of here, with Joe Fahey and Alex.[113] Jack decided at the last minute not to come. We parked the car at a little bay and were the only people for at least a mile. There was a very gradual beach with white sand. We had to walk so far out to get deep enough to swim that I was sure we were going to walk to Bahrain before it got to our waists. Alex got a half-bucket of shells, some nice ones. We had a picnic there and went walking along the beach. It wasn't until we were about a half-mile from the car that I noticed my feet. They were covered with tar-like oil, coated with sand, with shells, and seaweed stuck to them. They no longer looked like feet at all. The port refinery of Ras Tanura was about thirty-seven miles to the south and yet the oil had gotten all over the beach at Jubail. Anyway, we got lost leaving and ended up mired in soft sand fifty yards from the road we wanted. It took an hour of my pushing and digging to get the car out. I was so exhausted when I got home that Jack, Joe, Alex, and I went to the airport's restaurant for supper. I had a salad called tabbouleh and kifta—fingers of ground meat in a sauce served on rice. I would recommend the tabbouleh.[114] Very refreshing.

Eggplant and okra are very popular here. Eggplant is called the poor man's meat. I made eggplant eggah (omelet-like mixture) and put it in Syrian bread, split open and spread with tahini and chopped fresh tomato. It was a good meal.

---

113   Jubail now has an Intercontinental Hotel.

114   For recipe see "Tabbouleh" in appendix 1.

May 5, 1974 [Letter by Jack]

There was a notice put up in the language institute a week ago saying that the college was looking for two more English teachers for the summer session. We reviewed our decision about the summer and came to the same conclusion, that it is not worthwhile to stay.

Since there was a prince visiting today, Maralyn went to work at a co-worker's house this morning. Women aren't supposed to be working. She returned to the library this afternoon.

[Letter continued by Maralyn]

They have so many books in the library that last year they discovered that two floors were beginning to develop cracks. Two weeks ago they had a student art show and had cleared the fourth floor of books for the event. As they went to move them back following the show, they discovered the floors had gotten much worse. So they packed up half the Arabic book collection to ship them to the new library up on the jebel. They had loaded the books into trucks when somebody remembered that the prince was coming and it wouldn't do to have so few Arabic books in the library. So they unpacked them and replaced them on the shelves. Now they are packing them up again. The library is still standing.

The prince who visited was Prince Fahad, Minister of Defense.[115] He came to the airport with an entourage to spend the week attending the graduation ceremonies of the Royal Saudi Air Force cadets. The local police band, which I see practicing from the library window in the morning, was there in full dress uniform, bagpipes groaning. Prince Fahad is supposed to be King Faisal's successor.[116] The next morning at about seven or eight Jack said he heard two jets go over, then two more, then two more, until twenty passed overhead. He remembered thinking, "God, please don't let it be a coup." The jets seldom go over more than two or three at a time. It turned out that the graduates were showing off their stuff for the prince.

---

115 It was Fahad, but the office is probably incorrect. In 1967 Fahad was appointed as Second Deputy Prime Minister and in 1975 to Deputy Prime Minister and Crown Prince. He became king in 1982.

116 It was Khalid who succeeded King Faisal, Fahad succeeded King Khalid.

One of Jack's students dropped out. Jack was relieved when he did, since his English was so bad that he would have been the first student Jack would have had to fail. The guy then came to work in the library. One of the girls downstairs where he works said he was reading *The Three Bears*. He came to her with the book and asked, "What is this word?" She said, "Bears." Then he sat down and began reading. The more he read the more he giggled. He turned to her and said, "This is a very funny book."

Penny, who has her master's in library science, is leaving to go home because she can't stand it anymore. She wanted to go in March, but her husband refused to sign for her to leave. She's flying back on Royal Jordan Air, spending some time in Paris, and then to Minneapolis. The plane stops in Amman, Kuwait, and Rome before landing in Paris.

May 9, 1974

Alex and Jack were walking over to the college the other evening when the call to prayer came from the nearby mosque.

Alex: "Daddy, do you know what that is?"

Jack: "No, what?"

Alex: "That's calling the Saudis to parade."

He probably imagined a group of Saudis marching around the mosque in response to the loudspeakers.

I went into town this morning and bought favors for Alex's party, which we are holding the twenty-third of May so he can be a big shot for a day. A birthday without an audience of kids to impress is simply not the same, which is why we're having a party for him before we leave.

May 15, 1974

Found the *Betty Crocker Cookbook* in the library at Aramco. Made the brownie nut cake, "for small families." It is excellent. I ground the nuts in the coffee grinder. I think they come out a little finer than they would if I had chopped them.

Mohammed, the Saudi I work with, is twenty-four years old and somewhat sophisticated and worldly for the norm here. He majored in

English at Riyadh University and so is fairly fluent. He hopes to go to the States in the fall to library school. He told me he and a friend were walking around Aramco the other night, looking for girls. He said he walked where the single girls are housed, eight to a house, observing that they advertised their presence by hanging their underwear out on a line. He saw "rows of underpants" and (he didn't know the word for) bras. And he raised his eyebrows when he said this, as if he saw the girls in them. Trying to make a joke, I said, "Oh, I always hang all OUR underwear outside on the line inside pillowcases!" He said, "Oh, that is very good. You are very modest." I dropped the subject. What could I say? Saudis are very Victorian. Jack said, "When somebody asks you how life is in Saudi Arabia, tell them the story about the underwear."

I became so disgusted with the colors my sheets were turning from the water that I sent them out to the Dammam laundry. They came back white, starched, and ironed. They looked beautiful. It costs about twenty cents to have a sheet done.[117]

The college hired an extermination squad from the city of Dammam to come to the college grounds and spray DDT everywhere. They came into the library at half past one in the afternoon and began spraying books, offices, and personnel indiscriminately. Somebody dashed into our office, which I share with an Egyptian and a Saudi, screaming, "THEY'RE SPRAYING! LOCK THE DOOR!" Mohammed rushed to the door with a key. It was the wrong key so he ran back to his desk for the other. Meanwhile the exterminator stuck the nozzle in through a crack in the door and the room filled with a fog of DDT. Mohammed rushed back and locked the door. We gasped and roared and rattled the locked door, trying to get out. The only window was a plate of glass nine feet by six feet. Mohammed had locked us in.

One of the English teachers is a health food nut with a horror of DDT and anything unnatural. He was at his desk in his office with his back to the door when the exterminator came through and filled his office with DDT. He took one look at the sprayer and jumped out of the window. Fortunately he was on the first floor. Then he

---

117 A little over ninety cents by the 2012 dollar.

went around through the front door, grabbed the poor extermina-tor in a headlock, and dragged him out while warning him NEVER TO COME BACK! All the next day every ache and pain he had was attributed to the DDT and were considered signs of the onset of a long illness.

Related to the same spraying foray, one of my neighbors looked out her window and almost had cardiac arrest. She thought there had been a landing from space. One Arab dressed in a canvas suit with a Plexiglas face was plodding along, tanks slung over his back, holding a nozzle spraying clouds into the air. Another Arab walked three feet in front of him, apparently to lead the way. He had no protective clothing. She said, "The nozzle was pointed directly at the rear end of the first man. He didn't move it up, down, or to the sides. I don't know what good it was doing the neighborhood." The joys of living in a develop-ing nation.

We found a two-inch cockroach, or similar insect, in the bath-tub. It had four-inch antennae. I yelled for Jack. He whacked it with the flyswatter. The cockroach didn't even notice. Jack finally beat it to death with his shoe. A friend of Jack's in Peace Corps used to get up in the morning and find twenty or thirty of them in his tub. He couldn't imagine why all these bugs were climbing *into* his tub. Then someone informed him they weren't climbing *into* the tub, they were coming up via the drain. He began covering the drain after that.

The local radio station carries very dramatic Arabic soap operas. I can't understand them, but I can always pick out the villain by his laugh. MMBAHAHAHAHAHA! It would make Boris Karloff shud-der. The plots are along the lines of the bad guys foreclosing on the mortgage of the poor widow and then kidnapping the beautiful daugh-ter and tying her to the railroad tracks, etc. People with televisions tell me that the facial expressions on the television soap operas are right out of the silent movie era. Not very subtle.

May 18, 1974

At Arabic class this afternoon I learned of an accident the teacher's car got into all by itself. Miriam's husband and son parked their yellow Volkswagen outside the Al-Mana hospital, next to their dentist's big American car. A Saudi with two kids and no driver's license plowed into the dentist's car, pushing it against the Volkswagen, which sailed across the street into another car parked on the other side. Someone ran into the dentist's office screaming, "Who owns the yellow car?" When Miriam's husband identified himself, the fellow, an American, said, "You would not believe what I just saw!" The dentist's car was wrecked, but Miriam's was still drivable. However, the Saudi had connections in the police department and was not charged with anything. Instead they arrested the dentist's car. It was towed off to the police station grounds to be held. The dentist's insurance company is paying for everyone's damages. As many non-Saudis have learned when they've been involved in accidents, a Saudi is never at fault. Presumably after the dentist's company pays for everything, his car will be released. It was pretty much destroyed. Miriam's car just had a new paint job a month ago. Now it needs some more paint and body work, though it can be driven.

I have to go up to the gatehouse and pick up my laundry. The gatehouse attendant, Abdul Latif, who also sells cases of Pepsi and is in the laundry business, has the gift of looking continuously as if he just got out of bed and has the personality to match. His idea of dressing up is to tuck his shirt in. After an abnormally long stay at the gatehouse, Jack came back shaking his head, saying, "Abdul Latif has all the charm of an aging camel with a thorn in his foot." Ben Benjabril made the understatement of the year when he said, "I don't think he likes his job." Myra Anderson is convinced that Abdul has been making obscene phone calls in English from the gatehouse. However I don't think she has any evidence to support her convictions. It's only his overall attitude that makes one want to think the worst. Recently someone told us that it was best to tip him. Well, when Jack bought Pepsi, he didn't give Jack the right change. The amount held back was so small Jack let it go. We assumed he was tipping himself.

I am still getting ready for a birthday party for Alex, the twenty-third of May. I have eight invitations, which according to the custom here must be personally delivered by the birthday boy with his mother along to lend credence to the proceedings. Then there must be a gathering of at least six kids for perhaps one and a half to two hours, which is about as much as most mothers can stand. There must be games, ice cream and cake, and favors, consisting of a few trinkets, gum, and candy. Anyway, I'm *not* looking forward to it.

The sport among the single teachers in the English Department is sneaking into the Aramco-personnel-only movies. One guy carefully memorized an ID number at Aramco in case the guard stopped him. He planned to say he forgot his Aramco ID, but the ID number was such and such. Well, he got stopped, but the guard asked him his *house* number. He got so rattled he couldn't think of a number and was sent packing.

May 19, 1974

In about five and a half weeks we'll be out of here. High today 102, yesterday 104. A hot dry wind blows continuously. The sandstorm season is due anytime. Last year it blew for twenty straight days. I'm hoping it won't be like that this year. It goes in cycles of ten years.

Oh, scandal! The latest one involves a couple from California with two kids. She left two months ago for California, and rumors were that she was getting a divorce. It turns out she was having an affair with the guy across the way whose "wife" left him last year. This "wife," it turned out, was never really married to him because they got a divorce in Haiti just before he signed his contract here. She came along for the ride, hated it, and went off last summer to Nepal to teach English. He now has a contract in Iran, and when the girl in California has her divorce finalized, he will fly to California and marry her. Then they will all fly to Isfahan and live happily ever after—maybe. The administration hates things like that, the government here being puritanical to excess, but I'm not sure they know what's really going on.

May 25, 1974

Alex's party was incredible. It was from 3:30 to 5:00. And it convinced me that I don't want to have any more kids. One birthday a year is too many. Forty-five minutes into the thing, I took two Anacin; an hour into the thing, I began babbling and drooling. We rolled up the carpet, piled the furniture in the bedroom, blew up eight balloons and hung them around the living room, made colored marshmallow animals to sit on top of his yellow frosted cake and put four candles on it, had purple Kool-Aid, vanilla ice cream, pink napkins and cups, and paper plates with Road Runner on them, and a Happy Birthday tablecloth. The kids brought him two boats, a clockwork train, an airplane, a truck, and a toy Land Rover. Jack was running the games. He'd yell, "OKAY, WHO WANTS TO PLAY MUSICAL CUSHIONS?" (we didn't have enough chairs) and the same kid would yell back, "I don't wanna play!" to everything! By the time we'd played four games, only a half hour had passed, and the kid had gotten three recruits who all said in unison, "We don't wanna play." Jack decided it was time for the ice cream and cake. He said, "WHO WANTS ICE CREAM AND CAKE?" and one kid said, "I don't want any cake!" By the time 5:00 p.m. rolled around, I had looked at the clock one hundred and twenty times in ninety minutes, taken two more aspirin, cleaned up one overturned plate of cake and ice cream off the floor, discovered the mechanism on the clockwork train had been sprung, the airplane had been flown onto the roof of the house, the drive shaft on the battery-powered speed boat had been broken, and the spare tire had come off the toy Land Rover. I took two pictures of Jack climbing up onto the roof of the house on top of four end tables piled on top of each other near the back door. As he stood on the roof holding the airplane, the parents of Matthew, who gave him the plane, drove up. Jack waved the plane at them and said, "I think you're responsible for this!" They said, "We knew you'd have fun with it!"

May 31, 1974 [Letter by Jack]

Maralyn quit the library and is now working in accounting typing checks for all the people who are going on vacation. Graduation is in ten days and then this place should become very quiet. The shamals are overdue, and I hope they never come.

Maralyn went visiting at Woolrich's the other afternoon and ended up having some of his "grape juice." I went and got her after phoning twice, and she came home and flamed the shrimp for supper. The shrimp wasn't supposed to be flamed.

June 1, 1974

Just got back from the Woolrich's party. It was very nice. There was a punch made from some local brew and dishes catered from the Chinese restaurant in A-Khobar, and a variety of other dishes from various people in the department. My chocolate chiffon pie went immediately.

June 10, 1974

I am suffering from sinusitis. I went to the hospital today, along with Jack who is still having problems with his throat. The ENT man told him he should be operated on to have the last tonsil tissue removed. Jack had a shot of penicillin the first time, and the man gave him ampicillin tablets because he still had the infection. The doctor I saw was French trained and apparently right out of medical school. He was Arab and his English was hard to understand. He poked and prodded my stomach, then told me he found a "mass." The area was the size of an orange. I nearly had a heart attack. He said he was going to bring in another doctor to check it, and while he was gone I was mentally composing my last will and testament. He returned with Alex's pediatrician. The man poked briefly and said, "It's okay. That's her stomach." I offered, "I had tea for breakfast this morning." However, by this time I had lost all faith in the French-trained Arab doctor.

Two nights ago we ate at the airport restaurant. It is a great vaulted building, maybe three or four stories high. I noticed three little sparrows eating crumbs from the floor near our table. I said, "Jack, there are birds over there." Then I looked up and saw some flying around overhead, from one corner of the ceiling ledge to another. The building is enclosed. Joe Fahey said, "They're always here; haven't you noticed them before?"

A few days ago an Englishman came into town on an unscheduled flight. He couldn't find anyone to meet him, so he took a taxi to the gatehouse at the college and called a woman I happened to be visiting. He said he was at the gatehouse. She said, "My house is next to the gatehouse. I'll meet you." She came back and said he must be at another gatehouse. She tried the other two, but the night watchman only spoke Arabic. I said, "I'll try my Arabic." I called and said, "Fii rejul inglizzi ma'ak?" The man replied, "No speak English." I got the same response from the other man. I was depressed. My attempts at Arabic were mistaken for English! I checked with someone at accounting, and they said my Arabic was correct. Maybe the watchman didn't want to try to understand. The Englishman was eventually located.

The reason I am in accounting right now is because their Pakistani male secretary went on vacation. He borrowed money from everybody he worked with, got advances on his travel allowance, salary, housing allowance, and vacation pay. Also he borrowed three thousand riyals from the bank. And he hasn't returned! They think he might have immigrated to Canada. He has a brother there. The assistant director, a Saudi who shares his office with me, got a little steamed on the subject. He said, "I don't see why countries like Canada want immigrants from such uncivilized places as Pakistan!"

Jack is at graduation tonight. I am watching it on television. It's all in Arabic. Joe is leaving for England tonight, driving up Aramco's tapline road, which runs along the Saudi Arabian border to the Jordanian border into Syria. After graduation, he's coming back for supper and then leaving. No faculty members are allowed to leave until after graduation ceremony. Jack and Joe joked about the faculty flying down the jebel after the ceremony is over. They compared it to the beginning of the Monte Carlo—the cars waiting with their engines idling, ready to take off to the tapline road or to the airport. They're giving out diplomas now at the college. Jack and Joe should be back shortly

All the students are wearing the traditional Saudi garments. There was a big hand for a graduate in a wheelchair. I charmed the assistant director of the library into getting me an Arabic calendar, not the Islamic calendar, which is followed by no country except Saudi Arabia. The year is 1394 in case you're interested.

They're finished, marching out. Have to go warm up the chicken. Would you believe the students are filing out to bagpipe music?

June 11, 1974

People got their new housing assignments for next year. Neal and family are being moved to the other compound. Ben and Alice, my favorite neighbors, are going to the other compound. The Woolriches are going. I hope some people with kids move in here; otherwise it's going to be all childless couples or couples with infants.

One couple here, the Dmitrios, have raised hell about their housing ever since they arrived. Juraib, the housing director, is not very sympathetic. Anyway, after many complaints about their carpet being stained and worn, they finally, one dark night, threw it out on the lawn. At half past seven the next morning, Juraib and two of his heavies were banging on the front door. Serafina slipped out the back door, calling to her husband, "Oh, Chub, somebody to see you!" By the time Chub got to the door from his bed, they were gone. Later, he got on the phone to Juraib and complained bitterly about the "filthy Saudis" who lived in his house before he did. What he didn't know was that the "filthy Saudis" were none other than Juraib and his family. So when the new housing assignments came out, Chub learned he was reassigned to Ben and Alice's house, which is smaller than the one he now lives in. He's so mad Alice thinks he won't be back.

Chub's real name is Neville. His father was a great admirer of Neville Chamberlain. That was before 1938. Chub is Greek but got American citizenship a few years ago..

Visited a Saudi family in Dammam last week. They have eleven children, one is a student here. The family is well off. The oldest daughter is being married June 20 and we have been invited. The family is quite liberal, and we were very comfortable visiting them. The mother insisted we stay for lunch. Lunch consisted of baked chicken, a lemony tomato soup, a salad, bread, and milk custard for dessert. The salad had cubes of purple pickled turnip flavored with hot pepper, cucumbers, mint leaves, and parsley. It was delicious. The daughter showed me her trousseau, which she made herself on a hand-operated sewing machine. She didn't use patterns. One yellow crepe dress had a lined bodice sewn with lines of elastic thread, giving a puckered effect.

June 14, 1974

Things have quieted down considerably since Joe Fahey left town. Almost everybody has left, and the compound is like a ghost town here in this compound. There are a hundred or so houses here, and only a sixth of them are inhabited. As if to compound the eeriness, one neighbor across the street has shrouded his car in sheeting for the summer.

People who were departing brought over their unused groceries, and I am suffering from a compulsion not to throw anything out so I have been baking. I also have a French phrase book I intend to review in anticipation of our few days in Paris but haven't had a chance to look at it. There was a spaghetti Western, *Trinity Is My Name*, at the college last night.[118] You never saw such baroque touches in the Wild West. The architecture! The actors! I think that the sum total of the worst movies ever have been shown here at the college this year.

It is now late afternoon. We spent part of the day at the pool and then slept most of the afternoon. Alex is watching television, and Jack is still sleeping. Joe Fahey left his television with us for the summer.

The shamals, which were so bad last year, have so far failed to materialize. We have had three sandstorms. The shamal season is supposed to go from mid-May to the end of June. We've been very lucky. A Saudi at the accounting office told me that the shamals make the dates ripen. Mangos and apricots are in the vegetable souks now.

The night before Joe left, he drove me to Dammam to buy some material I wanted very much. After I bought it we walked around the town. The outdoor shwerma/Pepsi stands have television sets in them, over the counter, much like the bars in the States. Apparently the Dammam television station has been running a weekly serial/soap opera from Lebanon. Men were packed ten deep, in front of all these shwerma stands, watching the episode. Soap operas here are a very hammed-up affair. They also have mimed singing where the star breaks into song. The stories tend to be about star-crossed lovers, and the Arabs love it.

June 20, 1974

Husein, an Egyptian accountant, told me that last year the sand blew for twenty straight days and nobody could see his hand in front of

---

118   The name was either *My Name Is Trinity* or *They Call Me Trinity*; both names were used. The second is the dubbed version. This movie is a spoof on spaghetti Westerns. It was quite successful. Starring Terence Hill, Farley Granger, and Elena Pedemonte. Released in 1971.

him. They had to stop planes from coming into the airport on a couple of very bad days.

I am trying to use up all my odd ingredients here, so I don't have to buy any new ones before we leave for the States. The workmen are coming in to tear out the kitchen wall that all my cabinets are against. The Blairs next door were having fits about all the noise they were getting from our kitchen. They are putting in a double wall. So I have to move everything out of there.

I was supposed to finish work yesterday and take a week off, but they still have a lot of work to do so I will probably put in a few hours next week. It will keep my mind off leaving.

[No more letters were written this academic year.]

September 1974 to June 1975

Gerald Ford: President of the United States

Sep. 8, 1974: President Gerald Ford pardons President Nixon.

Jan. 1, 1975: Haldeman, Ehrlichman, Mitchell, and Marian convicted of Watergate crime.

Apr. 29, 1975: US Forces pull out of Vietnam.

Apr. 30, 1975: The war in Vietnam ends with South Vietnam surrendering to the North Vietnam government.

CHAPTER 5

Johnny Walker in the cockpit, the return of Joe Fahey, the Islamic Texans, the compassionate taxi driver, the stolen swim trunks, reading the Koran to chickens, purple satin underwear

September 2, 1974

This is our second day back. Our trip on Syrian Arab Airlines beggars description. We boarded the plane in Paris at 5:00 p.m. It had just flown in from Damascus. We stopped in Munich, where we waited an hour on the plane for the passengers. I spotted a stewardess coming out of the cockpit carrying a tray filled with five empty Johnny Walker nips. That is worse than walking into a doctor's office and finding him reading the *Merck Manual*.[119] The pilot also had the annoying habit of lowering the landing gear twenty minutes before the plane actually touched ground, giving the impression that mechanical difficulties were occurring.

By the time we left Munich for Dhahran, the flight was packed; the airline had overbooked the flight by seven people. Then the flight was delayed an hour while "documents" were en route. As the flight finally took off from Damascus, the door to the cockpit had to be held shut by the stewardess. This had also occurred taking off from Paris and Munich. Except that it blew open in the flight from Paris as there was no stewardess holding it then. Some of the air vents didn't work. They were short of safety instructions in case of emergency and had to hand them around. Two of the three bathroom doors didn't shut. Half the stewardess staff came from British Air. The airsick bags were from Pakistan Air. The metal molding on the wall of the plane had sprung.

---

119   *The Merck Manual of Diagnosis and Therapy.*

Some of the seats didn't recline. The plane out of Damascus was the same one that we had just taken from Paris. I suspect they have about two planes. I am not sure I want to fly Syrian Arab Airlines again.

It's really good to be back. I made gingerbread cookies today. I had a frosting-filled cake decorator and did faces on the snowmen I made. Then I got carried away and made them obscene.

I just learned that our air conditioner had been repaired only the night before we arrived. It broke down the morning we left. I had someone leave a note with maintenance. Three weeks before we left the States, I wrote to remind them. Our neighbor informed us that forty guys in twelve trucks worked ALL NIGHT the day before we returned.

September 6, 1974 [Letter by Jack]

Today everyone is supposed to be back, but there are still a lot of people missing. Eight of the twenty English Language Institute teachers are here, including two new ones (both Americans). We met them at a party of ELI people at Leo Blair's last night.[120]

Maralyn's been helping with acclimating the new people. She went with a group yesterday on a two-hour tour of a local fertilizer plant.

Since the road is torn up between here and town, it takes the bus a half hour to get to Al-Khobar.

Maralyn plans to check with accounting Saturday to see if there is a job there. In the meantime she's hoping Joe Fahey will arrive so she can get a ride to town with him and avoid the shopping bus.

September 9, 1974

I worked for the Housing Office yesterday because their Pakistani secretary was sick. The place was hopping. Everybody had complaints about their housing. There was a pile of nasty notes on the desk. The phone would ring again as soon as I put it down. Everyone wanted to talk with the director.

Every time a desk or bed is moved from one house to another, a computer form has to be printed by a secretary and fed into the com-

---

120   ELI is English Language Institute.

puter for "movement control." They do a lot of moving this time of year, and each piece of furniture right down to an ironing board has an inventory number. Anyway, I guess their secretary is back today because they haven't called. They indicated that they might like an assistant but said they would have to get a typewriter and office for her.

Yesterday our neighbor next door was out walking around on the compound green in 108-degree heat wearing a halter top and short shorts. The Arab gardeners were watering each other.

September 9, 1974 [Letter by Jack]

We'll only be teaching about three days when Ramadan will begin, and we'll go on a special schedule. Id al Fitr vacation will be October 10 to 20.[121]

September 10, 1974

I am still working on the house, trying to clean it up after a dusty summer and getting food in the cupboards again. Our friend Joe Fahey isn't back yet, but he was spotted at a campsite in southern Turkey, mugging it up with a big blonde. Must be that's what's keeping him. School officially opens Saturday.[122]

September 12, 1974 [Letter by Jack]

It is 100 percent humidity today and just unbearable. Still no Joe Fahey. I start Saturday, teaching five hours a day, four days a week.

September 14, 1974

Work is very confusing. Jack has double classes right now, and I can't work as many hours as they would like me to. It is a busy time for the Housing Office with all the new people, and they need help.

Jack is very upset with how muddled things are this year. Ramadan starts either Tuesday or Wednesday of this week, putting everybody

---

121   End of Ramadan holiday.

122   The beginning of the workweek. Thursday and Friday is the weekend.

on half days. Today and tomorrow all classes have been canceled until 11:00 a.m. while a national census is taken. They want—as I wrote last year—to pin the population down to something more precise than from three to eleven million.[123] The canceled classes must be made up on Thursday.[124] Jack isn't happy about that.

Joe Fahey came back unmarried. He wanted to get married, but his girlfriend Mildred wasn't ready. Also she didn't want to come back to Saudi Arabia. She rode with him from England to the Saudi border then took a taxi to Amman, Jordan, where she flew back to England. He says he's not coming back here after this year and plans to return to England to do another degree at the University of London. Mildred is an EFL teacher in London.

There are still very few kids around for Alex to play with. There is a flour shortage here, and most of the bakeries are closed. There seems to be enough American flour, and what bakeries that are still open must be using it because people say the bread is softer. I have been making my own bread and then last week found some frozen British bread. It is called "hovis bread" and is "made with genuine hovis flour" whatever that is.[125] The slices are smaller than Pepperidge Farm bread and thinner but quite edible and no bugs.

September 18, 1974

Food prices have gone up here, but they reduced gas prices. Now premium is fifteen cents a gallon.[126]

When Alex woke up from his nap and discovered that Joe had taken back the television he had loaned us, he announced, "If Joe Fahey comes back here, he's going to be under the arrent!" (That's

---

123   The census resulted in a total population of about seven million, but this figure included noncitizens. The CIA in their "World Fact Book" gives the population of Saudi Arabia as 26,534,504.

124   Thursday, being a weekend day in Saudi Arabia, is ordinarily not a workday.

125   Hovis is a brand name for a flour made by a patented process in Great Britain that is rich in wheat germ.

126   In 2012 dollars this would be about 70¢.

how he says "under arrest.") Alex was so upset at not having his cartoons and *Sesame Street* that we bought a secondhand television. Also Jack and I were going crazy for two days after Joe's television set went because Alex had nothing to do for two hours in the afternoon (from four thirty to six thirty) when we were usually busy getting supper. We were lucky and got a two-year-old Sony exactly like Joe's and in very good condition.

September 19, 1974

I am sitting under my hair dryer. Jack had to teach today to make up for the two mornings when classes were canceled due to the Saudi census being taken.[127] Jack is sort of disgusted with one of his classes because he has a couple of students in it who are going bananas over pictures in their textbook of secretaries with their legs crossed taking dictation (these are sketches, not photographs). And if they are acting that way over these pictures, wait till they reach the chapter in the textbook on ladies' underwear.

Joe Fahey has been presenting a problem. He's facing a year in Saudi Arabia without his girlfriend whom he hoped to marry, and things look pretty bleak to him. He has been spending most of his time with us, which is getting on Jack's nerves. Jack said, "I like Joe, but I don't want to live with him." I keep telling Jack that as soon as Joe accepts the fact that he's got to put in another year here without Mildred, he'll start finding other activities besides us. Jack isn't so sure. Anyway, if it keeps up much longer I think a showdown is coming.

It's funny to be back here for a second year. It is like a rerun. Already I have had it with the crush of people, and it took me until April of last year to feel that way. I would really like to have a car so I can get away from it and not have to take the bus in town with all the new arrivals.

There is a new couple here who are native born Texans and converted to Islam in the US. They were complaining on the bus one night that there were no mosques in Texas. She always wears long dresses

---

127   He was teaching on a Thursday, which ordinarily is the beginning of the weekend and not a workday.

with sleeves that cover her arms and a scarf that completely hides her hair. She has buckteeth and wire frame glasses. The scarf gives the impression that she has a continuous toothache. He is very thin, tall, and awkward and always wears a little embroidered silk cap. They have one surprisingly handsome son named Jamil. They consider themselves the resident authorities on Islam and are considered by everyone else as royal pains. She is in my Arabic class. She announced that a "man" had offered to teach her Arabic, but she refused because she didn't want to be taught by "a man." Another new couple is Mormon from Indiana. He's overweight, she's more so, and their six-month-old is the fattest baby I've ever seen. Then there is another new couple that belongs to some fundamentalist Christian church. The wife remarked to Jack, "Gee, I'd like to work, but the little church we belong to believes that the woman's place is in the home." I'd like to find out who did the recruiting this year for the college.

Then there is Joe's roommate, Jeff, who looks about twenty-three and is. He never taught before and has never been overseas. He kept asking Joe what he should say to his students. Then he went into Al-Khobar to buy a stereo, took a taxi back, and discovered he didn't know where he lived. When he realized that, he burst into tears. The taxi driver pulled over, hopped into the back seat, put his arms around Jeff, and tried to comfort him. They drove all around the college's three housing compounds, Dhahran village, and Aramco until they found an area he recognized and he managed to locate his house. He came in, took one look at Joe, and burst into tears again crying, "I've been robbed." The taxi driver charged him $2.80, which wasn't so bad considering what the taxi driver had been through.[128]

Speaking of "I've been robbed," Jack spent all last summer in the States looking for a bathing suit. In the last week he found one he liked. He bought it. He's worn it four times. Now it has disappeared off the clothesline. The kinds in Al-Khobar are the skinny knit Italian variety designed to expose more than to conceal. I had heard of ladies' underwear disappearing off lines, and baby clothing, but the Arabs are

---

128   In 2012 dollars, $1.30 is about $6.06.

not known for their love of aquatics, besides which Jack's suit was so modest that it looked more like a pair of Bermuda shorts than swim trunks. And I've NEVER seen an Arab wearing shorts.

To get back to Jeff, Harv Woolrich is so concerned about Jeff that he has asked Joe to look after him because he thinks he might quit before the year is out. Jeff didn't even know how to fix himself supper. Joe showed him how to make an omelet and open a can of soup. He was recruited at an EFL convention in Denver last spring.[129] They didn't let Harv, the department chairman, recruit this year but sent a Saudi instead. Because of the cultural differences, it is difficult for an Arab to size up an American with any validity.

September 21, 1974

Our garbage was collected today, nine days after the last time. I wouldn't have minded except that on day one I put out fish remains, and by day five the can was so stuffed we couldn't get the top down. It smelled pretty rank in the backyard. I began sending plastic bags of garbage to the south compound in Joe Fahey's car. Our sweet water container hadn't been filled. It looks as if we'll have no drinking water over the weekend. Between the water and garbage problem, I am frustrated.

September 21, 1974 [Letter by Jack]

I haven't been going to the pool the last week since my new bathing suit has disappeared. We theorize someone snitched it off the clothesline as happened to Frank Harris' suit two weeks ago. I haven't had much free time anyway with the extra teaching and Joe Fahey being to our house every free minute he's got. He's depressed over having to leave his girl behind in England and hasn't yet settled down to work. Also he doesn't have a double schedule like I have to keep him busy. We're on a Ramadan schedule now, and this morning after doing my first group of classes I called in sick for the last two. I

---

129   EFL, English as a Foreign Language (Studying English in non-English-speaking countries).

got up this morning with a headache, which instead of getting better just got worse.

September 22, 1974, 10:30 a.m.

Joe Fahey has been over every night for the past two weeks, and it is getting to be a problem. Jack is quite annoyed, and I am fast reaching that point. Last night when he showed up for the umpteenth time, we just went about our business like he wasn't there. I washed my hair, did dishes, studied my Arabic with the hair dryer on, etc. Jack read stories to Alex and lay down with him. None of this deterred Joe, since he stayed until ten fifteen. Joe goes crazy with time on his hands, so his solution is coming to our house. He gets all his work done in the office in the afternoon. Jack prefers to nap in the afternoon and work at home late at night. With Joe there he can't get anything done. We like Joe and would enjoy him now and then, but after spending the summer living with people, we would like some time to ourselves in our own home.

I have to go home—I'm typing this at work. Will continue later. Joe Fahey is putting a crimp in my correspondence.

Alex just received a birthday party invitation for the day after tomorrow, which means I've got to get to town to buy a birthday present.

The Pakistani secretary in the office where I am working was raving about what "dummies" the natives are, and how just because they've got oil they think they can rule the world and that most of them cannot write their own name. This was funny because in the last office where I worked—accounting—their Pakistani secretary had absconded to Canada on his vacation and in the process took with him money belonging to other people. The assistant director in that office was ranting about why places like Canada "take people like that from such uncivilized places as Pakistan" and "they must be hard up for people," etc. I guess it all depends on the viewpoint.

The king is supposed to officially open the new campus in November.[130] They've been working like mad to complete the eight-kilometer highway between Dhahran and Al-Khobar in time for the king's visit.

---

130 King Faisal. See "Saudi Arabia" in glossary A.

Every piece of road equipment in the Eastern province must be on that road right now. By law the equipment operators must be Saudis. Most of them seem to be learning on the job by the looks of the bark on the few trees left standing. Each time I go over that road it is different. Instead of building one road parallel to the old one, they seem to be doing it in sections and crisscrossing paths over it. People at the college have wrecked their cars going over the dirt paths, torn out their oil pans, ripped off their exhaust systems, punctured their gas tanks, broken their springs, etc. Now many of them are driving an extra nineteen miles around the city of Al-Khobar to avoid driving the three kilometers on the torn-up road.

I have been depressed the past week. This year holds no surprises except for the fact that everything is terribly disorganized due, I hope, to the religious holiday. Jack is teaching twenty-four hours a week instead of twelve like everyone else because three new teachers haven't arrived yet. He is exhausted. We've had trouble getting drinking water delivered, garbage collected, catching buses, etc. I am not terribly happy with my Housing Department job because I don't care to listen to the natives being run down, and they don't have enough for me to do.

September 28, 1974

I quit the housing job last Wednesday, writing a letter to personnel telling them that there wasn't enough work for me to do, which there wasn't, and not telling them I was having problems with the male Pakistani secretary, both physically and mentally. Now in the past six months I've quit two jobs and refused one. I figured it would be a while before they call me again and resigned myself to unemployment. As soon as I got back from Aramco's tennis courts today, my first free day, the phone rang and it was personnel, asking me if I wanted to be secretary to Dr. Hough, the chairman of the new Petroleum Engineering Department. The chairman *is* the department right now. However, he wants somebody who will work full-time and takes dictation. So I told them I took dictation, which I haven't for ten years at least, but said I couldn't work full-time. They said, "That's all right," and they wanted me to start tomorrow. However, Dr. Hough doesn't have an office for me or a typewriter, so what I am supposed to do tomorrow is beyond me. I also don't have any transportation to the new campus where he is located. It looks like another one of those jobs...

Joe Fahey's visits seem to be tapering off a little, l'hamdillilla (thank God in Arabic).

October 4, 1974 [Letter by Jack]

Maralyn has started her new job working for Dr. Hough. She is satisfied with it, although transportation to and from the jebel might become a problem in the future.

I got up early yesterday morning to get some fish and shrimp. I had to wait about fifteen minutes for the guy to arrive with the fish and open up his shop. Boy, do flies like fish shops. Every fly in Saudi Arabia must have been there, but they didn't bother me at all as there were better pickings where the fish were being cleaned.

The weather here has cooled off. The daily high is about ninety-eight degrees.

October 5, 1974

I am at work now employed by the Petroleum Engineering Department. The chairman, Dr. Hough, was dean of engineering at the University of Maine in Orono and has been hired to establish a major in petroleum engineering here at the college. He is the department, and my arrival just doubled the staff. His family is in Orono right now. He said he was flying back at Christmas. Dr. Hough told me that he was a full professor at thirty-seven. He received a PhD from California Tech in physics. Now he is a petroleum engineer. It's nice to be working for an American. The Saudis were okay, but the Iraqis, Pakistanis, and Lebanese are something else.

This gorgeous typewriter with which I am writing this letter has an "A" key which hits and then takes five seconds to fall back into place, stuck margins, a space bar that willfully decides how many spaces it will go no matter what the setting, and a touch that only George Foreman has.[131]

---

131   American boxer. Beat Joe Frazier for the heavyweight championship in 1973.

Jack took me to the airport restaurant for my birthday. Joe Fahey and Alex came too. I just got a notice that I have been granted a raise of one riyal an hour, so now I get ten riyals an hour, amounting to about two dollars eighty cents.[132]

Jack still has twenty-four hours of classes a week and is mad. He says if they don't do something by the end of the month he's going to complain. I think he should have been complaining all along.

October 9, 1974

Joe has been over less lately, as he seems to have found interests in the French community living in Dammam. He is going there tonight and tomorrow night. A two-week vacation starts today. We had hoped that he would go to Iran, but he couldn't get reservations in time. I will be working during some of the holiday, but the college will be shut down the sixteenth, seventeenth, and nineteenth of October, and Dr. Hough is going to Petra in Jordan on Monday. We might get to the beach, but we will surely be seeing a lot of Joe.

My written Arabic class begins the twenty-first. Joe is taking it. There are eight men and three women, one of whom audited the course at the University of Texas at Austin.

I have to take shorthand in my new job. I haven't done that in ten years. I am okay until Dr. Hough zips through terms like "high compression viscosimeter" and "well-reservoir engineering" and other petroleum engineering terms I can't get in longhand, let alone transcribe from my sloppy shorthand. I found a woman who loaned me a shorthand book for review.

Joe Fahey is still a problem. He is a compulsive doer. Any free time has to be filled. He's always after Jack to play tennis, do this, do that, and Jack gets annoyed with having his time planned out. Jack likes to think, and Joe does anything to avoid having to think about his situation.

I asked a Saudi how the Saudis afford food here. He said they all eat lots of rice and a piece or two of meat. Last week Jack was at the local fish market buying shrimp and fish. Shelled shrimp costs about

---

132 In 2012 dollars, about $13.05

twelve riyals for about 2.2 pounds. While Jack was waiting a man came in and asked for a riyal and a half (about forty-two cents) worth of shrimp.[133] That's about a sixth of a pound. There are rich Saudis who drive Mercedes and live in villas and vacation during the summers in Cairo, Syria, or Lebanon, but the majority seems to live on the edge of survival. And all the families are huge. The man who directs the airport post office has eleven children. Then he had a vasectomy, which must be the only one in the whole kingdom. But he is well off by owning a lot of property in Dammam. I don't think that there is the poverty here that you would find in Central American or Africa, but there is more than there should be for the wealth the country. Medical care is free. The government subsidizes rice, sugar, and flour, so the people are eating at least. Maybe these things take time. There doesn't appear to be a lot of discontent. But the religion fosters fatalism.

October 15, 1974

Ramadan didn't start today. The religious leaders have to look at the moon to decide when Ramadan starts, and about a month later they have to look at the moon again to decide when it ends. The month of Ramadan ends with a three-day holiday when everything shuts down.[134] This is the Moslem equivalent of Christmas because the kids get presents. Since the Saudi calendar is lunar, the year is eleven days shorter than the Western calendar year. Hence Ramadan comes eleven days earlier each Western year.

My food bill has increased about 25 percent, just over the summer. Bought a twelve-pound turkey for the equivalent of eighteen dollars.[135] The meat selection is sad, mostly Australian beef now. People live on Danish hamburg, which comes frozen in sausage-shaped plastic tubes and is adulterated with breadcrumbs and vegetable protein, or buy frozen Danish or French chickens. Jack and I eat a lot of shrimp and fish, but Alex won't touch shrimp and doesn't eat much fish.

---

133   In 2012 dollars, about $1.96.

134   Eid ul Fitr.

135   In 2012 dollars, about $84.

Got a good cornbread recipe and will make it the next time I make chili.[136] I soak dried beans overnight and cook them three hours the next day. Sometimes the beans are so old they never soften. However, the dried are safer because you never can tell how long the canned beans have been around.

We found a black scorpion between the screen and the front door the other night. It was three inches long not counting the tail, which is curled up over its body. It looked a little like a lobster. Jack finally cut it in two after the third blow from a big stick. Then the next morning he moved the bedspread from the bureau to the dressing table, and a pink lizard crawled out. He said he would have gone bananas if it had run up his arm. He carefully bunched up the bedspread, took it out the front door, and shook it. We couldn't see the lizard escaping, but we think it's not in the house. It was the fleshy pink variety, harmless, an insect eater. It's the third one we've had in here in the last month.

One more crawly thing in this house and I'm going home to mother.

October 19, 1974

The mail has been nonexistent since last Tuesday when the holidays began. The mailman at the college just dumped a sack of mail out all over the desk behind the glass mail window and left for five days. College personnel were going bananas because they could look through the glass window and see the mail strewn about, but they couldn't get to it. Then today two guys from the chemistry department managed to get into the mailroom to help a Saudi from the boiler room who was trying to put out the mail. The mail had fallen off the desk and was all over the floor. They were all squatting on the floor looking it over. Unfortunately the absent mailman had all the names and mailbox numbers in his head and they couldn't find the master list. The mailman is still on holiday. As of last report the mail is still strewn all over the floor, because there are no names on the other side of the mailboxes, the Chemistry Department professors have given up, and the boiler room man cannot read. So that's what happened to the mail this weekend.

---

136 For recipe see "Bessie's Cornbread" in appendix 1.

Dr. Hough seems to miss his family and to be very frustrated by the system here. He's used to an American university and where he dealt subtly with his contemporaries. What with the language problem, cultural differences, etc., a lot of subtlety just goes by the board. And what you think is really lowering the boom, by the time it has gone through translation and cultural differences, is just a slap on the wrist.

The chairman of Jack's department came to him and explained that he was going to give him all labs in the morning and he could double up his sessions. Jack, who is the only veteran teacher this year with a double load, told him he didn't like it and he was going to the dean about the extra class. Jack thinks that because he taught the extra class without complaining for a month that the chairman thinks he doesn't mind. The other two veterans who originally were given twenty-four hours along with Jack complained and were relieved as soon as the chairman could hire two British high school teachers from Dammam on an afternoon basis. He also told the chairman he was ready to quit. I think he is getting sick from the strain of the extra teaching. It is harder than high school teaching because the students need more work. So anyway, if things don't improve here I don't think we will renew out contract for another year.

October 20, 1974

Jack called the chairman of his department, ready to quit teaching today. He learned that new schedules have been drawn up with classes reassigned more evenly. He still has one of the heaviest loads. Joe Fahey got off very lightly. Joe comes down here and tells Jack what an idiot he is to be taken advantage of, which is annoying Jack to no end. Joe has cut down his visits somewhat due to a chilliness in the air. He is going back to England at Christmas to see Mildred. We just made reservations to Cairo today for a week starting December 20.

Jack's teaching hours got reduced from twenty-four hours to sixteen. The three new people still haven't come, although their visas have been issued, at long last.

Read in an uncensored *Time* magazine brought in by a returning vacationer, an article entitled "Chancing Sheik to Sheik."[137] It said that three members of the royal family lost six million dollars at the Monte Carlo Casino. Most certainly that story won't be found in the copies of *Time* carried in the Al-Khobar English language bookstore.

October 27, 1974

The movie *American Graffiti* came to the college last weekend.[138] It was cut all to hell. I found out from somebody who saw it in the States that one of the excised portions was of a bare bottom hung out of a car window. This was being done when I was at Northeastern University. It was called "hanging the moon." I am not surprised the censors cut that out. They were probably extremely puzzled, to boot.

The British here are going to celebrate Guy Fawkes Day on November 7—although it is Thursday it is our equivalent of Saturday night—with a bonfire and the burning of the straw dummy, Guy Fawkes. Alex and I visited Neal's dad tonight, who is in charge of supplying the dummy and building the bonfire. He dragged the dummy out of his bedroom into the living room, which scared the daylights out of Alex who didn't know what to make of it. The dummy was at least six feet tall.

October 30, 1974

Last night we went to a party. It was mobbed with people, half of whom I didn't know, which is quite unusual for here. When I inquired where they were from—expecting to hear Aramco, Northrop, BAC, Bechtel—I was told Germany. Thought I was being put on. Later learned that a Lufthansa crew had been temporarily stranded in Dhahran. There was some sidiqui from an Aramco source. It was a little more pure than moonshine. It didn't make me sick like the last product

---

137   *Time*, Oct. 21 1974. Among the three Saudi Arabian princes was Fahad ibn Abdul Aziz, Minister of the Interior, who later became king. The princes were not charged for their rooms.

138   A coming of age movie, pre-Vietnam era. Starring Richard Dreyfuss, Ron Howard, and Paul Le Mat. Released in 1973.

I sampled from the Aramco distillery. Found an interesting book in the Aramco library called *The Foxfire Book,* a compilation of mountain lore from the Ozarks with a quarter of the book devoted to making a still and how to hide it.[139] Very apropos here.

November 1, 1974

Husein, the Egyptian I worked with in the Accounting Department, visited us last night. He is going back to Egypt over the December 19 vacation to visit his family who live in Cairo. We are leaving the twentieth for Cairo. He is calling a friend there to make reservations for us at a first-class hotel, where he will meet us the day we get there.

Husein brought us a wooden plate with mother-of-pearl inlay work. He also brought me an ankh, or Coptic cross, to hang on a chain. The ankh design appears on the pyramids and symbolizes eternal life. The Copts adopted it later. Dr. Hough asked me if it was the women's lib symbol.

Halloween was last night. A neighbor gave Alex a jack-o'-lantern carved from a pumpkin raised at Aramco. Pumpkins are not usually found here. Alex went trick or treating with Jack.

At the last college women's group meeting, which is held in a new building that contains only men's rooms, I had to use the bathroom. One woman went upstairs to use the nearest men's bathroom during the meeting. I was afraid to do likewise, for fear somebody might be in there. So I got Myra Anderson's husband out of the chemistry office and had him check out the premises and stand guard. When I came out, I half-jokingly asked him if he had turned anybody away. He said, "Yes, a janitor." Later I asked the girl who had preceded me into the bathroom if she had any problems. She said, "Yes, a janitor walked in on me and there was absolutely no excuse for it!" Myra's husband said he saw the janitor watch me go in and then try to follow me. From the smell of the place, he never goes in any other time. Anyway, that's one way things are weird here. Peeping janitors.

---

139   Edited by Eliot Wigginton. Published by Anchor Books, 1972. The chapter "Moonshining as a Fine Art" has forty-three pages. The book has 384 pages.

The English language newspaper published in Bahrain contained an article about a huge poultry farm and processing plant being built in Dubai.[140] "In Denmark Emborg uses electric shocks to stun the birds before an automatic knife kills them. In Dubai, however, they will not use this method for religious reasons. The slaughtering will be carried out by hand in accordance with the Islamic rites and a quotation from the Koran will be repeated as each chicken is killed." The article said that Emborg planned to kill ten thousand chickens a day. Sounds like a full-time job.

November 5, 1974

This finds me in a depression. I guess lots of little negative things have happened of no individual significance and one big one. Yesterday a houseboy molested Alex's playmate, John age three, employed by the college to clean vacated houses. He got John into an empty house and apparently attempted sodomy or completed it. John related the incident to his parents last night by casually mentioning that a "painter wiped my bum." They questioned him further and found out enough to indicate that the man had attempted sodomy. John's father called the dean and told him. They found the man who was assigned to clean that house, and John identified him. John's father swore out a complaint at the police station. They took John to the hospital this morning to be checked out and to get a shot of penicillin.

I didn't go to work today. There was a possibility they wouldn't let me in the building because fourteen government ministers were visiting. Women aren't supposed to be working with men. So they banish us when dignitaries visit. Dr. Hough called while I was at Aramco and told Jack there were women all over the place today. Jack said he sounded mad.

Saw a few sugar beets in the vegetable souk the other day, what obscene looking vegetables! The Arabs are thinking about growing them here because they have a high salt tolerance.

I made deep-fat fried shrimp in a puffy batter the other night. The batter recipe came from Jack's father.[141] It's very good. They take a long

---

140   Dubai is a port on the Persian Gulf in the United Arab Emirates.

141   For recipe see "John's Batter for Two Pounds of Fish," appendix 1.

time to make. I cook six shrimp at a time, and Jack and I were eating them as soon as they were cool enough to hold.

There is a rare crew working this year as gardeners. They've knocked on the door twice, once asking for cigarettes and again asking for water. They worked Halloween evening and saw all the kids trick or treating, and then they started knocking on doors asking for things too. I can't believe it.

One of the women who was over to my place last night said that her purple satin underwear was taken off her clothesline. Then her husband had two car batteries taken off the front step. There never used to be a problem like this. Think it is being done by the Yemenis who are very poor and comprise the manual labor force in Saudi Arabia.[142] They are doing all the construction, gardening, houseboy work, etc., in the kingdom.

Jack's department is the one that the college would prefer to ignore. Its very existence admits that the Saudis' secondary school English programs are failures. These students have all had six years of English before they come to the prep year program. Then they have a year of English, twenty hours a week, just cut down to seventeen by the dean this year. The professors who get the freshmen still complain about their low level of English comprehension. Department meeting minutes, which I take, are full of such complaints.

November 15, 1974

Joe Fahey has gotten so busy that he hardly has time to show up anymore. The chilliness had gone, and I guess we are all friends again. Joe is in my Arabic class. He is teaching some French people English one day a week, is trying to work out ideas for a thesis for a master's in philosophy at the University of London, plays bridge one night a week, and is spending a lot of time talking himself out of marrying his girl back in London. He also plays tennis one night a week.

---

142   Still true in 2012.

The new campus will be dedicated November 29 by the king. It cost one hundred million dollars. The king will dedicate the campus and then travel around the Eastern Province. There are hundreds of workmen around cleaning up the college and the roads between here and the airport, planting trees, towing away junk, etc., in preparation for His Majesty's visit. The word has filtered down to the faculty that either they get haircuts or stay home while the king is here. The dean was too embarrassed to send out a memo to that effect, but the rumor is that the conservative Emir of the Eastern Province will be the king's host, and he told the dean to spruce up the faculty.

There is a large, shallow reflecting pool beside the modern mosque on the new campus. It's looking pretty sorry now, but that's partly due to the fact that nobody knows quite how to react to a body of water in Saudi Arabia. Joe Fahey said he saw three workmen in it sprinkling soap powder over themselves about a month ago. A student rode into it the other day, on his motorcycle. The cleanup crew for His Majesty's visit has been throwing cement bags, peat moss bags, old boards, etc., into it. And Aramco, located next door, has complained that the pool is breeding mosquitoes, which fly into their compound carrying malaria. They have sent workmen over with kerosene, which they poured on the water to kill the larvae. The architect claims that when the pump system starts circulating the water the mosquitoes won't be able to breed in the reflecting pool. There are channels a foot wide and a foot deep that run into the pool from all over the new campus, as part of the landscape design. They parallel the walkways around the buildings. It would be very easy to break an ankle in one if one didn't look down as one walked. Certainly no one in a wheelchair would be able to get around at all.

CHAPTER 6

Uniforms from Paris, earflaps in Saudi Arabia, love at 5:00 a.m., orange means passion, the coming of the king, to Egypt and back, the corpses on the bus, the frozen rabbit, three rules for Saudi Arabia

November 17, 1974

The department party was the night before last. The Chair Harv Woolrich and his wife Kerry had a turkey plus a five-pound ham. Everybody brought something. I made a chocolate chiffon and a banana cream pie. There was a sweet potato casserole, green bean casserole (with mushroom soup base and canned mushrooms added), carrots and peas together, stuffing, potatoes browned in butter, cranberry sauce, gravy, creamed onions, plus a British apple pie, which was very thin: one layer of apples, made in a big pizza pan, with a top crust. The turkey was very good, not dry. The green bean casserole had hot pepper in it, and I liked it but Jack didn't. The stuffing was too heavy on thyme or sage, and the British apple pie was made with the local golden delicious apples, which unfortunately, lack character. Someone once said that golden delicious is to apples what iceberg is to lettuce.

I will have to go to work late tomorrow because Alex won't be able to go to nursery school. He still has the flu, which he came down with yesterday. It is almost midnight and I am pretty tired. Played tennis yesterday because I am in this competition, called a ladder, in the beginner's category. I played someone yesterday who is a good thirty pounds overweight but naturally athletic. The best part of my game is my tennis dress. Naturally she beat me all over the place. I am creaking around now and know that the worst day will be tomorrow because whenever I get any unnatural exercise it always is the most painful two days later.

Jack not only had his bathing suit stolen off the clothesline but also his jock strap. He's steamed because they aren't available here. He bought two in the States this summer. A guy I work with had a double bed sheet taken off his clothesline. Things are a lot more chaotic this year. Lots of stuff stolen from the new campus: two calculators, lab tools, and things out of people's desks. The college is planning to establish a seventy-five-man security force, with uniforms from Paris.

November 17, 1974

When the temperature drops below eighty degrees, all the natives get out their woolly knit caps and start wearing plastic-visor hats with furry earflaps down and chinstraps fastened. All this over a cotton thobe. Some of them wear jackets too, and ski masks. Jack and I saw a four-year-old Arab boy who made us laugh. He wore a thobe and a black plastic hat with the earflaps down. No jacket or sweater. Jack says he would like to have the plastic hat concession for Saudi Arabia because it must be worth a fortune.

I usually cut through the lecture hall in my building on the new campus so I can avoid being stared at by the students in the snack bar. Today I stood in the doorway. It was dark and my eyes hadn't adjusted. Suddenly I heard shrieks and whistles and realized I had walked in on a movie. The students are easily rattled. They literally go to pieces on seeing a woman.

Husein, our Egyptian friend from the accounting, was complaining about his Saudi apprentice. Husein kept glancing at him and finally said, "What are you doing?" At first the apprentice didn't want to tell him. Then he finally admitted he was trying to divide 350 by 10. The apprentice is just out of secondary school. Husein thinks he has an IQ of about 55.

November 18, 1974 [Letter by Jack]

My students at the college know me as Mr. John. I went running today while my class was having physical education. When they saw me, they cheered me on. Today was the second time that happened. The first time, the physical education teacher had them on the track doing warm-up exercises when I ran by behind him. The students stopped their exercises and began waving, jumping up and down, and yelling, "Hello, Mr. John."

November 21, 1974

Always something! Alex just dropped the fever part of his flu, but now he has impetigo. That's quite contagious. Don't know how he picked it up. At first I was afraid that what he had was the result of a sand fly bite, which is quite painful to treat here.[143] It involves either surgical removal of the infected area or injections two to six times a week directly into the afflicted area.

Jack and Alex are at that elusive Disney film *Robin Hood*, a cartoon that had been scheduled and canceled twice previously.[144]

Today I helped Joe Fahey pick out two silver chains on which to hang a Greek and a Roman coin that he bought from a Bedouin at Petra.[145] It cost him sixty riyals each to have them set and sixty more for each chain.

Two gay instructors in Jack's department have "found" each other. Each of the two gay instructors shares a house with two straight roommates. One of the straights was getting a little steamed because at five in the morning he was awakened with, "But I love you!" coming from the next room. He dragged himself out of bed, stuck his head in the door, and said, "I don't care who loves whom, BUT NOT AT FIVE IN THE MORNING!"

We are having Thanksgiving with seventeen other people in a kind of potluck Thanksgiving dinner where we all share the cost of the bird

---

143   Sand flies can carry a variety of diseases. The least dangerous is sand fly fever, which is a viral infection that causes tiredness, nausea, red eyes, and pain in the eyes, limbs, and back. Symptoms may last a week. More dangerous is leishmaniasis of which there are two kinds: cutaneous and visceral. Cutaneous leishmaniasis causes skin sores that, if untreated can last for years. The visceral type is the most dangerous as it infects the internal organs: liver, spleen, etc. It can be fatal if not treated. Leishmaniasis is common in the Middle East.

144   Animated film by Disney. Animal characters play the roles of Robin Hood, Little John, etc. Released in 1973.

145   An ancient city in southwestern Jordan.

and bring another dish besides. It will be held in the South Compound the evening of the twenty-eighth. I'm making pies.

November 25, 1974

A group of people from the college went on an Aramco tour of Hofuf Oasis Thursday. They saw a foreigner getting his hair cut by the religious police (mutawa). Some were appalled, and some thought they ought to do that in the States, too. They really shave it off.

A tourist, a grandmother in her sixties, wore an orange thobe on the trip. She was told very seriously by the Arabs in Hofuf that orange was the color of passion and she should only wear that dress in the privacy of her home in front of her husband. Two Arabs were trying to sell her an abaya (black silk shroud-like garment worn by Arab women with the veil) to cover herself with. Another group is going to Qatif Oasis in a couple of weeks.[146] Qatif is supposed to be an unfriendly place full of minority Shia Moslems,[147] and a lot of people wouldn't go there unless they were with a tour.

The one shop where I buy fresh meat has a fairly reputable butcher and sells mainly American products like Rice Krispies, Libby's frozen foods, and Pepperidge Farm bread. I buy fillet there. Fillet is a long strip of beef thick enough for small steaks at one end and stew beef at the other. Last Thursday I walked past their service entrance where three employees were loading beef bones onto a dump truck. I watched as a huge rib cage came out, stripped of all meat. Trailing behind it was this lovely long brown tail with a big tuft of brown fur at the tip.

The latest in the saga of the reflecting pool beside the mosque on the new campus: a workman drove a cement carrier into it this week. The carriers are little buggies designed to ferry several hundred pounds of wet cement. Yesterday a mechanical engineer in his swim trunks was trying to repair the fountain, which is part of the overall

---

146   Qatif is the name of a city and oasis on the Persian Gulf. It is about eight miles north of the port of Dammam and southwest of the oil port, Ras Tanura.

147   The Shiites are discriminated against in Saudi Arabia. See "Saudi Arabia" in glossary A and "Shiites and Sunnis" in glossary B.

design, in order to get it working in time for the king's visit December 2. They had it running briefly yesterday.

That written Arabic course is getting complicated. What a confusing grammar. The teacher is quite good, and I have tapes now for pronunciation that accompanies the text. It is increasingly time-consuming to do. I'm almost sorry I got into it. Fortunately there are a number of scientific types in the class who don't have a clue of how to learn a language. I think I'm doing less work than they are. Maybe it will catch up with me in the end.

While Dr. Hough is attending the department chairmen's meeting, Ed Peattie—a faculty member in the department—thought he'd dictate to me an account of the Aramco group's trip to India last October. God, my shorthand is already so unreadable, and to be hit with words like BUNGLE, UDAIPUR, AGRA, TURBANS, and JEBEL makes them unbelievably difficult to read back. And wouldn't you know, he asked me to read all six pages back to him. It took me about twenty minutes. He kept yawning. I asked him if he thought he might be collecting Social Security by the time I finished.

Dr. Hough and a group of petroleum engineering students went to Ras Tanura, Aramco's refinery, last Wednesday. On the way back the bus was following two kids on bikes when one swerved out in front of the bus. The driver stopped short, jumped off the bus, grabbed the kid's bike, and threw it into a ditch. Then he got back in and drove on. He went about a mile when a blue taxi pulled up in front of him and stopped, forcing the bus to stop. The taxi driver claimed that the bus's first stop caused him to crash into the back of the bus and dent his fender. They argued for forty-five minutes, and the bus driver had to appear in the local court the next morning. I heard he sent a friend in his place.

The chief architect and resident engineer for the new campus construction are responsible for getting the place presentable for the king's visit next Monday. There were still several tin, scrap lumber, and cement block shacks used by the construction company near the campus. He tried in vain to get them torn down and finally, in disgust, burned down the building that served as the Yemeni workmen's cafeteria. A Yemeni claimed that his personal possessions were in the building and swore out a complaint at the police station. The police locked up the architect. Later that day he managed to get out of jail by signing a paper saying he wouldn't leave the country.

I found the lower quarter of a goat's leg on the walk not far from our house. Hoof, ankle, plus five inches. A dog must have dragged it into the compound.

Over the weekend we heard an explosion like a light bulb popping, only louder. Jack checked the closet where his homemade brew is stored. We keep it up on the shelf in a vacuum cleaner box. Sure enough several bottles had exploded. Liquid was seeping out of the corners of the cardboard box, all over my unironed laundry, my pattern collection, the vacuum cleaner, and the ironing board. Green glass was everywhere in tiny pieces. The place smelled like a brewery. One bottle must have exploded setting off the one next to it. The closet still stinks of yeast. We had left the air conditioner off that day. The heat must have set them off. The explosion wasn't as powerful as the one we had in our kitchen last year that blew open the cupboard doors.

November 27, 1974

The king is coming on Monday. They are cleaning up the area with a vengeance now. The fountain system still doesn't work, and the architect's office is working like crazy trying to get it operating before he comes.

December 6, 1974

The fly season is upon us. I got up, killed fourteen flies, went to work, came home, and killed fourteen more. It's cloudy today, a rarity. Gives a strange mood to the place. It's ordinarily so bright and sunny.

The king finally came to dedicate the college. He didn't make a speech. I guess if you're a king you don't have to make speeches. I didn't see him, but he walked through the college, and the fountain system was actually running for the duration of his visit. It hasn't run since. My theory is that they put one hundred and fifty Yemeni workmen with six-inch straws in the fountain and they all blew in concert while the king toured. The grand gesture that Jack envisioned him making (like giving everyone a raise) did not materialize. However, later it was announced that there would be another university created in the Eastern Province.

Something's crawling around in the wall besides the desk where I am typing. I don't like it a bit. Must go now and devein some shrimp and study Arabic.

December 16, 1974

Got the word on the Cleopatra Hotel (where we plan to stay in Cairo) from a couple here that stayed there last year. They advised us not to drink the water, not to use the ice under any circumstances, and to always eat at the Hilton. Other than that they said it was a nice place. I think we will go to Alexandria and forego the Valley of the Kings and Luxor.[148]

December 29, 1974

We got back from Egypt yesterday. Cairo was an experience. We came back with money left over because the city is so cheap. That plus the fact we were staying at the El Sleazo Hotel, because we lost our reservations that Husein (the Egyptian I worked with in the Accounting Department) made for us. That happened because Saudia's flight to Cairo was twelve hours late. And that probably happened because some Saudi prince commandeered the airplane for his own purposes. (That happens quite frequently.) Someone likened Saudia Airlines to a person who owns a private car and rents it out for a few days and then suddenly takes it back again. I'll never fly with them again if I can possibly avoid it.

After we got to Egypt, we spent an hour and a half getting out of the airport, which looks like it was bombed, was being renovated, or was just plain falling apart like a lot of other things in Egypt. We had a taxi take us to the Cleopatra, where they had never heard of us—ever. They suggested other hotels, and each place was booked up.

---

148   The city of Luxor is in Egypt, on the east side of the Nile. It has been called the "world's greatest open air museum" as it has an abundance of monuments, tombs, and temples. It is a popular tourist city.

By 11:00 a.m. Alex and I were sitting in the tourist office on Adlee St. with our suitcases, while Jack went around looking for hotels with a vacancy. At the same time the tourism lady made lots of calls looking for a room for us. About 1:00 p.m. she found a room with a bath, and Jack had located one about the same time. We saw hers first and it was pretty bad. Jack's room was pretty bad also but a little bigger, having another room and a bathroom in better condition, plus a more central location. It was not heated, and later we learned it only had hot water two hours a day. But we were glad to find lodging. The hotel, the Ambassador, is rated a "two" by our guidebook. The scale goes from one to three, three being the Hilton, Sheraton, etc. It had no curtains, no spreads, holes in the sheets, and four cockroaches, for which they didn't charge us. We managed to rent a small electric heater that took the dampness off the two rooms, a little.

We went to the Hilton that night and ate in their snack bar. We had no way of getting in touch with Husein because we didn't have his family's address. When we got back from the Hilton—which is a sumptuous place by Cairo standards and very costly by Cairo standards, but average by ours—the deskman handed Jack the phone. It was Husein. He had called twenty to thirty hotels before he found one with our name listed.

The next day he took us to the pyramids. We toured the temple near the Sphinx and rode camels around the biggest pyramid. Camels have a very swaying gait. I think you could easily develop whiplash symptoms riding on a camel for more than half an hour. That, or a rubber spine, or a terrible backache. They arise hind legs first, pitching you forward, a terrifying experience to the uninitiated. Then they straighten their front legs. By that time you find yourself clutching the saddle for dear life, and the camel driver is howling with delight.

We ate lunch near the pyramids at the Mena House, a famous hotel that has survived from British times.[149] It specializes in Indian dishes, though we hardly ever saw an Indian in Cairo. That evening he took us to the Khan Khalili, which is a souk consisting of lots of narrow winding streets with shops ranging from closets off the street

---

149   Named after the Pharaoh Mena, who was the first pharaoh of a united Egypt.

to rooms as much as fifteen feet square.[150] Many of the shops sold the same combination of items: brass, alabaster, leather, and Egyptian dolls, except now and then a small shop specializing in just one thing would turn up. It was in the old city. As it was the night before the Eid, shops were closing early. However there were a few open, hoping to catch the tourists.

I found a shop selling hand-blown local glass. I bought five cobalt blue glasses and a pitcher. I also bought a camel leather pocketbook. Unfortunately it smells as if the camel is still in it. In fact it smells like the camel crapped on it. Since we got home, I have been hanging it on the clothesline to deaden the odor.

In Cairo we also visited the National Museum, which houses the King Tutankhamen collection.[151] There were no lights on in the museum. Perhaps that was an economic indicator. Husein said that there had been a fire in a museum a while ago due to faulty wiring, so they just don't put the lights on. The mummy room required a special ticket. There were about forty mummies, unwrapped. It was rather unnerving. Jack was a little rattled by the mummy exhibit, too. Alex wanted to know how they "turned them into stone." Jack said, "Well, it's more like leather." They resembled thin pastry dough stretched over a skeleton and painted black.

That afternoon Husein took us to the Mohammed Ali Mosque, also called "The Citadel," which is up on a hill and affords a magnificent view of the city.[152] It also had no lights, and it was late afternoon, making much of the inlay and art work difficult to see. The Husein Mosque nearby—not named after our friend Husein—was broadcasting prayers.[153] Later that evening we met his friend Rauf, who works

---

150   The market was built in 1382. It is an important shopping area in Cairo.

151   The boy king, who died over 3,300 years ago. His tomb was discovered in 1922 by Howard Carter.

152   Also called the Alabaster Mosque. It was designed by Yussuf Bushnaq, a Greek. It was built 1830–1857. It has two slender minarets—270 feet high. The dome is 170 feet in height.

153   It is spelled "Hussein." The wood ceiling of the mosque is supported by forty-four white marble columns. The mausoleum on the side of the mosque was built in 1154, modified in 1236.

for a Swiss drug company in Cairo. Rauf took us up to the Cairo tower, where there is a revolving restaurant. It turns rather creakily and is probably bad for anyone prone to motion sickness. The restaurant makes one revolution every half hour, so we had a good look at all aspects of Cairo. I ordered Hammam Meshwi (grilled pigeon), an Egyptian specialty. The meat is like a very fine textured chicken. Husein and Rauf told me I wasn't cleaning off the bones well enough. Apparently they eat the bones, which are very delicate. I said my stomach was even more delicate.

Husein made reservations for our train trip to Alexandria. He bought the tickets in advance, and Jack paid him for them. He warned us he could not get tickets back to Cairo for us because everything was booked for the holiday. Probably, we would have to take a taxi. On Christmas Day, Husein left to visit his fiancée at Damanhur, a town about thirty-eight miles south of Alexandria.

That night we walked about downtown Cairo. It was flooded with people. The movie theaters were crammed, and many were walking in the streets. We went to a restaurant that Husein had recommended— the Aladdin. It was okay. We ordered steak, which was better than the steak in Saudi Arabia, but not as good as the US. The restaurant was very elegant, but the rice was gritty. We always had these problems no matter where we ate. Things just weren't very clean. We drank the native Pharaoh wine, which also wasn't very good.

The day after, we checked out of the hotel and went to the train station. A porter grabbed our bags and put us in the first-class car of the Hungarian made train. They served meals on snap-on trays, and there was a button for the waiter/conductor next to each seat. We pulled out through the industrial part of Cairo where the heavy industry and the big blocks of workers' flats were located. Then we began to travel through the fields and villages along the Nile. Roofs of the houses were piled with drying hay and twigs. It was very strange looking, the hay dripping off the roofs in soft mounds. We saw men riding donkeys, camels, women carrying baskets and jars on their heads, camels and donkeys heaped so high with bundles of twigs and hay that they looked like woodpiles or haystacks with legs. There were orange and lemon trees, palm trees, feluccas on the canals, and people laboring in the fields.[154] Although we went first class, this had its limitations as Jack killed a cockroach in our coach. Everything in Egypt is kind of threadbare.

Jack's Arabic was helpful in getting around, because English is not spoken as much as one would like. Most of the street signs were in Arabic only. French, it seems, is about as useless in Egypt as English.

The train passed through three small cities on the way to Alexandria, and Husein got on the train at Damanhur, the last city before Alexandria. We got off in a suburb of Alexandria and went to his sister's apartment. The brother-in-law manages a cotton processing factory with about two hundred employees. They have a very nice apartment by Egyptian standards. It had a dining room, den, living room, two bedrooms, a small refrigerator in the dining room, and a kitchen with a two-burner gas stove with a small oven. They owned a radio, a television, and French provincial style furniture. The apartment was not heated. Though they had hot water in the bathroom, there was none in the kitchen.

Alex has this absolutely rotten piece of velvet blanket binding he drags around when he sucks his thumb. It is of great comfort to him. When we were in the first class carriage of the train to Alexandria, he dropped it on the floor. The conductor came along, looked down, and froze. He just stood there for a moment, looking like he had detected a bad smell. Then he leaned over, picked it up, and started to stuff it in his pocket with a distasteful look on his face. I reached out and tugged on his sleeve. In Arabic, I said, "Give it to me. It is important," which was the best I could do with my Arabic. He looked at me like I was completely bonkers and handed it over.

We had the same experience at the apartment where we stayed in Alexandria. Husein brought us to his sister's house. The sister, her husband, and son arrived the next morning. Alex dropped his blanket binding on the floor of their hall. The husband came walking down the hall, stopped suddenly, and stared down at the floor, completely aghast, trying to fit this oddity into the scheme of things somehow. He stood there for two minutes, shook his head, and reached down to

---

154   A felucca is a small wooden boat with a triangular shaped sail.

gingerly lift it off the carpet. I said, in English this time, "It's Alex's. He likes it." Then he, too, gave me a look like I'd been in the Egyptian sun too long.

That night we went to downtown Alexandria and walked around. I bought two brass Turkish coffee pots with tin linings and wooden handles and an Egyptian carpet beater, which I presented to Myra Anderson when we got back.

We ate lunch that day at the San Giovanni, a hotel restaurant overlooking the Mediterranean. The rice was gritty again. We had shish kebab. Walked along the beach afterwards. Alex got his pants soaked by a fresh wave. Later we discovered that our feet were covered with tar from oil spills.

The next day Husein's sister came back from Damanhur with her husband and Mohammed, their six-year-old son, and Husein's fiancée, Nadia. We all went to the late King Farouk's palace, Montazah, with its gardens and a nice view of the sea. King Farouk was quite perverted.[155] He had an extensive pornography collection, which is not on display and a collection of sadomasochistic devices, which is on display. He is still hated in Egypt and, for a "playboy" king, was quite fat and ugly. The tour was in Arabic, and when the guard came to a collection of handcuffs and whips, he gave a long commentary. Husein refused to translate, except to say, "The guard said that Farouk was a very bad man." I had hoped for a few gory details. Afterwards we went on to the San Giovanni again for a late lunch. I had grilled shrimp, Jack had steak, and Alex had chicken. For dessert I had a fresh fruit medley with real whipped cream topping. We skipped rice.

For our return to Cairo, Husein had arranged for a taxi. From about four thirty to about eight o'clock we careened south on a four-lane divided highway loaded with trucks, insane asylum parolees, other taxi drivers, and donkey carts. All except the donkey carts were doing over sixty miles an hour. Sardine-packed buses were headed into Cairo. There was a full moon over the fields and the canals. I could make out the masts of feluccas tied up along the riverbank. It

---

155   King Farouk (1921–1965). The last king of Egypt. Assumed full power when he came of age in 1937. Forced to abdicate in 1952. Moved to Italy.

was beautiful, if I could have relaxed enough to enjoy it. I didn't think we would make it back alive.

Cairo is so overpopulated that the public transportation can't accommodate everyone. People travel hanging from buses, out the windows, and from the doors. We saw a train coming into Cairo with twenty-five or so people sitting on the roofs of the cars. People were clinging to the sides of the engine like so many cutout paper dolls. It was unbelievable. The taxi driver kept telling Husein that lots of people are going to Cairo and he was lucky to get a taxi. He kept hinting that he should get more than the usual price. In the end he did.

We saw a Christian hearse on our way out to the airport. It was like a black 1930s model-T, except with a truck back. It had life-size gilt cherubs springing from each corner of its roof, plus gold crosses in between and grill work at the doors in back. Jack though it looked like something used in a Mafia funeral in Sicily.

When we got into our house, Santa had visited and left presents under our artificial tree! (We arranged for Myra Anderson to put out the Christmas gifts before we returned.)

January 4, 1975

I am in the process of getting over some kind of affliction with nausea and diarrhea. I didn't go to work this morning. Since I came down with this the day before New Year's, I don't know if I can blame Egypt or not. Jack laughs at me for trying to find out what caused it, because he thinks it's hopeless. I ate a salad the day before we left Egypt, and I am blaming that. However, that would have been on the twenty-seventh. Four days later I get sick? Such problems afflicting returning visitors to Cairo are referred to at the college as the "Cairo Crud." There is also the "Delhi Belli," but not so many people go there. There was a tour to New Delhi the end of October. Of the forty people who went, all came back with stomach problems except one couple. They all blamed the salad served on the Air India flight, which they had assumed would be safe.

I expect Jack home any minute from his first two classes. He thinks I am at work. I would have gone, except that there is no ladies' room in my building at work. The buildings on the new campus are numbered in consecutive order from one to fourteen. I am in number four. There is a ladies' room in building one and in building eight. It is quite a walk between buildings. A good attack would get me as far as the main door. And forget the rest.

Joe Fahey must have gotten back from England by now. Wonder if he got Mildred to marry him. This past week was very peaceful without having to worry about whether or not he was going to drop in on us unexpectedly.

My Egyptian pocketbook is beginning to lose some of its pungency. I have been hanging it on the clothesline. Learned from a girl who was in the import business in Texas that dry cleaners can process leather from the Near East to remove the odors. Unfortunately I am not in the US. People like to buy fur-lined suede parkas in Iran and Turkey. I have listened to many stories about the coat being put outside while the owner visits. They are rumored to be especially bad in the rain.

There is a big sign up at Aramco's dining hall indicating that as of the new year no one will be admitted with an ARAMCO ID card.

January 7, 1975

Heard on BBC that there were three hundred cases of cholera in Mecca. According to the Saudi government, pilgrims from Nigeria brought it in. Rumor has it that there are now cases in Dammam, ten miles from here. Also all the schools and colleges in the Western Province (Jeddah, Medina, Taif, Mecca)[156] have been closed for at least a week. The college sent around a notice that everyone should get their cholera shots up to date. We just got them at Christmas time to go to Egypt. Actually, cholera shots are only 50 to 60 percent effective.

We had some heavy rain here in Dhahran while we were in Cairo. About fifty feet of sidewalk was completely washed away when a lake

---

156   Jeddah is a major port on the Red Sea. It is the second largest city after Riyadh. Mecca is inland from it, due east, about fifty miles. Medina contains the Mosque of the Prophet, making it the second holiest city in Saudi Arabia, Mecca being the first. Medina is north of Mecca and about 110 miles inland from the Red Sea. Taif is a two-hour drive from Jeddah and is at an elevation of six thousand feet. Mecca is the holiest city to Muslims. Not only was the Prophet Muhammad born there, but the Ka'bah (House of God) in Mecca is supposed to have been built by Abraham and his son Ishmael.

built up on the other side of the road, flooded across, and washed the sand out from under the clay tiles of the walk, causing it to collapse. There is no provision here for rain, no storm sewers, no trenches for drainage, nothing. Not even any means of collecting the rainwater for use. It really makes a mess when it rains.

Last year I wrote you about my neighbor who had leaks in her roof. Well, this year the maintenance men came to tar her roof. They put the ladder against one side of the house, then got on the roof, and tarred it until they were on the opposite side of the house from the ladder. So, sprock, sprock, sprock! They walked across the tarred section of the roof back to the ladder and climbed down. During the next rainstorm her roof leaked so badly that both glass globes in her kitchen filled up with brown water, and the kitchen was suffused with a warm, brown glow because she'd left both lights on when she went out to Arabic class. She got stranded there with me during the storm. She also had a leak right over her bed. They gave her a different house over the summer, same problem though. In the first rainstorm of last fall, the light in her kitchen exploded and blew a neat hole through the globe surrounding it. The rest of the globe remained in place without even a crack.

Joe Fahey has come back from England after visiting his girlfriend at Christmas. He appeared the first night, stayed for supper, and said he would return the following night. We put all the lights out and went to bed at nine. He didn't show. He then showed up last night about half past seven, and Jack and I were steamed. We just went about our business. I washed the bathroom, washed and set my hair, sat under the dryer, and read my mail. After watching some television with Joe, Jack did the dishes. Then Joe wandered out into the kitchen, talked a while with Jack, and left about quarter to ten. I'd like to be more blunt about our feelings and frustrations, but Jack has to work with him and this is a very small community. We plan to buy a car this month, and Jack intends to get his Saudi driver's license. So in the future, we won't be home as much. Now without a car, we're like sitting ducks.

In the mass of humanity crowding into Mecca during the Hajj season, a few people inevitably get crushed to death. This December a million and a half made the pilgrimage to Mecca. The Iraqi pilgrims usually come overland, packed like sardines in brightly painted, ramshackle buses, with suitcases and boxes piled high on the roof. Two relatives of one family got crushed to death, but they didn't want to bury them in Mecca. So they put the corpses in the bus to bring them back to Iraq. In Dammam, one thousand miles from Mecca, the bus stopped to let the passengers out to walk around. The Saudi police noticed that two didn't get off and seized the bodies over great protests. The authorities buried them immediately.

January 12, 1975

Jen, on the other side of our house, left for good on Thursday. She stopped by to say good-bye. She said she couldn't take Saudi Arabia anymore, had been depressed since she got back from Greece this summer, and had been having one-and-a-half hour crying spells, which in turn depressed Leo. She said she needed to be alone for a while; she was too dependent on Leo and hoped to get herself together in the States. She said if he signed another contract next year she would come back, but personally, I doubt if she will because the place holds nothing for her. Leo never was home, always at the office, playing chess with the bachelors. She was home going batty, no kids, nothing to do, no company.

Found out how to take the phone off the hook without having a little guy on my doorstep from the switchboard half an hour later. Just have to dial the number one and it's taken care of. This came from Jen next door. She said the other day she got all her work done, dialed one, and went to bed for a nap. But she forgot to lock the door. The next thing she knew some people who couldn't get her on the telephone came over to her house, walked in, and woke her up. She was mad, but she said it was her own fault for not remembering to lock the door. Now if we could just find out how to disconnect the doorbell.

A British couple from the college computer center went to London over the last vacation. She came back with two half pints of whiskey hidden in the pockets of a raincoat she was carrying. They got through customs and had their bags marked by the inspector. As they were leaving the customs area, the guy who checks for the chalk marks on the baggage looked at her and motioned that he wanted to see the raincoat. He discovered the whiskey. They were taken back to an office, and the whiskey was poured into a barrel. Then they were let go! Usually they give you twenty-four hours to get out of the country or lock you up in jail for a while, ranging from overnight to a month or more. They got away with a warning.

January 20, 1975

The erase key on this typewriter no longer works. I wonder whom I should call. They have this ham-fisted auto mechanic, Abdullah, who is posing as an IBM typewriter repairman. I have been warned through the grapevine here to avoid him at all costs. He has been known to bolt things down so that the typing element can't be removed. Things are never the same again after a visit from Abdullah.

January 25, 1975

Marcie Wildermann, one of the American secretaries here, has been at the college for ten years. She worked as a secretary for just about everybody at one time or another. Her kids are grown up and her husband, Fritz, is teaching in the Physics Department. I visit her in her office when Dr. Hough is away. She's funny and entertaining. She was complaining to me about how bad the Australian beef is and how a friend at Aramco used to keep them supplied with good American meat from their commissary. Then the friend got transferred to Jeddah, on the west coast, and now she is back to eating frozen Danish chicken and hamburger just like everybody else. One day she got word some guests were arriving for supper, so she sent her husband to Omar's Supermarket to buy one of those Australian beef filets that resemble frozen baseball bats. He got it and left it on the sink to thaw. When she got home, she unwrapped it and discovered, to her horror, a RABBIT! It had apparently been thawed and refrozen so many times that the shape was disguised. It had also been stretched out to be frozen. So she rewrapped, refroze, and returned it to the store. Someone suggested she should have put a slip of paper inside that said, "If you have discovered that this was a rabbit, initial here and return to Omar's."

So I had to tell her about my experience eating hammam meshwi (grilled pigeon) in Cairo. Grilled pigeon is a dish for which Cairo is famous. I got so engrossed in formulating a plan of attack that I didn't pay much attention to the actual pigeons. They were split down the backbone and spread-eagled on the grill. I was served two of them on my plate. They weren't very well done, so it was hard to pry the legs off the breast, etc. About halfway through eating the first pigeon, I noticed these comma-shaped appendages protruding from the middle of each pigeon. Upon a closer examination, I saw two eyes and a beak on the head of each comma. I let out a little yell, threw my hands in the air, and then looked around, embarrassed. They left the HEADS on the pigeons! I could hardly finish them.

There is a lot of suspicion among the foreign community here that American companies are sending their seconds to Saudi Arabia. For example, a load of seventy-five IBM typewriters arrived. They are all older models, which were ordered by the architects of the new campus. The architects get an 11 percent commission on everything ordered for the college. Most of these typewriters do not work, adding insult to injury. The faculty members saddled with these typewriters suspect that IBM is unloading otherwise unsalable equipment here. I have one of the new models only because the college purchasing department acquired it downtown from the local dealership, since Dr. Hough urgently needed a typewriter. The local dealership is miffed because they didn't get the order. Consequently they have refused to install, repair, or improve any of those ordered by the architects.

We heard last night that Leo, our neighbor whose wife left last week, is planning to leave. I can't believe it. He was never home when she was and even went into the office on weekends. It seems unbelievable that now that she's left, he suddenly can't stand it here anymore. He is home a lot more than he used to be. I think it must be one of those rumors. Maybe it started out that he was leaving in June and by the time it got to me he was packing his bags.

Jack called and said he had been to the Personnel Office to check on his driver's license. They will take him to Dammam on Wednesday for the preliminary round. Procedures for getting a license here are incredible. They want to know everything except, "Can you drive?"

We went to a big party Thursday night. Just as we arrived, the electricity went off and didn't come back on again until half past one in the morning. There were at least one hundred people invited, and although there was no music at first, the din was incredible. Everyone brought snacks. David Goodbout donated one hundred bottles of his homemade beer. They had some stronger stuff, but I stayed with beer because the other stuff gives me headaches, hangovers, and other unpleasantness. The lights weren't on so it was impossible to see what one was eating. I picked up a canapé that was very beautifully made. A little round of rye with a spread carefully placed and an olive decoration in the middle. It turned out to be mashed sardine and horseradish, heavy on the horseradish. One very good hors d'oeuvre consisted of a slice of smoked German sausage wrapped around a cream cheese filling and held with a toothpick. Jack said he tried a slice of pizza, but it was so bad he couldn't finish it.

I got a chance to talk with some people I don't ordinarily see. Someone finally located a stereo that would function on batteries, and everybody started dancing on the porch outside the master bedroom. I was hoping it wouldn't collapse, building specifications being what they are in this part of the world. I am sure the porch wasn't designed for eighteen people hopping up and down on it.

There was a terrible wind out of the northeast last night. When I came back from the movie, it literally tore the breath from my lungs. I got dust in my eyes and grit in my mouth. The treetops were being tossed this way and that. It is very easy to uproot trees here. The root systems are so shallow that a good wind tips them over. The Maintenance Department sets them up again, trims off all the leaves, and wires the trunks to several stakes. Then the trees take root again like nothing happened.

Thunderstorms were predicted for last night, but never materialized. Usually the storms come when the wind is from the southeast, warm, moist air from the Gulf and India.

In a strange way it's terrible having Joe Fahey gone. I didn't know what to do with myself yesterday, since I didn't have to worry about contingency plans in case he dropped by. It's like leaning against a post all year and suddenly somebody takes it away. But in two weeks he will be back.

January 27, 1975

I am still at work. The only reason I am still at work is that the IBM repairman still hasn't shown. I called and he said, "Put the typewriter in a car and bring it to Dammam. I can fix it in ten minutes." I told him it was quite impossible since 1) I can't drive, 2) I don't have a car, and 3) the college isn't going to pay attention to any woman calling them expressing the need for a car to take a typewriter to Dammam for ten minutes. So he said he would send his assistant who was just now working on a caterpillar tractor. I said, "Is he as good as you?" (Opinion on that is up for grabs: there is much debate around here over how good he is). He said, "Oh yes, he's very good." So here I sit, with one hour left to go, and the repairman still hasn't appeared.

The name of CPM (College of Petroleum and Minerals) has been changed to UPM (University of Petroleum and Minerals). People have been going around all day saying, "UP EM!" to each other and getting "UP YOURS, TOO!" in reply. I thought CPM was a little snappier. I don't know how it is possible to have a UNIVERSITY of Petroleum and Minerals, university being a term for a collection of different colleges, and we do not have a collection of colleges called "Petroleum and Minerals."

At four o'clock this afternoon I will leave for a tea at the dean's new home. They just moved in, and it is supposed to be fabulously furnished. I was told to wear my track shoes because the living room is fifty feet long. I hear that there is a huge L-shaped couch in sea green at one end of the living room and a matching one in pale blue at the other end. I understand that people converse with bullhorns. Everyone is going to check out the house. This will probably be the biggest turnout for a tea in the history of the college.

I am using my Egyptian handbag now. The smell seems to have given up and left.

January 29, 1975

The chemical engineering secretary has quit, so the faculty is bringing all their work to me. I have been pretty busy. That IBM man still hasn't appeared. The joke in the Computer Department is that IBM means Inshallah, Boukra, Mumpkin (God willing, tomorrow, maybe).

Three handy rules for Saudi Arabia:

1. Never EVER get onto an elevator. Always take the stairs. (Most of the elevators don't work, and if they do, they can stop working at any time with you in them.)

2. Don't bother setting your watch to the exact time. Nobody else does, and no two clocks in Saudi Arabia tell the same time, even if they are working, which most of them aren't.

3. Just because the driver in front of you is signaling for a left turn doesn't mean he won't turn right. Act accordingly and don't pass him.

CHAPTER 7

*"The Yellow Rose of Texas" and other hymns, air-conditioning for
cows, kissing in public—men only, the religious police strike again, the
US Consulate tennis party, only the Jews evolved, the shaking minarets*

February 2, 1975 [Letter by Jack]

We've had six days of light rain or drizzle, which by the looks of
this morning's sky has now broken. Many people around here
have the flu, but (knock on wood) we're doing fine with this New England type weather and no air-conditioning. In general we've had very
good health since we shut off the air conditioner.

All the yards and walks are dug up around here as they are laying new gas pipes. The trenches selectively hit all of Maralyn's gardens
including her tomato plants and parsley. I don't know what we'll be
able to save from it.

The tennis lineup came out, and Joe and I are in the semifinals at
the Consulate on February 12. One of our opponents is Ben Benjabril,
our neighbor from last year. He used to beat me regularly last year, but
I'm a lot better now. It should be an interesting match. I have not been
getting any exercise because of the weather.

February 3, 1975

My office has no privacy. I got so damned sick of the students
staring at me from the hall (the door has a long window down
the side) that I hung a long Snoopy calendar over the upper part
of the window. Being stared at drives me nuts! Now I see thobed
legs through the lower part of the glass as they stop to look at the
calendar.

Jack got his license to drive. If we ever get our contracts, which are supposed to be out this month, we will be able to decide whether to buy a car or not.

The year before we arrived, a carillon was installed on top of the college's new water tower on the jebel.[157] It played "South of the Border" and the story is that they wore it out the first year. Well, the latest version of that story is that not only did it play "South of the Border" but also the "Yellow Rose of Texas" (a Texan was the contractor). Some Saudi thought that the "Yellow Rose of Texas" was a hymn and that the bells were "Christian" and it was silenced forever.

Ed Peattie, a chemical engineer teaching with Dr. Hough, was at Aramco about fifteen years ago. Then the only Americans in the area were either at the US airbase that used to be here or at Aramco. They both had football teams and played their big game at Thanksgiving. They called it the "Wajid Bowl," but couldn't understand why the Saudis laughed and laughed and laughed when they heard the title. (Wajid means big, great, very much, lots, in the local slang.) They found out why the Arabs laughed, when a nurse at the Aramco dispensary told them that "bowl" was an Arabic word for urine. Maybe the Arabs thought the Americans were planning to knock the "piss" out of each other on Thanksgiving Day.

That IBM repairman finally showed and told me it was a good thing he came when he did because something was about to give out in my typewriter. I had been chasing him for three weeks. They charge twenty-eight dollars for a house call.[158] I said, "That's more than a doctor," and he replied, "There are lots of doctors around, but I'm the only IBM typewriter repairman in the Eastern Province."

The dean, Bakr Bakr, is Saudi with an American PhD. His last name is the same as his first name, in case you think you're seeing double here. When the university got university status via royal decree, Dean Bakr became "Rector Bakr," causing no end of merriment among the foreign faculty who are now referring to his office as the "rectory."

---

157   A carillon consists of at least twenty-three bells and is played from a keyboard or is automated. They are usually placed in towers.

158   In 2012 dollars, about $120.

Jack announced that when he just now answered the phone there was only heavy breathing. I suggested that he tell the guy to get a chest x-ray the next time he calls.

Jack and Joe Fahey have made the finals for the American Consulate Tennis Tournament Doubles. If the next game is won, they both get brass trays from Iran as prizes, and I want one.

There was a blueprint for a US invasion of the Gulf oil states in the latest *TIME* magazine.[159] It was pieced together from Pentagon sources. I couldn't believe that it wasn't censored, but the whole article was intact. Since they mentioned Dhahran by name, naturally I got a little concerned.

February 22, 1975

All kinds of rumors continue to fly about regarding the new contracts. They still aren't out yet though everyone expects them this week. Jack says he won't sign for less than 10 percent.

A new shipment of Brazilian-made Volkswagens arrived at the dealership in Al-Khobar. The model we want is there in several yucky colors, like screaming yellow, bastardized blue, and passionate purple. We may change our decision on a model if we can't find a color we can live with. One cannot imagine these colors.

We made plans to take our next vacation in Iran, and I'm really looking forward to it. People are starting to get to me. Speaking of which, the bane of our existence, Joe Fahey, hasn't been around for two whole weeks. One time we invited him, but that doesn't count.

I just made Jack some hot fudge sauce for his ice cream. We can buy Nestlé's canned cream here, and I dump a can of that into the butterscotch sauce recipe.[160] We can't get fresh dairy products here, except for frozen New Zealand, Danish, or Irish butter, and sterilized bottled frozen cream from Germany. In the near future the Saudi government has plans to import two thousand Michigan cows, combination Frisian and Holsteins. They will be flown in and boarded in air-conditioned barns.[161]

---

159   *Time*, Feb. 10, 1975. "Excursion in the Persian Gulf." Securing the Dhahran airstrip is part of the plan outlined in the article.

160   For recipe see "Butterscotch Sauce," appendix 1.

161   The Saudi government is doing its best to increase its internal food supply, which is insufficient for its growing population.

February 24, 1975

Interesting things have been happening here. A friend here went to the drugstore to buy birth control pills. She learned that they would no longer be sold after the end of the month. The Saudi government did a census last fall and learned that they have fewer people than they thought. Since most of the Saudi families I know have anywhere from nine to twenty kids, I can guess that it will mainly affect the foreign residents. Many of the wives have already been to Al-Khobar drugstores buying up a year's supply. My friend called a Saudi girl she knows who confirmed what the druggist said, saying it had been in the newspapers, on the radio, and on television the past few weeks. It doesn't affect me, but I know about half the faculty wives are going to be in a frenzy over it.

Flies crawling across one's face are tolerated to an unbelievable extent in the Arab world. I don't understand it. Jack went mad trying to talk to a student of his one day, while a fly crawled across the kid's face. Jack didn't want to brush it off but at the same time couldn't stand watching it. Consequently he couldn't concentrate on a word the student said.

Non-Moslems are not allowed to go to Mecca or Medina. At one time Riyadh, the capital, was off limits to foreigners too. The diplomatic community is in Jeddah, not Riyadh, the capital. If non-Moslems are found in either of these two cities they can be killed.

Yesterday at four in the afternoon, Dr. Hough, two other women, and I were coming down off the jebel in Dr. Hough's Volkswagen. We thought we saw a fire at the old administration building, a half mile away. Then the cloud of smoke, three stories high, went around the building. We decided the fire must be a car engine. The car went around the building three more times, smoke pouring out in great white clouds. We were headed for the mailroom, which is in that building. The fog was so great we couldn't see the door, so we kept on going. Then we spotted the culprit, a DDT tank truck spraying for bugs, right behind us. We went straight for the north compound the spray truck in hot pursuit. The two women with me were having fits. They had wash on the line. So did I. They flew out of the Volkswagen, and Hough drove me to my house. Jack helped me get my wash in. Then for the next three-quarters of an hour the truck sprayed the compound four times. It is amazing there are any birds, dogs, cats, or kids alive today.

March 3, 1975

Jack and Joe Fahey lost the final tennis match and consequently did not win any prizes. They were playing in the middle of the closest thing to a sandstorm that we've had this year.

We saw our new contract last Wednesday. It was 21 percent more than the last one, and we are signing up for another two years. Jack's chairman said that Jack got the highest percentage raise of all the people up for contracts in the English Language Institute. He did the most work, teaching all those extra classes last fall. Our former neighbor Leo is on a four-month emergency leave of absence in the States. He wrote to friends here stating that if they paid him $50,000 a year, gave him TWO houses in the south compound, and WEEKLY repatriation, he still wouldn't come back.

We just bought a car this morning! A white Volkswagen station wagon, not much different from the one we had in the States except this one is Brazilian made and has no radio. They take care of the registration and the plates. We hope to have it by Thursday morning.

One thing I learned recently was to avoid being quoted in the newspapers. There are a lot of newspaper and television people floating around Saudi Arabia looking for people to interview and doing articles about customs and lifestyles here. Also, my Arabic teacher's husband was told to leave after this semester because he apparently made some disparaging remarks about "something Saudi" and was quoted in an article in a US newspaper. A minister in Riyadh read the article, so the story goes, and he called the dean ordering him to get rid of the man. The dean had all he could do to let him finish the semester. They intended to depart after this year, anyway. Word is out that at least two people here didn't get their contracts renewed. As usual nobody knows why, including the people involved, or at least they aren't saying if they do know.

I did know that last year in May the religion editor of the *New York Times* stayed as a guest in my Arabic teacher's home. The editor tried to take pictures in the neighborhood mosque during Friday services. His camera was confiscated. Taking pictures in a mosque during Friday services is unthinkable. I'd be willing to bet it left a bad taste in the editor's mouth, so he wrote the offending article. Unfortunately he queered things up for my Arabic teacher and her family.

Americans with companies like Northrop or Lockheed, the US military, and the Consulate have APO privileges, which is a big advantage over using Saudi mail and having to deal with customs officials. Certain companies also provide commissaries for their employees. The Aramco commissary has a special license to carry pork products, which are sold in a separate section of their meat department. The Saudi government does not allow local merchants to sell it, consumption of pork being forbidden by the Koran. I imagine people with companies offering these advantages have a problem because all the have-nots in the Eastern Province must be badgering them for this or that all the time. The people with APO get uncensored magazines and can use mail order companies in the States to buy clothing. If I tried to order something from J.C. Penney's, first of all it would take forever to come by sea mail, then I'd have to try to get it out of customs at the Port of Dammam. But if I had those privileges, I would really be annoyed with people asking me for favors all the time.

Iran is generally considered to be a better place to live and work than Saudi Arabia. It is more modernized, industrial, colorful, scenic, liberal, and interesting, among other things. However, I have the suspicion that sooner or later the Shah is going to want to use all those lovely arms he is buying.[162]

March 10, 1975

After foreign faculty children reach age fourteen here, they have to leave the country to continue their education. Many go to the American School in Bahrain. Another popular American School is in

---

162   The Shah and his family fled Iran in January 1979. He was opposed by the traditionalist movement led by Ayatollah Ruholla Khomeini.

Beirut, and a few families here, next fall, are sending their offspring to the Woodstock School in northern India. The daughter of the head of the College of Industrial Management goes to the American School in Switzerland at six thousand dollars a year. The Woodstock School costs about half that. UPM contributes up to three thousand dollars per child.

I am quite sick of women's thobes. They are ubiquitous because they are the only inexpensive outfit a woman can get that covers enough so that public appearances don't attract too much attention. Consequently, all the new people immediately go out and have two to ten thobes made up in various fabrics. A married couple in this compound both had thobes made; hers just like a man's. They put on thobes, gutras, and egals (head cloths and black rings to hold them in place) and strolled up and down Al-Khobar's main street hand in hand. They said they got a kick out of walking around Al-Khobar holding hands. She could pass for a man because she's flat chested, had her hair up, and wears glasses. Normally, a man and a woman seen holding hands are absolutely riveting. It stops traffic and is considered very bad form by the Arabs (opposite-sex touching is reserved for the bedroom). Yet men hold hands and kiss in public, which is considered quite riveting by the foreigners and evokes mutters of "damned queers" from the Aramco hardhats who happen to be in Al-Khobar shopping. Another perfectly acceptable local custom is scratching oneself in the groin area.

Every week Dean Smith types up the minutes of the engineering chairmen's meeting. I call him the Walter Cronkite of UPM because that's the only local news there is here. This week's minutes went two and a half pages, and item number 27 reads: "Dogs are becoming a problem in the south compound. One of them ate Dr. Husein's sheep." I'll bet universities in the States don't have items like that in their engineering chairmen's meeting minutes.

We picked up our new Volkswagen wagon on Thursday. It is like having walls fall away to have a car. We can go to Aramco whenever we feel like it, or to Al-Khobar, or Dammam, or even to the beach.

March 17, 1975

In two weeks we will be in Iran, assuming we can get a hotel. The Iranians are on a strange calendar. Their New Year celebration, called Now Ruz, comes about the twenty-first or twenty-second of March each year. They celebrate it for thirteen days. The hotels are usually booked. We are going on the third of April. Hopefully they will be tired of celebrating by then and have gone home. I have to visit a neighbor soon to check out her carpet purchases in Iran. She offered to give me some tips on carpet buying.

Our car is fine. It is nice to have one even if I can't drive it.

The religious police were on a hair-cutting binge in Al-Khobar tonight, and there were many assorted hanks of hair in the gutter. Jack saw them doing it, but I missed the actual performance. I thought they had quit last year, but it appeared they were at it with a vengeance tonight. I told Dr. Hough about it, and his only remark was "I wish they'd do that in the States." I told him the civil liberties people wouldn't like to hear him say that.

March 20, 1975

Tonight we are going to the consulate tennis party. It cost fifty riyals (fourteen dollars) a couple and included a buffet type supper.[163] The charge also covered the cost of the prizes and drinks. It is quite cold out, and that orange nylon jersey dress I plan to wear isn't very warm.

Two books recommended to me by Marcie Wildermann, who has been here since the college was founded, are *Golden Swords and Pots and Pans*, written by José Arnold,[164] a former Aramco employee, who set up the royal household for King Saud, and *Around the World and Other Places* by Ilka Chase,[165] who describes a trip she and her husband made across North Africa, through Jordan, Saudi Arabia, Iran, and

---

163   In 2012 dollars, about $60.

164   Published by Harcourt, Brace & World, 1963.

165   Published by Double Day & Company, 1970.

India. Ilka writes, "Saudi Arabia is about as dry as the US in prohibition."

Ilka is married to an eye specialist, and they are now at Aramco where her husband is setting up a clinic. They came here under her married name, Brown. Nobody knew Mrs. Brown was really Ilka Chase. She got a reputation for bitchiness from the start, and Marcie, who had been invited to a party in honor of the Browns, declined saying, "If she's as bitchy as everyone says, I don't want to meet her." Later when she found out who Mrs. Brown really was, she kicked herself. The "other places" in the title include towns and cities in Saudi Arabia she visited. When she came to the Dhahran airport, two officials from the college whisked her off to the college guesthouse over her vehement protests that they were here as guests of Aramco. She gives an account of this in the book and also describes Robert King Hall, the senior advisor at the college, as "the man who whispers words of wisdom into the ear of God."

March 24, 1975

The Consulate party was a swinging affair. The word got out that the real booze was in limited supply, so everyone was drinking as soon as they arrived. The Consul had some sidiqui, the local distilled product, in reserve for when the other ran out. Since people can drink the other anytime, anyplace, they wanted to belt down the good stuff. The affair involved giving awards followed by a meal. If Jack and Joe had defeated their opponents, the prize would have been a silver chalice maybe five inches high. They also gave out silver baskets, silver trays, and silver flower holders. Unfortunately they decided to give the awards after everyone had been drinking for an hour and then serve the meal. By that time I had had two gin and tonics, and Jack had three and wondered if he could keep them down long enough to get through the buffet. It was a cold evening. I had borrowed a white crocheted shawl, but that wasn't enough.

They had tables set up outside with candles burning at each end and a buffet that included barbecued beef, lasagna, potato salad, stuffed eggs, coleslaw, liver wrapped in bacon, rolls, roast turkey, roast beef, relishes, etc. I don't know if they had dessert or not, but if they did, I missed it. They also had a big platter of sanbusi, which is a triangular, deep-fried pastry with a ground meat, parsley, and onion filling.

By the time the evening was halfway over, hands were roving, wives and husbands were holding each other up, and the jokes were getting raunchier. Denton Edes, who we drove to the party, came by and said, "Percy Avery's wife is blonde, right? Well, he's got his hands on the fanny of a brunette right now." (Percy Avery is a very scholarly, quiet, very British fellow of about forty with a degree in Arabic from Cambridge University.) What Percy didn't know was that the husband of the brunette was after his wife, who is seven months pregnant and huge. Percy's wife acted very insulted over the attention she was getting from the brunette's husband, but I don't think she knows about the brunette and her husband.

At the party we met a busty, blonde Northrop wife of about forty-five in a skin-tight black dress with bare back and a black feather boa wrapped around her neck. She came with another guy from Northrop Aircraft, not her husband. Denton Edes in an attempt to make conversation, said to him, "Oh, you work for Northrop. Are you the guy who flies over my house at nine thirty every morning?" The blonde looked at him and went, "HA! HA! HA! Baby, he flies but not over your house. It's my husband who flies over your house at nine thirty every morning." Then the blonde and her escort jabbed each other with their elbows and rolled their eyes. Denton concluded something was going on there.

Later the Ayers, the young couple who we think will be moving into the other side of our house, began throwing pretzels at the people at the next table. Jack got up and danced with me for the first time in his life. Joe Fahey went to the men's room with John Mathew. Both of them were having difficulty standing. When they came out they walked straight into the Mormon assistant principal at the Consulate school whose jaw was hanging down to his knees and eyeballs were bulging out over whatever he thought was going on in there.

Jack's watching British soccer right now, thereby avoiding correcting papers, etc. Today he passed back some tests. One student immediately began bitching over Jack's taking a point off for leaving out a period. There are no periods in Arabic. They just connect everything with "and" and go on forever and never come up for air. The student argued with him for a few minutes, trying to persuade Jack to give him the point. Suddenly the student noticed it was not his paper. He handed it to the guy next to him. Jack said to the owner of the paper, "If you have any questions ask him," and pointed to the student who had just been arguing with him.

I will enclose a computer-drawn portrait of the king done in honor of his visit here last fall [See next page]. The student who did it told me he spent a hundred hours on it. It's quite a good job.

We got that young couple, the Ayers, as neighbors. They are supposed to be moving in today. I later learned that the other couple I thought I would have preferred as neighbors owns the only operating still in the college. Now the idea of somebody running a still in the other half of my house with the attendant danger of fire would have driven me to the Housing Office with a complaint. I just have fits thinking about it. At Aramco there have been fires caused by stills, but people mostly keep them in a tool shed outside the house or in their garage.

My raise came through. I make twelve riyals and not ten an hour. They justified it on the basis that I take shorthand. This is equivalent to $3.40 an hour.[166] I work about eighty hours a month.

The television movies Aramco buys are so old that they have W. C. Fields starring in them and Model T's everywhere. And they aren't trying to be campy.

Jack got an interesting version of the theory of evolution the other day in his reading class. As with most fundamentalist religions, they view it here as a heresy. The class found that there was a city in Australia named "Darwin." Jack explained where the name came from. One of the students said that Mr. Darwin came up with the theory of evolution but that Islam had disproved it. He said Darwin was a Jew and that the theory of evolution really said that the Jews were descended from monkeys. Jack went on with the lesson and didn't rise to the bait.

---

166   In 2012 dollars, about $14.52.

March 29, 1975

On Tuesday we learned that Faisal, the king of Saudi Arabia, was assassinated by his nephew. We were relieved that it was not the CIA, a Palestinian, or any group that could be blamed by the people. The king was well liked and respected for his honesty, wisdom, and ascetic lifestyle. Even the foreigners thought well of him. His brother, the new king is not well known and apparently preferred it that way.[167] Because this is such a conservative country, I doubt if there will be any great changes. It was a shock. Everything was closed for three days, the Aramco television and radio stations did not broadcast, the movie was canceled, and the college was locked up.

---

167   King Khalid succeeded King Faisal.

Aramco is rumored to have ceased its television and radio broad-casting for forty days, out of respect for the late king. However, I am ready to stick my head in the oven. At 4:30 p.m. Alex is tired and out of sorts and doesn't know what to do with himself. If he can sit down in front of *Sesame Street* or cartoons until suppertime, he gets some rest and likes himself better. The rest of us like him better, too.

We are scheduled to leave for Iran next Thursday and hopefully our visas will have been processed by then, despite the shutdown of government offices.

March 31, 1975

There has been no change here since King Faisal was killed. Aramco television and radio are still off the air. Rumor has it that people are even discovering reading again. I may have to teach Alex to read, out of desperation.

There was a fire in one of the new houses in the new south compound the day before yesterday. It was caused by faulty wiring and started in the master bedroom clothes closet. The trash men discovered the fire when, as they were picking up the garbage, a window blew out. They concluded something was wrong. The couple living there had very nice clothes, and the college is going to reimburse them for a new wardrobe. There was a lot of smoke damage. They have plans for ten more of those houses to be built by the same contractor, the fly-by-night construction company of Beirut. As a variation on what they used to say about airplanes, "Would you like to live in a house built by the lowest bidder?"

I think the safest thing around here is to live in a tried and true house already broken in by a number of other people, with all the bugs out of it—a house like we have. Although I'm not sure about the bug part.

April 2, 1975

We leave for Iran tomorrow.

Concerning the assassination, the magazines and newspa-pers here were censored to hell, and nobody could learn much of any-thing. Absolutely nothing has been written in either English or Ara-bic about the assassin, the king's nephew, and there has been no news about him on the radio. Of course in such a situation wild rumors are rampant. The newspaper clippings that I received from the States are the first facts I have about the assassination. The only news since is that the nephew has been declared insane. Even here, I believe, a crazy person isn't responsible for what he does.[168]

Some people have gone to the bank and sent all their money back to the US, but I don't think it is necessary to do that and neither does Jack. I must say though that after reading the clippings from the States, I had the feeling that things were much more uncertain here than they seemed—living in our fool's paradise with no news. If anything happened here, we'd be the last to know. Dr. Hough is very nervous about the little guys with machine guns in the baggy green uniforms that have appeared on every street corner in Al-Khobar. He said that those guns can fire one hundred bullets a minute, and if one of them tripped and the gun went off, a person could be cut in two. He made it a point to walk along the side streets where the little guys with the guns weren't.

Half the college seems to be going to Isfahan on this vacation so getting away from the same old faces I am not.[169] Hopefully they won't all be in the hotel we plan to inhabit. Jack has dreams of drinking gin and tonics while sitting around a pool with Alex happily splashing away and not bothering him. However it will probably be too cold to swim, and I want to do some shopping and take some tours.

I am going to make a trek to the fourth floor ladies' room in the next building. This morning after I virtuously ran up three flights of stairs I discovered that the water to the building had been cut off and the facilities were not functioning. Sometimes the door is locked from the inside, the room being occupied by an Egyptian lady, who is commonly thought to be bathing in there due to the excessive amount of water left on the floor. I think she's one of the Arabic typists. Sometimes there is no toilet paper to be had. This is because the local custom

---

168   The king's nephew was found guilty of regicide and beheaded in June 1975.

169   Isfahan is Iran's third largest city, known for its wide range of architectural styles, from the eleventh to the nineteenth century.

is not to use paper, but water. Sometimes there are footprints on the toilet seat, caused by the men who use the bathroom marked "Ladies." Since the existence of a toilet presents a problem to them, they squat on the toilet seat.

I just got back from my sprint to the fourth floor. It was open, but there was a good deal of water around the sink. The bather must have come and gone.

The last time I was in Al-Khobar I found that a shipment of Geisha brand smoked oysters had arrived. I have never seen smoked oysters in Al-Khobar before. There is neither rhyme nor reason to the way shipments of food come to the markets here. Sometimes there is just one shipment of something that they've never had before and never will have again.

Just heard that a wife of a physical education teacher was given twenty-four hours to get out of Saudi Arabia for making, consuming, or selling alcohol. Can't seem to find out the specifics.

According to the resident expert on Iran, a former Peace Corps volunteer, we shouldn't have any trouble getting a room in Isfahan even though it is the end of the Iranian New Year celebration. We hope to get a room at the Ali Qapu Hotel (sounds dirty, like, "I gave him the old qapu"), which is nice but not costly.[170] The best hotel in Isfahan is the Shah Abbas, which is also considered to be one of the best hotels in the world, but not the most costly.[171]

April 13, 1975

We left Saudi Arabia without our health booklets, which show we have had vaccinations for smallpox and cholera shots. The booklets are required for entrance into Iran, but they let us through without them. When we got to the airport in Shiraz, we sent a postcard to our neighbors, the Al Sayids, asking them to go into our house, find our booklets, and bring them to the Dhahran airport when our flight comes in. Then, in case they didn't get the postcard, I sent my keys back with

---

170   The Yahoo Travel User Rating (2012) gives it four stars out of five.

171   This hotel was a seventeenth-century caravanserai, which was renovated and expanded to a 216-room hotel. A caravanserai is an inn on a caravan route.

Ben and Alice who left a day before we did for Dhahran. Al Sayid didn't get the postcard, but Ben found the booklets with their help and managed to meet us at the Dhahran airport when we returned. The alternative was vaccination on the spot for smallpox and possibly quarantine for the cholera.

We had all sorts of problems traveling in Iran. The ticket from Shiraz to Isfahan wasn't written out properly, so we had to stay two nights in Shiraz waiting to get a flight. Alex fell into the swimming pool of the Park Hotel in Shiraz (where we were staying) twenty minutes before we were to take a taxi to the airport. Jack broke his sunglasses the last day we were in Shiraz. The taxi got a flat on the way to the airport. Alex got sick the night before and threw up four times from 2:00 a.m. onwards. We finally got to sleep about six, and at six thirty the desk called to wake us up. They had the wrong name, confusing Doyle with Boyle or something. Everything was more expensive than we had anticipated, including the hotel rooms, which were about a third more expensive than we had read in our tour books.

We had many problems communicating in Iran. Although Arabic and Farsi have a great many similarities,[172] the basic vocabulary (yes, no, 1–10, stop, go, etc.) is different, and nobody there seems to know Arabic, English, or French. I have a basic vocabulary in Arabic and better than basic in French, although I have difficulty in understanding what anybody says to me in either language.

We stayed at the Park Hotel in Shiraz for two nights.[173] The Park is comfortable and old, and was once the place to stay in Shiraz, but has since been outclassed by a huge chrome and glass Inter-continental on the outskirts of the city. Yet the Park Hotel seems to invite people in with its flowers and tree-shaded courtyard, small pools, garden furniture, and a screen aviary behind some bushes. It contained fifty or so parakeets in shades of blue, green, and combinations of colors, which added their spring sounds to the atmosphere. The entrance to our hotel was surrounded with hundreds of pots of stock, purple, pink,

---

172   Farsi is the Persian language. It is the language of Iran (which was Persia) and is spoken by about 25 percent of the population in Afghanistan.

173   The Park Hotel Shiraz is rated four out of five stars by the users in Yahoo Travel for the year 2012.

white, and variegated. The courtyard breathed the scent of them, a heavy sweetness. It was nice to experience spring again. Here it goes from a kind of winter in the fifties to mid-July overnight. Shiraz is five thousand feet above sea level. They have real seasons there and snow in winter. It is high season in Iran right now. The weather was in the high fifties to low sixties. In Saudi Arabia it is getting into the high eighties now, and Iran was a pleasant contrast. I would like to go back.

The hotel had the most amazing accoutrements in the bathroom. Even in France I had not seen anything like it. There was a bidet with a spray mechanism coming out of the center. The ones in France merely filled with water like a sink and you lowered yourself into the water. Toilet paper is not regarded to be as good as water in this part of the world, although my first impression was of some kind of hand shower system. Anyway Alex had a good time making everything work, but he got a shock when he turned on the bidet and got a face full of water.

In Shiraz I went on a tour that took us to the mausoleums of two of Iran's famous writers. Then we went to a shrine where the brother of the eighth Imam is buried.[174] I had to put on the chador, one of the cloaks that the Iranian women wear, about a seven-meter circle of fabric that covers their heads and wraps around their bodies. I found that they are almost impossible to keep on, let alone trying to manage with a camera in one hand and a large pocketbook in the other. All shoes had to be checked at the entrance to the shrine. Entering the shrine was like walking into a crystal. The whole interior was made of bits of mirrors in mosaic patterns. The sarcophagus was enclosed in a silver cage, and the faithful circled it, touched it, and clung to it. Then they backed out, kissing the wall and the doorway as they went. I was having enough trouble with the thing on my head without backing out the entrance. I kept stepping on it, it kept falling off, and one lady in the tour who stepped on hers fell backwards into me almost knocking me out the door.

After the shrine we went on to the bazaar and had a glass of tea at a caravanserai located in a backwater of the bazaar area. Its courtyard was hexagonal in shape and in the center was a pool with a fountain and

---

174   The Eighth Imam is Reza (765–816). He was the only Imam to die in what is now Iran.

three ducks. Several shops owned by the government sold handicrafts. Caravansaries were places where people on caravans could spend the night, get water for their camels, and food for themselves. The camels were left in the courtyard. In this establishment the only kind of food served is that which was served in Persia two hundred years ago. The tables were covered with hand-printed cloth, and cushions lined the walls. If you desired, the waiter would bring a water pipe to smoke. The waiters had on old Persian dresses with baggy pants, dervish hats, and silk tunics with full sleeves and cummerbunds. It was not a place just for tourists because there were lots of working-class Persians there, and the waiters didn't know French, Arabic, or English.

We tried a kind of sherbet, which was like rose-water-flavored ice with something that looked like coconut frozen in it. It wasn't coconut, and nobody has been able to tell us what it was. It seemed to melt as it was eaten. With the sherbet came a cruet of lemon syrup to be poured on the dessert. Sherbet originated in Persia and comes from the Arabic word "shorbah," which means soup.

We finally got to Isfahan about six o'clock on a Saturday night. Our hotel was on the other side of the river and walking to the bazaar area took us across this bridge of yellow stone, one layer of archways on top of another. The river itself was mostly marsh grass with a fast-moving stream through the middle of it. The Park Hotel in Isfahan (the Ali Qapu Hotel had no vacancies) was not as nice as the Park Hotel in Shiraz, but Alex had somebody to play with and cartoons to watch on the television in the early evening. We had heard a lot about the Shah Abbas Hotel in Isfahan, which is an old caravanserai converted into a luxury hotel and priced out of our class. But I wanted to go there and have tea in the garden. We walked into what looked like the pictures I had seen of the courtyard of the Shah Abbas, but I could not see a main desk, waiters, or doormen. A group of men were standing in a line under the onion dome, and more men were joining them. I asked a man with a camera what was going on. "It's a funeral," he said. I thought, "What kind of hotel is this?" The next day I discovered that it was a theological school. Next door was the Shah Abbas Hotel. We did have tea there, and it is beautiful with fountains, flowers, and a bridge over one long pool in the courtyard. Tea is the drink in Iran. Ask for coffee, they give you a pot of hot water and a tin of Nescafe. When in Rome, etc.

One of the specialties in Isfahan, besides carpets and handcrafts, is nougat with pistachio nuts in it. The Persians call it "gaz." It is coated with confectioner's sugar and cornstarch to keep it from sticking. It is delicious. Another specialty is pistachio nuts, which are superb. Iranian rice is also unsurpassed. They steam it and it has a different quality from any rice I have had anywhere else the world.

We had recommendations from two different people that a craftsman named Ben Mayeri had the best brass work in Isfahan. We had verbal directions on how to get there. We walked a quarter of a mile out of the bazaar area past dozens of little shops, took a right down an alleyway, a left, another right, and we found ourselves in a courtyard. We had been warned that Ben's crooked nephew had a shop downstairs and would tell you he was Ben. We went straight upstairs to Ben's living room. I commented to Jack, "It would take the CIA to find this place."

They were right. Ben did have the best brass in Isfahan. We saw a beautiful little brass teapot with a tin lining with no engraving or metalwork on it. There was a tray of brass and silver about two and a half feet in diameter with an Aramco woman's name on it. It cost $1,100.[175] And a brass filigree lamp had been made for a Mrs. Helms of Teheran, wife of the ambassador to Iran, who was the former head of the CIA (so the CIA did find the place).[176] I bought a plain rectangular tray for a wedding gift and a plain round one for myself. We thanked Ben politely for showing us his work and left. An emissary of the crooked nephew downstairs pointed to his shop, but we kept going. Ben's craftsmanship spoiled me for anybody else's work. Ben and Alice rented a taxi and took us on a two-hour tour of Isfahan to see the historical places. I went with Alex and Jack to the Armenian Church where they have a museum. There had a particularly gory painting of the crucifixion. Alex just stood in front of it and said sadly,

---

175   In 2012 dollars, about $4,700.

176   Richard Helms (1913–2002), director of the CIA 1966–1973. Fired by President Nixon in 1973 and in the same year became Ambassador to Iran.

"Poor Jesus." The Armenian Church had a museum displaying a Bible verse inscribed on a human hair. It had to be viewed through a microscope, which brought "Why did they write on a hair?" out of Alex. We went on to visit the shaking minarets.[177] It seems that there is an old mosque with two small towers or minarets on top. Everybody has to climb to the roof of the mosque and stand around while the official shaker climbs up inside the left minaret and throws his body around until we can feel the vibrations and the other minaret begins shaking all by itself. Ben complained that he couldn't see the other one shake and asked for his money back from the ticket seller. He didn't get anyplace. The tower seemed to be parting from its base one-half inch with each shake. My prediction is that the tower and the shaker have about another six months before they find themselves on the ground in a heap of bricks.

After the shaking minarets, we went on to the fire temple outside the town. There are four major religious groups in Iran: the Moslems, the Christians, the Jews, and the Zoroastrians or fire worshipers. The temple seemed to be on top of a volcanic cone, and there were no roads to the top. One had to leg it. Ben, Alice, and I decided we could see enough of the fire temple from the bottom, but the kids all wanted to climb to the top. They had to take a rain check, and we went on to the Friday mosque, which beggars description as do most of the mosques in Isfahan.[178] All the mosques have blue tiles, onion domes, and courtyards with fountains or pools. We ended up at the bazaar in a huge square with the sheikh's mosque on one side, the Ali Qapu Palace on the other,[179] the old bazaar on another side, and the shah's mosque opposite it. The nobility used to stand on the balcony of the Ali Qapu

---

177   The Shaking Minarets (Manar Jombar) are part of the mausoleum of Amu Abdolah, a mystic and scholar of the fourteenth century.

178   Other names for this mosque are: Great Mosque, Masjid-e Jame, and Congregational Mosque. There are several mosques throughout the Islamic world with the name Friday Mosque. The Friday prayer is an obligatory, congregational prayer that is performed on Friday, just past the noon hour. The Friday Mosque in Isfahan is famed for its beauty. It was in a state of construction and renovation from 771 to the twelfth century.

179   The walls of the palace are decorated with paintings and floral patterns. The palace is seven stories high.

palace and watch polo being played in the square. The shah's mosque is the most beautiful one in Isfahan. The acoustics in the main prayer area are so good that if you clap your hands once, it echoes clearly seven times.

I have never been searched as I was searched before boarding the Iran air flight back. The woman inspector pushed my breasts together (did she think I had a pistol in each one?), felt between my legs, and even went through every single thing: cards, photographs, etc., in my wallet. I sort of staggered out of the booth, stunned, and the lady who followed me had a surprised look on her face as well. She said they even clicked off a picture on her camera, apparently thinking it might be a bomb in disguise.

Taking a taxi is a unique experience in Iran. One stands near the gutter—gutters are two-by-two feet deep channels on either side of the road in Shiraz—and shouts the name of one's destination. Since most of the Persian names are unpronounceable to a foreigner, it is difficult to get a taxi. Ben said that he would hop in the taxi as soon as it stopped in the hope that it was going in his direction. Other people from the college told us that they were at the Iran Air office and wanted to go to the Saudia Airline office in downtown Shiraz, about a mile down the road. They asked the clerk in Iran Air what to yell to get a taxi. She said, "Saaadi." So they yelled, "Saadi," got in a cab, and got taken to Saadi's mausoleum, about three miles away. They screamed, "No, no!" and someone who spoke English appeared. They told him they wanted to go to the Saudi Air office. The man explained in Farsi, and they got taken to the airport five miles away. I don't know if they ever made it to the Saudia office that day. The taxis as they go along take on other passengers, if their destination pleases them. Once we had eight people crammed into a car little bigger than a Volkswagen. The driving styles are also very exciting. I was in a taxi that got caught in the middle of a "V" press. Fortunately he stopped just in time, and the cars to his right and left just managed to avoid each other.

The crafts in Isfahan range from carpet weaving, cloth printing, ceramics, glasswork, brass work, enameling, as well as miniatures, and inlay. The turquoise in Iran is famous, and much of it is set in silver filigree designs. The miniatures are very expensive and the best are painted on ivory.

We got back the night of the tenth and were met on the runway by an airport employee carrying our health booklets. Since then I have been doing laundry, six loads already, taking time out to tie a few knots on the end of the carpet we bought. Otherwise it will wear faster. But it is a time-consuming job.

CHAPTER 8

The body in the pool, dancing girls not appreciated, the dictionary game, dangerous lizards, traffic lights and Saudi drivers, the police make an arrest.

April 14, 1975

One of the students was reported missing from the student dorms last week. He was gone about three days before anyone noticed. Shortly after that, his body turned up near the deep end of the student swimming pool. Since it is sandstorm season, the pool water has been very cloudy. They think he dived into the pool, hit his head, and never resurfaced. And nobody noticed! For several days the physical education swimming classes were conducted while a body lay at the bottom of the pool. Shudder!

April 20, 1975

Last evening was "International Night" at the college. I was asked to wear a costume made from a hand-printed Iranian tablecloth. It was a gored skirt with fringed bottom and a top with short sleeves and stand-up collar and fringe on the sleeves. It was a good fit, so I modeled it.

Then at the last minute someone refused to wear a Moroccan wedding dress made out of satin, silver net, and silver embroidery. It was a caftan design with a net covering. I was asked to model that, too. The complete outfit must have weighed twenty pounds. It was also very long. Even though I was six feet tall with heels, it was touching the floor! No wonder the first person didn't want to wear it.

There were about twenty other women in the show, modeling everything from Saudi Arabian and Mexican wedding dresses to Thai costumes, and Finnish and German peasant dresses. People kept coming up to me afterwards and asking if I had been a model in the States and if not I should have been. Heady stuff. I was the tallest one there. Dr. Hough said I should have had a more disdainful look, like I was bored. Actually, I thought all I had to do was to wear the costume and mill around. I never thought I was going to have to walk down a runway, turn, and stand there while someone described the outfit.

The show consisted of booths displaying things people had brought back from different countries. I contributed two wooden blocks used for cloth printing to the Iran booth. For some reason nobody remembered to exclude the students, and they composed about half the audience. I thought this was great. Unofficially the policy is to keep the faculty and students as far apart as possible. One of Jack's students from last year came up to me and said, "My friends have never seen anything like this (the fashion show). Only here at the college could they see something like this."

I think it's good for the students to see that their teachers have families and an existence outside the classroom and to meet them on an informal basis, although the administration doesn't think so.

Those damn lizards have returned with the warmer weather. I am going to have a heart attack someday when one of them darts across my path. Two got into our house last year, the fleshy pink ones that look like rearview mirror ornaments won at carnivals. Speaking of which, car status symbols here include fake fur covered dashboards, smocked pillows artfully placed in the corners of rear windows, acetate fringe dangling from the edges of the windows, and a wicker birdcage complete with plastic flowers and fake bird hanging from the rearview mirror. Enough to give a New Hampshire Department of Safety officer an embolism.

We had a violent windstorm late last week. A huge locust tree next to our house blew down. Trees here have extremely shallow root systems because their only source of moisture is surface water. Two days later Jack, Alex, and I were all trying to have a nap in the afternoon when another shamal (wind/sandstorm) started up. Despite the blowing sand a crew of about fourteen gardeners set to work with the dullest axes ever made and began hacking away at the branches of the fallen tree and making merry. As soon as the sandstorm died down and we gave up on the idea of sleeping—they left.

Jack said, "What do they want to stick around for? There is no sandstorm blowing and nobody's trying to sleep. They won't be back until there is another sandstorm." However, he was wrong. They were back with their dull axes the next morning at half past six to cut the remaining branches off the tree. They replanted it; hopefully it will have new branches. My yard looks like a jungle. Locust tree branches all over the place. And these have thorns on them.

April 22, 1975

Daily temperatures are in the high eighties to low nineties. I may inherit a neighbor's cat for the summer, if we are still here at that time. It will take care of the cockroach and field mouse problem that comes with summer. Cats think it great sport to chase the large cockroaches. A neighbor told me not only do they catch all the ones in the house, but also they go outside and bring in a few. That is fast queering my desire to take care of the cat.

Oh, another thing cats do is chase lizards. Myra Anderson's cat went after a lizard on the kitchen floor. It pounced. The lizard dropped its tail and took off into a corner, while the tail continued to flop around on the floor. The cat was paralyzed with indecision. It didn't know whether to chase the lizard or the tail.

April 26, 1975

Things got very exciting around here last night. After Jack and I got home, we put out all the lights and went to bed. About fifteen minutes later we heard a noise like a bird flying around the bedroom, crashing into the Venetian blinds and the walls. Jack leapt out of bed, punching the light switch as he did, yelling, "I think it is over there!" But it had disappeared. He searched the room thoroughly, to no avail. We went back to bed, and Jack put the flyswatter on the bedside table, just in case. We were both almost asleep again when the crashing around the room began again. Jack screamed, "I think it's on the bed!" I dived under the covers. The next thing I knew, the lights were on again, and Jack was whapping away at the bed with the flyswatter while the air was filled with a whirring of wings. He managed to knock it on the floor, and I came out from under the blankets to see what it was. Jack finished it off with a rubber sandal, but even then it continued to twitch. It turned out to be the biggest moth I had ever seen. The body was five inches long, and the wings in flight were nine inches from tip to tip.

The latest minutes for the Engineering Chairman's Meeting reported that a dump truck drove into the big reflecting pool by the mosque, but nobody was hurt and the truck was towed out. Things are always falling into that pool. And Yemeni workmen still bathe in it.

April 28, 1975

I made a tomato soup cake with cream cheese frosting. The recipe was Campbell's own, and it didn't call for any salt, which I thought was strange.[180] I added a little salt.

April 30, 1975

I heard a bit of Arab lore. Humans know ninety-nine attributes of Allah.[181] The Arabs say that the supercilious expression of the camel is due to the fact that he alone knows the one-hundredth attribute.

The latest rumor making the rounds of this rumor factory is that the college's Egyptian doctor got FIRED! A drunk driver hit three students last Wednesday night. One was killed instantly, another critically injured, and the third hurt. Witnesses called the college doctor at home, and he refused to come. His contract had already NOT been renewed, but was not up until the end of August. The doctor on duty at Aramco, nearby, finally came to the scene. The doctor who was fired was treating one of my neighbors for gout. The medicine made her

---

180   For recipe see "Tomato Soup Cake," appendix 1.

181   These ninety-nine attributes (or names) of Allah are the names that Allah revealed to man by the Quran. Some of these attributes are (not in order): the Highest, the Creator, the Shaper, the Judge, the All Powerful, the Just, the Witness, etc.

deathly ill. She finally went to another doctor at a hospital in town and learned she had a broken bone in her foot and did not have gout. The story got around. I've never gone to him, preferring the Ash Sharq Hospital, a Lebanese establishment. Their doctors are mostly trained at the American University of Beirut Medical School.

We just received a notice that the electricity will be off tomorrow from seven in the morning to three in the afternoon for maintenance work on the high-voltage wires. Since it got up to ninety-eight degrees today, having no air-conditioning tomorrow should be a real treat.

May 2, 1975

You don't know how difficult it is to place a call out of here. The last memo we received on the subject involved going to the airport when the Bureau of Posts and Communications was open, depositing thirty dollars, and then going through the complications of actually placing the call.[182] Some businessmen here who have needed a quick answer on some deal they were negotiating have actually flown to Beirut for the answer rather than wait three days (it can take that long) to make the call.

May 5, 1975

Jack and I took the nine-by-twelve foot living room rug outside and hung it over the clothesline so we could beat the dirt out of it. The rug was heavy, and we probably would have been killed instantly if any of the wire clotheslines had snapped. Alex's plumbing collection came in handy for once, and we used his various lengths of pipe that are strewn about the yard to beat the carpet. Despite the fact that the rug is vacuumed daily, great clouds of dust and sand appeared with each whack. Alex got into the spirit of the endeavor and whacked away, too. No matter how much we beat it, great eruptions of dirt kept billowing out. Finally we dragged the rug back in the house, ran a vacuum over it, and turned it around so that the worn end is now towards the furniture side of the living room. It looks like a new rug.

---

182   In 2012 dollars $30 is about $128.

The last time we moved the rug we discovered a long dead, leathery, wrinkled-up pink lizard under the carpet. Jack had been complaining so much about the smell coming from that side of the room that I was sure we would find at least the body of a cat under there. I think the smell must have been coming from the dampness due to the terrific wind and rainstorm we had about two weeks back. Water just poured in around the windows.

We had eighteen leaks. I was stranded up on the jebel at work, and Alex was into everything. Jack gave Alex eighteen empty plastic ice cream containers and told him to put them under all the leaks. Water was just pouring in a steady stream down from the ceiling. The light bulb burst in the kitchen because of water dripping through the wiring. The glass globe over the light in Alex's room filled up with water. As soon as a bucket got two drops in it, Alex would grab it, run into the bathroom with it, and empty it in the toilet. Meanwhile the deluge continued. When I finally got home, there was water everywhere, ice cream containers with brown water everywhere, a blown light bulb in the kitchen with the filament exposed and no apparent way of removing it, a big tree blown over in the yard, and the rug near the exterior wall of the living room was soaked.

May 6, 1975

The labs at Aramco ran tests on the Pepsi from the local bottling plant. Enough bacteria, dirt, and insects were discovered to lead them to the conclusion that the returned bottles were neither washed nor sterilized before being refilled. I never drank much of the stuff anyway, but I can say with assurance that I will be drinking a lot less now.

The creepy crawly things here will be the end of me. Just walking down the tiled walk to the house sets in motion all kinds of insects and lizards who have been sunning themselves on the sidewalk. I live in fear that one of them will become confused and slither over my sandaled foot someday.

May 10, 1975

All three of us, we discovered, have worms. Alex was positively infested. Jack discovered he had them first. Then we checked Alex that night. Then last night I found I had them. Now we're all taking medicine for it. I would like to know where Alex picked it up. I went to the bus stop to catch the nursery school bus to work and told John's mother that Alex had them. She said, "I know, he just told everyone at bus stop." There were about seven mothers and fourteen kids there. Cringe.

May 14, 1975

The students have come out with a science journal. One of them wrote an article entitled "Visit to the Math Department," which describes the Math Department. At the end of the articles are some items about the proposed summer activities of the department members. One entry reads:

> *Dr. Al-Moajil will be busy in the summer on what is called an internal research. He will get married! Congratulations and a happy life, Dr. Al-Moajil.*

Since the editor of the journal was Saudi, he missed the double entendre.

The Pakistani male secretaries at the college are just incredible. Most of them spend all their time telling the faculty members that they are too busy to type anything or that they can't do any typing unless they get it ten days in advance. One of them has it down to a science. He sits at his desk and reads the Koran all day. Not even a Saudi can touch him. Who would dare tell someone not to read the Koran?

A Civil Engineering Department professor came in to borrow twenty-five ditto masters. He said his department Pakistani told him that they didn't have any. The department member had a big project to be typed. Of course, if there are no masters there will be no typing. So since I hate to see idle Pakistani secretaries, I generously gave him twelve of my twenty-four masters.

The Pakistani secretaries also go around telling everyone how much better they are than the American women who work part-time. I worked under one, Hanfi, for three weeks last September before I quit. Hanfi corrected MY English, which insulted me no end, with remarks like "That's not how we write it here." Hanfi fancies himself quite an authority on the English language. These Pakistanis write sentences full of "most respected sir" and "Kindly please thoughtfully direct your attention to the aforesaid subject." Subordinate clauses dangle like bunches of bananas from the ends of sentences. They also write letters of the stomach-turning variety to the college like, "I would be so happy in my heart to work in your most esteemed country where the Prophet once trod. It would be my heart's desire most honored sir," etc., ad nauseam.

Hanfi also had other unfavorable qualities like a tendency to run down the boss as soon as the boss left the office. Once he and a Saudi graduate student had a big discussion about whether or not the director of housing, Juraib, was a good Moslem or not. Hanfi had this disconcerting tendency to run down Juraib's personality and then look me in the eye with a "Don't you agree?" expression on his face. Once when he did this, I ahemmed and harrumphed, then he grabbed my hand and said, "My, what a beautiful watch!" ($8.98 Timex), looked straight at me, and said, "And the person who's wearing it is too." That convinced me it was time for my exit and I quit.

Two friends of mine work under Pakistani secretaries. They both complain that the Pakistanis spend most of their time trying to make the women's work look inferior, either by telling them to type slower, giving them the wrong forms and then waiting for the boss to appear to correct them publicly, or by not giving them any work, and then giving them all the work to do at the last minute.

May 22, 1975

Jack took the car into the Volkswagen dealership yesterday, again, for the one thousand kilometer free checkup and oil change. The last time he took it in, a week ago yesterday, he presented them with a list of things to be fixed, and they used the list and fixed somebody else's car. This time they did about half the things on the list, and Jack pointed out to them what they missed. They had the list the second time, but apparently just read the first three items or so. He checked the oil before he took it in to see how dirty it was, so he'd know if they actually changed the oil or not. I don't think he has checked it since he took it home. Dr. Hough suggested that Jack look to see if we had *any* oil, because sometimes one guy drains it and the other guy forgets to put new oil in.

The local grocer, Omar, used to sell "Polish beef" with big winks and refer to it as "special meat." Everyone concluded that he was putting one over on the customs officers by labeling pork as beef. But a Pole, head of the Mechanical Engineering Department, claims it was really beef all along. I guess Omar was adding to his mystique.

May 26, 1975

The college featured the movie *The Way We Were* with Barbara Streisand and Robert Redford Thursday night.[183] I enjoyed it despite the fact that all references to the female lead's Jewish heritage had been deleted.

There was a scene earlier in the movie where he comes to her apartment, falls asleep in her bed, and she gets in with him. He starts to make love to her, and she isn't sure he knows who she is or even where he is. The bed scene seemed to last ages. I kept wrapping my legs around each other, sitting on the edge of the chair, gnawing my knuckles, saying to myself, "Oh God please end this." This kind of scene is terribly sensitive in this culture. A bunch of Saudis sitting up back were making clicking sounds with their tongues (tsk tsk), and I was sure somebody would throw a fit.

Dr. Hough told me about a presentation given by the British Iron and Steel Institute last week at the college. They had a reel of film with girls in body suits covered with steel mesh and nothing on under the body suits. They danced and generally displayed what they had. The audience, mostly Saudis and some foreign faculty, became increasingly uncomfortable. Then the projector broke down, and they had to rerun the whole reel. By this time one student stood up and said, "This is NOT Europe. This is Saudi Arabia!" The director of the program got flustered and said, "Go on to the next reel!" Many industrial presentations throw in a few sexy girls to get the attention of the audience and then move on to its real purpose.

---

183   Starring Barbra Streisand and Robert Redford. About two college students in the late 1930s who fall in love although they have different personalities and political views. Released in 1973.

Next Thursday is the department party, and the chairman has bottled about thirty gallons of wine. The only wine I have had recently that is worse than what most people here make was the three dollar a bottle wine we had ordered in Shiraz. It tasted like white grape juice added to vodka. I almost choked. Neither of us could finish our glass let alone the bottle. And the Persian poets wrote ecstatic stanzas about the wine of Shiraz. Maybe compared to the alternative: swamp water.

Last night we had two couples over. One of our guests had been an English teacher with the Peace Corps in Afghanistan. He said intestinal problems are legion there, and when you see a doctor the first question he will ask is, "How are your stools?" After the English teacher missed classes for three days with the usual affliction, the doctor sent an Afghani English teacher to inquire about his health. Not knowing the English word for "stools," the Afghan turned to his English/Farsi dictionary and asked, "How are your manures?"

June 6, 1975

Tomorrow afternoon there is a tea for Dr. Hough's wife. I said I would bring a pineapple upside-down cake.[184] Found the recipe in the *Boston Globe* and it's great.

Dr. Hough's wife finally got here the first of June, after having a wild time trying to replace her passport and her son's, which were lost in the mail, but she made it. I took her around Al-Khobar Wednesday night to show her where to buy souvenir gifts, fabric, have thobes made, dresses, and batiks. I think her head is still spinning. Dr. Hough is having problems adjusting to having a family again, after spending the whole year getting used to being a bachelor.

[Letter continued by Jack]

We will be here June and most of July as I was offered a good salary for teaching summer school. It won't be easy, but we can use the extra money.

---

184 For recipe see "Pineapple Upside-Down Cake," appendix 1.

There are a lot of activities going on here this week as everyone is entertaining before going away. Besides the department party, we went one night with Jeff and Joe to the Edes' where we played the dictionary game. One person picks a word out of the dictionary, and everyone writes what they think might be a definition. The person with the dictionary writes the real definition, and then when all the definitions have been read, everyone votes for what they think might be the correct definition. If someone votes for your definition, you get a point, and if you vote for the real definition, you also get a point.

June 7, 1975

I am working more hours now since Jack has no classes and can stay home to take care of Alex. Joe Fahey is packing to leave. Graduation is the thirteenth, and after that everybody will be leaving. I'll be glad when they're gone. I have to stay because Jack is teaching summer school.

The latest hot rumor, of which there are many this year, is that foreign women will be allowed to drive in Saudi Arabia and that they are already trying it experimentally in Jeddah, which is on the west coast. I am not sure I would want to take on the male drivers here, but it is frustrating to want to go someplace when Jack is at class and the car is sitting in the yard.

Last night I spotted the big pink lizard that hangs out near the back door light. He was hiding behind the plastic plate over the door that has our house number in Arabic and English numerals. Jack saw him dart at a moth. The moth tried to get away as the lizard munched on him and attempted to swallow him wings and all. I can't stand the fauna of Arabia much longer. The warmer it gets, the more fauna there is. The air-conditioning repairman who lives in our compound captured a dhub, "a four foot dangerous lizard" as described in the locally written English language guidebook to Arabia.[185] We couldn't decide if that meant the lizard had four feet, or was four feet long, or

---

185   Considered a delicacy by the Arabs.

both. Anyway, Alex indicated that it was two and a half to three feet long. I didn't make the pilgrimage over to see it, so all this is hearsay.

I found the first good steaks in Saudi Arabia last week. Flown in from Australia.

June 14, 1975

Graduation was last night. We watched it on television. Couldn't find Jack, but he was there. The cameraman was easily distracted. He once followed a janitor across the auditorium. There were a lot of shots of people's backs. I saw Dr. Hough. After the ceremonies a dinner was scheduled for twelve hundred people: the graduates and faculty plus guests of the college. Jack had no intention of going. It was males only, as most of the official functions here are. They killed twenty sheep and roasted them. It was chaos. Dr. Hough said there were police at the door manhandling the guests and when he finally got in, there was no food left. People were scooping up rice with their hands and piling it on their plates. He said he wasn't going to eat from a serving bowl that somebody else had dipped his hands in.

Last Wednesday this Pakistani secretary (male) down the corridor came into my office and asked me if I would go into Al-Khobar and buy him a Rolex watch and an Akai tape recorder. He was to go on vacation the twenty-fifth and planned to visit his girlfriend in Canada. She had asked him to bring a watch and a tape recorder with him, saying she'd pay him for them. Last year, just before his vacation, he went into Al-Khobar and the mutawa got him. The mutawa or religious police cut men's hair, if it's too long, or forcibly escort them to the barber. His hair was pretty bushy. Anyway, they shaved it all off, and he was too embarrassed to go back to Pakistan, so he postponed his vacation a month until it grew a little. He wasn't taking any chances this vacation. I declined his request. Last year they grabbed one of our neighbors whose sideburns were deemed too long. They escorted him to the barber and told the barber to cut them off. The Britisher sat there as the guy trimmed his hair and said, through gritted teeth, "If you cut off any more, I will kill you." The barber didn't cut off any more.

Just had a conversation with Ed Peattie about how difficult it is for Saudi drivers to adjust to traffic lights and highways with lanes. They just completed a six-lane divided highway from Dhahran to Al-Khobar, complete with traffic lights. The natives aren't used to being told when to stop and go. Three cars will line up side-by-side at the light. One will inch forward. The others inch forward too. Then the first guy moves up some more. Sometimes, before the light changes, one of the three may decide he can't stand the suspense anymore and will drive right through the red light. When the light finally turns green, the two remaining hotshots just sit there. If there is an American among the front three, he's usually a half-mile down the road before they get their act together.

Another interesting phenomena occurs the very second the light goes green. A chorus of horns will shatter the air. Most Westerners are infuriated when the eighth guy back in the third lane will honk his horn the very second the light changes to green. One Frenchman actually got out of his Peugeot and walked back to the Arab behind him to inquire what the problem was. The Arab probably came very close to homicide. Jack's reaction to a chorus of horns behind him is to make a great show of peering about to see what the problem is. Once, when the symphony started before the light even changed, he was so busy swiveling his neck around that he didn't see the light when it did change green and just sat there while the fellow behind him almost lost it.

Dr. Hough's wife has a sunburn, and his son is housebound and frustrated by the confined existence he has to live here. He went walking up towards Aramco and was stopped by a taxi driver who insisted on bringing him home despite his protests that he liked to walk and he had no money to pay him with. Dr. Hough says the boy likes to range all over and can't here because the Saudis are suspicious of somebody "just walking" when the temperature is one hundred and ten degrees. From Dr. Hough's description of his son, I was expecting a blond bushy-headed Zulu, but his mother prevailed upon him to get a haircut before he left.

June 18, 1975

This is my last day in this department full-time as the academic year is ending. The summer session will start in five days. I will be putting in about an hour a day here and then will work about four hours a day for Industrial Management. Dr. Hough left this morning for Europe and the States with his wife and son.

I shall describe an average day, which usually begins about half past seven, when Alex gets me up. He has to have breakfast and be outside to catch the nursery school bus at a quarter after eight. I usually catch the same bus and get off at the jebel where the college is, as the bus passes by on its way to Aramco. I spend anywhere from four to seven hours at work, depending on Jack's schedule. Dr. Hough used to bring me a sandwich from Aramco when he got back from lunch there. When I get home I collapse for a couple of hours, depending on what I have to do, and when I recover I start cleaning the house. Now that most of the faculty is gone, Alex doesn't have any kids to play with, so he usually wants to involve me in what he's doing. We eat supper anywhere from five to seven depending on how long it takes to cook and how insistent Alex is that he wants something to eat "immediately." We go to bed about midnight. Jack sometimes stays up later because he says he does his best work after twelve. Unfortunately I am good for nothing after twelve and he's just coming alive. Alex is in bed about eight. I read, sew, and cook for recreation. We go town to shop about once a week but sometimes more often, because we run out of things or need something like medicine.

Most of the people who are leaving the college for the summer have left. It has been hot but not humid, and there has only been one moderate sandstorm so far this month. This is the season for them. I am mostly going from an air-conditioned building to an air-conditioned house and vice versa, so the heat hasn't bothered me.

June 25, 1975

The daily temperature is 110° in the shade. Last year at this time it was around 116°. We've been lucky. Also there were three or four minor sandstorms this June, and June is the season.

Jack has started teaching summer school as of yesterday.

July 2, 1975

Since Dr. Hough left, I have been working for Isa Al-Sayid in Industrial Management. He is also head of food services for the college. They call him if somebody over there sneezes. I spend all my time answering calls from food services. The other day there was a fire at 5:00 a.m. in a big freight elevator in the food services building. They called him at home and got him out of bed. He told them to call the fire department. They called back about fifteen minutes later and said it was still burning. He got dressed and was almost out the door when they called back and said it was out. By this time he was up!

Yesterday he was yelling in Arabic over the phone. I understood enough of what was being said to be intrigued. He explained that the week before the cash registers in both cafeterias were robbed. About eighteen dollars in riyals had been taken from each machine. The drawers had been pried open. Somebody called the police, who came with their fingerprinting kit. They took fingerprints and arrested the cashier. He's still in jail. Isa doesn't think the man did it. "Why would he break into the register when he knew how to open the drawers? Why would he do it when there was comparatively little money in the registers? Why would he come all the way to UPM on a weekend from his home, which is forty miles from Dhahran?" But the police matched the fingerprints, so they think they got their man. Isa said he would never have called the police over such a small amount. All cashiers in the kingdom will probably wear gloves from now on.

Don Smith is about to get bumped as dean of the graduate school. The administration is putting Saudis into all key administrative posts. The dean of sciences, dean of engineering, dean of graduate school, and all the department chairmen will all be Saudis next fall. Most of these appointees aren't seasoned department members and earned their doctorates less than three years ago. Some of them were made department chairmen before they'd even been here a year. The new Saudi math chairman took twelve years to get his degree in math history at George Peabody College in Tennessee. His thesis was on Arab mathematicians in the Middle Ages. Not exactly a heavy-duty math degree.

July 11, 1975

Things are quiet here. Daily temperature is around 110 degrees and we had a sandstorm yesterday. Busy packing.

July 18, 1975

It's Friday night (the equivalent of the end of the weekend). I stopped work on Wednesday. It has only been two days, and I'm already going bananas waiting to get out of here. Alex has his nursery school graduation tomorrow. We leave a week from Wednesday.

July 20, 1975

It is 4:15 p.m. and ninety degrees in the house. The electricity went off at 12:15 p.m. The temperature outside is 108. I am stark naked, having just taken a bath to try to cool off. I filled the tub from the COLD tap, and it was warmer than I was. Some blasting was being done on a new road nearby, and I wonder if that had anything to do with the power outage. Jack took Alex to the student pool up on the jebel. Women aren't allowed to swim in that pool. The family pool has a broken pump so they closed it.

We leave the morning of July 30. I am counting the days. Since I'm not working anymore, I have all kinds of ambitious plans for the house, cleaning shelves, drawers, closets, etc., but today I got one cabinet done before the power went out and now it is too hot to attempt anything.

On Thursday we went to the Saudi government hospital in Al-Khobar to get cholera shots, which we will need to get back into Saudi Arabia in September. They are free, and they stamp the health booklets in Arabic so the airport officials can read them. In the States we would have to go to our doctor, get the shots, and then chase down the local county health official to stamp and certify our booklet. It's easier to do it here although whenever I go into the government hospital I am afraid of coming OUT with more than I went IN with. They do use disposable needles and their vaccine is refrigerated, but the other patients there look like they might be suffering from diseases no

American doctor has ever heard of. I saw what looked like elephantitis the other day. A man was sitting on the sidewalk with his left leg exposed. It was enormous, just huge. The skin was stretched to the point that it was shiny.

After phoning inquiries around the college, I have learned that a cable burnt out, and they hope to have the power on again by tonight. Now when Jack returns from the pool I will have to strong-arm him into taking me either to Aramco or to the airport for supper. Since I am getting out of here in less than two weeks, I would prefer Aramco to the airport, but since Aramco costs more he will probably opt for the airport.

Speaking of supper, there are a number of interesting cheeses available here. But sitting on the docks in Dammam under a broiling sun awaiting clearance through customs makes them even more interesting. We bought five pounds of New Zealand cheddar the other day and it had the gamiest flavor imaginable. Jack can hardly stand it. It tastes as if some little old lady in New Zealand had a cow and made her own cheese and sent it by slow boat to Arabia. We had bought this cheese before and found it to be a mild pleasant go-with-anything cheese. But this would rank out Roquefort.

Enclosed is a memo from the Juraib, the housing director that has a certain quaintness.

July 23, 1975

That cashier who was arrested because his fingerprints were on the snack bar cash register is free, but he was beaten in jail. Some of his family even came to the police station to say he was at a wedding that day, but the police wouldn't believe them. He was back at his old job just before I quit work. They must have given up trying to get him to admit guilt.

I can't wait to get out of here, what with the summer session it's been a very long school year

[The End of the Second Year in Saudi Arabia]

MEMORANDUM: UPM—DHAHRAN
Date: 18 June 1975
To: Prof. E. W. Hough
From: Housing & Services Department
Subject: FILE CABINET/PURCHASE REQUISITION

First of all, I would like to point out that several circulars have been shot out in regard to procure office equipment as well as furniture, all purchase requisitions must be processed through this department. In case of requirements arise, Housing and Services is to be contacted and as such, purchase requisition is returned with this memo.

Instead of buying 3-drawer file cabinet from the market, we can supply you with 4-drawer file cabinet from the ready stock. This can also be locked as desired.

Please advise us as soon as possible so that action required could be arranged and assuring you of our cooperation. Thanks.

A. M. Al-Juraib
Director

September 1975 to June 1976

Gerald Ford: President of the United States

Sep. 18, 1975: Patricia Hearst captured by FBI in San Francisco. Charged with bank robbery.

Dec. 29, 1975: Eleven killed, seventy-five hurt by terrorist bomb at LaGuardia Airport in New York City.

Mar. 29, 1976: Eight Ohio National Guardsmen indicted for shooting and killing four Kent State students on May 4, 1970.

CHAPTER 9

*Fermentation fun, imitating grandmother, working for the Dutch,
Halloween party, my driver—Mohammed Al Sharif, death in a
parked car, the five-kilometer foot race, party in
the Dutch compound, Pakistani English*

September 26, 1975

Our British Airways flight landed on time at Dhahran Airport at about eight thirty Tuesday night. The plane was mobbed with people from the college, and all the kids knew each other. They ran up and down the aisles, played, and fought. It must have been pretty tough on all those people who weren't from the college.

Our car seemed in pretty good condition, but had about five hundred miles put on it since we left the end of July. Husein had even swept out the inside and washed it for us. Our house was not painted, but they did fix the washing machine and gave us a new toilet seat. The workmen had spit out the shells of their watermelon seeds on the rug. The housing situation at the college this year is really grim. They are moving couples that had been assigned to this compound—some with one or two kids—to Dammam, which is about ten miles away. The houses in Dammam have all kinds of problems, irregular bus service to the college, electrical failures, no phones yet, no place for the kids to play, and Turkish toilets. One couple refused to live there and said they would go back to the States unless the college could accommodate them elsewhere. They are in this compound now.

The other new department member, Fred Priest, a former vice president at Aramco, was met at the airport and taken to a bachelor apartment at the college. They couldn't find the gatekeeper who had the keys, so he had to be put up in a hotel in Al-Khobar. Undoubtedly he had a fabulous house at Aramco and isn't going to be too pleased with his quarters. His wife will probably feel the same way.

September 29, 1975

The night before last we brewed our first six gallons of wine with all the professional ingredients brought back from a brewing supply shop near Boston. My linen closet smells like the Carlsberg Brewery we toured in Copenhagen last summer. Jack keeps taking readings on his new hydrometer, and when the sugar reaches a certain level, we transfer the juice to an airtight jug for a longer time. In approximately three months, we will have about six gallons of a dry grape wine. Tonight we add the yeast and the yeast nutrients to the sugar/water/grape juice mixture and will let it ferment about fifteen days. This has to be superior to what everyone else at the college is mixing up. Most of them just dump everything together in a vat and let it stew. We sterilize everything and measure carefully and add wine nutrients with special wine yeast. Necessity is the mother of this hobby.

It has been 105 degrees. The humidity reaches 100 percent in the evenings.

October 1, 1975 [Letter by Jack]

Fred Priest, the petroleum professor, is going to move in next door to us. He's the American with only a BA, but he's a retired vice president from Aramco. His salary is twice as much as the Egyptian in his department with an American PhD. There will be hard feelings when that comes to light.

October 1, 1975

This promises to be a very chaotic year. Last spring they were having difficulty recruiting students because several new colleges had opened up around the kingdom. For fall they managed to locate a "record number" of prep year students. This is going to overwork the faculty because in Jack's program they have the same number of teachers as last year and one hundred more students scheduled. They were overworked last year. Jack suspects they sent college officials out to stand on street corners to buttonhole anyone between the ages of eighteen and forty who passed inquiring, "Howja like ta go ta college? We'll pay ya!" or the local equivalent thereof. He also suspects, accordingly, that the quality of the incoming class will be worse than last year and, consequently, more work for him to teach them.

October 4, 1975

Yesterday was my birthday. Jack surprised me with a pair of earrings. Alex insisted on helping me open my present. At my advanced age and feeble state...and what with being short of wind I thought he might help me blow out the candles too, but he lost interest at that point.

I found the "Mark Eden Bust Developer" in a pharmacy downtown. Instructions were in Arabic. It is (TA DA!) two wooden disks separated by a big spring in the middle. You press the disks together and presumably it gives you the chest of Johnny Weissmuller.[186]

October 14, 1975

Work is still not too great. I have been working seven to eight hours a day, and it is very frustrating to see a department pulled this way and that when it looked so promising last year. I think the two new guys resent their dependency on me because I am the only one who knows anything about university procedures and the only link to the department last year. Neither of them thinks Dr. Hough intends to come back and want to make all manner of changes in the curriculum and laboratories he planned. It is frustrating for me to watch this because Dr. Hough is very well known and well published in his field, and these guys don't even know what some of the lab equipment he ordered is used for. As you can see, I am emotionally involved in the department.

Jack has been doing the shopping lately. He teaches from two to six in the afternoon and doesn't feel like shopping afterwards. I work from half past seven to half past one. Today he bought a fresh lamb leg.

---

186   Johnny Weismuller (1904–1984) won five Olympic gold medals in swimming. Known for his role as Tarzan. His first *Tarzan* movie was released in 1932.

I just put it in the oven about an hour ago to cook according to directions given me by Isa Al-Sayid. Unfortunately, still on the leg (which included part of the rib cage as a bonus) was an appendage, which either is the poor animal's tail or part of his other equipment. I about had a fit. Of course, I removed it before cooking. In the back of my mind is the possibility that it could be tumor, but I'd prefer it to be one of the first two possibilities. Anyway, I excised it and saved it for Jack for his opinion. After examining it, he will probably swear off lamb for the rest of his life.

October 15, 1975 [Letter by Jack]

Maralyn got a call tonight and learned that there is a Dutch construction company—the Naarden-Meuse Groep —looking for a full-time American secretary who can take shorthand.[187] They would pay her the equivalent of my salary. There would be many problems, but if she could get the summer off and if it's a good working situation, then it is possible. In any case, she is going to find out more about it.

[Letter continued by Maralyn:]

Working outside the college community has advantages. I am not too happy with the situation in the Petroleum Engineering Department this year. I had a lot more responsibility and independence when I worked for Dr. Hough. The two new guys regard me as they would a piece of office furniture, and I resent it. With Dr. Hough I knew every detail of the department operations, but these guys don't bother to tell me what's going on. To them I'm just a secretary. Dr. Hough used me at another level. I had already spoken to Darya Al-Sayid, in personnel, about another position, and asked her to keep me posted on what came up. At the time she said there would be absolutely no problem in placing me anywhere in the college. I had specifically requested a position where I would be using shorthand. Neither of the two new professors gives dictation.

Bought two two-pound bags of Betty Crocker flour and sifted them as usual before storing them in five-pound tins. With each sifter full, I

---

187 The name of this company has been changed.

got little mahogany-colored beetles and white worms. Jack bought me three pounds of Uncle Ben's rice. Again, maybe twenty-five mahogany beetles, one-quarter inch long. I put the rice in a plastic bag in the freezer to kill them. Then each time I make rice, I will flush water through to float the debris out. If I thought I had an odd box, I'd toss it and buy another, but the next one, and the next will probably be infested too. So I comfort myself with the fact that it will all be cooked. My sifter has a very fine mesh and it removes everything living, but I don't relish the idea of eating some insect's house. The last box of Cheerios I bought had a coupon in it that said "expires Jan. 1975." Terrific.

One of the older women here observed, "It's like living back in grandmother's day." She meant all the extra work one has to do to live here. Everything has to be ironed, milk made from powder, vegetables disinfected, wash hung instead of tossed in a dryer, drinking water poured from a jerry can, flour sifted, vegetables prepared from scratch, and meat thawed before cooking. She makes her own mayonnaise because one of our mutual acquaintances spotted Arab ladies in Omar's opening mayonnaise jars, sticking their fingers in, and tasting the mayo to see if it was okay. After hearing that, I may start making it myself in my small blender. The expiration date on all the mayonnaise jars is this month. I can't imagine what the mayonnaise has been through in getting here from the US.

Maxim's, a new steak house, has opened in Al-Khobar. Alice and Ben went with a guest. They were served a very ordinary soup, a bottle of apple juice, small portions of fish, vegetable, rice, coffee, and cake for dessert. It came to forty dollars.[188] The fish was hamur, the local haddock. Nothing unusual. Darya and Isa (Darya works at the college; Isa is her husband) will take us to the fish market with them next week. The market in Dammam has a very good selection, and Isa will tell us the Arabic names for the different fish. I want some red snapper and shrimp.

October 18, 1975 [Letter by Jack]

Maralyn's job with the Dutch company sounds more promising, but the guy that might hire her has gone to Riyadh on business. Maralyn has an interview with this guy at his home Wednesday night.

---

188   In 2012 dollars, about $171.

[Letter continued by Maralyn]

Made a very good casserole for a potluck supper we went to—chicken almond casserole. I lined the two-quart casserole dish with cooked chicken, almonds (whole blanched), chopped onion, another layer of chicken, and topped it with chicken sauce made from the broth of the cooked chicken. It was served with noodles.

I am still investigating a position as confidential secretary to the director of a Dutch company, who has many Saudi contracts. They would provide me with a car and driver, and a very good salary. Problems: it is full-time and would require that I find a sitter in the afternoons, and it is not near the college but in Al-Khobar about seven miles away. Full-time would be a strain, but for two and a half times what the college is paying me—and I'm one of the college's better paid secretaries—I might put up with the strain. A big plus, aside from the salary, is getting away from the college community.

The first batch of our homemade wine is in the secondary stage of fermentation. This stage requires a fermentation lock (pressure lock, filled with sodium bisulfate solution to keep it sterile). The first night Jack filled the five-gallon jug, it burbled and gurgled all night, three to four times a minute, keeping him awake. He finally turned the air conditioner fan on to drown out the sound of the wine in the bedroom. When it stops making noise, it is ready to be put in bottles. We will get about seventeen bottles from every five-gallon batch. We have a glass hydrometer to measure alcohol content. We got a 12 percent reading on the first batch, which came out like rosé, not bad. It must settle some more before it is potable. The second five-gallon batch is from cranberry juice and fermenting very slowly. The third five-gallon batch is "grapple" (grape/apple) and has already gone into the secondary fermentation stage. We expect to drink it before the cranberry. It's an interesting hobby. My next batch will be made with dates, which are a very available commodity. All this will be ready to drink in about three months.

October 21, 1975 [Letter by Jack]

We went to the Dammam fish market yesterday with Darya and Isa. They had many types of fish I hadn't seen before in the local market including thin, needle-like fish with long mouths, many sharks about one and a half feet long , and a hammerhead shark about four feet long. Isa said he had never seen sharks there before.

October 28, 1975

I accepted the job of working for that Dutch civil engineering firm. It pays one thousand dollars a month.[189] A driver comes to get me and to take me home. My boss, Mr. Kanterman, had an American secretary, but she left with her husband when he was transferred to the States. He tried a Syrian and a Lebanese male and neither worked out, especially at taking minutes of the weekly meetings with the company's subcontractors. The minutes were the critical area, it seems. The company deals with many different nationalities, but the official language of communication is English. I took the minutes at the meeting today and got about three typewritten pages out of it. Maybe I messed up some of the civil engineering terms, but I think I got what they wanted, mainly who was responsible for what and who promised what to whom. That obsequious Syrian is still hanging about the office, and the Lebanese is operating a telex machine. It's hard to be their replacement and still have them on the scene. But being out of the college walls is very liberating, and the Dutch community seems very interesting. My hours are from seven to two. The part of the company I'm in will be moving out to the Dhahran airport, where they have a contract to build several structures. That's about a five-minute drive from my compound.

Incidentally, I found out that all phone calls from outside the kingdom are not only monitored but taped as well.

November 1, 1975

I am starting my second week of work today. It seems to be going well. Thursday the college women's group held a Halloween party in the south compound with a spook house, a fortune-teller, games of chance, a cookie and Kool-Aid table, and a pumpkin-carving contest. Everybody at the party wanted to know about my job. Lots of people

---

189   In 2012 dollars, about $51,260 a year.

told me to keep them in mind if I heard of anything outside the college. I went to the mail desk that morning, and the man there, who can hardly get out a simple sentence in English, said, "You no work here?" I said, "No, in Al-Khobar." He then said, "Wish you luck new job!" I got tired of talking about it after a while. It really is an advantage to be outside the college community, just for a change of face. It isn't bad in the fall, but by February or March, working, living, and partying with the same people becomes too much.

Last night we were invited to an adult Halloween party. We were supposed to come in costume. Well, we have nothing kicking around the house that could pass for costume gear, so I put my hair up, put on Jack's hounds tooth knit pants, blue dress shirt, red tie, and his shoes and socks. I drew a moustache on my face. He put on the slinky gown I wore to a consulate party two years ago. It had a halter top. He put a tennis ball in each side of the front, shaved his moustache, wore lipstick, eye shadow, a scarf, and white beads. He carried a white purse and reminded people of "Klinger" on M*A*S*H.[190] The gown exposed his hairy chest, and people told him he could at least have shaved under his arms for the occasion. It seemed as if people looked at us, trying to place us, and then a minute or so later the light dawned. I think the fact his moustache was gone confused them. Alex got up this morning and told Jack he looked "stupid." Jack assured him he planned to grow the moustache back.

A neighbor of ours came dressed as a shower, with shower cap, wrapped in a shower curtain, with an old shower fixture stuck in the back of his swim trunks so that it hung about one and a half feet above the top of his head. Julius Caesar was there, along with a guru, Moshe Dayan,[191] a banged-up, blood-stained karate expert, and Wee Willie Winkie,[192] among others.

---

190   M*A*S*H (Mobile Army Surgical Hospital) was a TV series that ran from 1972–1983. Klinger was a soldier hoping to get a discharge by dressing as a woman.

191   Moshe Dayan (1915–1981). High-ranking military officer in Israeli who became Minister of Defense in 1967. Wore a patch over his left eye.

192   Character in English nursery rhyme: Wee Willie Winkie runs through the town,/ Upstairs, downstairs, in his nightgown./Tapping at the windows, crying through the locks, "Are all the children in their beds? It's past eight o'clock!"

About ten thirty somebody decided we should go visiting. Fifteen of us left the party and wandered down the street. We knocked on the door of the maintenance director, Mr. Porro. The shower man was up front, and when Porro came to the door he said, "Mr. Porro, can you fix my shower?" Porro thought it was funny, and then we went off to some other houses. Meanwhile, the gatekeeper was standing in front of his shelter with his mouth down to his navel and his eyes like saucers.

I just read where the company I am working for has a four hundred million dollar contract with the Saudi Ministry of Defense. They have civilian contracts as well, related to sewer and water services, etc.

There is a big solar energy conference going on at the college. Rumor has it that even Jews and Russians will be admitted to it. They are very short on hotel space and sent a circular around asking people to take in guests. They got a few more rooms for the attendees that way. All the hotels were full.

November 5, 1975 [Letter by Jack]

Next weekend is the English Language Institute faculty party. Thanksgiving is two weeks later, followed by a big evening party to which we have been invited.

November 7, 1975

Frank Jones, the best bridge player in the college, was killed in a head-on collision with a Mercedes last week. Frank drove a blue Volkswagen beetle and was an instructor in mechanical engineering. The Volkswagen is behind the police station and is about two-thirds of its original length. It happened at night, and they took him to Aramco's hospital. He died at eight the next morning. He had no identification on him and they still didn't know who he was when he died. The police located something with his name on it in the back of his car and called the college. The Personnel Department tried his home, no answer, and then sent a faculty member in his department to check his 7:30 a.m. class. The students were there but he was not. Then they sent the instructor to identify his body at Aramco. The body will be flown back home. No information about the driver of the Mercedes sedan. This weekend an accountant for the Dutch company was killed in a crash with a tanker truck just outside of Riyadh. They flew his body back to Holland this morning on KLM. He had been here a month, and his family was to come in three weeks. It's been a bad week.

November 12, 1975

Cockroach update: our cockroach population this year is minimal, knock on wood. Occasionally I find baby cockroaches, which can't be a good sign. At least the big mothers aren't making themselves visible. Probably because they're making babies someplace where I can't see them.

November 15, 1975

Jack's workload was reduced from twenty-four to sixteen hours. He teaches four hours a day, four mornings a week. He doesn't teach Saturday, giving him a three-day weekend.[193] Two nights a week he's attending an advanced Arabic course.

The humidity has been terrible the past few mornings, accompanied by a pea-soup fog. Mohammed Al Sharif, the man who drives me to work and back, is an excellent driver. I feel safer with him than I do with Jack, who is a nervous wreck after driving just one mile here. Mohammed has been driving for Naarden for eleven years and never had an accident, an extraordinary record. This is as much attributable to Allah as to his skills, because one can be the world's best driver and still get creamed on the roads.

November 19, 1975

Jack had been pretty sick for two days with excruciating stomach pains. It turned out to be a virus that was going around. Several neighbors had it as well. He called the college doctor at two in the morning, who told him to call the doctor on duty that night. This doctor, a Saudi

---

193   A three-day weekend, since Thursday and Friday is the weekend in Saudi Arabia.

woman trained in England, told Jack to go to the hospital in Al-Khobar. He figured he would just be put in a bed for the duration of the night, so he decided to sweat it out at home. He went to the college doctor the next morning, who was angry that the woman doctor hadn't gone to see Jack. He said he would speak to her. A Saudi woman doctor is a rare thing in this country, where few women go to college, let alone medical school. She has a small baby, and her husband is a graduate student at the college.

Jack and I have been invited to a dinner/dance at Mr. Kanterman's house on the fourth of December. All the administrators from my company will be there, plus some Swedes who are working with Naarden.

Our latest wine is now about the strength of a US wine. The beer ingredients arrived from the States. Envelope A, which had all the identifying literature removed, was marked "For Cooking" to mislead customs. It arrived before the letter explaining its contents. Jack and I both tasted it trying to figure out whether it was corn sugar or a particular yeast. We couldn't decide. Then the next day the letter came telling us that envelope A contained a beverage settler. Envelope B, which contained the special yeast, never arrived. We may substitute Fleishmann's baking yeast if it doesn't come soon.

The new faculty center opened last weekend. It looks like a country club in the States. The pool is furnished with white, wooden furniture with flag-blue cushions, chaise lounges, and umbrella tables with a blue-and-white design on the canvas. There is a magazine library with copies of *Vogue*, *The New Yorker*, *House and Garden*, *Good Housekeeping*, *Redbook*, crafts magazines of different kinds, etc. The Center also includes a ceramics room, a snack bar, bowling alley, locker rooms, playground, tennis courts, basketball court, and shallow wading pool for the very small children. There will be a hairdressing salon as soon as the couple hired to run the facility arrives. The wife is a hairdresser.

We will be spending Thanksgiving Day with the Woolriches. That evening there is a party in our compound put on by three couples. The following Thursday is the party given by my boss. I am debating what to wear.

The family of Frank Jones, the mechanical engineer who was killed in a head-on collision, wired that they wanted to have the body cremated and the ashes sent to England. Cremation is against the law here. This was mentioned at the Engineering Chairmen's Meeting, and the Pakistani who has been taking the minutes since I quit wrote, "Frank Jones' body has not yet been sent to England, because the family wanted the body incinerated."

We have a small plastic Christmas tree, which stands about two feet high. It doesn't feel like Christmas here, and without a real balsam tree to smell I just can't get into the spirit. Whoever heard of Christmas with green outside and temperature warm enough to go around without a coat?

November 25, 1975

My geraniums are doing well, and I will try to find the time to transplant them into my new dirt and a couple of white plastic pots I bought. There aren't any clay pots to be had. In Hofuf, about two and a half hours from here, there are potters who make clay water jugs, like the kind you see in illustrations of Bible stories—usually the woman is carrying one of these big clay jugs on her shoulders. They also make smaller pots, which would be good to put plants in, but unfortunately I am not going to Hofuf.

Jack's Arabic teacher assigns homework like writing out the conjugations of verbs in Arabic. Jack usually doesn't have time to do the homework, but the guy has been bugging him about it. So yesterday Jack decided to get his students to write out the conjugations for him. Well, they got into a big argument about how they should be written and told him that even at the college level, some teachers didn't know that stuff, etc. Jack said he didn't think they were putting him on and was sorry he asked.

The father of our Jordanian neighbor, Dr. Deeb, was killed two days ago when two Saudis racing sports cars collided with his parked car. He died instantly. The man sitting next to him is in critical condition. The man in the backseat was hospitalized. I don't know what happened to the Saudis who smashed into him.

We all ate dinner at Jeff's house last Thursday night. Later that evening we picked up a sitter for Alex and saw *Alice Doesn't Live Here Anymore* at the Aramco movie theater.[194] One ingredient I can't get here is sour cream. Sometimes I can substitute yogurt, but it doesn't always work.

I am now working eight to three instead of seven to two. I just wasn't functioning at seven. When the operations move out to the construction site at the airport, the engineers and laborers here will be working six to six without a full hour for lunch. Terrible hours. Fortunately they don't expect it of me. But seven hours a day is strain enough.

Just found out it is against the law to give somebody a letter to take out of the country to be posted. This fact is in the company files. I also learned that this company has permission to bring in a certain volume of spirits, which are dispensed from the Riyadh (head) office. Boggles the mind.

November 29, 1975

Thanksgiving passed uneventfully. We went to Jack's chairman's home, and I brought pies and rolls. That night some of the people in Jack's department held a party and one hundred and twenty were invited. It was mobbed. They had a turkey buffet with cold salads, beer, and wine punch. There was no punch to the wine punch, so I drank it all evening without feeling a thing. Sidiqui is a good thing to avoid, unless one has a cast-iron stomach. We left about eleven thirty because we had to get the sitter home, but it went on until about three in the morning.

After he ate Thanksgiving dinner, Jack ran in a five-kilometer cross-country race against a freshman team, a sophomore team, a junior team, and some faculty members, mostly from the Physical Education Department. Jack had been sick the week before with an intestinal virus, so he hadn't been doing much running. Anyway, he

---

194   Starring Ellen Burstyn and Kris Kristofferson. About a recently widowed woman with a young son trying to succeed as a singer. Released in 1974. Movie got good reviews.

came in twenty-second out of twenty-three. No. 23 was a student with a cramp in his side. The course was across the desert, around the US Consulate, and back to the old physical education complex. Students took the first four places with faculty members coming in fifth, seventh, and eleventh, and of course twenty-second. One of the physical education teachers told me that the students have to run that course to complete one of their requirements in physical education. I said we had had our car stopped to let the students cross the road on one of those runs, and five minutes later students were still jogging past. This was out of a class of thirty, and it was the beginning part of the course. He said they've been known to jog smartly out of sight and then rest behind dunes. Others would run approximately half of the course until they got to the part where it paralleled the main Dhahran-Al-Khobar road. There they would flag down a taxi and ride back to the vicinity of the physical education complex, so they could jog the last few hundred yards.

November 30, 1975

Mr. Kanterman, my boss, did not return this week, so it looks like I will have another week of little to do. He went back to Holland; his wife was hospitalized unexpectedly, and he sent a Telex that his return to Saudi Arabia would be delayed indefinitely.

I brought a book to work, but Jack says if I sit at the desk reading a book someone I shouldn't be working for will ask me to do something. This could lead to problems. Unfortunately the male secretaries in this company feel threatened by the presence of a female one. Once I did some work that a male secretary should have been doing, and the man nearly had a conniption. Never saw such carrying on. It came about when one of the Middle East managers who was visiting the office saw I had nothing to do and told the other man to give me part of a claim to type. This made his secretary very nervous.

Finally, yesterday it started to get cold. The low was predicted by Aramco news to be fifty-one degrees. When we got up this morning it was sixty-one degrees inside. I am going to have to put a blanket on the bed. We put the heat on in the house when we got up. We are lucky because we have one of the newer air conditioner/heat units and can easily switch from heat to air-conditioning. Most of our neighbors have to withstand the cold until the conversion crew makes a visit to their house to adjust the mechanism from within. The weather is very strange because the day before we were still running the air conditioner and now we have to put the heat on.

Last week I bought a box of Weetabix, a British breakfast cereal that I suspected of being Shredded Wheat under an alias.[195] When milk is added it actually tastes like a combination of Cream of Wheat and crushed Shredded Wheat. Very soggy. Alex likes it and they don't even offer something free inside, which is generally his criterion for buying cereal. Sometimes there's no explaining his taste.

One of the Dutchmen in the company I work for dropped a filing cabinet on his toe. They took him to the hospital, but the doctor could not prevent the black on his toe from moving progressively closer to his body. The doctor has decided to amputate his big toe. The company has decided they want a second opinion and are sending him back to Holland today. He's been here less than a month and is probably delighted to leave, despite his toe.

December 6, 1975

Did you ever work in an office where you could hear a flock of sheep maaa'ing outside? Very strange. These sheep belong to some Bedouin family who gave up their old way of life, except the sheep apparently, and settled in an apartment house across the way. The sheep wander around this part of Al-Khobar, supposedly the choicest section, living off whatever they can find. I saw them nosing through a pile of garbage the other day, which I'm sure will give an unusual flavor to the meat. The driver told me that a Bedouin knows exactly how many sheep he owns.

We were invited to a New Year's party at Goodbout's. They sent the invitation out in the form of one of the memos that inundate our mailbox in "Pakistani English." It was a very good imitation and very funny. The following week we received a memo from the Security Office, which people agreed was the worst English they'd seen so far.

---

195   This company is still going strong. It has a website.

You have to read this kind of prose for a least a year before you can see the humor in it. Also it helps to have personally known a Pakistani secretary.

My boss still is not back from Holland. Most of the office has moved out to the airbase, closer to our compound, but I won't go until Kanterman comes back.

On Wednesday afternoon, my driver stopped by the house with two presents for me from the company. They had been flown in on the morning's KLM flight from Amsterdam. One gift was an almond-flavored pastry, a puff pastry outer layer with a coconut filling. The other was semisweet Droste chocolate in the shape of a solid chocolate letter "S." Alex was impressed. I learned that the Dutch usually give their children a solid chocolate letter, the initial of their first name, for their birthday. They give Christmas gifts the fifth of December. They also celebrate the twenty-fifth, but I don't know how.

This year Aramco is going to have their outdoor Christmas pageant again. They do it every other year. We still haven't done any Christmas shopping. I hope to get in town before the Eid (Dec. 13–16) because shops will be closed then, and after that there will be a pretty picked-over selection.[196]

Thursday night we went to a party at the Dutch compound, the dinner/dance that Kanterman planned to host. It was lovely. Two of the Dutch wives had cooked Indonesian food, which is difficult to describe. It isn't like Chinese, which is the only point of reference I have in Far Eastern cooking. It also isn't like Indian food, though I would say it is closer to Indian than Chinese. They located a case of Johnny Walker for the event. I had three drinks and didn't feel so well Friday morning. Jack had considerably more than three drinks and was quite sick all day Friday. There were thirteen couples there, five of them from TVA, a Swedish firm that is the supervising contractor over my company.[197] We left about one thirty in the morning, but I heard today it went on till five. Jack danced. There were some fast and some slow numbers. It was quite nice. Jack said it

---

196   Eid al Adha, the festival of sacrifice. See glossary B.

197   The name has been changed

was the best party he'd attended since he's been here, including the Consulate parties.

I baked Alex's Halloween pumpkin and scooped out the pulp. I had enough for three batches of pumpkin bread.[198]

This was the joke memo:

THE KINGDOM OF SAUDI ARABIA
PLAY SCHOOL OF PETROLEUM AND MINERALS
DHAHRAN, SANDY ARABIA
TO: Some UPM Community
FROM: Committee for the Preservation of Sanity
SUBJECT: Party

We wish to call your fact to the attention that on the 28th Dhual hij-jah 1395 (31st Dec 1975) the year is to end. Your kind cooperation in this matter will be much appreciated.

This unusual event will be celebrated from 8 pm until 1976 at house 226. All adults are welcomed including men and women.

Bus service will maybe be available. The line 111 route 7 schedule will be adhered to stopping at stop 1 at 7 pm, stop 11 at noon and stop 111 at 8 am and arriving house 226 some time around Jan 4th 1976.

Better come by own vehicle, but since parking of same under trees and toileting near bushes is causing lot of damage to our plantation you are kindly requested to avoid parking your car/motorcycle/donkey/camel under trees and going to toilet in bushes, rather use parking lot meant for these purposes.

Committee for the Preservation of Sanity
   The Greens
   The Taggets
   The Monroes
   The Goodbouts

---

198 For recipe see "Pumpkin Bread," appendix 1.

This memo was voted the worst English:

KINGDOM OF SAUDI ARABIA
UNIVERSITY OF PETROLEUM & MINERALS
DHAHRAN
TO: All Faculty, Staff and Students 26 Nov 1975
FROM: Security Department

NOTICE CIRCULAR
We would like to draw you attention that there are some vehicles having been parked under the shade on the westside of Building #1 since long.

We are in process of moving those vehicles from there so as to use that area for storage after proper fencing it.

If you have any information about those vehicles, kindly help us finding the owner by calling on telephone Numbers 390 or 524 enabling us to communicate with the person concerned.

Thank you for your valued cooperation,
    SALEH S. HALWAN
    Director, Security Dept

CHAPTER 10

Christmas pageant and stampeding sheep, at work with Woo and Wee,
supermarket special—ice from Greenland, pornography in miniature,
an amorous driver and related problems, the Al-Khobar land
boom, international office: Dutch, Italians, Scots, Swedes,
Koreans, Lebanese, Syrians, and Palestinians

December 8, 1975

Jack is on vacation now. He's been taking Alex to the faculty recreation center for a hamburger lunch the past two days. Alex has kindergarten through Wednesday. Then I am off work until the morning of December 17. Big religious holiday, the Hajj. They are expecting two million pilgrims in Mecca this year. Each pilgrim is supposed to kill a sheep during the course of the rituals performed in Mecca. The wealthier ones kill two or three. There is a meat shortage predicted for next month. Naturally nobody eats a whole sheep, so the remains are buried in pits by bulldozers.

Tomorrow Naarden moves out to the site office at the Dhahran Airbase. The office buildings look like a combination hospital/warehouse, with twelve-foot ceilings, blue tile floors, and yellow concrete block walls. There is also a bathroom problem. No ladies' room! One big room has two urinals, two sinks, and three toilets with partitions that have one-foot spaces below the partition doors where the users' feet can be spotted. Terrific. Something MUST be done. When the last of them arrive, there will be about two hundred Korean laborers out there, plus a few Arab laborers, the men from Naarden, as well as the TVA supervising engineers the Saudis have hired to supply the site plans and check up on Naarden.

Yesterday at Omar's Supermarket I spotted an unopened carton of twenty-six or so two-pound bags of flour. I opened it and removed three perfect looking bags. When I got them home to sift and repack in metal tins, I found them loaded with those tiny beetles we call cereal bugs

December 9, 1975 [Letter by Jack]

Winter has come to Saudi Arabia. The high temperature is now about sixty-eight to seventy degrees and the low about fifty-two to fifty-five. It's been quite cloudy this last week, and I wouldn't be surprised to see rain any day.

Maralyn's boss is still in Holland, and since he didn't tell anyone what Maralyn was to be paid, she's drawing only what they paid the last secretary until he gets back.

December 21, 1975

My boss came back from Holland last Wednesday night, and there has been a lot of work to do.

Yesterday Jack got me a poinsettia. It is beautiful but the pot is too small. I should repot it. All the flowers here are flown in from Europe.

We are having a number of bachelors from Jack's department over on Christmas Day. The volume of cooking wouldn't be a problem except that I have no time to do it. We were invited to a company Christmas dinner on Wednesday night, but I don't think I can afford the time. Besides Christmas Eve is a nice time to be home. I don't think it's fair to leave Alex with a sitter on Christmas Eve.

Friday night we went to a Christmas pageant at Aramco. It was a whole movie set, real camels, sheep, shepherds, donkeys, and a manger in a stable. The pageant was held in Aramco's baseball stadium. We sat in the bleachers. Afterwards Alex wanted to come back for the part where they nail Christ to the cross. He complained that they didn't finish telling the story.

The pageant included sixteen shepherds and ten sheep, but the sheep wouldn't cooperate and refused to come out on the field. They dug in, and the shepherds cursed and swore, kicked, prodded, and tugged, trying to get the sheep out there. If there had been twenty shepherds, they could have carried the sheep on, two to a sheep. Finally, after a good delay, the sheep were pushed onto the field. Then, after the shepherd scene, they were supposed to gently wander off behind the Three Kings of the Orient. But the sheep suddenly stampeded off, en masse, which spooked the camels carrying the Three Kings, driving them off the set. The shepherds fled after the sheep apparently hoping to catch up with them before a posse was necessary to round them up. The audience was half Saudi, and there were students behind us. They thought the sheep incident quite amusing. Our seats were at the end of the L-shaped bleachers, and we got to see the comings and goings of the camels, sheep, and angels at close hand.

A large choral group sang appropriate songs for each scene. Unfortunately the director was "inspired" and dug up some Christmas music nobody had ever heard before. Playing obscure Christmas music doesn't enhance the experience. Also one of the heavenly hosts was chewing gum.

Last week Alex discovered that a four-inch lizard had met its doom by getting shut in the front door at the hinged end. Flatter than a pancake. He was intrigued.

December 24, 1975

Tomorrow we are entertaining the Ayers next door, my boss Mr. Kanterman, and three bachelors from Jack's department.

Every single food shop in Al-Khobar is out of turkeys. They are held up in customs at Dammam harbor (maybe they think something is hidden in the cavities). I was really depressed because there wasn't so much as a large chicken in sight Monday night. Then someone with a friend at Aramco came through with an eighteen-pound American turkey. It is thawing now. I will make mulled wine with our first batch of homemade brew. Jack is quite pleased with it, except for a sediment problem.

We have been invited to the Dutch company New Year's Eve party, but I haven't been able to get a sitter. All the potential sitters here want to stay up and set off firecrackers at midnight. If we can get a sitter, I think we'll stop in at the Goodbouts' and then go to the Dutch compound about ten o'clock or so. We can take a guest to the Dutch compound party so we invited Jeff, who wasn't doing anything for New Year's Eve.

December 28, 1975

Jack surprised me for Christmas. He gave me a gold pendant, which is a replica of a Dilmun seal.[199] Dilmun was an ancient civilization on Bahrain about 3,000 BC. It was a center of trade, and the seals— which Danish archaeologists unearthed—were used for business purposes. Mine is called "the beer drinker." But there is also one called "the star gazers" and one called "the gazelle." Myra Anderson, who has done excavating on Bahrain, once found a seal of an animal.

The Korean tea/office boy at the company came to me yesterday and introduced himself, "My name is WOO." I replied, "I'm Maralyn." All day I hear people going up and down the hall yelling, "WOO! WOO! WOO!" There is also a Mr. Lee, and some of the staff here can't say "L's" so they go up and down the hall calling, "WEE! WEE! WEE!" It is most distracting if one is trying to do some work.

My Christmas dinner wasn't bad. The food was quite good, but my boss, Mr. Kanterman, didn't know any of the people there and they didn't know him, so it was a bit stiff at first. The weather finally got cold for us, down into the forties at night and the mid fifties in the daytime. It seemed a little Christmassy. I made some mulled wine, and it was excellent and actually had an effect.[200] Last night we put up a second batch of wine and made up a wine starter bottle for assembling five gallons tonight. What I find frustrating about making home brew is that it takes so long between the making and the evaluating of the product. At least with cooking you can try it an hour or so later.

The turkey was stuffed with bread, parsley, Bell's Seasoning, celery (three stalks donated by Myra Anderson who inherited two bunches from Aramco—it isn't in season in Saudi Arabia), onion, and finely chopped Westphalian sausage (an all beef, smoky German sausage). I fixed sweet potatoes, French beans with browned butter, slivered almonds and mushrooms with garlic salt, hot rolls, which I made the day before, gravy, cranberry sauce, lemon chiffon pie, Christmas

---

199   A Google search on "Dilmun seals" will yield a lot of information on the subject.

200   For recipe see "Mulled Wine" in appendix 1.

cookies, and mince pie and a Christmas cake brought by my neighbor, Diana Ayer.

My boss, Mr. Kanterman, brought me a bouquet of white spider asters. Jeff brought Jack some Dutch cigars, Alex a huge inflatable KLM jet (usually suspended from travel office ceilings), and gave me a very silky fringed brown scarf.

One of the Christmas cards we received showed a resigned look-ing lion covered with lambs. Alex thought it was STUPID. I asked him why, and he said, "Because that lion is gonna eat those lambs! "Alex," I said, "that's what Christmas is all about. The lion and the lamb get along." "Yeah," he said, "THE LION'S GONNA EAT THE LAMBS AFTER CHRISTMAS!"

January 2, 1976

The Dutch New Year's party wasn't as much fun as the dinner party on December 4, but they served some Dutch delicacies that had been flown in via KLM.[201] I ate several pieces of sliced smoked eel. The eel, freshwater variety, was oily like mackerel, but fine textured and very good. I could develop a real affection for eel. The salted raw herring has small bones in it; the Dutch eat it with raw chopped onions bones and all. I found the bones disconcerting. I'm sure eating the two together guarantees no intimate conversations for at least a week.

They sang a Dutch New Year song—in Dutch—and then the Swedes sang Swedish New Year songs and they all sang "Auld Lang Syne." After that all the Dutch people went around shaking everyone's hand and kissing everyone and wishing them Happy New Year. They had dancing and served sidiqui—they couldn't afford real booze. They also had tiny lamb and shrimp shish kebabs with peanut sauce.

January 7, 1976

Believe it or not, Jack is talking like he's had it with Saudi Arabia. After this contract is over, he doesn't want to stay. There is a pecu-liar absence of both negative and positive things here that's difficult to

---

201   Royal Dutch Air Lines (Koninklijke Luchtvaart Maatschappij).

describe. The two things that get to me the most of late are the local attitudes towards women (the Saudis treat women like children, but with fewer rights than a son), and the driving is absolutely insane. The whole lot of them is like children in dodge-ems. I gave the finger to a car full of clowns the other day. They forced Jack over, and then cut in front of us while two in the backseat turned around to look, grinning from ear to ear. Something short-circuited, and the next thing I knew I was waggling my middle finger at them. I am not sure it means anything here, but I felt better afterwards.

We will go into Al-Khobar tonight to shop for the week and to also make reservations on Iran Air for our trip there next month. I finally decided to buy a Persian miniature when we are in Isfahan. They also paint pornographic miniatures. One of the milder ones showed a well-endowed young Persian lady squirting a stream of milk from one breast into a bowl held by a bearded poet kneeling at her feet. I hear they have more explicit ones under the counter that are much more expensive.

January 8, 1976

Yesterday I found the ultimate in Omar's. A box of ice from a Greenland glacier. This ice is chipped off a freshwater glacier, boxed, and shipped to Saudi Arabia. I couldn't find a price on it anywhere, but there were a good number of boxes in the freezer case.

Instead of importing Greenland ice, I wish he would concentrate on getting more staples in. There still are no frozen turkeys, though he did get some turkey breasts in after Christmas. There is no molasses, no decent cheddar, no Parmesan, no Romano, no chicken parts, no malt syrup, which Jack uses to make beer, and no nutmeg. Rumor is that the government discovered it was hallucinogenic and took it off the market.

My boss is still in Holland; he flew there after having spent Christmas with us. Nobody has heard anything, and nobody knows how his wife is doing. Mr. Krotz, the man who temporarily is in charge, has an abrasive manner and can be quite insulting. Everyone is complaining about him. I hope Kanterman comes back soon.

My driver, Mohammed, who takes me to work in the morning, is very westernized. His English is excellent, and he is generally much more sophisticated than most natives. He is forty-one, is married to his cousin, and has three children. Through astute investments in real estate, he's moderately wealthy and could retire comfortably, but prefers to work. I can be at ease with him. He has been very helpful in giving me good advice about handling the Dutch people in the company and explaining to me the way the company is run.

Last week after helping me move equipment and files from the Al-Khobar office to the Dhahran office, I turned to pass by him, and he tried to kiss me. I was astounded; I didn't have a clue he felt this way. I pushed him away. He apologized that afternoon, and I thought that was the end of it. I pointed out that I was married, he was married, and there could be nothing between us.

At the beginning of this week, he said he wanted to take me to Al-Khobar to buy me a $2,500 Swiss watch.[202] I said my husband would never allow it. I had joked about owning such a watch when he drove me downtown to buy Christmas cards for my boss. He said he would give it to me in front of my husband. I said it was impossible to accept such a present from someone who was not my husband. Then he offered to give me the money so I could buy it. I told him my husband would know I didn't have that much money to spend and would demand to know where it came from. I said it would make a great deal of trouble for me if he gave me such a gift. The driver told me he wanted me to have a present that would make me think of him every time I used it.

At that point, I decided that if he was thinking of buying me a $2,500 gold watch, who knows what else he was thinking about. I decided that I had to tell Jack what was going on. Jack felt that my protestations to Mohammed, that I did not love him, that I loved my husband, that I was not interested in him, were just adding to the fun. He said in the Arab world to a man "NO, NO, NO" really means "YES, YES, YES," and women were expected to be like that before eventually giving in. Well, yesterday, he kept coming into my office and even came back from lunch early; he never did that before, and tried to touch my face. I turned my head and changed the subject. On the way

---

202   In 2012 dollar, $2,500 would be about $10,097.

home, he said something about being twelve hours before he saw me again. Again I told him that there could be nothing between us.

Jack and I talked about what should be done. I suggested he talk to him, and then I changed my mind because I felt that that would be like stabbing Mohammed in the back. Jack felt that I was too naive and that he would eventually try something because he was playing by different cultural rules than I was. The whole area of male/female relationships is in a totally different context here. For example, single women at Aramco are bought gifts like cars by Arab boyfriends, although they can only be driven within the Aramco compounds. Of course they get to kiss or maybe even go to bed with them. The women, to whom virginity didn't matter much, would be thinking, "These crazy Arabs, boy, are we taking them!" And the Arabs, to whom virginity is a *sine qua non* and to whom sex is simply not available outside of marriage, would be thinking, "Boy, are we getting something! Those crazy European and American women!" Jack said both sides thought they were getting the best of the deal, but only because each side was playing by a different set of rules.

To sum it up Jack and I finally came to the conclusion that he should speak to him, harsh as it sounded, because the only thing an Arab male would understand was the righteous wrath of a husband whose property was being trespassed upon. I know it all sounds melodramatic, and I could hardly keep a straight face thinking about it, let alone having to say it. But Jack can ham it up from his long experience in dealing with disciplinary problems in his classes.

So the next morning when Mohammed came to pick me up, Jack went out to the car pretending to be mad and told my driver that he didn't like what he had been hearing about his behavior towards his wife, he knew it was not right, etc. The driver apparently feigned innocence and said, "Me or someone else in the company?" Jack said, "Well, you're her driver…" Anyway, I got into the car and expected reproaches and a scene, but he said nothing. Conversation in the car was stilted, but he answered everything as if nothing had happened. I'm still expecting a confrontation about "Why did you tell your husband?" and when it occurred, I planned to say that I was not getting across to him, that his behavior was out of line, that I am not interested in getting involved with him, so I had no choice except to tell my husband. I was going to say all this in words of two syllables or less, then to cut off further discussion of the subject.

The whole thing really makes me feel sad because now I can't be myself with him. My behavior towards him was no different than towards anybody else, and I can't imagine that I encouraged him. Probably in his context, my friendliness was a real come-on.

I learned yesterday that Krotz, the man filling in for Kanterman, worked for six construction companies in the three years before he came to work here. They must be running their personnel operation in Holland from the depths of an asylum. He has more enemies than friends now, and people are talking about quitting. Even I have considered it, but I am holding out for Kanterman's return or June 30, 1976 (the date that we leave Saudi Arabia), whichever comes first.

In my entire life, I've never seen a personality like Krotz's. Whole conversations are initiated by implying that the person is a liar, and he has the most hostile approach to employees that I have ever seen. Arabs are very volatile, and he pulled this with an Arab employee whom I suspect is playing fast and loose with the company, but was apparently blameless in this particular case. This Arab got so mad that he grabbed Krotz by the necktie and shook him. The European employees are quite meek in reacting to the thrust of Krotz's barbs, but he usually backs down when challenged. Most nationalities find him intimidating. A Lebanese employee predicted that some night he would be found beaten in an alley.

January 18, 1976

The latest rage at the college is to invest in land shares. The price of land in Al-Khobar has reached astronomical heights: $28,500 for a quarter acre lot on a street.[203] People are borrowing money to put into land. My driver told me that they are even selling lots off Al-Khobar that are under water, apparently in anticipation of a government landfill operation. Foreigners must have a Saudi partner. One person bought a piece of land several years back for $17,100, and it is now

---

203   In 2012 dollars, $28,500 is about $115,109.

worth $428,600.[204] I expect the government to begin regulating it any time and then the bottom will drop out of the market. It reminds me of what I heard about the stock market in 1929. The Dutch company I am working for would like to build a bigger compound, but they can't afford the price of the land. They are hoping that the government will grant them some acreage. A number of non-Saudi Arabs in the company, and all of the Saudis, are busy speculating and borrowing money to put into property. Such speculation makes me nervous. I feel better with my money in a sock under the mattress.

My driver has not renewed his offer to buy me a watch. I do not get offers like that every day of the week. I think I better get a decent watch before I get an anonymous donation. He talked about his marriage yesterday. Apparently his parents decided he would get married when he was seventeen. He could say nothing about it, although he wasn't looking to get married. His wife (a cousin) was fifteen. The parents set them up in housekeeping. He said, "I am not going to try to do this with my son. I don't care whether he marries an American, a European, or an Arab girl. It is up to him. This kind of system causes a lot of unhappiness."

I agreed with him. At least if you pick your mate yourself, you have only yourself to blame. Of course, the divorce rate in America reflects how good that system is. I wonder if the social conditions here were the same as in the US—meaning that a Saudi woman could freely divorce her husband and be self-supporting afterwards without the taint of scandal—how many divorces would take place. Here there is this attitude that you will grow to love the person you are forced to marry. I suppose if you have a dog around long enough...

Jack's having a good time brewing beer. He drank five gallons in three weeks. My only point of reference is consumption of six-packs, and I can't make the mental transition. At any rate, I have no reaction whatsoever to his brew, so he can't be doing himself any harm. On the other hand, he claims to have no reaction to my wine, and if I have more than three small glasses of it, I get numb. Maybe it's all psychological.

---

204   In 2012 dollars, respectively about $69,066 and $1,731,085.

January 29, 1976

The meatloaf recipe I received in the mail came just in time.[205] I had thawed a pound of Danish hamburger and didn't know what to do with it. If I make American Chop Suey or chili one more time, Jack probably will start eating in the student cafeteria.

February 1, 1976

We're thinking that next year will be our last year here. The money is good, especially with my working, but the problems are not financial, they're psychological.

I couldn't begin to convey the difficulties of this existence to someone who has never experienced them. Most of the hardships are not physical, except for the poor quality of medical care, lack of good meat, power outages, etc. Living in a very foreign, developing country is fascinating at first. After two and a half years, the charm has worn off. It is like Chinese water torture. The little drips that didn't matter at first gradually become irritating and then painful. Pretty soon you're screaming in pain. I think Europe might be better because the cultural differences aren't as pronounced. People react to these little annoyances in different ways. The driving has really gotten to me, along with the attitude towards women. Neal's father says he'd like to ban thobes. Other foreigners are absolutely convinced that not one native has an ounce of brains in his head.

All the money in the world isn't going to help if you get flown home in a straitjacket.

February 10, 1976

A neighbor requested my recipe for making my potato salad dressing. I boil the potatoes, drain the water from them, and pour over the hot potatoes a mixture of oil, dill pickle juice, chives, pepper, and salt. Then I stir in chopped onion and let it stand for a while. Then I stir in celery and at the last minute add mayonnaise.

---

205   For recipe see "Easy Meatloaf," appendix 1.

February 11, 1976

In class the other day, Jack used the expression "the pot calling the kettle black." Later he was worried that the students might have taken it as a racist remark. I thought that this possibility was rather remote. Then he came home yesterday and related a conversation with two of his students. One was black, from the Sudan. The other was a Bedouin, who the urban students view as rural hicks. The Bedouin said something to Jack, and the black Sudanese interrupted saying, "Don't pay any attention to him, sir, he sleeps with sheep." The Bedouin didn't show any expression, then suddenly announced, "And don't pay any attention to that black man, sir." After telling that story, Jack said to me, "And I was worried about something I said." A short time later Jack came up with the following: "He who sleeps with sheep wakes up with a case of the blaa-aa-aahs."

Mr. Wee, the office coffee boy, must be the most highly referred to office boy in Saudi Arabia. It is impossible to call him just Wee because of the confusion it causes. A while back one of the Dutch accountants was trying to bend his ultra-cheap filing cabinet back into shape. I said, "Wee has a hammer." He looked at me and said, "We has?" I said, "No, WEE has a hammer!" He looked puzzled and asked, "You mean the company?" I said, "No, Mr. Wee." Then one afternoon last week Wee was out sick. Everybody in the office was going up and down the hall crying, "WEE! WEE! WEE!" because they wanted coffee. I finally stuck my head out the door and announced, "Wee is sick." They looked at me and said, "You are?" So now I call him Mr. Wee because I don't want to go through THAT again. You have to remember that for 90 percent of the office staff, English is a second language and non-agreement of subject and verb doesn't jar their ears.

February 14, 1976

Marcie Wildermann knows a couple that was hired by Northrop. The couple had arrived in Saudi Arabia to find a completely furnished house awaiting them, right down to a vacuum, television, and small appliances. The deal the college offers is nothing compared to what private companies give. Naarden also supplies cars to its employees, along with small freezers and very nice furniture. Jack's salary at a place like Northrop would be at least 50 percent higher. Northrop would send him back to the US every year and on leave locally every six months. Employees have commissary and APO privileges. Of course, his hours would be much longer than they are at the college. It is a matter of weighing advantages and disadvantages and deciding what you can live with.

I find the longer I live here the less tolerant I become. It's terrible. One would think it would be the other way around.

Our good friend, Jeff, is leaving for Amsterdam tomorrow on the KLM flight. He has this tendency to take off for Amsterdam every time there is a vacation. It must be costing him a bundle. Bachelors here have it so much harder. Jeff's contract is up this June. He says he may sign on for another year.

My boss has gone to Riyadh, and I have absolutely nothing to do. The second-in-command, Krotz, is filling in, but I have managed to avoid him all morning. Krotz is being transferred to Tabuk, a town near the Jordanian border where there is a military base. He has three children ages eleven, twelve, and thirteen, but there is no school there that I know of. When he was offered the job, he accepted immediately, without even talking to his wife first. That's the kind of man he is. At any rate, 90 percent of the people here will cheer his leaving. He reminds me of the final sentence in Kevin Cash's book, *Who the Hell Is William Loeb?* which is "He lost a lot of friends, but he never lost an enemy."[206]

Jack is temporarily out of homemade beer. Some should be ready about the time we return from Iran. He mixed up another lot last night, and that should be ready to be put into bottles when we come back. It keeps us busy. I am beginning to have nightmares about being overwhelmed by bottles. We have thousands of them. There is a sparkling, German apple juice that comes in tall green glass bottles with a porcelain stopper and rubber seal. A couple of years ago we started buying the apple juice for the bottles. Then we developed a taste for the apple juice. Now we are inundated with bottles. They multiply like

---

206   Published by Amoskeag Press, 1975. William Loeb was the owner of the Manchester *Union Leader*, the largest newspaper in New Hampshire.

hangers in a closet. They are always piled up in the sink. I trip over them in the hall. The house is suddenly too small. It's awful.

A friend of mine sent me two German cookbooks that had been translated into English. They are written by the German Betty Crocker, named Teutonically enough, Dr. Oetker.[207] Unfortunately, Dr. Oetker, like Betty Crocker, has a line of baking products in every German supermarket. Naturally he calls for his own ingredients in his recipes, like Oetker vanillin sugar and Oetker custard powder (corn starch). I am rather at a loss in trying to follow the recipes since the Oetker line isn't carried in Omar's. (Omar is getting so rich that he'll be putting out his own line.) The recipes look very good otherwise.

February 15, 1976

This office is truly international. There are the Dutch, most of whom speak good English, but with a fairly strong accent. They imported two hundred Koreans as laborers, few of whom speak English, and those few who do, have a very strong accent, sort of singsong. The supervising engineers, from TVA, a Swedish consulting company, speak limited English with a strong accent. Their written English is something to behold. My company has an Italian subcontractor for plumbing and air-conditioning work. The firm Zompa is represented by an Englishman, an Australian, and two Italians, neither of whom speaks English, Dutch, Korean, or Swedish.[208] The Australian and the Englishman spend most of their time trying to communicate with the two Italians via pantomime. One of the Italians has a tendency to sleep in the storehouse during the day where there are a few extra mattresses stored. I suggested that maybe he worked better at night. Then yesterday a Scottish electrical engineer from Glasgow arrived, and his accent is worse than the Dutch, Swedish, and Koreans put together. In the site office there are three Saudis, one Lebanese, a Syrian engineer, and a Palestinian translator. One Saudi speaks good English, one not bad, and the third very little. The Lebanese is pretty good, along with the Syrian, and

---

207   His books are no longer in print. The last one, *German Cooking Today: The Original*, was published in 2003. Secondhand copies are obtainable.

208   The name of this firm has been changed as noted previously.

the Palestinian is about the best. Since I am used to an Arab accent, I can understand them better than some of the others can. The English-man with the Italian subcontractor told me that his last job had been in Jeddah where he worked with a bunch of Texans. He said they called him "Limey." I said I hoped he called them "Yanks." He said once he got used to their mannerisms he liked them.

There is a good amount of hostility between the Swedes and the Dutch. I can't decide whether that is because of personality problems or national antipathy. The Dutch think the Swedes are cold and stand-offish. The Dutch and Italian firms have some friction between them, because of problems in Turin (Zompa headquarters) about getting things done on schedule. Since the Dutch communicate with the Ital-ian company through its English-speaking employees, I can't say how the Dutch get along on a personal basis with the Italians. But I suspect they don't. Their national characteristics are too opposite. A Dutch-man wouldn't be caught dead sleeping on a mattress in the warehouse.

The hardworking Koreans and Dutch seem to do pretty well together. I think the Koreans must be the Germans of the Orient. However the Dutch are suspicious of the Koreans, and they always think they're up to something. The Oriental mind does puzzle them. It is hard to pick up how they feel about Americans. Although they all admire American expertise, since the Dutch are much more welfare minded they feel that people are treated brutally by big American cor-porations.

The Arabs and Koreans have both said they like working for Americans better than any other nationality. They have nothing to gain by telling me that, so it is probably true. One Saudi here told me that no matter how hard you work for a Dutchman, he won't give you praise, but will instead give you more work. He said working for the Dutch was like "dancing for a blind man." But, he said, "The Ameri-cans weren't like that. They noticed and thanked you and didn't keep trying to work, work, work you." He worked at Aramco and then came to work for Naarden

The Dutch also seem to think that all the Arabs are spies, and don't trust them. The only exception is my driver. His family comes from Iran, and nobody thinks that the Saudis would recruit him for spying.[209] Last month Naarden had to fire their legal adviser, an Englishman, plus three other Englishmen who held important positions in the company, because they were spying for a big English company! They should worry about the Arabs! The legal adviser saw all the contracts, agreements, etc., anyone in Naarden made anywhere in the country. I don't know how the Dutch found out about the spying.

The Koreans seem a bit fanatical to me. From my window I can see them doing calisthenics, which they do every time they have a few spare minutes. They hate the Pakistanis. The catering service here is Saudi with Pakistani cooks and laborers. There have been several incidents already with Koreans hitting Pakistanis. They think the Pakistanis are trying to cheat them out of their daily bread—literally. Once at lunchtime when a supply of bananas ran out before the Koreans got any, a riot nearly started. Personally, if there is any nationality I have had negative experiences with, it is the Pakistani. Here I sympathize with the Koreans. They probably are stealing food from the Korean mess. Most of the Koreans have been in the army, and some are still in the reserve. Many came from Vietnam. There they worked for the US Army or were in the Korean army. They are very polite, like the Japanese. The guards at the entrance site to Naarden are Korean. They don't speak English. There have been complaints that the guards are letting everybody through. The problem is that once they've stopped a car, they can't communicate with the driver. They are too polite to put themselves in that position, so they just wave everybody through.

Aramco has gotten more and more responsibility from the Saudi government. They continue to expand. Now they are in charge of providing electric power for the whole Eastern Province and supervising all industrial development for this area. The best features of working for Aramco (which unfortunately we are not) are that they solve all your problems for you, send you back to the US every year on leave, provide quality housing and reliable utilities, a commissary and post office, and you can save money like crazy because you aren't spending it on anything.

---

209   The vast majority of Iranians are Shiites, which are not looked upon favorably by the Saudis, who are mostly Wahhabis. See "Wahhabism" in glossary B.

February 17, 1976

At work today, the big excitement was a loud fight between a Swedish engineer and a Dutch engineer. What with the friction between the Koreans and Pakistanis, Saudis and Italians, Dutch and Swedes, World War III ought to break out right here on site at any moment. Yesterday I was talking to a Saudi engineer working for TVA. His job is to keep an eye on our Italian subcontractor. He has to deal with the two Italian engineers who don't speak any English. He complained that the Italians were difficult to work with. Every other word they use, he said, is a bad word. He said the Americans use "shit" or "damn" once in a while, but they are nothing compared to the Italians. He was most unhappy with them. I almost asked him how he managed to talk to them at all since I am sure he doesn't know any Italian. The other two engineers working for the Italian subcontractor, an Australian and an Englishman, use sign language a lot, since they don't speak Italian. Maybe the Italians punctuated every other word with a rude gesture.

It is almost official. Husein, our friend in accounting, told us that he spent late nights at the office this week working on the 12 percent retroactive raise—back to October 2, 1975—for the foreign faculty. This summer Jack should get a mid contract increase of seven and a half to 10 percent as well. Since they took the Saudi income tax off last May, things have been improving rapidly. I really didn't expect the dean to give us this increase even though the government made it clear it was for ALL government employees. He gave it to the Saudis last month. He does everything with such bad grace. It was clear that he didn't want to do it.

My driver again expressed his desire to replace my $8.98 Timex with a gold Girard-Perregaux last week.[210] He also brought me four and a half pounds of pistachio nuts from Kuwait. Jack said I shouldn't have taken them. I thought I was showing great restraint not taking his offer of the watch.

---

210   Girard-Perregaux is an expensive Swiss watch. In 2012 dollars this watch in gold would cost at least $10,000.

CHAPTER 11

The high price of an orgy scene, airline ticket agent—a dangerous job,
one woman and three hundred men, a Korean and a religious spin,
Mrs. Wee is Wee's dog, a gem from the Security Office

February 29, 1976

On Saturday my boss, Mr. Kanterman, got word his mother-in-law died of a stroke in Holland. His wife had a breast removed in December and is recovering. They both left on Sunday via KLM to go to Amsterdam for the funeral. So I am on my own again this week with not much to do. Fortunately Mr. Krotz was transferred the week before last to another site, and I don't have that thorn in my side.

Two days ago Mr. Wee's new assistant, Mr. So (I have to refrain from saying "Ah, So!" when I see him) brought me coffee at half past ten accompanied by a hard-boiled egg and a little salt. They must have cooked it at in the office pantry. It was a little odd.

The fact that I wear an $8.98 Timex still bothers my driver. He has been muttering things about improving the situation before I go to the US this summer. The oddity about this situation is that I like him very much. However, I'm not crazy enough to accept an expensive gift from him. I brought him a box of "gaz," rose water flavored nougat with pistachio nuts from Isfahan. I bought a box of almond gaz for myself with no rose water flavor. That additive is popular in this part of the world. It tastes like perfume, but the Arabs love it.

As for our vacation to Iran, I came back with bronchitis. It is terrible to be away from home and sick. The whole experience is colored by it. It snowed in Isfahan and I take back all the nostalgic things I ever wrote about missing winter, although Alex enjoyed it. After the first lovely ten minutes of fat flakes floating down and my breath making clouds in the air, the novelty wore off. The cold and my sickness made sightseeing out of the question. Because of the altitude there, about five thousand feet, the air is terribly dry.

For two mornings in a row, our flight from Isfahan back to Shiraz was canceled. The second morning the fog was quite thick. We went back to the hotel where we had spent the previous night, and I decided to try to eat breakfast, but my stomach was still too unsettled. Most of the hotels in Isfahan are occupied by Grumman Aircraft person-nel, because of a shortage of housing in Isfahan.[211] Some families with children have been living in hotels for as long as five months. The Park Hotel in Isfahan was about half filled with Grumman people.

In the breakfast room at about nine o'clock, all the Grumman wives were sitting around over coffee. Alex and I were the only non company people there. I ordered corn flakes for him and tea for me. Then another American woman came in, speaking fluent Persian to the waiter. She began to address the group in English about how to deliver a baby at home. Alex was spellbound, entranced; he couldn't take his eyes off her. The lady explained that if the woman starts to deliver at home, don't tell her to cross her legs or try to hold the baby's head back. Put her on a bed with her buttocks resting on the ends of the mattress and each leg resting on a chair. Never take your eyes off the baby's head for a minute or she might deliver on the floor. She recommended using newspaper because the printing process has sterilized it. At one point Alex piped up with "Ma, what's buttocks?" I whispered, "Fanny." He then asked, "Ma, what's a fanny?" I said, "Be quiet." Finally, I'd had it and led him from the room. This caused quite a stir behind me as apparently they thought I was a part of the Grumman family. Later that day Alex wanted to know how they got him out of me in the hospital, etc. I could have done without that breakfast.

On our trip we bought two tribal rugs, an Ardabil and a Turkoman-Bokhara—the man called it that, but it seems most unusual for that type. I bought two miniature paintings for myself for forty-eight dol-

---

211   Grumman Aircraft was found by Leroy Grumman and Jake Swirbul in 1929. In the twentieth century, it was the leading producer of civilian and military aircraft. It became Northrop Grumman in 1994 when it merged with Northrop.

lars each.[212] The obscene miniatures, and there weren't many, cost much more than the presentable ones. One rather risqué scene of a disheveled looking beauty riding on the back of a bearded Omar Khayyam type,[213] with bare legs wrapped around his chest and offering him a sip from a bowl of wine, cost three hundred dollars.[214] Jack's theory was that they didn't bring the really obscene ones out from the back room if a woman was present. There was a large orgy scene about twenty-four by eighteen inches, and the man wanted one thousand dollars for it.[215] It wasn't much of an orgy by Hugh Hefner standards.[216]

The two I bought were about three by five inches. I will bring them to the States this summer to have them framed. One is a scene of a shah under a canopy in a garden with a pond, a duck, and people sitting around. There is some Persian script in the top left corner and bottom right. The other is the facade of a building with a shah sitting cross-legged on a throne-like chair watching a girl dance. There is a very finely drawn pattern on each tile on the building. The paintings are watercolor and done on compressed ivory. One absolutely enchanting miniature was of a lovely girl and a bearded poet. It cost one hundred and thirty dollars.[217] I wanted it but hesitated to pay that. You could discern each hair on the man's beard, the perfectly round pearls on the girl's neck, their eyelashes, etc. It was about three by five inches. After spending time examining the good ones, buying the cheap ones were out of the question.

The Ardabil carpet is about four and a half by seven feet, wool on cotton warp. The colors are faded blue, brown, green, and salmon. None of the rugs we saw in Isfahan really hit us. This one was differ-

---

212   In 2012 dollars, about $194.

213   Omar Khayyam (1048–1131). Astronomer, mathematician, philosopher, scientist, and poet. But best known in the West for his book of poetry called the *Rubaiyat*. The most popular translation was by Edward J. Fitzgerald. His poetry, contrary to the way he lived, preached hedonism and asked astute questions concerning free will, God's intentions, and the meaning of life.

214   In 2012 dollars, about $1,212.

215   In 2012 dollars, about $4,039.

216   Hugh Hefner (1926–) is the founder of *Playboy* magazine.

217   In 2012 dollars, about $525.

ent in design and colors. The majority are red carpets, but they cause decorating problems. When we got it home and spread it out on the floor, I discovered it was about two inches wider at one end than at the other, that apparently the carpet weaver had bit off more than he could chew on the design, leaving bits of the pattern out here and there. The borders were slightly wavy and uneven. If the dealer were living in downtown Al-Khobar, I'd have returned the rug. It looks okay on the floor of our bedroom, and these things aren't noticeable at first glance but they bother me. It cost about three hundred dollars, which is on the high side for the quality but considering the size, isn't outrageous for a hand-knotted carpet.[218]

When we got to Shiraz we took a walk through the rug souk, and both of us simultaneously spotted THE rug. The man, who spoke little English, said it was a "Bokhara," a catchall phrase, besides Bokhara almost always is a red rug. This rug was about four by six feet in pale gold, rust, flag blue, and turquoise. The pattern was even. It was a nice densely knotted rug, wool on cotton warp. It is gorgeous and cost only about ten dollars more than the Ardabil.

The meals were disappointing—the food was much better last spring. There is a lot of poverty in Iran. But the country is beautiful with dramatic mountains rising into the sky just outside the city, rivers with many-arched bridges. The people are handsome; the blue-tiled buildings are exquisite. I think I would like to go back once more.

I have heard from a reliable source that an electrician working for British Aircraft Corporation in Teheran, Iran, named his cat Shah-an-Shah (king of kings), a title reserved solely for the Shah of Iran. His janitor overheard him calling the cat that and reported it to the local police. The poor electrician and his wife got twenty-four hours to leave the country.

When we got back from Iran, we were told there had been a couple of wild rainstorms, one that continued for twenty-four hours. On our kitchen floor and on the counter we found large brown spots where it had leaked in and dried while we were away. Now for some reason the

---

218   In 2012 dollars, $300 is about $1,212.

oven won't work. I can't live without an oven. I am afraid by the time they finish fooling around with it what I will have will be a screwed-up thermostat, a not uncommon affliction in the college housing.

We asked that the work be done in the afternoon, so they sent three guys to our house around noon. Jack had gone off to class and just missed them. So Alex sent them packing. Then I called and they sent out two guys who somehow managed to light the oven, told me it was fixed, and departed. Of course I couldn't duplicate their accomplishment. Then I called maintenance again and they sent out a Pakistani plumber. He arrived just as I was about to boil some spaghetti for supper. This delayed supper an hour and a half, which was not good as we had invited someone to eat with us. He fooled around and fooled around, then departed saying he needed a part and would be back the next afternoon.

Then, the next afternoon, two disreputable looking fellows arrived, neither of them resembling the Pakistani and barely speaking English, saying they'd come to fix the stove. I said that a Pakistani was here last night. They looked at me, made a face, and said, "Pakistani no good." (My sentiments too, but I didn't say so.) I tried to explain that the Pakistani said the stove needed a part and he was getting it. The two went into the kitchen, dismantled the stove for the third time, and then told me, "Stove no good!" and "Need new stove!" and "Call Foreman Yazmi and tell him stove no good." Well, the stove was new when we had arrived in Saudi Arabia and worked before we left for Iran, so I couldn't imagine why it should now have to be replaced. So I called maintenance again, talked to three different nationalities, and fifteen minutes later the two disreputable looking fellows, plus one I never met before, appeared on the back steps. After a half hour of work, the stove now works better than ever. But in the meantime, I made the mistake of trying to learn what had happened to the Pakistani plumber and heard a few more "Pakistanis no good!" out of them. Then at half past nine last night someone I never spoke to called and wanted to know if we got the stove fixed, and if so, what time the men left. I couldn't pinpoint it exactly, but it was before four o'clock. Where those three went and what they were up to after they left my kitchen, I can't imagine, but somebody was checking up on them.

Mrs. Priest told me about watching the first three men come to my kitchen door to fix the stove. Alex had refused to let them in and wouldn't even open the door to speak to them, preferring to yell through the glass. She said they were so mad they went to HER house and banged on the back door to complain, "SMALL BOY NO LET US IN!" She told them, "You're damn right. His parents have told him not to let strangers in. Come back when they're home." She gave them no sympathy. She says what she thinks. No question about it. They were on the trip to Iran with us. They had been with Aramco from 1946 to 1972, and she is very interesting when she gets going on how things were in Saudi Arabia way back then.

My boss is supposed to come back from Holland on March 6 with or without his wife. This morning Mr. Wee brought me a semi-hard-boiled egg with my coffee. At noontime the Lebanese administrator at the office brought me a banana. The other Korean left a small package of toffee. I am trying not to eat since I haven't much of an appetite since I got back from Iran. Hope to lose a few pounds. But it looks like circumstances are conspiring against me.

March 6, 1976

Aramco's dining hall has tacked a surcharge for outsiders of about five dollars for lunch and about eight dollars for dinner onto their normal meal costs.[219] I guess they want to discourage people from using their facilities. We can't afford to go there anymore.

We've been hearing that TWA is now supervising SAUDIA (the airline) operations. The International Air Transport Association complained about SAUDIA's random honoring of reservations and the Air Pilots Association threatened to refuse to land in Saudi Arabia. Also a prince recently commandeered a plane for his whole party. The people sitting in the airport who had reservations for the flight threw a small riot, leaped over counters, and beat up the ticket agents. I couldn't believe it and asked my driver about it. He said, "This happens all the time." I asked, "Why do they beat up the ticket agents?" He replied, "What are they supposed to do? They had reservations,

---

219 In 2012 dollars, this is respectively about $20 and $32.

they are angry." Now there will be Americans behind the ticket counter. Jack says it is probably much easier to say no to a prince if you are American than if you are Saudi.

The college recently has instituted two movies a week, Sunday and Thursday, in response to the students' complaint that there is nothing to do here. Jack says he hears this especially from his foreign students. Nothing to do here is everybody's complaint!

The sun finally came out. I called Jack from work at the air base and asked him to bring rubber-soled shoes for me to wear to Mud City (Al-Khobar) this afternoon. I wore them as boots in Iran.

I HATE dialing out of this site office. If I am lucky enough to get off the air base and through to the college switchboard and the operator is awake and there, then I have to get them to dial correctly our phone number 147, which isn't all that easy. They frequently hear it as "174." We get a lot of calls at home for 174 because of the way numbers are given in Arabic—one hundred, four and seventy is 174. But if they get the number right, Jack happens to be home, and we don't get disconnected thirty seconds into the conversation, then I KNOW it's my lucky day.

March 9, 1976

Today the Palestinian translator who works here brought me a kilo of dried apricots. He found them in Dammam. I need them to make apricot wine. We already have six forty-eight ounce cans of apricot juice. I will boil them up and throw them in. Maybe add a jar of apricot jam for good measure. He wouldn't take any money for them. He said, "If you insist, you will make me very angry." I tried to tell him that if he wouldn't take any money for them I would hesitate to ask him to do anything for me in the future because I would feel like I was asking for a gift. He said, "Next time." I'll bake him some cookies.

There is a hassle about my working at the air base, because I am a woman working among three hundred men of various nationalities. I have a security pass, but the situation makes people nervous, especially the Saudi Air Force Administration. Officially I am not here, and they cannot give me a contract. I am budgeted off somebody's miscellaneous expense (not so miscellaneous, actually). I was also told, if asked, to say I was not working here, but just doing a little typing as a favor to an old friend, Kanterman. To me this sounds more suspicious than telling the truth.

We are leaving at the end of June, but I am not sure I can last until then. There are two hundred and five Koreans on the site now. One of them who works in this office is not all there, if you get my drift. He shares his office with a Dutchman, van der Waal, who brought in a block print done by his ten-year-old daughter, Sabrina. It shows a bird with one leg bent walking through grass. The sun is shining and rays are coming down. There are two clouds in the sky. The bird, sun, grass, clouds, and rays are white on a black background. The Korean told me the bird was Jesus Christ. He said, "The road is rough," referring to the grass, I guessed. "The weather is bad; it is raining," referring to what I saw as the sun's rays, and "The bird has a broken leg and is suffering." I had assumed that the bent leg was a childish way of showing that the bird was walking. The Korean ended his interpretation by saying, "Yet with all these bad problems, he keeps on going." Some people can put a religious spin on anything.

An American woman who use to work here—she left last June— used the company postal address for all her correspondence. Unfortunately some of her mail didn't make it and was sent back by the US Post Office. On some of these letters she didn't put her name above the return address, so they were opened. One of them contained a long and involved description of her marital and sexual problems with her husband, plus all the lovers she had while in Saudi, who she referred to by initials. The person who opened her letters, van der Waal, was intrigued by this and checked to see if any of the initials matched a company employee. However, they didn't. It sounded as if she was in the sack with a different guy every night of the week. I don't know where her husband was while all this was going on.

March 14, 1976

My driver, Mohammed, hates dogs, as practically all Middle Eastern people do. Mohammed dislikes them so much that when the head of the company in Saudi Arabia arrived at the airport with his wife, dog, and two kids, he refused to carry the dog in the car. So Kanterman brought his car along. The man, wife, and kids got into Mohammed's car, and Kanterman followed behind with the dog.

I just got back from a trip to the Aramco vet this noon with Mr. Wee, who speaks almost no English, Mr. Wee's dog (who is named Mrs. Wee), and my driver, Mohammed.

Mrs. Wee (the dog) needed shots. Mohammed likes Mr. Wee very much and wanted to do something for him. Mr. Wee only earns about forty-five riyals a day, and the sixty-dollar cost of the distemper and rabies vaccinations means almost a week's salary to him.[220] So Mohammed decided he would forget his principles and drive Mr. Wee and his dog to the vet's, and pay for the shots. I went along to talk to the vet because Wee can't and Mohammed didn't want to. I thought it was very decent of Mohammed to pay for these shots considering his feelings about dogs.

During the trip the dog got nervous and peed on Mr. Wee's leg. He wasn't half as nervous as Mohammed, who kept looking over his shoulder to see what else the dog was doing. Maybe he was afraid the dog would do more than pee. Mohammed doesn't want anybody to know he took the dog in his car because all the Dutch people have dogs, and he's afraid if they found out, he will be running a dog taxi.

When we got to the vet's, the girl wanted to know how old the dog was. Wee didn't know. Then she wanted to know its name. Wee had been calling it Mrs. Wee around the office, but he didn't come out with that there. She said to give the name on the next visit. While we were in the waiting room, Mohammed kept pointing to pictures of cats, trying to convince Wee he ought to have a cat instead of a dog.

When he drove Wee back to the barracks with the dog, I saw that Wee had built a little doghouse around which he had pieced together three strips of cyclone fencing to keep him penned in.

Aramco's new cafeteria policy of tacking an eight-dollar surcharge for the evening meal on the bill is going into effect tomorrow, so Jack is taking me there tonight. They are going to require a person to have

---

220   In 2012 dollars, $60 is about $242.

a "blue card" in May to enter their library. Going there is the benefit I would hate to lose because they serve meals we can't get anywhere else. I hope college people will be issued blue cards.

An update on my latest effort at wine making—the apricot mess fermented like crazy. After five days the apricots looked like a pulsating grayish mass in the five-gallon bucket. We had to fish them out with a strainer and transfer the five gallons of juice to a jerry can with a pressure lock for another couple weeks of fermentation. I didn't know what to do with the remains, a mucky mess in the bottom of the bucket. It occurred to me that I could flush it down the toilet, but the idea made me sick. Finally I dumped it on the bushes next to the front steps. Fertilizer! Yesterday I checked to see what it looked or smelled like, but I couldn't find a trace. Maybe it crawled off. Fruit seems to ferment much faster than juice alone.

March 21, 1976

Mr. Wee had to get rid of his puppy. The other Koreans were complaining that the dog whined and barked all night and was keeping them up. He gave it to someone who worked at the Swedish consulting firm.

March 20, 1976 [Letter by Jack]

Marcie's husband told me one of his students came up to him and announced he was planning to spend the summer in Germany. The student asked what it was like. Fritz said, "Well, Germany is pretty expensive for a whole summer and..." The student interrupted with "Well, I think I've got that taken care of, sir, I've put aside 280,000 riyals for my expenses." That is about $65,000.[221]

March 22, 1976

Annual spring depression has set in. Everybody at the college is in a bad mood, including us. I really don't know how I could stand to spend another contract here. Next year should be our last if I am

---

221   In 2012 dollars, about $262,530.

to stay sane. This place is really getting to me. Some of the bachelors seem almost suicidal. Problems of compound living, overexposure to the same people, and loneliness seem to peak about spring. I think they should hold graduation next week and send everybody home for the summer.

Since those clowns fixed my oven, everything I cook burns on the bottom. Did you ever cook a rice pudding in a 300°F oven for ninety minutes and have it burn on the top? It was in a pan of water, even! I need an oven thermometer.

March 27, 1976

The maintenance men came to adjust my oven temperature yesterday afternoon. They told Jack it was fixed. I made a big chocolate cake last night, and it burned top, bottom, and sides before the center was cooked. I was furious.

April 7, 1976

Two days ago one of the Italians with the subcontractor at Naarden was heard sobbing at the top of his lungs behind a closed door. A telegram had come, it was in Italian, and since the Dutchman who could decipher Italian was not around, the only word anyone could figure out was "mother." It was assumed that his mother had died. Arrangements were made to get him an exit visa and book him on an Air France flight out that night. His boss, who is British, had been trying to get rid of him for months. He was sent to Dhahran as a plumber, but they later learned that his last job had been as a bellhop in a Turin hotel. He also has a habit of sleeping in the warehouse during working hours. Anyway, he arranged for this fellow to get an exit visa, but did not obtain a reentry permit for him. So he won't be back. When the one Dutchman who could read Italian got back to the office, he read the telegram and said that the Italian's mother had been operated on for kidney stones!

My oven still is not fixed. Yesterday I dragged my driver into the house and had him explain the problem to the maintenance crew in ARABIC. Today we will see what we shall see! Unfortunately my driver goes off to Riyadh tomorrow morning and won't be able to follow up on it.

The maintenance crew installed a new thermostat. The oven is now about one hundred degrees hotter than what it reads, but at least I can control it.

April 10, 1976

I learned that one of the factors that made a faculty member at the college decide to resign mid contract was a deflating incident at the jebel (pun intended). He was trying to make a class, couldn't find a place to park, and so put his vehicle in an unauthorized area. When he came back he had some tire changing to do. The college security guards let the air out of his tires. He had several other reasons to resign as well, but this one definitely clinched it.

Last night Jack took me out to the Marroush, a Lebanese restaurant in Al-Khobar. I had grilled boneless chicken and tabbouleh. When we got back the Priests, our neighbors, were sitting on their back steps, drinks in hand, grilling a steak. They insisted we come in for one (not a steak). He told Jack that the bottle of homemade beer Jack gave him was the best homemade beer he had ever had during his twenty-eight years in Arabia. It's true. Jack makes the best around. I think our wine is up there, too. Mr. Priest really likes Alex and kept going on about what a great kid he is. Both of them were pretty sloshed. I think they start about 9:00 a.m. on weekends. Jack said if thirty years in Arabia makes you drink like that, then we'd better get out soon.

April 13, 1976

The university sent a "Dear John" letter to Dr. Hough terminating his contract. Dr. Hough has been on medical leave. The college insisted he take a year off, when he had only asked for a semester. They figured they didn't need him anymore because they had two faculty members and a Saudi chairman. Mr. Priest told me all this.

The following [see next page] is a gem from the Security Department of the university:

UNIVERSITY OF PETROLEUM & MINERALS MEMORANDUM
DHAHRAN—SAUDI ARABIA DATE: 13 April, 1976

TO: ALL UPM CAMPUS RESIDENTS
FROM: SECURITY DEPARTMENT
SUB: PROTECTION TO UPM BELONGINGS/PROPERTY

This is to draw your immediate attention that on many occasions your kids were found playing with UPM belongings like as listed below:
(i) Climbing up the Water Tower where entrance is strictly prohibited.
(ii) Damaging Light bulbs hitting by stones all around light poles.
(iii) Roaming around new hoses under construction and play with building material—cause damage to Doors/Windows and likewise stuff.
(iv) Climbing up the Recreation Center walls and jumping in and out from time to time.
(v) Shaking and spoiling recently developed plant (Palm Trees) on which UPM has spent huge amount for plantation.

Resident-kids have been advised politely as well as repeatedly to avoid all such naughty mischieves but no attention was paid to our verbal advice.
Now we are constrained to direct all of our Security guards to watch closely and carefully the children playing around so that appropriate solution could be sorted out.
You are, therefore, requested to extend your full cooperation by advising you kids to evite nuisance and to cause vexation to us as well.
Thanks.
SALEH HALWAN DIRECTOR

April 18, 1976

This past winter has been the rainiest winter in recorded history (which means as long as Aramco has been keeping records).

April 24, 1976

A m enclosing a picture of Alex and me in my office the day he visited me at work. My boss just told me he is leaving for Holland on the second of May for two weeks. I will be relieved because the pressure has been getting to me. I can't unwind at night and have been having problems sleeping. Jack's on vacation this week, which will take some of the pressure off of me temporarily.

A few days ago the Koreans here got a hold of a supply of local booze, got roaring drunk, and several did not show up for work the next morning. They also got hold of some blue movies and were showing them in the evening. Anyway, the top Korean here has been canned. Lively place.

The Italian who got the telegram and who carried on sobbing for half an hour is back. It seems that when he got to Italy, his mother was on her deathbed from the operation, and she extracted from her son a deathbed promise that he would clean up his act and be a good boy from now on and go back to his job in Saudi Arabia. He went to the head office in Turin with that tale, and they sent him back to Saudi Arabia. The two Brits who run the office here had obtained an exit visa for him but NOT a reentry permit, thinking they had ditched him for good. He came back somehow, without the proper visa, and spent the night in the local jail. He was in the office by this morning, however, and for the time being looks

as if he has cleaned up his act.

April 27, 1976

Jack just finished translating *The Little Red Hen* from Arabic to English. He was working on a biography of Louis Pasteur in Arabic, but that proved too ambitious for him at his level.

Tomorrow I take Alex to a Dutch children's party in honor of Queen Juliana's birthday.[222] The following day we go to a grown-up party celebrating same. It is an annual event with the Dutch. There are so many invited to this party that they are serving local booze. My driver went to the airport today to pick up smoked eel and salted herring. Only the eel was there, though herring was on the shipping documents. I can't imagine who would want to steal herring. It is an acquired taste.

---

222   Queen Juliana of the Netherlands (1909–2004) became queen in 1948, abdicated in 1980. Her birthday is April 30.

CHAPTER 12

Lethal sea snakes, twenty-five cups of coffee a day, husbands advised to cover their wives, AA and AAA, both needed, Arab justice for obscene phone callers, Mohammed and the new secretary, Margaret, toilet squatters—hard habit to break

May 3, 1976

Jack wasn't terribly happy about going to the Dutch party on Thursday night. We went anyway. He did not have anything to drink. The refreshments were great. They had Indonesian delicacies, such as a deep-fried fish and shrimp ball appetizer, tiny shish kebabs with peanut sauce, smoked eel, salted herring (which finally materialized), stuffed eggs, canapés, sanbusi, which are the Arab version of egg roll but triangle shaped. I quite enjoyed the food. When we left about midnight Jack observed that everyone was getting progressively stiffer, and I later heard that it went on until 3:00 a.m. amid, by that time, loose behavior—couples in bushes, etc. My driver was slightly taken aback by what went on and wanted to know if this went on at parties in the States. I said not in my circle.

Bob Asa a Californian we met in Iran, is temporarily staying in Al-Khobar. He is the Middle East representative for Tremont Corporation (plumbing, porcelain, and generators).[223] His company stationed him in Amman and he does regular tours of the Gulf, North Africa, and Iran. He took us to the Al-Gosaibi Hotel, Al-Khobar's answer to the Ritz, for dinner. I ordered fillet; it was the oddest steak I have ever eaten. It was tenderized to the point of mushiness inside. Jack ordered the same thing. Bob had veal. The vegetables were excellent. The bill

---

223   Name has been changed.

for the three of us came to forty-one dollars.[224] This is with no liquor, of course. Later our neighbors told us that we got away cheap. They paid twice that much for their meal. The dining room was carpeted, chandeliered, linened, candle-lit, and elegant. However, the waiters weren't too polished. They rammed Jack's chair with a trolley and then giggled about it.

We saw Bob's room, which was poolside. It looked like a country motel room. He said that morning while he was taking a shower and was covered with a fine froth of soapsuds, the water went off. So he slipped on his swim trunks and jumped into the pool just outside his door, leaving a trail of soapy bubbles in the water. Water and power outages happen at the most inopportune times. Jack has been caught in the shower too when the water went off.

I will add one thing about the Algosaibi's dining room: the gold letter menu did not have one English mistake in it. You would not believe some of the spelling in menus at other restaurants.

Jack plans to mix up his last batch of beer soon. This is before we leave for the summer. We will return well stocked! Our wine production has finally caught up and passed our consumption. There must be about twenty gallons in one stage or another. I am curious as to how the apricot will turn out. We want to do another lot of cranberry soon, though the juice is so acidic that it takes a while to ferment properly.

The Dutch people are having a big farewell party for a fellow I work with who is leaving Saudi Arabia after four years. This is on the twenty-seventh of the month. Jack is reluctant to go. He feels that the Dutch are bigoted and class-conscious in the extreme, which is true. They see the Saudis and Koreans as some subhuman species. It really is most unexpected among these liberal-minded people. Jack has had it with that attitude and told me a while back that if he heard one more person tell him that you can't teach "these people" anything he was going to level with them. At the last party we went to, a Dutch fellow walked up to him and started in. I kept trying to change the subject, knowing what would be coming if I didn't. When Jack told him, "Well, I think that's a lot of crap." I

---

224   In 2012 dollars, about $166.

said, "I think I'll go see if they've put out the smoked eel" and didn't hang around to hear any more. I too get exasperated with the way things are done in Saudi Arabia, but I don't leap to the conclusion that they all must be stupid or that they should do things our way, because there is a whole social and cultural tradition outside of our own operating here.

I have to go to this forthcoming party, since the fellow they're having it for fills in for my boss when he is away and then I work directly for him. I am really running out of things to wear!!

May 7, 1976

I am rapidly becoming up-to-here with Kanterman. If I quit I would be giving up one thousand dollars a month. Jack says I can, because he is more disgusted than I am with my boss and a few other people at the company. Unfortunately, one's standard of living rises with one's income. Kanterman is an extremely nervous man. He flies off the handle before he half investigates the situation. I don't like being told I am wrong when I am not wrong. Over 75 percent of the time, Kanterman is wrong, but he hops on me first. Very aggravating. He called me at home Wednesday afternoon five minutes after I came through the door to ask me where something was that I typed. It was smack in the middle of his desk pad when I left, with nothing on top of it, and I told him so. I know he found it because the next day I talked to the person who had to translate it into Arabic, but Kanterman never mentioned it to me.

May 11, 1976

Work went a bit better today. My boss was mad at forty different individuals for sundry reasons and had a lot to get off his chest. He dictated about nine pages to one employee. The madder he got, the faster he talked. I just don't go that fast. I've discovered that in taking dictation I can ad lib. Put in what sounds good and they rarely notice.

The nights are getting steamy and tropical again. Going outside is like walking into somebody's mouth. The fleshy pink lizard is back hiding under the outside light. Big cockroaches are out in large numbers. Horrid things. I jumped up on the toilet as one scurried past me in the bathroom. Alex thought that was pretty funny. Jack said I must be getting used to them because I didn't yell this time.

May 16, 1976

We went to the college beach on Friday for about an hour. It was too hot to walk on the sand, so Jack and Alex went for a stroll up the coastline. During the walk Alex picked up a banded sea snake, which is poisonous with no known antidote.[225] He waved it by the tail at Jack and yelled, "Hey, Dad! What's this?" Jack screamed, "Drop it!" because he could see it was groggy, but still alive. Jack gets cold chills thinking about what might have happened. Alex said he thought it was an old piece of rubber. He likes to go wading in the water, picking up and examining small pieces of flotsam and jetsam. It was the first time I had seen one of these snakes. People who go snorkeling have described them to me. This one was about the size of a garden snake, but they can reach five feet, and all of them are poisonous.

I decided I should have a new refrigerator. I sent a memo to housing with a copy to maintenance listing six reasons why I should have one. To my surprise the next day I got a copy of a memo from maintenance to housing saying in effect, "We think Doyles should have a new refrigerator too, please give them one." Four days after that we got a copy of a memo from housing to maintenance saying, "Re: Mr. Doyle's memo about his refrigerator. Please do the needful and repair it." At this point we decided relations weren't too good between maintenance and housing and awaited developments. Yesterday we received a copy of a memo from maintenance to housing saying in effect, "Apparently you guys in housing can't read. We said the Doyles need a new refrigerator. Please give them one if you have it." I can anticipate that the next development will be a memo to us from housing with a copy to maintenance saying, "Sorry, we don't have any refrigerators in the Storehouse." They always say this even when they have a whole storehouse full of refrigerators. I knew a girl who worked at the storehouse. People called her after they had gotten a song and dance from housing about not having something

---

225   As mentioned in footnote 100, there is more than one species of poisonous sea snakes live in the Persian Gulf. The deadliest is the beaked sea snake, whose venom is a hundred times more deadly than a king cobra.

or other in stock and learned that they had at least five or six of whatever they had requested. Housing lied to them.

A year ago last fall I worked for three weeks in housing, and it was a real circus. I quit. The Pakistani secretary there who worked for Abdul-Mohsin Juraib, director of housing, hated his boss, and as soon as Juraib left the room he would start in on me with "Abdul-Mohsin isn't a good Moslem. He lies to people. I never used to lie when I was in Pakistan. Now I come here, and Abdul-Mohsin has made a liar out of me too." Then he would massage his stomach because he was developing an ulcer. Occasionally he would get into a heated discussion with some disgruntled Saudi graduate assistant who wanted better housing over what kind of Moslem Abdul-Moshin was, and both of them usually agreed, not a very good one. Everyone seemed to spend a lot of time checking out Juraib's stories through other departments.

Jack isn't too happy that I sent off the original memo because he gets stuck with following it up. However, I never expected it to be as interesting as it turned out. We still do not have a new refrigerator. The other day Alex almost got a concussion from a frozen chicken that came flying out as he opened the freezer door. The floor of the freezer is warped and battered. All our problems would be solved if I could figure out a way to disable the refrigerator permanently without it looking like sabotage. My neighbor Diana came over last night and told me how the motor on her wringer washing machine finally burned out. Her husband took the motor apart and also removed a key part. Then they called maintenance and said they needed another washing machine. Maintenance has to say something can't be fixed before housing will replace it. Maintenance came on Sunday, took the washer away, leaving the Ayers sure they would finally acquire an automatic. On Monday they returned with the same washer but a new motor. Diana says it sounds like it is going to take off straight through the roof now. The old one was quieter. So even sabotage can be self-defeating.

Must telephone my driver. His wife, who is thirty-eight, just had her fourth child, second son, via Cesarean. He decided this was it and had the doctor "close the road" as he put it.

May 29 1976

Mr. Wee, the Korean coffee boy, once kept records of how much coffee and tea everybody in the office drank and found out that Kanterman drank twenty-five cups of coffee a day. He always takes a full glass of water with each cup of coffee, however. Wee's English isn't too crispy, so he goes into great pantomime to get his point across. The other day he went into a routine of Kanterman drinking coffee, drinking water, running down the hall to the bathroom, running back to his office, calling Wee on the phone, drinking more coffee, more water, running down the hall to the bathroom, etc., and had all the Arabs in the office roaring.

There is a dog up the street that hates Arabs. (The feeling is mutual.) Jack has watched groups of gardeners pass this house while the dog lunges and strains at his leash, snarling and baring his teeth ferociously. And when the dog is out, but not on a leash, you don't see those gardeners for dust. Jack followed a group of them into the compound one afternoon. The dog went into his act, and the gardeners reacted by yelling back at the dog and waving their arms at him, aggravating him further, but they backed off as they did so. Jack came along and the dog dropped his aggressive posture, came bounding over to Jack, wiggling all over with delight, wagged his tail, and waited to be petted. He said the gardeners just couldn't figure that out. I saw a notice posted in a supermarket in Al-Khobar that read, "Welsh Corgi needs a home.[226] Not suitable for children or locals." Probably had the same problem as the aforementioned neighborhood dog, but add children to that.

May 30 1976

I would recommend wine making as a hobby. It really is quite rewarding. The wine we made from apricots is a lovely golden champagne color and not too sweet.

---

226   The breed originated in Wales. The average Welsh Corgi is about ten to twelve inches high and weighs around thirty pounds. They make good companions and are very intelligent.

May 31, 1976

I am enclosing a copy of a memo we got [see next page], further restricting the coeducational use of the recreation center. Jack is quite upset about it, along with almost everyone else. It is very depressing to see this place go backwards so fast.

The college seems to be getting more conservative all the time. A notice came out last week asking women to cover their arms, legs, and dress conservatively. Now the recreation center, one of the few places one could go with one's husband, is segregated. It will now be limited to women one day and men the next. Also it is rumored that all women working at the college will be terminated tomorrow. I heard different reasons why: (1) very religious students have complained in Riyadh that women are "running around naked" at the university, and (2) the university is being transferred from under the Ministry of Petroleum to the Ministry of Education. The latter is a much more conservative ministry.

This would be in effect as of the next fiscal year—June 28. If it gets much worse, for sure next year will be our last. I can't stand it now. Of course it is the end of the year, and we are both very fed up. To make matters more aggravating there is now a self-appointed guardian of public morality in our compound. He is a Saudi and calls up husbands whose wives he believes to be under clothed. Like, for example, walking around within the compound wearing shorts and sleeveless top. He advises the husbands to cover their wives. The frame of mind Jack is in at this point would probably get us twenty-four hours to get out of the country if that fellow called him.

UNIVERSITY OF PETROLEUM & MINERALS
DHAHRAN, SAUDI ARABIA
May 30, 1976

To: *All faculty and Staff*
From: *Dr. Abdulrahman Al-Zamil,*
Sub: *Dean of Educational Services*

UPM RECREATION FACILITIES
 Since the opening of the faculty recreation Centre a number of allocations in the program have been instituted. This memo is to draw your attention to the main schedule changes and to again request your cooperation in observing the regulations that are in force at the Recreation Facilities.
 Saturday 7:00 p.m.–10:00 p.m. FACULTY AND MALE
 AUTHORIZED STAFF ONLY
 Sunday 8:30 a.m.–11:30 a.m. LADIES ONLY
 Monday 7:00 p.m.–10:00 p.m. LADIES ONLY
 Tuesday 8:30 p.m.–11:30 p.m. LADIES ONLY
 Friday 8:00 a.m.–11:00 p.m. FACULTY AND MALE
 AUTHORIZED STAFF ONLY
 During ladies sessions no male staff or faculty may use any part of the Recreation Center.
 Your attention is draw to the memo circulated by the Physical education department (10 September 1975) which stated that ladies are not permitted use of the swimming pool at Building 11 nor may they use the main gymnasium facilities.
 Finally you continued co-operation is solicited with regard to dress as particularly in the Recreation facilities it is expected that all concerned will dress in a manner appropriate to the customs pertaining within the Kingdom.
 Your co-operation in these matters is much appreciated
 ABDULRAHMAN AL-ZAMIL
 DEAN OF EDUCATIONAL SERVICES

June 6, 1976

L ast week Bob Asa was our houseguest for four days. When he is in
this area, he generally stays at the Al-Gosaibi Hotel.[227] This is a posh
hotel in Al Khobar and is booked up at least three months in advance,
but the local Tremont outlet (Bob works for Tremont) bribes the desk
clerk with a bottle of Johnny Walker (worth about sixty to one hundred
dollars on the black market) and gets a room for Bob. This time they
were either out of Johnny Walker or the company was steamed at Bob for
refusing to dump $100,000 of inferior toilets in the Middle East. Either
way, they neglected to get him a room. So he called us from Jeddah,
one thousand miles to the west, to tell us he was coming that evening.
Alex answered and told him we had just left (we had). The message as
Alex gave it to us was: "Hey, Bob who lives in Khobar called." After we
thought about it for a while, we decided Bob must be at the Algosaibi
and called there. Jack spent ten minutes spelling Bob's name for the desk
clerk whose English was not too crispy. Halfway through Jack got disconnected. He dialed back and went through the routine all over again.
Finally the desk clerk declared that no one by that name was registered
at the hotel. Jack was 95 percent convinced the clerk was lying, because
he was fed up talking to Jack. Fortunately, Bob called again from Jeddah
that afternoon and Jack answered. Originally he was to stay with us two
nights, but because his flight to Abu Dhabi was canceled, he ended up
being with us two more nights. Jack has a lot of time off (compared to
me) so he entertained Bob. We got him a pass at the recreation center.
He is looking for a position with another firm because he feels Tremont
is completely unethical, and he is tired of putting the screws to custom-
ers on Tremont's orders and then taking the flak. Apparently his boss in
the States took a course from the American Institute of Management in
doing business in the Middle East. He's never been to the Middle East,
but thinks he knows all about it. Some of the stuff he's ordered Bob to
do is quite unbelievable.

We've had a few days of sandstorms, moderate ones. June is the
season for them.

---

227   This hotel is still in existence and has a website. Search Google on "Algosaibi
Hotel."

There was a college department party Thursday night to which we brought Bob. Several people arrived drunk. One fellow, who was high, but not from alcohol, said to one of the crocked teachers, "Do you like my soft shoes?" pointing to his Hush Puppies. The other fellow said, "Give me that old soft shoe!" and the first individual did literally. Then the second fellow took the shoe, tucked it under his chin, and began tap dancing while he sang to himself, "Give me that old soft shoe...!" Honestly, a chapter of AA is needed in Dhahran. I said this to Jack earlier except I told him AAA, and then corrected myself.[228] Jack said, "We need that too!" (Referring to the highway fatalities).

I am fed up at work. There is one man there, van der Waal, whose mind is occupied with sex most of the time. Both he and his wife have an arrangement that they are free to relate to whom or whatever. He spends a lot of his time trying to relate to me, and I spend a lot of time dodging and weaving (figuratively speaking). He hasn't tried to get physical yet, except on the dance floor at company parties. Jack does not care for him at all, and not because he knows he's after me, although that may be part of it. Van der Waal made it with the Dutch nurse and then told everybody. From what I hear, the whole construction company goes in the front door of her accommodations and comes out the back on a regular basis. If everybody who claims to have made it with that single Dutch nurse actually did, then she would have to spend all day and all night in bed. I saw an evaluation of her written by the Dutch doctor for the company. He gave her high professional ratings but observed, "Miss de Veen seems unable to suppress a certain chaotic streak in her character. As far as I know her personal behavior has caused no scandal in our compound." The Arabs think she's crazy. But when she visits Dhahran, all the Koreans are suddenly sick and need to see a nurse. She is about thirty-five, not unattractive, but very bizarre. She is stationed in a remote part of Saudi Arabia near the border and there are no hospital facilities at that site.[229]

---

228 Respectively Alcoholic Anonymous and American Automobile Association.

229 It has an elevation of 7,500 feet, has a moderate climate, and is in an attractive part of Saudi Arabia.

June 7, 1976

The college seems to be going back into the dark ages. The latest plan is to separate men and women at the movies next year, having one night for the men and the next night for the women. They have the impression that all the men are lust crazed and all the women are wanton harlots. Give them ninety minutes together at the movies and the inevitable will take place. The same thing for men and women swimming together at the pool.

June 12, 1976

I am getting no time at work to type letters because of Margaret, the Pakistani woman who is replacing me. Like so many people from the Middle East and Far East, she thinks that if she has everything down in writing, then she is all set. She has reams of notes. Explaining the job all day to her makes me hoarse, not to mentioned peopled out. It is so typical of Kanterman to hire my replacement six weeks before I leave. The job doesn't require that much explaining. Kanterman is so nervous. I get the feeling he is afraid of losing his grip on things and that the slightest tremor, like his secretary going on leave, might cause him to lose everything. Somebody like that is very aggravating to work for, believe me.

I was talking to Mike, a Britisher in Jack's department, yesterday. He was going on about some of the more conservative turns the university has taken lately and then related an incident last year when he went to a doctor at a local hospital in Al-Khobar. As he went into the office, he passed an older Saudi couple with a young girl, about eighteen, leaving the office. The doctor was all upset and said to Mike, "I wish they wouldn't ask me to do these things. That girl just got married and her husband doesn't think she is a virgin. He wanted me to examine her to tell him. How the hell do I know?" and he just shook his head. Virginity is a very big thing here. If there is no bleeding on the wedding night, then they consider that a sign that she must have had somebody else and they can turn her back to her parents. I think this system is just insane. Producing a bloodstained piece of cloth as proof is also part of it. The partying goes on while the couple retires to the bedroom. Then the cloth is shown to all present. I have heard stories of the husband inflicting a wound on himself in order to have the stained cloth to show. Mike's comment was "Suppose the doctor says she was a virgin, then what kind of relationship will they have, her husband having made the accusation that she wasn't a virgin." Then he remarked, "Maybe they expect to be unhappy with this kind of relationship."

From several reliable sources I have heard that next year the recreation center will be open to women all the time and to men only if they bring their wives along. The theory is that you can't go there and stare at everybody's wives unless you tow your own along to be stared at back. I suppose, since the Saudis feel like staring at women in bathing suits, they think everybody else does too. Since I am working more hours than Jack, he takes Alex up there for a swim and a hamburger for lunch. Now he won't be able to do that unless I come long. The bachelors are really worked up over it since they don't have wives to bring. The word is that some very religious students took photographs of the women working at the college (a bunch were fired last week) and of women playing tennis and swimming, then sent them to Riyadh to show them what was going on at that den of iniquity in Dhahran. The rector here is getting squeezed from the top and is in turn trying to tighten up at the university.

June 14, 1976

Alex came home yesterday and announced, "Christian told me a man said dirty words to his mother but they caught him and he got arrested." Later I found out that an obscene phone caller had been bothering people in the college. Christian's mother has been getting a lot of the calls and complained to the administration. They told her to keep the guy on the line while they traced the call. Maybe there are three to four thousand phones at the college. It took them forty minutes to trace the call. I figured the guy's English had to be pretty good to keep it up for forty minutes. They found a teenage boy, son of a Pakistani secretary in the Physics Department, still on the phone in Building 6 on the jebel. I heard he was thrown out of the country, but don't know how true that is.

The usual variety of nuisance call involves heavy breathing. The Palestinian translator at work, who has lived in this area for twelve years, told me when automatic dial was introduced, a rash of obscene calls occurred. One fellow got caught because he would repeatedly call one particular Arab woman who complained to her husband. When they caught him, they hung a telephone around his neck and drove him in a convertible through the main streets of Al-Khobar. That diminished the problem somewhat. I noticed recently when I tried to call Jack from the gatehouse that the phone there had a plate over where the dial holes should be. The plate contained one hole over the number "0". So the phone could only be used to call outside the compound. That was probably done to discourage bored gatekeepers from entertaining themselves.

The enclosed memo from the acting dean of business at the university has the Americans steamed because the notice is not in both English and Arabic. The implication is that the Americans are making the obscene phone calls.

June 20, 1976

There have been a lot of parties this month. Last night we were invited to Kanterman's house for dinner. We came at half past seven, and there were four other couples besides us there. He served real scotch. I had an empty stomach when I arrived, but by nine that evening I didn't care if I ever ate. This was after one scotch on the rocks. The company has a fantastic Indonesian cook who prepared the dinner. He served first a light tomato-based vegetable soup with tiny meatballs. The buffet consisted of tiny shish kebabs with peanut sauce (called saté) and two kinds of chicken dishes I hadn't tried before. These were on the hot side. There was rice with raisins, fried bean sprouts, a beef dish in a thick sauce with broad beans, a crisp, fried shrimp-flavored "bread" that is supposed to be Indonesian-Chinese. There were condiments such as sliced bananas, sliced tomatoes, hot sauce, etc. He made a delicious Indonesian version of egg roll. After dinner we had coffee and chocolate pound cake. It broke up about half past eleven, and I had a much better time than I expected.

June 29, 1976

Jack will pay for our tickets tomorrow or Thursday. British Air flights
out of Dhahran have been delayed a minimum of two hours lately,
and one flight over the weekend never showed up. It is very depressing.
Rumor has it that Heathrow authorities have cracked down on Saudia's
random ways, telling them that either they take off in the slot allotted
to them or they will just have to wait three or four hours and will not
be given priority anymore. The Dhahran Airport delays are supposedly
Saudia's retaliation for London's hard line. We should be leaving here
on the sixteenth for London and arrive on the twenty-second in Boston.

Nothing new with us. Graduation is Wednesday and a lot of people
are leaving on Wednesday night while the rest seem to be booked out
of Dhahran on the second of July.

July 1, 1976

Graduation is tonight and Jack decided to stay home. Unfortunately almost everyone else has the same idea, and I am afraid
the dean will take attendance. The administration built a special section for the women to sit in with a screen separating it from the men's
section. Last year somebody's son graduated and the Saudi mother
jumped up, cheered, and clapped to everyone's delight—the foreigners' anyway.

UNIVERSITY OF PETROLEUM AND MINERALS
Administrative Services
ADM/110/174
June 12, 1976

MEMORANDUM
TO: The University Community
FROM: Fahed Al-Hazzam
Acting Dean of Business
SUBJECT: Obscene Telephone Calls

The academic community has been plagued by a series of obscene telephone calls emanating from within the University. The problem has reached such an extent that the surrounding municipalities of Al-Khobar and Dammam have also been receiving obscene calls. The telephone company and the police had traced the Al-Khobar and Dammam calls to the University.

A number of individuals responsible for some of the calls made within the University community have been apprehended and punished. Until the problem is completely solved surveillance from both within and outside the University will continue.

The penalty for making obscene telephone calls is severe. In addition to immediate dismissal from the University, police action will be taken. This is applicable to both Saudi nationals and foreigners alike.

With your cooperation, this entire matter may be brought to a conclusion. Should you receive any sort of improper telephone call, please notify Saleh Helwan, the Director of Security, (ext. 524 or 390) immediately.

Thank you.
FAD/ead

July 4, 1976

The Pakistani secretary at work, Margaret, is making problems. She is accustomed to servants and expects people to wait on her. She's also working hard to make a job for herself, mainly by increasing the volume of paperwork. Jack says Kanterman may be a lot of things, but he's not dumb and after two months will be on to her.

My driver, Mohammed Sharif, also has to take Margaret to and from work. He is not one bit happy with her because of her attitude that he should wait on her. He told me unless people treat him as an equal he can't work with them. He does much more for the company than drive and is quite wealthy. He says he is working because he likes it, but he can afford to quit anytime. She expects him to ring her door-bell in the morning, open the door for her, drive her directly to the office door, check with her when it is time for her to leave to see if she is ready, etc. The first morning he sat in front of her apartment building and blew the horn. A neighbor came out to see what he wanted. He said he had come for the "Hindian." The neighbor rang the bell. She, thinking he finally gave in, came sailing out the door and was surprised to find her neighbor there.

Mohammed has a new car but refuses to run the air-conditioning, telling her the engine is too new to put such a strain on it. Last Wednesday he parked the car in the mud at the far end of the office building. She sat there waiting for him to come round and open the door. He got out and went into the office. She gave up, climbed out, picking her way through the mud "like chicken" the driver said. I gathered he looked at her out of a window.

Lately she has taken to ordering other people in the office to inform Mr. Sharif that she is ready to leave. He usually attempts to distract them and talks of other things. They leave forgetting why they came. Then she has to ask him directly. She never leaves when she is supposed to but expects him to be ready and waiting the minute she decides she is finished for the day.

Wednesday afternoon when she was ready to leave, the Palestinian translator, who also dislikes her, decided Mr. Sharif should check something on his car and took him outside. They both lay across the front seat pretending to look under the dashboard for twenty minutes. She stood in the doorway of the office building for ten minutes, and then sent Mr. Wee to inform Mr. Sharif she was ready to leave. Mr. Sharif told Mr. Wee to beat it, and Mr. Wee hightailed it back to his kitchen. Finally she came over and told Mr. Sharif she was ready to leave. He managed to delay for another five minutes by going to the bathroom, saying good-bye to Kanterman, getting a drink of water, and pretending to hunt for his car keys.

Another morning he sat out front of her house blowing the horn. Her maid passed him on the way to Margaret's apartment, and he told her to "Tell the Pakistanian I'm ready." I usually hear of these events through the Palestinian, a guy named Mizian, who has been good friends with Mohammed Sharif for about ten years. Sometimes the driver relates these stories to me and sometimes I happen to be on the scene.

It's funny but every single Pakistani I have ever had anything to do with has left me with a negative impression. All I can conclude is that Pakistan is a dog-eat-dog place and people come out of there with a concentration camp mentality that they can't seem to shake, no matter the subsequent circumstances. Obviously this woman is upper class and used to having people wait on her. Saudi Arabia is not that kind of society. Even when slavery was common here, slaves were treated as equals and ate with the family.[230] Her attitude, coming first from a Pakistani, secondly from a woman, and thirdly towards a Saudi is quite offensive. I related all this to Jack, and he tells me I should pay them to work there, because that kind of entertainment is hard to come by in Saudi Arabia.

Margaret's husband has been in jail for forty-one days. Anyone in a car accident here that results in more than a damaged vehicle, such as personal injuries, is likely to be thrown in jail for fifteen days by the police. He was in an accident nine months ago, and everyone thought the matter was settled, damages paid, etc., and he was found not at fault by the court. Now he has been put in the local lockup with no water, food, or air-conditioning. The family or sponsor must take care of the needs of the prisoner. A guy at Naarden was locked up two weeks ago and another about a month ago, for being in car accidents. All this locking up of people has made Jack nervous, and he is saying he will take the bus into Al-Khobar until we leave in two weeks.

---

230   Slavery was abolished in Saudi Arabia by King Faisal in 1962.

Margaret has been trying to get her husband out of jail. She has been carrying on at work, crying, and generally milking the situation for all the sympathy she can get. Kanterman has been putting pressure on Mohammed Sharif to arrange something and get her husband out of jail. Mohammed, since he dislikes her intensely, won't do anything to help her. Just a week before her husband got locked up, she was in Kanterman's office complaining about the way Mohammed treated her and about me as well. Mohammed's connections are remarkable, and he says he could make one telephone call and solve her problem, but he knows she would just go back to treating him like a servant the following week.

Her husband works for the Netherlands Airport Company, which is building a new runway at Dhahran Airport. She thinks the people at the company aren't doing enough to help and wants Kanterman to visit the Emir of the Eastern Province and ask him to order the police to release her husband.[231] Kanterman told Mohammed today that the director at the Netherlands Airport Company doesn't like her husband because he acts just like she does in the office.

The other secretary and I are the only two in the office right now. It is lunchtime. There is a crew of cement-dusted Yemenis waiting in the hallway for their money. They just finished unloading several tons of cement. I explained to them in Arabic that the cashier would be back in one hour and to please rest themselves and wait a little bit. They are arguing among themselves now, and I suppose they will be back soon to ask me some more questions I can't understand, since my Arabic is very limited.

Yesterday the office in Riyadh hadn't made any cash transfers to the Al-Khobar office's account, and they had no money to pay the Yemenis. They are frightening. I thought they would start a riot yesterday. They fought and argued and pushed each other, along with the poor company Arab who was trying to talk them into being patient. This crew would have to be seen to be believed. Yemenis dress in plaid kilt-like skirts wrapped around their waists and wear shoes, socks, and military-type shirts of beige or gray, with turbans on their heads.

---

231 An Emir is a prince of the royal family in charge of a province.

They are dark skinned with black hair and penetrating, dark eyes. Sprinkle all this with cement dust and you have the ingredients for a scary movie.

July 6, 1976

Yesterday we went into Al-Khobar. I got a gold chain: square, braided, eighteen karat, and Italian made. It is about thirty-one inches long and a nice weight. I won't go into the price, but I have been keeping about sixty dollars a month out of my salary and had been saving it up. It is very elegant looking and will look nice with anything. My only problem is what to do with all my jewelry over the summer. If I leave it here, I will worry about somebody making off with it. If I take it with me I will worry about somebody stealing my bags. The only solution seems to be to wear it and look like an Arab bride.

Speaking of that, last night when I got home Husein, Jack, and a former student of his were in the living room. The student brought me a pair of Bedouin silver earrings, the old kind of Bedouin silver work with a rough turquoise stone set in each one. I hung them in my ears, and they came down to my breasts. I might add that if Bedouin women wore them all day they must have calluses on their earlobes. I had a time getting them off because the silver ear loop is considerably thicker than the wires found in European earrings. But they are a nice souvenir of Saudi Arabia. He also gave us some tassel-like decorative yarn and beading to be hung on the wall. I think it too is Bedouin. Perhaps they use them to decorate their camels or tents.

July 10, 1976

My driver, Mohammed, has finally decided to turn on his air-conditioning for the "Hindian," because he met her husband (who finally was released from jail) and decided he was a nice guy. Mohammed still does not like her, complaining she is "heavy blooded," "has a funny smell like the Hindians," "is heavy in my car," "talks too much," and "is like a queen."

Some days he tells me he is going "to make her crazy," but is waiting until after I leave so she won't think I'm behind it. The Arabs here refer to her as "malika," which means "queen" in Arabic, because of her superior attitude. Since she arrived, she has been working her wiles on Kanterman, which Mohammed calls "polishing." In his vernacular, this means making the surface look good but not actually doing much. Lately he has been talking about taking a vacation, so he won't have to take her to work anymore. She must be wearing him down.

Last Friday we were invited to Mohammed's home. He has four children, a boy sixteen, girl thirteen, girl seven, and son two months. His wife made tabbouleh and sanbousa. Sanbousa reminds me of egg rolls, but the meat filling is more like a paste.[232] The family lives in an Arab-style house with an inner courtyard open to the sky. The rooms all open onto the courtyard, and there are stairs to the second floor where there are two more rooms.

The house has Turkish toilets that are squatted over and flushed with a bucket filled at a nearby faucet. Last year a Dutch family with a seven-year-old boy visited. The boy had to use the bathroom. He came out immediately complaining that the toilet was broken. I have so far managed to avoid using this variety of plumbing, much to my discomfort on occasion. At the college, the architect installed Western toilets in the men's rooms. They have been experiencing a rash of broken toilet seats because most of the students insist on squatting on the seats, which of course, breaks them. The Arabs complain that the Westerners don't know how to use their toilets, and the Westerners complain that the Arabs don't know how to use theirs. The Arabs say Western toilets smell, and the foreigners say the same thing about theirs.

July 14, 1976

This will be the last letter we mail from Saudi Arabia before leaving day after tomorrow.

Got a note from Dr. Hough who asked that we call collect when we get into town. I wrote him what I had done with his personal effects I had been keeping for him. He had two size forty-four suits and a sun hat. I told him I had put the suits in a brown paper bag, with the hat on

---

232   It is sometimes called the Arabic egg roll. The meat is either ground beef or lamb. Recipes may be found on the web.

top, out by the garbage pail and speculated that probably some Yemeni gardener was wearing them now. He wrote back saying that he wanted a picture of a Yemeni in a size forty-four suit, because they are all small of stature (built like India-Indians). Well, if I see one wearing his suit, I will send him a picture of the fellow.

July 15, 1976 [Letter by Jack]

Travel nerves have got us. It was 2:00 a.m. when I got to bed last night. I was up at 4:45 a.m., and we were both up for good at 6:15. At 6:15 Maralyn said to me the clock just stopped ticking, which will show you how "hyper" we are.

Tomorrow at this time we'll be in London sipping gin and tonics. Inshallah.

September 1976 to June 1977

Jimmy Carter: On Nov. 2, 1976—President of the United States

May 9, 1977: Patty Hearst is let out of jail.

Jan. 18, 1977: Scientist identifies bacterium that is the cause of Legionnaire's disease.

Jan. 21, 1977: Jimmy Carter pardons Vietnam war draft evaders.

Aug. 16, 1977: Elvis Presley, forty-two, dies at Graceland. (We were home in the United States at this time.)

CHAPTER 13

First car accident, Hermann Schenck and the tree, his only English,
"My teacher," the male nurse gets beaten up, the leaking roof bridge
party, the four companions to the companions of the prince

September 17, 1976

Our trip back was exhausting, but we got through customs with a minimum of hassle. I went back to work almost the next day. I had telephoned my boss, Mr. Kanterman, tonight. He leaves for vacation on Sunday for six or seven weeks, and it looks like he won't sign another contract in November. Now I just have the *other* secretary, Margaret, there to bear. My driver told me she threw a big party for all the Dutch people a while back, and her son is having his first birthday next week and she plans another big party to which she is inviting all the Dutch wives and their children. This he calls "polishing." Tomorrow I expect to find she has changed my office all around and I won't know where anything is, so I will have to ask her where things are.

September 20, 1976

I have had a glass of wine. We resampled our apricot and strawberry batches. I think I prefer the strawberry. There is a big holiday on—Eid al Fitr. The college will close tomorrow. This is the Moslem equivalent of Christmas, except bigger.

I have worked only a week, but now have a five-day holiday. I go back on Tuesday. The first day back Kanterman called Margaret and me into his office. I expected the worst, since I had already heard she was working overtime for nothing, coming in on weekends, throwing parties for the Dutch people (ignoring the Arabs in the office), accumulating more and more authority for her position, redesigning the whole filing system, etc. He told her that she would be administrative secretary, taking care of the filing, circulation of documents, registering telexes, keeping a follow-up file. I would be his personal secretary, taking his dictation and minutes of all the meetings. I was delighted because I hate the paperwork anyway. She was upset and pressed him for reasons why. She felt we should share the job equally. He finally told her my shorthand was better than hers. She was insulted. I suspect what he meant was that my English, my grasp of technical matters, and my writing were all better than hers. But for simplicity's sake he seized on the shorthand.

That afternoon she handed in her resignation. The next day I had a chance to talk with her without her trying to show me who was better, and she said that all summer everything she did was described by Kanterman as "terrific, wonderful, and fantastic." He never criticized her once. Suddenly in front of me he informs her that my shorthand is better than hers and she wasn't going to take that!

He left the next morning for six weeks in Holland, so when she came to work, she couldn't confront him. She wanted him to take back his words. I avoided gloating and was quite pleasant to her. She came in the rest of the week to finish changing the filing system around and filing all the stuff she had backed up to last July. As for me, I am not crazy about Kanterman either, but keep these opinions to myself. The duties that I had last year have changed so much that it now looks like a new job, and I have no notes to follow or anything to help me figure it out. Margaret has made a regular paper factory out of the job, but I will admit that her filing system is superior to mine.

We got a notice in our mailbox this afternoon saying that the college would have a dinner party at the recreation center in honor of the religious holiday and SEPARATION OF THE SEXES would be strictly observed. Marcie Wildermann says they can hang it in their ear, she's not going. Jack's sentiments as well, among others.

September 24, 1976

Since I got back I am trying to get the house clean, curtains washed, Venetian blinds soaped down, woodwork scrubbed, etc. Things got so dirty from sand blowing all summer. I cleaned before I left, but the blowing dust seemed to find spots I missed.

September 26, 1976 [Letter by Jack]

I had my first Saudi Arabia car accident. I was stationary in a line of traffic at a stop light when three Arabs in a big truck behind me saw the light go green and started up, driving into the back of my car. I have a nice, neat dent in the back of my Volkswagen. They were mad at me because I got out to look at the damage and they missed the light.

[Letter continued by Maralyn]

The king has just made a speech calling for a return to the values of Islam and asking that foreigners respect them.[233] He added he had instructed the religious police to see that the rules were followed. Translated this means no bare flesh for women or long hair for men.

October 1, 1976

This morning at nine we went to the college beach with Rick and Marleen Connelly and their two boys. The Connellys are from Vermont. He's with a Boston engineering firm. Connellys will be leaving for the States for a month at Christmas. I get the impression that he likes it here better than she does, but that's the way it goes. All the men seem to like it better in Saudi than their wives do. One of the wives enrolled the kids in school and herself in nursing school and wrote her husband she'd see him when his contract ended. This is not uncommon.

Finally Margaret finished up most of her work. I went in on Tuesday, after having the first three days of the week off (holiday), and she didn't appear. She left about fifty pieces of paper in my desk drawer with a note "Just a few pieces of paper left to be registered and filed." At this point I am going to try to stay with the job until June, at which time I will quit, since commencement is scheduled for June 13.

---

233   This speech was made by King Khalid, who was more conservative than his predecessor King Faisal.

Jack is going to take me out for my birthday. I may also buy a green plant for the house. The other day my driver remarked that my house did not look like the houses of the Europeans or other Americans because I did not have antiques or flowers or bric-a-brac around. Actually, I don't want to accumulate a lot of stuff to airfreight back, but the house does look as if we are camping out in it, and this is our fourth year! Coming here just a month before the Arab-Israeli war in 1973 burned into my brain the fear of accumulating anything, because I might have to leave in a hurry.

Jack still hasn't started teaching yet, maybe next week at this time. Just what the college is doing about the segregation of the sexes is not clear yet. Meanwhile I am trying to avoid contact with the college community as much as possible. All the best houses at the college have gone to Saudi faculty, regardless of their rank at the university, while the foreign faculty was given lesser accommodations. This irritates me despite the fact we are in a fairly decent house that meets our needs. Many of them are millionaires and can afford to build themselves a house off campus.

October 3, 1976

Jack took me out to dinner tonight to Maxim's Steak House, one of the more costly dining places in Al-Khobar. This restaurant has the flashiest neon sign in town. They turned it on when they spotted us standing outside wondering if it was open. Apparently we dine early. The steak was excellent, but there were three waiters hovering about at all times. To make matters more uncomfortable, we were the ONLY people there until we were ready to leave. Naturally a whole fleet of underemployed waiters stood in the corner and observed us.

I had heard that the atmosphere was nice there, but there were strange lapses. It would have taken Houdini to undo the napkin gracefully. I suspect it was tied in a double knot to make it stand upright on the dinner plate. The walls were operating room green, and the damask on the tables was hospital pink with matching napkins. Little pots of toothpicks sat next to the salt and peppershakers.

When the steaks were ready, one waiter brought over a silver platter with fried potatoes on one side of the steaks and canned vegetables medley (sans can) on the other side. On top of the steaks were what looked like a potato pancake topped with mushrooms. However, when we cut into it later we were unable to identify it. The mystery vegetable had been canned and marinated. It was a banana color and about the size of a pineapple slice with the hole intact. As the waiter entered with the tray, his assistant produced a cloth-covered serving table. They removed our plates to this table and served using two implements in one hand—tricky. Our plates were returned, and the assistant disappeared with the serving table.

Jack could imagine the fight that ensued over the tip he left. Now I can say I have been to Maxim's.

Afterwards, since we still had an hour to kill having told the babysitter that we would be back at half past eight, we went into Al-Khobar to look around. Jack bought me two plants for the house. One is some kind of miniature palm tree and the other is English ivy. These plants are flown in from Holland, so they're not cheap. Sending palm trees to Saudi Arabia is like sending coals to Newcastle.

Once again the college is flying with rumors about separation of the sexes. The recreation center is supposed to alternate women's and men's days. The faculty dining hall will require the wives to be put in another room by themselves. God knows what would happen if men and women ate together. Orgy! Scandal! And sharing the swimming pool. My God, it boggles the mind.

October 9, 1976

Because I felt so awful and because of the trends at the college, I was very depressed last night. Jack and I spent an hour talking about going back to the US next summer, for good. I felt as if I couldn't face the coming nine months at the college, let alone another year.

Last week the college sent out a circular announcing that alternating days of the week would be segregated at the recreation center. I can go today but Jack can't. He can go tomorrow but I can't. The weekends are strictly limited to families: we both can go together, but neither can go separately. The faculty dining hall has a room for women. The husband can join his wife there, but she can't eat with him in the main dining facility. Rumors are flying that the movies will be for women one night and men the next. We all know what goes on in movie theaters when the lights go out. I told Jack that UPM is suffering from a terminal case of dirty mind.

My good friend Marcie, who was secretary to the dean of science, was told that a man was replacing her. If she wanted to stay on, she was told that she could work in a closet and have work brought to her by her replacement—a male Pakistani secretary. She declined. The problem with a Pakistani bringing you work is that he becomes a "supervisor" and doesn't do anything. And two Pakistanis are only worth half a Pakistani. One becomes a supervisor and doesn't do anything, while the other spends half his time running around telling gossip about the first.

I have given Marcie's name to the Personnel Department at Naarden, and maybe she can fill the other position recently vacated by Margaret. For the few women still working at the college, there are new rules requiring that they be escorted to and from work by their husbands, that they be covered neck to ankles, not to mention wrists, that they not be working with or seen by men while they are at the university, etc., ad nauseam.

I am starting macaroni and cheese for supper and will look through my English translation of Dr. Oetker's German cookbook to see what one can do with one pound of veal, now thawing. My meals lack originality. Just found a recipe for braised veal, but it calls for juniper berries. Now if I had some gin…

There is a faculty-rector meeting tomorrow in the new auditorium. I think there will be some tough questions asked. People are seething about the new restrictions. Any kind of labor organization is against the law. The rector claims to be fighting it all the way, but suspicions are that he is covering his tail with Riyadh to hang on to his job.

October 10, 1976

Jack started teaching yesterday and he has a slow group. He tells me that's part of teaching, some groups are smart, some average, and some slow. He tried to get a student in his group to say, "What is that?" and the student—misunderstanding—kept answering, "That is a book." Jack never did get through.

Not only is the university becoming sexually segregated, but also the bus schedule to Al-Khobar has been changed. There used to be nine buses a week to Al-Khobar: one six mornings a week, and one three evenings a week. Now on Saturday and Sunday there are one evening and two morning buses and that's it. Al-Khobar is a mob scene on Thursday (equivalent to our Saturday). Everybody likes to avoid it then. Someone called transportation to complain. They were told it was done on strict orders from the rector. Theory is that he doesn't want UPM buses unloading unescorted women to wander through the streets of Al-Khobar. Tonight's faculty meeting should be a free-for-all.

October 12, 1976

This place is getting crazier and crazier. Supposedly the college is going to require that all women who are travelling or going outside of the compound to cover their hair. There is talk of separate, segregated buses for men and women into Al-Khobar. Jack and I couldn't ride together.

At a faculty meeting with the rector of the university night before last, a bachelor asked why the recreation center was segregated this year. The answer was that immoral things had been going on—immoral by ANYONE'S standards, not just the Saudis' and that men had made comments to women in the pool. People have complained, he said. Now if anything immoral by MY standards had been going on, I know it would have gotten around. Somebody remarked that the Saudi lifeguard appeared to be getting pretty worked up over the women in the pool and maybe that was immoral.

Yesterday I visited Kathy, a Scottish girl with an outstanding build, who is married to a physical education teacher. We talked about the dress restrictions on women working at the college and the new rumor about wearing head covering. She said it made her so mad that she put on her tightest, shortest shorts and her most negligible halter and walked around the compound three times until she felt better. Afterwards at least three Saudis had to be hospitalized.

October 13, 1976

The Dutch don't appreciate the Germans, which probably goes back to World War II. The acting site manager at my company, Hermann Schenck, is Dutch but very direct and imperative. Loveniers, a Belgian who works under him, was complaining that Schenck's family came from Germany about eight generations back. Loveniers said, "Hermann Schenck approaches a tree. Either the tree falls or Hermann Schenck falls. If a Belgian finds a tree in his path, he goes around it." Loveniers declares he will not work with Germans. I think he is looking for excuses.

Jack told me that they are still switching students around from one group to another to get uniform classes in ability. I overheard Jack tell Mike Mullins, "Hey, thanks for that guy you gave me. All he can do is smile pleasantly and say, 'MY TEACHER.'"

October 16, 1976

I am excited about the trip to Athens we are planning. We got several travel books from Aramco that had chapters on Greece. Our hotel that we will be staying in is a year old and has a stunning view of the Acropolis. I've been reading about what to buy in Athens and, would you believe, one of the best buys is a Greek rug called "Flokati."[234] We asked Alex if he wanted to come or to stay here, thinking we could arrange something with somebody. He wants to come. He will miss three days of school because the holiday—Eid al Adha—starts November 30.

I went swimming today up at the Recreation Center and guess who was there sans family? Four Saudi PhDs: the head of personnel, two department chairmen, and the head of administrative services. I was very angry, since Jack couldn't get in, according to the new regulations, unless I accompanied him. I found out who they were and called the head of the Recreation Center, who is British. He said he also had com-

---

234 Flokati rugs have been made in Greece for over 1500 years. They are made of wool and were originally used by shepherds as a bed, blanket, or clothing.

plaints the day before and took down the names. Some of the names I gave him were repeats of yesterday's violators. It just infuriated me that they should be imposing their standards on Westerners and then breaking the rules themselves.

October 18, 1976

Marcie Wildermann started work today with my company. Marcie is about fifty-seven, with gray hair. There are a lot of new people here this year. Many of them are Dutch and Dutch names are hard to remember. The new Korean tea boy, Mr. Son, speaks less English than his predecessor Mr. Wee (who was unceremoniously shipped back to Korea for nonperformance of his duties and an incredible number of sick days). However, Son wanted to tell me something about Marcie. He pointed towards her office and said, "My mother." Then he pumped his fingers up and down like he was typing, grinning like a cat. I know he wanted to say more, but he lacked the English and I lacked the Korean. She told me later he stood in the door of her office, moved his fingers up and down, and grinned at her. Maybe he thinks she ought to be home in a rocking chair.

Two nights ago I mixed up five gallons of rice, raisin, and white grape juice. Last night I checked on the mix, and it was fermenting to the point that the raisins were moving around. It should come out like a saké or a sherry; I'm not sure which. I threw in the rice for body.

October 22, 1976

Marcie likes working with me at the company. We spend all our lunchtime talking. However, the Palestinian translator and my driver keep saying, "She likes it now but how will she feel when Kanterman comes back?" Kanterman is still on annual leave and will be back either the end of October or the sixth of November. We are hoping his plane gets hijacked.

October 25, 1976

Today I attended a meeting between the Swedish consultants and my company consultants. While discussing personnel changes the assistant site manager, Schenck, mentioned that they now had an English male nurse on site to assist the Korean nurse. I remember seeing a telex sent to Riyadh about a week ago saying, "Please send us an English male nurse to assist our Korean nurse, Mr. Chi. Every day he grows more nervous." Come to think of it, I have noticed Mr. Chi running around the office like a chicken with its head cut off. At the meeting Schenck went on to say that Korean laborers would come to Mr. Chi, who had to decide whether they were sick enough not to work. Later, after work, Mr. Chi would get beaten. Since I am supposed to keep quiet and take the minutes, I didn't ask for details. I assume that if he decided somebody wasn't really sick, the disappointed laborer beat him later. If he decided the laborer was too sick to work, he got beaten by his coworkers who had to take on the additional work. They figure if they got a big, strapping English male nurse, nobody would beat him. Also the Englishman would be living in Al-Khobar and not in the barracks on the site, so he wouldn't be so available for retribution.

I have been indulging in all sorts of travel books about Greece. The food sounds like a great change from what we've been eating, and there are museums, flea markets, beaches, and ruins to see. The temperature will probably be in the forties, and it may be raining some of the time. I suppose I should bring my raincoat or maybe my wool jacket.

October 26, 1976

We have been invited to a Halloween party on Thursday. Jack came up with the ideas for costumes. At first he was going to put on a peasant-style dress of mine, with elasticized empire waist and puff sleeves, shave his moustache, put on a scarf, and go as a pregnant woman. I said if he went as a woman again this year people would start to talk. So he is going as a "50s" greaser, with tattoos, tight jeans, T-shirt with sleeves rolled up, etc. He decided I should go as an Indian wrapped in a blanket, with feathers in my hair and Red Rudy (Alex's stuffed animal) in a papoose cradle on my back. The party is being held at Diana and Michael's, but usually migrates around the compound later in the evening.

Marcie isn't coming into work until noon today because she had to have a gall bladder X-ray at the local hospital. There she heard the UPM doctor complain that he had treated more cases of depression at the university in the past three weeks than he had in his whole medical career. This is due, I suppose, to the additional problems and restrictions this year.

Things are running quite smoothly here without Kanterman, although he'll find that hard to believe. He was so nervous about leaving the assistant site manager in charge that he divided authority among three people; the assistant site manager, the chief of planning, and the quantity surveyor, and gave me strict instructions not to let anything out of the office without being sure all three had seen and approved it. I ignored that, since I don't feel it is my place to sneak around behind the site manager's back to make sure the other two know what he is doing. If Margaret, the Pakistani secretary, had been any other kind of personality, she could have had the job as Kanterman's secretary with bells on. I would prefer working for anybody else in the whole office. But if I had done that, she would have made it her place to boss me around, and I could never take orders from her. Anyway, I'm very glad Marcie is here. Mohammed Sharif, my driver, likes her very much. She is easy to get along with and very warm and friendly.

November 4, 1976

Last week the woman dietitian at the college told us to use the back stairs to the faculty cafeteria, because religious students had been complaining that women were passing them while they prayed. Jack was furious and told her what he thought. I said it wasn't her fault that she got stuck with the job of telling everyone the unpleasant news. He said the college should send out an announcement. The attitude and new rules here make me feel, as a woman, like an emissary of Satan. Then, adding insult to injury, we got a memo written in English describing the establishment of a charity fund at UPM. The Moslems have something like tithing in their religion, except the money goes to the poor.[235] The

---

235   It is customary for a Muslim to give 2.5 percent (1/40) of his income to the poor.

memo asked for faculty members to send in their names and amount to be deducted from their pay each month. Except for the memo on obscene phone calls, everything we've gotten from the university in the past is always in both English and Arabic. This memo was only in English. All the people I've talked to about it say they threw it away, because (1) there should be no need for a charity fund in a country as rich as this, and (2) they have a lot of nerve asking, in English, the non-Moslem faculty members to contribute. Most of the Moslems here are of Arab origin.

An article from the Arab culture editor appeared in the Women's Group Journal stating that Arab women already have the status that women's liberation is seeking. I felt like writing her a note asking her to please stop insulting my intelligence with such rubbish. If women have so much freedom in Saudi Arabia then why do they have to go around with bags over their heads, why can't they drive, or work, or leave the house by themselves? It is good that we are going off to Athens in three weeks or I am sure I would be in jail for assault by December.

Tomorrow is Jack's birthday. I went into Al-Khobar yesterday and bought him a brass plaque, maybe eighteen inches long, of Arabic writing. It means something like "Welcome."

November 8, 1976

I had forgotten how irritating my boss, Kanterman, could be until he came back from vacation. He's as obnoxious and arrogant as ever. I introduced Marcie to him. He was so cold I couldn't believe it, and he made it sound like she would be here only temporarily. He doesn't even say good morning to her when he arrives at the office, and if he wants to see me when I'm in her office, he acts as if she's invisible.

The Dutch are rather cold. There are, however, a few nice ones. Hermann Schenck appears to be on his way out. Kanterman and Schenck locked horns this morning, and a shouting match ensued.

Jack spent most of the day with maintenance trying to get them to cover our roof with a tarp or polyethylene. Finally they came after we went into Al-Khobar shopping and put a ten-foot square canvas on top of the roof and secured it with concrete blocks. Diana, on the other side, says she can't wait for the next storm to see where it will leak after it seeps in under the canvas.

When I came into the house this afternoon Jack told me he had some bad news. A lizard got into the house and he didn't know where it was, but it was last seen on my side of the bed. He thought it might be in my closet. I told him to get me a room in the Al-Gosaibi Hotel for the duration.

November 9, 1976

Last night we had a bad thunderstorm. The power went out about ten minutes into the storm. Our roof leaked terribly with water pouring through the kitchen light fixture like out of a faucet. I accumulated at least a gallon of muddy water in a five-gallon bucket that was put under it. There were leaks in Alex's room, leaks all over the kitchen, and leaks in the living room. In several places it was running down the walls so we couldn't catch the drips. Our neighbors, Diana and Michael Ayer, had seventeen leaks in their half of the house. They came over about eight in the evening with a gas lantern, and we played bridge until ten to a symphony of plink, plank, plonk all over the house. We had to move furniture to get out from under the leaks. This morning the house looks like a typhoon went through it. I went to work anyway. Of course, Alex had to be in the middle of everything. It was a very exciting time for him.

Kanterman is objectionable as ever. Marcie was so upset today about the way he ignores her that she began to cry. There is no excuse for the way he acts. I told Marcie that I can't wait to lay on him that I am taking a week off to go to Athens the end of the month. I bet he does a one hundred and eighty degree turn when he finds out she will be taking my place. Her reaction was "By then it will be too late." Marcie said she doesn't know how I've put up with him for a year. I plan to resign in June when we go back to the US.

November 10, 1976 [Letter by Jack]

Yesterday I spent my spare time on the phone to maintenance trying to get them to do something about the roof. I finally ended up screaming at one guy, "That's the problem with the fucking university.

You can't get anything done until it's a fucking disaster." When I came home from class at nine thirty this morning, our roof was covered with plastic held down on the edges by cinder blocks.

November 11, 1976

Suddenly the college has decided to stop paying tuition for Consulate School students whose parents are Moslem. This affects a lot of families. There are a number of Moslem children with American passports, because they were born in the US. Also some Moslem Arabs here are US citizens. The tuition is three thousand dollars a year per child.[236] Some families have three children making the Consulate School prohibitively expensive. The alternative Saudi schools devote 30 percent of the curriculum to memorizing the Koran. They are segregated by sex, boys' schools and girls' schools. Some of the teachers pinch, hit, and pull hair. There are sometimes two students to a desk. Not to mention no air-conditioning. The girls' schools seem to be even less well equipped than the boys' schools. As a result, American Moslem families are considering leaving.

November 15, 1976

I had six people over Thursday night to play bridge. I made cocktail franks, a walnut cheese ball,[237] and tuna pate recipe from a Boston newspaper. Supposedly this recipe is requested over and over again. It required three cans of tuna, mayo, chopped onion, hot pepper sauce, chili sauce, cream cheese, parsley, and had to be mixed with an electric mixer. The guests consumed about a third of it, and I had at least two cups left over. I have been eating tuna sandwiches all week.

Kanterman is in Riyadh for today, so I don't have any work to do. Last Saturday I told him I was going to Athens for a vacation in two weeks, and his first remark was, "What is that new secretary's name again?" Of course, the personnel person who hired Marcie told him all this. I spelled Marcie's name for him. Then he wanted to know if

---

236 In 2012 dollars, about $12,117 per child.

237 For recipe see "Walnut Cheese Ball," appendix 1.

she could take shorthand. I said she could. After that he asked if I was showing her the office procedure so she could take over while I was away. Then he said good morning to her, and when he came back from lunch, he said good afternoon. Maybe she'll decide to stay after all.

The Arab student Jack has in his English class who can only say "My teacher" is hanging in there. A few weeks ago Jack put a sign on the door when the classroom changed to one across the hall, but the student came late and couldn't read the sign so he missed the class. Last week Jack gave a ten-question quiz to be answered on a standard twenty-five-answer space form. He happened to look at this student's answer sheet and saw him writing answers for questions #13, #14, #15, etc. Jack doesn't expect this guy back next semester.

November 18, 1976

A week from today we leave for Athens.

Jeff came down a couple of nights ago. He brought a red, black, and gray rug with him, a Baluchi (Afghanistan) that he bought in Dammam from a hajji (pilgrim) who was on his way to Mecca. The big Hajj is this month. Millions of pilgrims are on their way to Mecca. A pilgrimage done now is spiritually worth more than one done any other time of the year. The poorer pilgrims bring rugs with them and sell one on the way to get money for the Hajj. And they sell one on the way back to get money for their trip home. All this week pilgrims are passing through Dammam selling rugs there. Maybe I can get Bob Asa and Jack to go look this afternoon, although I don't have any spare money to put into a rug now.

Marcie despises Kanterman. She says she's never seen anyone so immature in her life. He's fifty-three but acts like two. She said she couldn't believe the way he spoke to me the other day. He was really in a tear, and everyone was avoiding him like the plague. I nearly quit that day. When Jack came to pick me up, I was close to tears. Kanterman continuously accuses me of having papers and reports that he's never given to me. Later he finds them on his desk or someone else's. Also he is always insisting that he told me something, when he's never mentioned it. Marcie says if I quit, she'll quit. Mohammed, my driver, says if I quit, he'll walk out too. If I quit I'm afraid I'll be leading a parade out of the office.

Yesterday I asked for my bonus—one thousand dollars—for one year with the company.[238] I left the accounting form in Kanterman's in basket waiting for his signature. Marcie works till 4:00 p.m. and I leave at 2:30 p.m. I told her to check his *out* basket to see if he signed my bonus request. I met Marcie when she got home, and he had signed it. I'll collect that before I go to Greece.

Bob Asa, who is now staying in Al-Khobar for a few days, took us to a Chinese restaurant last night. Bob, who oversees Tremont sales in the Middle East, had a local salesman from Tremont with him. At the next table a single American or British woman was eating with a Saudi couple. The salesman said the woman was a companion to the wife of Prince Turki. The wife has four companions of different nationalities. They have free reign over what goes into the prince's villa and have changed the plumbing in the prince's bathroom three times in one year. Bob told us they've had purple toilet fixtures this year. Tremont has a deluxe five thousand dollar toilet, sink, and tub set that is a very big seller in Saudi Arabia.[239]

Bob has invited us to visit him in Amman, Jordan, for a week in April. He has a luxury apartment there costing one thousand dollars a month, and we could stay with him.[240] In Amman either you have a luxury apartment or you have a tin hovel. We are considering it.

---

238   By 2012 dollars, about $4,039.

239   By 2012 dollars, about $20,195.

240   By 2012 dollars, $1,000 is about $4,039.

CHAPTER 14

Northrop's heavy drinkers, the Swedish party—real scotch, getting homesick, a nuclear physicist flips out, the Egyptian who didn't want to eat chicken pox, death on the road, fun pronouncing "Foking"

November 19, 1976

Today we went to the central mosque in Dammam where the hajjis are selling their carpets to pay for their pilgrimage to Mecca. They were mostly red and black tribal rugs from Afghanistan. Whatever language the hajjis spoke, it wasn't Arabic. They held up their fingers to say the price. I spotted one I loved. It was about two feet by four and half feet, a Baluchi I think, but gray, cream, and black, a tight little carpet, neatly done. An enterprising Saudi who was asking three hundred and fifty dollars for it apparently had purchased the rug from a hajji.[241] Jack refused to consider it since the thing should have cost around one hundred and twenty dollars. It was by far the nicest rug on display. Further down the street some Bedouin women were selling flat-woven, striped rugs sewn together down the middle by hand. One lady wanted about eighty dollars for an attractive beige, purple, and maroon rug. That kind of thing would be nice for a porch.

Now that the temperature is down into the 70s during the day, all the Yemenis are wearing their plastic hats with the fur earmuffs.

November 24, 1976

Alex has taken to doing a very authentic imitation of the call to prayer by cupping his hands over his mouth and going ALLAH

---

241   By 2012 dollars, about $1,414.

HU AK BAARRRRRR! Unfortunately he has been doing this in places like the middle of the main street in Al-Khobar and in the hallway of the student activities building where the faculty cafeteria is located. Jack is afraid he'll get us all in jail because doing that in Saudi Arabia is like wearing the American flag as a bikini at an American Legion Fourth of July picnic.

November 26, 1976 (Postcard from Athens)

Getting out of Saudi Arabia is never easy. I was exhausted. We took a quick tour of Athens today and went to the National Museum. It's been snowing here today and is cold! The Greeks tell us this is most unusual, but you couldn't prove it by me. Near us are Hadrian's Arch[242] and the Temple of Olympian Zeus,[243] which took six centuries to complete and is why there is always a time limit on construction contracts now. However in the next six centuries it fell down and there are only a few columns left.

December 5, 1976

Concerning our trip, you would not believe how the tour's Northrop Corporation contingent drank. They took bus tours of the Peloponnesus and swigged from brown paper sacks. One guy nipped all the way to the airport when we were leaving, drank in the airport lounge, drank on the plane, made passes at the stewardesses, and even at the married women with children. We sat behind two couples from the college: the Filinskis and the Bishops. Betty Bishop bought a rattan carpet beater in Athens. The drunk staggered down the aisle, grabbed Betty Bishop's carpet beater, waved it in the air, and bellowed, "What's this? A Polish fly swatter?" I thought Filinski might deck him, but he showed great tolerance and ignored him.

I made the mistake of buying one of those carpet beaters in Egypt. It was about four feet long, made of bamboo bent into a butterfly

---

242   Constructed in 131 AD by the Athenians in honor of their emperor—Hadrian.

243   Construction started in the sixth century, but was halted for some reason. It was finished by Emperor Hadrian seven hundred years later.

shape. The thing wouldn't fit in my suitcase, and I had to hand carry it all the way back to Dhahran. When I got back I presented it to Myra Anderson as a gift. She thought it was so cool she nailed it on her living room wall. Later I wondered how an Egyptian would react to that. Would it be the same if an Egyptian nailed a Hoover vacuum cleaner to his living room wall?

Athens was clean, fun, good food, but not cheap. Athens' prices compare with those in the States. The streets were not littered, and the bathrooms didn't smell. However, the air pollution was pretty heavy. There wasn't the poverty, like in Cairo, Damascus, or Iran. It was a nice break from Saudi Arabia. Toys were twice as expensive as in Saudi Arabia, so we didn't get anything there for Alex for Christmas. I bought a two-by-five-foot Flokati, a fluffy white wool rug and some presents, mostly edible, for the people I work with: Marcie, my driver, and the Palestinian translator.

When I returned, I discovered that Naarden was not working Saturday and Sunday because of the Moslem holidays.[244] Not only that, but Marcie told me Kanterman hurt his bad knee refereeing a soccer match between the Dutch and Koreans and will probably have to go to Holland for surgery for six weeks! The whole time I was in Athens all I could think of was, "How can I go back to that job?"

December 12, 1976

In the good news department, Kanterman told me last Wednesday that he is being transferred to Riyadh in January. His knee surgery isn't possible till January 20 so he didn't leave today as promised. Hermann Schenck, who recently had been going over the edge, made the world's fastest recovery from a nervous breakdown when he learned Kanterman had to go to Amsterdam for surgery. For a man who was crying over everything and was so depressed that he was going to be transferred back to Holland, he pulled himself together remarkably— miraculously—as soon as he found out he was to be in charge. Now he is his old Teutonic self, marching around, shouting imperiously, and demanding to know when people got to work. I can only surmise from

244   Eid al Adha.

all of this that his problem was either (1) Kanterman, or (2) not being the boss. However there will be a replacement for Kanterman. Hermann Schenck won't get to run things forever.

Yesterday Kanterman told me at 9:30 a.m. to inform four people that there was a meeting at 2:15 p.m. As they were all in the field, I put notes in their mailboxes. At 2:10 p.m. he limped down the hall and asked me if I remembered to tell the four about the meeting. I said I wrote them all notes immediately. In his best snotty tone, he inquired, "And did you see that they read them?" I said, "NO." He went, "Tch, tch, tch," and left. I steamed about that for a while. He can't leave soon enough for me.

December 16, 1976 [Letter by Jack]

The holiday season has begun. We have a tree and put some lights up, and everyone is inviting us to parties, but we really miss the States this year and Maralyn is thinking more and more of the house we bought in New Hampshire. At most we will spend one more year here and then back to the States for a while, regardless of finances and job situation. We might come back here again, but right now we're very tired of Saudi Arabia. We realize that the States has its problems, but new problems are easier to bear. We think of home a lot lately, much more than before.

[Letter continued by Maralyn]

Our car has something wrong with it. Actually, a lot. Small details. Shoddy workmanship. Brazilian made. One night Jack pulled into the yard and went to turn off the lights. He shoved the rocker switch right through the dashboard. Unfortunately the lights were still ON. He had to find a flashlight, get down on the floor, and grope around trying to locate the missing part so he could turn the lights OFF before the battery went dead. It took him twenty minutes before he succeeded. He's told me to keep my mouth shut about what's wrong with the car because when we try to sell it, all my complaints will come back to haunt us. Right now there is no power in second gear and we don't have any idea why. Our Egyptian friend Husein has been in Cairo. He came back today. We have Husein's car, but Jack is afraid of having an accident with it so he won't take it anyplace. I'll get Husein to take me to the man who worked on the engine once before. He did a good job. Husein will translate for us.

December 16, 1976

Last night we went to a party held by the Swedish company that supervises my company. They served real scotch. Some of the Swedish staff performed skits, and a husband and wife team sang English folk songs between acts. They were excellent. Marcie and Fritz were there and really enjoyed themselves. It was the best live entertainment I've seen in Saudi Arabia. And wouldn't you know it, Kanterman had to go to the bathroom in the middle of the show, and the only way he could get to the john was to go across the stage. I am feeling slightly hung over from last night. I had three scotches in four hours, and it was too much. I'm not used to the real stuff.

Kanterman's knee seems to be getting better. He has been stumping up and down the hall with a cane. However, they are transferring him to Riyadh sometime in January. Rumor has it the new manager will be coming from Kuwait.

Last night Celia, an English girl, came over to me while I was at the bazaar with Marcie and said, "Did you used to work with a girl named Margaret?" I said I did, and the English girl said, "Well, she has a message for you." Marcie interrupted and said, "What is it? Drop dead?" because Marcie knew what went on when Margaret and I worked together. Celia informed us that Margaret wanted me to know that she is now working for Northrop. I almost bit off my tongue trying to keep my mouth shut and not ask any questions. I figured in a month Celia would be telling ME all about Margaret. Anyway, Celia didn't pick up on Marcie's comment.

December 20, 1976

We managed to get to customs in Dammam to pick up two Christmas packages from the States: Alex's space helmet and a package marked "puzzles." What confusion. The college had over one hundred packages that nobody had bothered to pick up. A man from the purchasing department is supposed to clear airmail packages through customs. Apparently he had not been doing his job because one package was mailed the fifteenth of October. It is typical of the college administration to take so little interest in whether or not anyone gets Christmas packages in time for Christmas. The word "morale" is not in their vocabulary. If it hadn't been for my driver, I wouldn't have my packages either. I managed to recall sixteen names of college people I had seen while sorting through the dusty piles of parcels. I called them all to tell them they had something at the customs building in Dammam. They could contact either purchasing or administrative services to ask for their stuff. I imagine the college didn't appreciate it very much when they started getting calls on Saturday morning.

Yesterday our neighbors, the Priests, full of Christmas cheer, came trekking in our back door at half past five in the afternoon while I was decorating Christmas cookies. She carried a big long present for Alex, and Fred had a bottle wrapped in foil for us. I was afraid Alex would burst a blood vessel. She put Alex's gift under the tree. Alex was having a nervous breakdown looking at it. After they left he came into the kitchen and made an effort at pleading temporary insanity BEFORE the fact, that is, "Pretty soon if I keep looking at that present I'm afraid I might run over and tear all the paper off!" I advised him he'd better control himself. Later after he went to bed, Jack and I checked it by opening a corner of the paper. Another neighbor had bought him a Polaris submarine kit, and this box was the same size. The printing on the box was in German, but I think it might be a truck. We may yet have to hide the present on him, since it has become such an obsession and may cause him to run amuck or something.

Mrs. Priest also gave him a white, felt Snoopy Christmas tree ornament. Snoopy is wearing a gutra, the red-and-white, quintessentially Saudi Arabian, checkered head cloth. Mrs. Priest told me her friend who makes them was discouraged from selling them at Aramco's Christmas bazaar. The natives frown on such frivolity. First they don't like dogs. Secondly putting a gutra on a dog is committing an obscenity on their native dress. I thought it was adorable. Alex's judgment consisted of, "I think it's kind of silly."

I went to Arabic class last night. The first time in a week and a half. Wouldn't you know he gave a quiz. I think I must have scored somewhere between zero and forty. That class is driving me nuts; mostly it's the people in it. There is a German lady named Gerda who giggles shrilly and hysterically every time she makes a mistake. Then there is a middle-aged, goateed professor who over pronounces everything and is going to suffer a collapsed lung someday from aspirating his H's. Behind me is a very gay physics professor, dressed to the nines, who giggles like the German lady and recites as if he were trying out for a part on Broadway. There are five Pakistanis in the class, one of whom picks at his nose for the whole hour and thirty minutes. Of course there is also the perennial quota of show-offs who like to ask questions to let the rest of the class in on how brilliant they are, or how much Arabic they already know. I can't imagine anything worse than trying to instruct a class full of PhDs in anything. Their egos are enormous and correcting them is like walking on cracked eggs. Also I have an attention span of forty-five minutes, and the class runs forty-five minutes over that.

December 21, 1976

Jack and I went into Al-Khobar last night to look for something for me for Christmas. Everything I wanted was either sold out, hasn't come in because of the embargo on air freight (too much freight piling up in the warehouses), or is expected within a couple of days. I think he'll give me money to buy something later.

A nuclear physicist in the Physics Department flipped out last week. We were at a dinner party with him Thursday night at John Dakin's house. The physicist drank steadily the whole evening. We drove him home. Later we learned he visited somebody else and drank the rest of the night. The next morning he was with John, talking of committing suicide. Then he tried jumping in front of several Mercedes diesel trucks while John tried to stop him. At one point the Arab driver of one truck stopped and wanted to call the police to prosecute. He was talked out of it. John and two other faculty members took the physicist to his apartment where they stayed with him trying to keep him from harming himself. He turned violent and cut all the furniture into little pieces. They called the college doctors, but none of them would touch the case. Then the college sent an ambulance to take him to an Al-Khobar hospital. None of the three hospitals would take him. Then they tried Aramco hospital, who also refused until John said he would have to be turned over to the authorities. He was American and Aramco didn't want that to happen. The Aramco doctors put him in a straitjacket and shot him full of tranquilizers. As of last night he had calmed down and wanted to remain in Saudi Arabia. However, the rector at UPM is furious, because he had enough alcohol in his blood to deck a horse. The latest rumor is that they will send a UPM doctor back to the States with him. Some people have begun questioning the thoroughness of the Personnel Department in screening prospective faculty members. The physicist admitted to having been institutionalized in the States before coming to Dhahran. There are absolutely no facilities for psychiatric cases here. I think Aramco has a psychiatrist, but his caseload is probably all neurotic Aramco wives and disturbed kids.

Jeff stopped by last night, and I made mulled wine and served Christmas cookies. He's coming to the house for Christmas dinner along with another bachelor from Jack's department and the Ayers and the Greens.

We bought a poinsettia from a small florist shop in Al-Khobar. Oddly enough, this florist has a side business in crèches made in Bethlehem and carved from olive wood. They cost a fortune, but are quite cheap if one happens to be in Jordan. If we get to Amman next spring I may get one. You'd think the Saudis would ban these Christian symbols.

Marcie heard a rumor that the government was planning to stop all foreign wives from working. But it's kind of hard to prove who's working, and it's hard to enforce. Probably I can last until June.

Kanterman expects to be gone by mid-January to his new job in Riyadh. His knee has improved to the point where he no longer requires an operation in Holland. He doesn't have to use the cane anymore. As I mentioned in an earlier letter, Hermann Schenck made a miraculous recovery from his nervous breakdown when he heard Kanterman was going to leave the site. He's second in command. The company medical officer, Dr. Hendrik, recommended that Schenck be sent to Holland for treatment of his nervous condition. He also recommended that Kanterman have surgery on his knee. I think Dr. Hendrik might be selling newspapers in Amsterdam by January.

December 27, 1976

My Christmas dinner party went well. There were two babies, one nine months and the other three weeks. Both cried either together or in shifts in the bedroom where we had put the television for Alex to watch. He kept coming out and complaining that the babies were giving him a headache.

Alex received a box of rubber dinosaurs for Christmas. He had dinosaur wars all last night on the dining table. They are German made and names of each are printed on the legs in German, "urvogel" for example. We also gave him a microscope and a walkie-talkie. Neal got a walkie-talkie, too.

The Priests gave Alex a German-made tractor and trailer. Tools were enclosed so that can be taken apart and reassembled. Unfortunately the Ayers gave Alex a complex Polaris submarine kit that Jack is going to have to assemble. Jack does not want to get involved, not that I blame him.

Jack bought me a Saudi gold piece, set in a very plain frame. Most of the frames here are quite ornate or else in horrible taste, sun burst setting, etc. This holder is the bare necessity and displays the beauty of the coin with good effect. The face of the coin is covered with fine Arabic writing and in the center is the crossed palms and sword symbol of Saudi Arabia. The coin is twenty-two karat gold and was used as currency at one time in Saudi Arabia. Aramco used to pay their employees with little bags of these gold pieces. He also bought me a bright purple outdoor grill. The grill was a surprise, but I knew about the coin and was with him when he chose it. Jack had hidden the grill in the trunk of the car. I gave him a brass hanging lamp, which I had wired at the local electrical shop. They did a most peculiar job. Probably when we get back to the States, I'll have it rewired.

Jeff Crossley gave all of us Christmas gifts. He gave me a bottle of "4711," which I like.[245] Jack got two boxes of Dutch cigars. Alex got some metal airplanes.

Jack didn't have Christmas off because the weekend here is Thursday and Friday. His classes were from half past seven to half past nine in the morning and from one to two in the afternoon on Saturday. However, when the students indicated they wouldn't show up on Saturday, he didn't show up either. Christian holidays are completely ignored in Saudi Arabia, and it's business as usual. Countries like Bahrain recognize it as a holiday.

December 30, 1976

Alex has chicken pox. The college pediatrician confirmed it. Night before last Husein, our Egyptian friend who has been on leave for three months, stopped by to visit and to bring us a Christmas present. Jack asked, "Did you have chicken pox?" and Husein replied apologetically, "Thanks, but I already ate." With the help of an English-Arabic dictionary, we managed to sort that out. He brought me five meters of navy Egyptian wool, very nice material. But five meters is enough to slip cover the living room with drapes to match. I don't know what to do with it all. A long skirt and matching jacket maybe? He brought Alex a cowbell from Munich, which impressed Alex not at all. But I hung it on the front door so I can hear people come in. Our back door has a chain of six camel bells. People tend to sneak in the back door more than the front. So the more the warier.

December 31, 1976

Our sitter for New Year's Eve has the flu, and Alex has the chicken pox. We've been invited to two parties, one at Naarden and one in the other compound. I'm not unhappy about not going. We may sneak over to the other compound after Alex goes to sleep.

---

245 4711 (pronounced "forty-seven eleven") is an eau de cologne originally made by a French friar who moved to Koln, Germany. The name is from the street number of the Muelhens perfumery that marketed the scent in 1794. The scent is for both men and women. It is a blend of sandalwood oils and citrus fruits.

The weather has been unseasonably warm. Year round good weather is terribly dull. Mrs. Priest was complaining about the weather this morning. She said that she met Ed Peattie in Al-Khobar yesterday. He cheerily said, "Isn't this weather marvelous?" She remarked, "He'd say that if hell reached up and grabbed him."

Everyone has the flu. I was praying for a wild rainstorm to wash the dust off everything. It hasn't rained since early November, when we had forty leaks and the crew from housing rushed up on our roof (I use the term loosely; nobody in this country rushes anywhere) and spread out sheets of polyethylene. It sounded like they were rehearsing for a variety show up there. Paint flaked off all over the living room. I was expecting a Yemeni on my coffee table momentarily. Later that day it began to rain again. The house still smells soggy from the soaking it got. This week the crew appeared to scrape tarpaper off our roof. I presume they intend to tar the roof, but the tarring machine is still over on the other side of the compound, so why the rush to scrape ours is beyond me.

It rained quite hard last night. The roof leaked merrily in the bathroom but otherwise the plastic tarps seem to be effective. I've been ironing most of the afternoon and *trying* to cook.

January 3, 1977

My typewriter at work finally went. It was going tick tick tick when Alexander Gordon decided he could fix it. Always be suspicious when somebody's idea of fixing something involves pulling, pushing, prodding, or kicking. When Gordon got through, it went tick-tick, tick-tick, tick-tick. So I got Nasser, the Naarden printer and resident fix-it man, to help. Nasser got the typewriter apart, held up a tiny screw, grunted, "Screw no good. I go garage, find new screw." I must admit I had my doubts Nasser would find a replacement for my typewriter screw in a place where they service bulldozers, cranes, and diesel trucks. However, Nasser did find a screw, and when he had reassembled the typewriter, the noise stopped. Unfortunately the rewind wheel for the ribbon no longer works. Now I am waiting for a service representative from the local IBM distributor to come and probably do worse than Nasser. Their motto should be "Sales but No Service."

Finally after ten months of complaining, the college has seen fit to re-tar our roof. Now we have blobs of tar all over both steps, on the side of the house, and in the yard, not to mention great sheets of plastic, concrete blocks, flora, fauna, detritus, and debris from fourteen Yemenis lunching in the backyard. When they all climb on the roof, it sounds like they are either practicing judo throws or rehearsing for a minstrel show.

January 10, 1977

I made my mother's recipe for hermits last night.[246] They were delicious.

January 12, 1977

Yesterday on the way to Al-Khobar Jack thought his Volkswagen's directionals weren't working. He pulled at the switch, and it came off in his hand. Fancying himself quite the home mechanic, subcategory car electrician, he decided to try to fix it. While he was poking around under the dashboard, he blew a fuse three inches from the end of his nose and scared the daylights out of himself. I might note that this is the fourth time he's fooled around with the car's electrical system. However this is the lowest number of fuses he's blown while doing so. Maybe things are looking up. I used to have a hepazootie (as my neighbor Mrs. Priest would say) every time Jack headed for the car with a screwdriver. Now I just laugh at him. I can't drive it, anyway. Then, following the inevitable disaster, he usually goes into a deep depression and threatens to turn to drink.

My boss, Kanterman, had a falling out with the head office in Riyadh. He is on his way to Riyadh this weekend to hold a showdown. There is a distinct possibility he may quit the company. At any rate he's being transferred out of this site office to Riyadh at the end of the month, no matter what. The funny thing is that as arrogant and stupid as he can be, they're nailing him on something he was 100 percent correct about. There is no justice. Well there is, but it's a peculiar kind of justice.

---

246   For recipe see "Soft Hermits," appendix 1.

January 14, 1977

At work I met an engineer from an American construction company. He's been here since March. His firm is in road construction. He told me about the heavy equipment accidents he has witnessed. Two graders were in the middle of the desert preparing a road base. They had a head-on collision. Both drivers disappeared over the dunes never to be heard from again. He wondered how anyone could have a head-on collision in the middle of the desert, especially in two lumbering graders. Another accident involved a line of dump trucks. One stopped suddenly, and the other four folded into each other.

We have to go into town for food today or tomorrow. This place is driving us nuts. There was a head-on collision between two Mercedes dump trucks last month. Marcie passed the accident when the body was still in one of them. I don't know how they got it out. A couple years ago, an oil tanker truck rolled over onto a Japanese sedan with six people in it. The authorities brought in excavating equipment and buried the car, bodies and all, at the side of the road, rather than try to extricate the victims. I would estimate the accident rate here to be ten times the US rate.[247] Jack's car has been hit twice, and both times his car wasn't moving. We now have some chrome off the front and a dent in the back. A local Saudi who works for Naarden was driving to Hofuf, a three-hour trip south, in October with his best friend, the friend's wife, and four of the guy's kids in the back. He was doing one hundred or better when the car went off the road and overturned several times. The wife and two kids were killed, the friend had a concussion, the Saudi had a cast on his foot for a month, and the other two kids were hospitalized. The friend declined to press charges. However this was the Saudi's eighth accident, according to another guy in the office. I don't know how he's driving now. Even if the friend does not press charges, the Saudi may be serving a jail sentence because there were fatalities.

---

247   Traffic accidents were the leading cause of deaths in Saudi Arabia in 2011 and probably was in 1977 as well.

January 19, 1977

Kanterman cleaned out his desk today. The new guy looks like he was shot out of a cannon. Unkempt to say the least. His name is Foking (pronounced "Fucking"), and this has the whole place in stitches. Kanterman took him around and introduced him to everyone. When they got to the materials lab, Tom Spender, the very British and very black lab engineer, had had no advance warning of the new site manager's name. As soon as he was introduced, Tom went to shake his hand, "Good morning, Mr. GAFFAW! GAFFAW! GAFFAW!" After I heard what had happened, I told him that he had wasted no time getting on the new manager's black list. My driver, Mohammed, says he's never going to be able to call Mr. Foking by his real name. Everybody claims they can't say the name without smiling, so he'll probably be "Mr. Manager" or "Sir" to everyone. His name doesn't carry the same impact in Dutch as it does in English, but apparently all the Dutch people know what the English meaning is and they too think it is very funny.

This guy's previous job was with a different company in Nigeria where he supervised construction of a brewery. I suppose for the Saudis that could be compared to having been the manager of a pig farm in terms of previous experience. Anyway, obnoxious and arrogant as Kanterman can be, I actually felt sorry for him as he cleaned out his office and made room for the new man. Mr. Foking has said very little so far, which impresses me more than if he were shooting his mouth off about the job the first day.

That sycophantic Korean coffee boy, Mr. Son, who always broke his neck to carry Kanterman's briefcase to the office, didn't lift a finger to help him carry his gear to the car. But he took one look in the conference room yesterday during a meeting, saw that the new site manager, Mr. Foking, smoked, and tore in with an ashtray and a coaster.

Kanterman got five smoke bombs in the mail yesterday. They look like nine-inch tubes, the kind decorative matches come in. They weren't gifts from his detractors. When air-conditioning ducts are tested, they use smoke bombs.

Jack and I sent a maintenance slip requesting that the two sixteen-foot oleander bushes in front of our picture window be trimmed so we could get more light in the living room. Yesterday afternoon I came home from work and saw that the gardeners had been working in the yard. They did such a subtle, delicate, skilled pruning job. They hacked off the top thirteen feet of each bush. We do get more light.

Just put the air-conditioning on. Our house is very damp. We had a spell of cold weather. A week ago Saturday the temperature dropped to an unbelievable thirty-six degrees at night. In the morning, about quarter to seven, it was forty by our thermometer.

One of the Korean administrators at our site, Mr. Lee, brought Kanterman a Korea Oil Company calendar with lovely Korean watercolors on it. I've had the hots for that calendar since it arrived. Unfortunately I also made it very obvious. Kanterman hinted that it might go to me when he left. But now Mr. Foking is in the office and his desk faces it. If it disappears everyone will know who took it. My driver, Mohammed, says he's going to steal it for me. That doesn't help. I'll be suspected anyway. And I'm a terrible liar.

January 23, 1977

We acquired a batch of *Playboy* magazines from someone who drove into Saudi Arabia and didn't want to deal with the problem of disposing of them when they left the country last June. The problem now is hiding them from Alex and his friends.

Yesterday Alex and Neal came tearing into the house:

> ALEX: You would not believe what we just saw!
> ME: What?
> ALEX: A Saudi showing his bum!
> ME: What?
> ALEX: And he was doing pooh!
> ME: Oh yeah?
> ALEX: And he pulled his pants up before he was even finished and it was this long! (Spreads arms to show about thirty-six inches)

I figured that Neal and Alex came bursting around the compound wall and spoiled his concentration. I told Marcie, who has been here twelve years. She said, "Hasn't he seen that before? They do it on my lawn all the time! That's why I never go out there." But she has lovely green grass.

Two Royal Air Force officers stopped in here. It was lunch hour, and only Marcie and I were in the office. They had a big problem. They parked their car in a field, and the excavator from Naarden dug a trench all around it. Now they want their vehicle. Naturally we were no help. They had come up with the idea of finding two boards and bridging the gap with them. I sent them to the Korean mess hall and they haven't returned.

Headquarters in Riyadh sent Mr. van Hout to be assistant site manager. Hermann Schenck, currently holding the title of assistant site manager, didn't have a clue he was to be replaced by van Hout and would be demoted to construction manager (a kind of limitation of authority). Now Schenck has been out sick for three days. Everyone has been going around saying, "It's nervous breakdown time." Van Hout speaks no English and looks like a Spanish dancer.

CHAPTER 15

The pilgrim from Ireland, farewell to Kanterman, swiping the Korean calendar, the super prompt Saudi driver, the magic coffee cups that change color, the suicidal bisexual Englishman, Mr. Foking reframes complaints, Saudi Boy Scouts

January 29, 1977

I tried a cinnamon yogurt pancake recipe last night.[248] It turned out well.

Mr. Foking made an emergency trip to Riyadh to see the company doctor. It seems he has suffered from dysentery ever since he left Nigeria. And the dead have risen. Hermann Schenck appeared this morning. He's been out sick at least a week, ever since van Hout arrived. Perhaps the idea of the top man being out of commission for a while appealed to him. But he's hardly his old self. In fact, sitting at the desk, he looks like somebody stuffed him.

Kanterman's farewell party is this Thursday night. They plan to give him a tape recorder as a gift. Jack doesn't want to go. I do since they always have delicious Indonesian hors d'oeuvres. The invitations to the party indicated, "Dress formal." I asked what this meant, exactly, and somebody said it means to wear socks.

Recently I had conversations with two couples, British and American, who have lived overseas for a long time. They thought it gets in one's blood. Both had tried going home to live, and it didn't work out. I wonder it if will be that way with us.

---

248   For recipe see "Cinnamon Yogurt Pancakes," appendix 1.

February 4, 1977

Kanterman had his farewell party last night. He greeted me like a long lost relative, kissed me on both cheeks, even. Then he asked me to dance twice, put his arm around me and said he hoped we wouldn't lose touch. I hope nobody thought something was going on.

They had fantastic food, as usual. Indonesian specialties like saté (shish kebab with peanut sauce), a hors d'oeuvres resembling triangular egg roll, cold meats, stuffed eggs, raw vegetables, etc. And real scotch plus the sidiqui. I had two scotches and this morning regretted the second one. Last time I had three real scotches and regretted the whole evening.

Jack is sorry he ate three Indonesian egg rolls at the party last night. I'm sorry we didn't stay later, so I could eat more.

There hasn't been much going on at work. The new manager, Mr. Foking, hasn't gotten hold of things yet. But seven guys were canned last Wednesday. Rumor has it some hanky-panky was going on, but you could have fooled me. I'm waiting—nervously—for them to decide that two secretaries are one too many.

February 6, 1977

Jack says he is going to take me to the Marroush Restaurant for our anniversary. It falls on a Thursday, which is like a Saturday in the States. The Marroush is a Lebanese restaurant, and the food is pretty good.

Marcie was reading over some government statistics on participants in the Hajj (pilgrimage). She told me there was one pilgrim from Ireland and she's bound and determined to find out who it was. She still has relatives in Ireland.

Just after Mr. Foking got back from lunch, he went into Marcie's office and told her he had orders from Riyadh to cut back on staff. Since they really didn't need two secretaries and she came after I did, they were going to have to let her go. I think she's going to work out the month. I felt like somebody punched me. The administrator, van der Waal, who hired her went into Foking's office and told him there was too much work for one secretary. Foking said, "Well, the one we've got is going to have to work all the harder!" Sounds like he's going to be fun. Marcie was upset about it, but not crushed. I'm going to miss her terribly. The quantity surveyor, Alexander Gordon, was upset about it—his department generates most of the typing. He said he would recommend that Marcie be kept on part-time, which she is willing to do.

My driver, Mohammed, has been so upset about the seven people who got fired a week ago and Marcie's firing on Sunday that he went to Mr. Foking and demanded his vacation, immediately. He's leaving the sixteenth of February and will go to Shiraz for a month where he has family.[249] I don't know how I am going to get to and from work. The administrator here, van der Waal, who should be arranging such things is gone three quarters of the day. He has a girlfriend at Aramco that he's sharing with the native broker and, rumor has it, a Bedouin contractor as well.

I doubt that Mr. Foking will agree to Marcie working part-time. She's through February 23.

I finally took the Korean calendar that I had the hots for. After Kanterman left, I slipped into the office one day and swiped it, putting up a Korean calendar of photographs in its place. Mr. Foking must have assumed Kanterman took it.

February 13, 1977

It turns out that Mr. Foking has a nineteen-year-old daughter who just arrived last night. As soon as she gets used to the place, she will probably be looking for employment. I can't wait to see how that develops.

A close friend in administration told us Jack is being offered an 8 percent raise to sign a new contract. This person saw all the contracts and tells us 8 percent is the maximum increase. Jack is not happy and neither am I. The college is showing no sign of doing anything about the US tax situation whereas all other organizations here will take care of the tax for their employees.

I was right. Mr. Foking informed me that he didn't think we should keep Marcie part-time. I feel like quitting and leaving them with their problems.

---

249   Shiraz is a city in Iran.

February 19, 1977

It's almost nine o'clock, and that horse's neck of an administrator has forgotten to arrange transportation for Marcie and me this morning. Mohammed, the usual driver, is now in Shiraz and we have no regularly scheduled ride. A Korean finally came to pick us up, Mr. Son. That's a first. Usually the drivers are Arab.

I found a recipe for slow-cook meatballs that calls for cardamom. Cardamom is a very distinctive spice. The Saudis use lots of it in their coffee. Sometimes as much as 50 percent. Mohammed, my driver, bought a kilo of cardamom pods to take to his family in Shiraz. They cost him almost forty-five dollars.[250] It is supposed to be the second most costly spice, saffron being first. Arab coffee is more like a medicinal tea made with very lightly roasted coffee beans in a blend of three parts beans and one part cardamom. Bayouni's, the coffee shop where we buy a blend of half Italian and half American roasts, reeks of cardamom. For our coffee, we grind French roast beans in a small French coffee grinder. A kilo (2.2 lbs.) of coffee here is about fifteen dollars now. Most of the beans come from Africa—Ethiopia, Uganda, Yemen. I put cream in it. We can get tinned Danish cream here. It's very strange. And any resemblance between canned and fresh cream is purely on the label.

February 20, 1977

Jack and I went to the Marroush on our anniversary. I had my usual tabbouleh and shish taouk—marinated chicken shish kebab. Jack boldly ordered the special, which turned out to be a mound of rice with chicken on top, a bowl of melokhia in broth (an Egyptian vegetable something like chopped spinach),[251] a bowl of vinegar, oil, and chopped onion, and a bowl of Arab bread squares toasted. We never did find out how one eats it, since the waiter disappeared after he served it. Jack ate some of my shish taouk. I thought it was underdone. But the light was so dim I couldn't tell. For dessert I ate what came with Jack's special,

---

250   In 2012 dollars, $45 is about $171.

251   Often called "Egyptian herb soup."

custard with chopped pistachios on top and burnt sugar syrup. It was very good. He ordered chocolate ice cream. Less than twenty-four hours later, we both had bad cases of diarrhea. I went to work yesterday morning, but Jack canceled classes. My options were either to stay home and try to get in the bathroom with Jack in there all the time or go to work where only Marcie and I use the ladies' room—van der Waal was off at Aramco. Fortunately I didn't have any meetings to attend. I think I'm okay now. We figure it was the shish taouk, since we both ate it. Normally I'd blame the tabbouleh, since it is raw, but Jack didn't eat any of it.

Marcie's last day is Wednesday. Today she said she never laughed so much at a job as she did at this one. We're always snickering and giggling over some of the English that goes through here. The setting has a lot to do with the humor. The Dutch have no sense of humor at all. Ever since Marcie learned that Mr. Foking has a nineteen-year-old daughter, she's convinced he's going to bring "Brunhilde" in to replace her.

February 24, 1977

Contracts came out and our salary increase at the college was 8 percent, as expected. We are very undecided about what to do. We have until March 1 to decide. They don't give us much time. One of the overriding factors is the official move against women working in the kingdom. Supposedly the religious leaders have inspired it, and nobody can oppose them.[252] We're afraid to sign up for another year and then find out that I won't be able to work. Today I heard that the fine was two thousand riyals per day per woman and that the government has said the woman, not the company she worked for, must pay it. However, my company has not received a letter yet.

My driver is still in Shiraz, and the latest driver, Abdullah, ought to be in the *Guinness Book of Records* as the world's most prompt Saudi. I have actually been getting to work EARLY as a result and have been observed flying out of the house eating an English muffin with one hand and zipping up my skirt with the other. This guy has got to go.

---

252   The Wahhabis (ultraconservative Muslims) were exerting their influence over the kingdom.

He sits out there behind the shrubbery in a company car, blowing his horn. With all the horn blowing that goes on in this country, I'm supposed to recognize his? Mohammed used to pull up about 7:30 a.m., and if I objected to being fifteen minutes late in arriving, he'd tell me, "These people don't care." (They do, with a passion.)

Another problem with Abdullah is that he doesn't speak English, so I have to use my pidgin Arabic on him. Because I can toss off a few words in Arabic, he thinks I'm fluent and makes comments about the other drivers and observations about the company in Arabic. Once in a while I pick up "majnoon," which means "crazy." He said something about a camel this morning, "howar," but I didn't catch the rest of it. However, I kept looking hopefully out the window expecting a herd of them. There weren't any.

Anyway Mohammed will be back soon, and Abdullah will probably retire and work on the Saudi Railroad where his gift for promptness will really be appreciated.

Marcie gave me six cups and saucers for my anniversary gift. She wanted to buy brown and tan striped ones to match the four I already have, but the store was all out. So she got the blue striped cups. At work in the tea kitchen there are twenty brown and tan striped ones that match the four I have at home. Marcie convinced me to ask Dawood, the purchasing agent, to let me swap. I had planned to switch them one at a time. Marcie figured it would be better to do it all at once. Mr. Son, the Korean tea boy, always locks the kitchen at lunchtime, so the next morning I brought in a cardboard box with the six cups and saucers. Dawood didn't come in all morning, so I decided to swap them without his permission. Halfway through lunchtime I passed by the kitchen door and noticed that Mr. Son had forgotten to lock it. I raced down with my box of cups and made the exchange. Marcie said she could hear the clanking and chinking of crockery all over the building. I taped up the box—that now contained all brown and tan striped cups—and put it in Marcie's office on top of her filing cabinet. At one o'clock Mr. Son came back. Fortunately he speaks very little English, but he was plainly disturbed. He nabbed me as I came down the hall on an errand and led me into the kitchen. He pointed to the cups, showing me one of the brown cups and saucers and then pointing to the blue. I observed that the blue were lovely. That wasn't what he wanted to hear. He kept indicating he was puzzled. I grabbed a box of TIDE and suggested that maybe his detergent caused the color change. He finally gave up on me. Later I told Marcie I must have been pretty dumb to think Mr. Son wouldn't notice six blue cups. All he does all day is wash them and serve tea in them. Apparently my stupid act convinced him of my innocence, and he went down the hall to confront Marcie. He noticed the box on her filing cabinet. She pretended ignorance, but Mr. Son wasn't buying that. Twice more that afternoon he appeared accusingly in front of her. At half past two, when we were about to leave, I felt uneasy about marching past the kitchen holding the box full of dishes, so I asked the Arab driver, Abdullah, to get the box and take it to his car while I sent Mr. Son to another building to deliver a letter. Something got lost in the translation, and by the time Abdullah understood what I wanted him to do, Mr. Son was back and on his way into Marcie's office. At that point if he had any doubts before, they vanished upon seeing the driver leave with the telltale box. The next morning Marcie told Mr. Son that Wednesday would be her last day. Mr. Son raised his eyes heavenward with a knowing Oriental "AHAAAA!" Marcie said, "He thinks I got fired for switching the crockery."

February 26, 1977

First of all I have some good news: Jack resigned. As rumored, the increase was only 8 percent. The dean gave inflation and the new US tax laws as a reason. I don't know where we will be next year, but it won't be at UPM. I feel like one hundred pounds fell from my shoulders. It's time for a change. Our car is falling apart, our house is falling apart, Jack's department is falling apart, and the country is becoming more conservative every day. Jack did say in his resignation letter that if the university took any positive significant action to increase the faculty benefits (higher salary, paying part or all of our US taxes, better housing, etc.) we would be willing to reconsider. However, the biggest problem was one we couldn't mention in the letter and that is the recent conservative trend against women working in the kingdom, except nurses and teachers. If I'm not working, our income and tax exemption is almost cut in half. The factor that pushed us into our decision to resign was the tax law and the college offering a contract with an increase of only 8 percent. There is a 40 percent inflation rate in the kingdom.

Now I'm trying to decide what to sell and what to ship.

The local English language bookstore was almost sold out last week. All the Harold Robbins novels and the lurid romances are gone, and his stocks are reduced to comic books and censored *Time* magazines.[253]

March 3, 1977

Marcie has been gone over a week now. Mr. Foking has one of his daughters working at the clinic. A Korean was removed to make room for her. Van der Waal is having fits because Foking told him he wants to bring in either his other daughter or his wife, whom Marcie refers to as "Maxine the Truck Driver," to work in the office. Marcie suspected this all along, but I thought she was being prematurely judgmental because he had fired her.

We went to the Clerons' for supper. They had a black American couple there from Northrop. I was surprised. For a long time the Saudi government wouldn't let in black Americans. He is a computer analyst. He said people are always taking him for a native and speaking to him in Arabic.

There was an attempted suicide last week, an Englishman in Jack's department. Smedly, the Englishman, had been at UPM for five years. First he took twenty-four Valium and drank a quart of the local distilled product. Then he locked himself in his bedroom with the gas on. Meanwhile he telephoned the rector to say he was being persecuted. They came and took him away. Smedly was locked in Aramco hospital's padded room. He was booked onto a British Airways flight out Thursday morning, accompanied by another Britisher. British Airways got wind of the fact that he tried to kill himself and refused to take him without a physician along. Meanwhile Smedly claimed the whole thing was a misunderstanding, and he didn't really try to kill himself.

---

253   Harold Robbins (1916–1997) was an American author, published over twenty novels, including *The Carpetbaggers*, *The Dream Merchants*, and *The Raiders*.

Smedly is bisexual, flamboyant, and a heavy drinker. This is such a difficult living situation for stable personalities, let along marginal ones. Jack's chairman had been recommending that they not renew Smedly's contract for the past two years. Not that the administration paid any attention.

One female IRS representative came from the Teheran regional office to speak at the college about the new tax law.[254] It was a hot session. The law is ridiculous, and people's anger was directed at the IRS rep. I asked Jack if he saw any Saudis in the audience, thinking there might be a college administrator monitoring the proceedings. Jack saw a former Saudi student of his in the audience, which goes to show you how desperate people in Saudi Arabia are for live entertainment.

Alex's school sold sweatshirts with SAIS (Saudi Arabian International School) and a picture of a scorpion on the front. One of Jack's students told him he knew another word for "scorpion." Jack asked him what it was. "SAIS!" the student said proudly.

I have enough work to keep me busy the whole day. I complained to Mr. Foking that at the end of the week I wouldn't have time to get everything done, like his monthly report in particular. He said, "Maybe we can get you some help." But before he could say who, I said, "Well, Marcie isn't working yet and she knows the office. I could call her." He said, "Okay, but it is just temporary."

March 7, 1977

Would you believe I inherited two more Korean art calendars!! The coffee boy, Mr. Son, gave them to me and in exchange wants me to bring him an American calendar.

A British teacher in Jack's department was put in jail in Dammam last week for a hit-and-run accident. He drove into a Saudi pedestrian, who is in critical condition. There were two witnesses, one rumored to be an Englishman who followed the car to the college and who copied down the number of the UPM parking sticker on the windshield. The

---

254   The new tax law added what we would have had to pay for housing to our taxable income, plus the free education that the college gave to the children of the faculty.

teacher claims to know nothing about the accident, but with two witnesses it is rather hard to believe him. He's going to be locked away for a long time, and if the Saudi dies, he's in even deeper. The British embassy is notoriously useless in helping British citizens in such cases.

Jack refuses to go to the Chinese restaurant in Al-Khobar with me since the last time we were there he saw a two-pound cockroach crawling up the wall next to the kitchen. Everyone has cockroaches here. They are probably in every restaurant in Al-Khobar. The food is better there than anyplace else, but he won't go again. There is another restaurant in Al-Khobar called "The Floating Restaurant," which is a misnomer. Actually it's a tacky-looking building on piles twenty-five feet out into the mudflats. The tide always looks permanently out. If that restaurant isn't infested, then there's not a cockroach in the Eastern Province. I suspect just sitting next to a window there would result in a case of the vapors.

March 9, 1977

This morning I went to look for a blouse in my closet and saw something black move. I looked again, and a two-pound cockroach was crawling up one of my tops. Immediately I shrieked and Jack flew off the bed. It seems he had a guilty conscience about a lizard he saw in the bathroom the night before and just assumed it was now in my closet. In trying to find the cockroach, he knocked half my clothes off the rack. The cockroach, having had the bejesus scared out of him by all the commotion, crapped all over two of my dresses. Jack finally squashed him after five minutes of hot pursuit.

Last night we noted an advertisement for a 1974 Pontiac station wagon on the college bulletin board. A local person owned it and had carefully written in English, "STATION WAGIN (LEMINS) SR 11,000." That's about $3,100.[255] I said, "No wonder it's so cheap. It's a lemins." Jack assumed he meant "LeMans."[256]

Jeff, who teaches the new site manager's daughters English, told me that the last time he was there they were showing him pictures of

---

255 In 2012 dollars, about $11,756.

256 At this time, Pontiac had a model called the "Lemans."

a Korean funeral. A Korean mason was electrocuted a month or so ago. They had a funeral at the company site and sent the body back to Seoul. I saw some of the proceedings from the office. They brought the body from the Aramco morgue in a station wagon. All the Koreans were dressed in suits, and there were flowers. I was furious to see one of the Lebanese clerks taking photographs of the whole thing, because it seemed to me that the Lebanese saw the proceedings like something in a zoo. Well, the site manager's daughters had photographs of everything, even the body. Of course Jeff was telling us about it while Jack was trying to eat his dinner and keep from turning green at the same time. Neither the Dutch nor the locals have any respect for the dignity of these Koreans. Photographing the funeral, I think, shows atrocious taste.

Tomorrow night my neighbor and I are entertaining a family of Palestinian origin who are now Saudi nationals. We had dinner there last spring. These cross-cultural encounters are difficult, in that it invites criticism for an Arab lady to serve less than twelve different dishes. We are going to barbecue chicken, serve potato salad, three-bean salad, homemade rolls (mine), and pies. I haven't decided yet what to serve as dessert. They will probably think we are chintzy. There is nothing more American than a barbecue, so maybe we can sell it on that count. The meal they served last spring was superb. They cooked for days and the neighbors assisted. The result was a feast.

An army of fruit flies has invaded the Eastern Province. Jack sets glasses of wine around the house to attract and drown them. I think he's just attracting them. I pointed out they use fruit flies for genetic research in the US. We could set traps and make our fortunes.

March 13, 1977

Jack finally received an acknowledgment of his resignation from personnel, with carbon copies sent to about ten different people and departments including one Yahyah Ayoob, whose name we cannot find in the college phone book and whose department was not given. Probably he is that man in the college mailroom rumored to have the job of pulling departing faculty's job offers before they reach the mailbox.

We're trying to work out a route to Europe from here on Saudia Airlines. Unfortunately they don't fly to Rome, and our tickets are limited to Saudia or a pooled flight with another airline. The annual sport at the college come spring is to figure out a route home via some city Saudia does not fly to and thereby avoid the requirement that departure be made on Saudi Airlines. Our neighbors the Priests are going home via Dubrovnik, Yugoslavia, then to Italy. I think she's being a little extreme. I'm trying to think of a good reason they should let us go to Rome from here. Alitalia,[257] which Jack says is the only airline worse than Saudia, flies out three times a week direct to Rome. We ought to be able to work out something. People make up reasons like, "My sister is in Rome being treated for a rare disease. She may not have much longer to live, and I'd like to see her one last time," etc.

March 15, 1977

One puzzling telex came across my desk the other day, and I didn't know what to do with it. It read: "WHEN WILL *BIRDY BACK* RETURN TO S.A.? Signed SCHENCK." I've been trying to figure out who *BIRDY BACK* is ever since.

On every Korean Camp Supervisor's report the quality of "dishi washing" is mentioned. An item frequently washed in an unsanitary fashion is "bowels." And nobody seems to notice except me.

Mohammed, my driver, will be back from his trip to Shiraz this weekend. Then I can give the air to Abdullah who was outside my house blowing his horn at ten past seven this morning.

I learned yesterday that there are three Abdullahs who are drivers. The Dutch distinguish among them as "Big Abdullah," "Little Abdullah," and "Abdullah Sammy Davis Jr."

March 21, 1977

Mohammed returned from Iran last Wednesday. He stopped by last night with a rug he had for us. It is a woven rug from his village, which is located 350 miles out of Shiraz. We tried to find out the name

---

257   An Italian airline, not to be confused with Alitalia S.p.A.

of it, and all he could tell us about that rug was that "Turkoman" people made it. I think Turkomans are nomads.[258] It is a runner rug in natural sheep's wool and goat hair with stripes in brown, black, and white. Jack and I like it very much and have put it in the hall. In Iran rugs are often displayed outside on the ground and people walk on them, and sometimes cars and trucks drive over them. They get quite soiled. I decided to wash some of the dust out of it. After three tubsful of water and stomping around on it in my bare feet, the water was still brown. I reeked of a barnyard odor and so did the rug. I took a shower and hung the rug out on the line. It attracted flies for two days, but when it did dry the odor disappeared. I never saw this particular kind of rug in Iran. Mohammed said they are common in the small villages and among the tribes that weave them, but are seldom sold in the cities. The nearest approximation here is the kind of flat runner rug woven in wild colors by the Bedouin women, but this is nicer. It is tightly woven and even. Mohammed tells me they last forever.

March 23, 1977

We had the first staff meeting under the new manager, Mr. Foking. I had to take minutes. First, somebody complained about getting month-old Dutch newspapers and said the firm should buy more papers so everyone could get the latest news. Then there was a complaint about the smell in the toilets. The new manager said this was good because then people would not spend a lot of time in the toilets reading newspapers. Someone else objected to the new hours that gave him Saturday morning off because at that time their kids were in school. Mr. Foking pointed out that this allowed everybody to have some time home alone with their wives. Then someone requested that the company supply special seats for the cars (those wire and straw things) so that they would be protected from the hot plastic. Mr. Foking told him to show him where in the labor agreement it said Naarden had to provide cushions for the employees' cars. I can't wait till the next meeting on the tenth of April, except I will be in Jordan on that date. This guy is very earthy.

---

258   The Turkmans came from central Asia and have been living in Iran since 550 AD. They speak Turkish, albeit with an accent. Most of them are Muslims.

March 27, 1977

The UPM administration is making an effort to bargain with people to get them to remain. They must have had a record number of resignations because they've NEVER bargained before. The attitude has been "We can always find replacements." Jack was approached last night with a suggestion of a 25 percent raise. We gave four reasons for leaving, including the 8 percent increase and the US tax situation. They are making an effort to lift some of the tax burden, and if they gave 25 percent, it could be a significant factor. His chairman wanted to know if Jack got this increase would he be willing to stay? We spent a lot of time talking about it, and Jack feels it's a perfect circle. There are so many factors. Psychologically we are ready to leave.

I finally got through on the phone to Jack to try to find out what happened. He talked to his chairman this morning, who said they had only six interested people to fill twelve positions. And none of these six have been checked for references or necessarily will come if offered a position. Jack said he couldn't make an intelligent decision on the matter until after he returned from Jordan. Frankly I'd like to get out, but the money is tempting even if we pay taxes on it. It would be a financial cushion for us, but is mental disability worth it? It really is a dilemma.

April 3, 1977

The Saudi Boy Scout troops are out in full force checking cars for proper registration, license plates, driving licenses, and the mandatory safety equipment—fire extinguishers and safety triangles.[259] There is a three hundred riyal fine for no safety triangle. They've been holding up traffic for as much as twenty minutes doing their thing. People are avoiding going anywhere by car during Safety Week. There are banners across intersections with safety slogans in Arabic and English. One read, "DO NOT DISTURB OTHERS AND THEY WILL NOT DISTURB YOU!" The others were equally irrelevant. Some old wrecks have been resurrected, decked out with

---

259   There have been Boy Scouts in Saudi Arabia as early as 1946. In 1961 the Saudi government issued a decree that officially established the Saudi Arabian Scout Association.

signs in Arabic, and parked on median strips. One gaggle of scouts stationed themselves outside of one of the big foreign compounds when everyone was coming home from work. A British professor was delayed half an hour by the line waiting to enter the compound. He was furious and claimed they were all practicing to work for the national airline.

Last night we met Frank Harris in Al-Khobar. He had taken a taxi in to town to look for a fire extinguisher, which cost him sixty dollars, and a safety triangle, which cost fourteen dollars. Frank is one of three people in Jack's department approached with an offer of more money if he would reconsider his resignation. Yesterday Frank had had it up to here with Saudi Arabia and complained that all year people are being killed left and right on the roads, but for one week everybody goes berserk in the other direction, stopping cars and fining people, then next week they'll be back to driving like maniacs and killing people all over the place.

Unexpectedly, Bob Asa came to Dhahran over the weekend. He had been in Beirut and brought me an eight-kilo box of strawberries. What a treat! I haven't had real strawberries in four years. When we go home for the summer, we always arrive in New England just after strawberry season. I found an excellent cheesecake recipe in the *Al Hasa Cookbook*,[260] so I made that recipe, put real strawberries on top, and cooked a strawberry glaze using a cup more of strained strawberries, to cover the strawberries. I also made shortcake, ate strawberries and cream, and delivered boxes of strawberries all over the neighborhood because no way could we finish eight kilos of strawberries before they spoiled. It was a delightful gift.

April 6, 1977

This is my final letter before our vacation trip. We have to be at the airport tomorrow at 4:30 a.m., according to the ticket agent for Alia (Jordan) Airlines. The plane leaves at 6:00 a.m. with one stop in Baghdad.

---

260   The *Al Hasa Cookbook* is a collection of recipes put together by the 140 wives of the faculty of the college (UPM), the Aramco and Northrop employees, and other expatiates. The first printing, 1976, was done by General Publishing and Binding: Iowa Falls, Iowa. It was reprinted in 1981. Appendix 2 has some of my favorite recipes from this book. For recipe see "Cheesecake—Never Fails," appendix 2.

I saw the ultimate in automobile decoration the other day—a huge Mercedes diesel painted with bucolic scenes, purple-fringed valance around the truck cab, and a huge feather duster stuck upside down where a hood ornament should go. Jamilla! (That's Arabic for "beautiful.")

CHAPTER 16

The wind of sheep, Mount Nebo and the Promised Land, the five-foot Yemeni with the one-foot iron spike, the bed in the parking lot, garbage pickup halted by Playboy magazines

April 15, 1977

This is our second day back from Jordan, and there is a terrible sand-storm outside, one like the first year we were here. I can't see fifty feet. The air is yellow with dust. Jack and I got up and ran strips of three-inch masking tape around the windows. We covered the kitchen fan with plastic and tape. My nose is still filled with dust. I feel bad for the people coming back from holiday today. It probably is too dusty for the planes to land. Maybe they will end up in Bahrain.

Surprisingly enough, our respite from Saudi Arabia resulted in our being convinced that the best thing to do would be to leave. Maybe the US tax business will blow over. We NEED a year in the States. After that, maybe something like Algeria will be a possibility.

Jordan is a lovely country, and I think the people we met there were the friendliest Arabs in the Middle East. It made us realize what we were missing by spending our lives in Saudi Arabia with no dis-tinctive culture, no cultural contacts, no history, no scenery, no ruins of castles, or attractions of any kind, save the beaches.

We met Bob in Amman, and the next day of our visit was spent making the three and a half hour drive to Damascus. We spent four hours there, and it took another three and a half hours to get back. Visas at the border are time-consuming. We had a buffet lunch at the brand new Hotel Meridian. They served a variety of cold salads, meats, marinated vegetables, olives, pickles, etc., for the first course. The second course consisted of two meat dishes and boiled potatoes.

Would you believe that one of the meat courses was sliced tongue in gravy and the other was a medley of braised kidneys, sheep gonads, and hearts? This is allegedly quite a delicacy, but the kidneys put me off, not to mention one of the other items. I had a few slices of tongue, and Jack skipped the second course altogether.

On the way to Damascus, we had passed the Roman ruins at Jerash. On our way back, Bob wanted to stop, but we were anxious to get back to Alex, whom we had put in a nursery school for the day. We could see a lot of the ruins from the road.

We visited the rug souk in Damascus, but it was rather disappointing after Iran. The rugs were almost all used, were not very good quality, and the prices were high. I wanted a small prayer rug but decided against trying to find it there. In the Damascus souk, nobody lets you alone. People are running up to you, pulling at you and yelling, "Come to my store I have the lowest prices!" There is no peace. Fighting off eighty people is extremely irritating.

The second day we were in Jordan, Bob took us to the Dead Sea. It is the lowest point on the earth. The Jordan River empties into the Dead Sea. Because of the intense heat there is tremendous evaporation leaving salt and minerals saturating the water. We have some pictures of Jack and me floating in the sea. It is not only very salty but also very bitter. I attracted a lot of attention by being the only woman in the water. When I went to the ladies' showers to rinse off, I found them locked. I also found I had accumulated a following of locals, so I went directly to the car and sat there, white from the minerals, waiting in the hot vehicle for Bob, Jack, and Alex.

The descent into the Jordan valley Dead Sea area is very steep and cliff hanging. We passed many ancient trucks straining up the hills loaded with produce from the valley. There are no guardrails at the edges of the roads, and they are barely wide enough for one large vehicle. I was quite nervous riding both ways, given the many S and U curves.

On Saturday we left Amman for Petra, an ancient Nabatean trading city that flourished about the time of Christ. Petra is on the road to Aqaba, Jordan's only port on the Red Sea on the south. Because it was the Easter holiday and there were many Holy Land tours booked into hotels and rest houses, we were told we couldn't get reservations in Aqaba and maybe not at the Petra Rest House either. When we got to Petra, they said there were no rooms. We decided to see the ruins and then check back at suppertime. For $7.50 we could have rented a horse, led by a Bedouin, to ride the two kilometers through a very narrow canyon of red stone to the city proper. We decided to walk. It was very rocky underfoot. But when we got there, we had to do more walking, a lot of it up into the mountains, and by the time we were ready to go back at dusk, there wasn't a horse to be found, and we had to walk back downhill through the canyon. I thought my legs would drop off.

Alex loved exploring all the holes in the rocks and had to check out every single cave we passed. The Nabateans in these caves carved very elegant classical facades out of rock. They had an elaborate system of collecting water and built steps out of the rock to reach higher "apartments." Bob led us up a long climb to the top of the mountain, accessible by carved steps in the stone walls, where there is a very impressive four-story cave building called "El Deir" ("the monastery").

As we laboriously climbed and climbed, I whined and complained. Bob kept promising me that an incredible monument was just around the next bend. We must have done at least a half-mile of steady climbing. Meanwhile, as we slowly scaled the stone steps, an aging but agile Bedouin passed us. Carrying four Pepsis he sprinted effortlessly ahead of us on the path. When we finally arrived at El Deir, breathless and thirsty, he was waiting for us at a small stand made out of wooden packing crates. He had four Pepsis for sale! We bought them all! And would have paid twice the price.

A flock of sheep grazed in the grass around us as we sat there on a rock and caught our breath. Suddenly our tranquility was interrupted by a noise that sounded like an inflated tire being punctured by a blunt instrument. We couldn't figure out what it was. As the staccato outbursts continued, we realized the sheep all had gas! It was the most surprising sound.

Jack climbed a bit further up the hill where Bob said on a clear day you could see the whole Jordan Valley and the Tomb of Abraham, but there was a light dust haze and Jack couldn't see much. On the way to Petra, we passed the Well of Moses where Moses caused a spring to rise out of the ground. People sometimes take water from this well for baptisms. Jordan is filled with biblical places, and it made me wish I knew the Bible better.

After we got back at dusk we ate dinner in a Nabatean house that had been converted into the Government Rest House dining room. It was all carved out of stone and still had smoke marks on the wall where oil lamps had been burned. Bedouins camped up in the ruins, furtively trying to sell visitors tiny oil lamps they had unearthed or ancient Roman, Greek, or Nabatean coins. Signs put up by the Jordanian Department of Antiquities warned tourists against buying these items, saying it was against the law and besides the majority are fakes. It was tempting, nonetheless. I did find a couple of shards of pottery in the ruins, but that was all. After we had finished eating, the desk clerk told us a tour of sixty had canceled and we had rooms.

The next morning we left for Aqaba at half past six in the morning. At about eight o'clock we reached the Wadi Rum Guest House.[261] The view was spectacular, and we could see into an endless valley of lunar mountains and jagged canyons. We ate breakfast of olives, eggs, labneh (a strong yogurt), Arab bread, butter, and tea. All along the wadi were Bedouin tents of black goat hair and flocks of sheep, goats, and camels tended by children in black embroidered tunics worn over pants. A railroad ran parallel to the road, a few hundred yards from it. There is a phosphate mining industry in the Wadi, and a very narrow gauge train runs along the edge of the canyon. The phosphates are sent to Aqaba to be loaded onto ships. Bob said the gauge is so narrow that occasionally the train falls off the track if the load is not balanced. We saw an old rusting chain of crumpled boxcars about ten miles out of Aqaba.

In Aqaba town we got oranges to take to the beach with us. Across the harbor is the Israeli port of Eilat where oil is delivered and stored. Its population is about fifteen or twenty thousand people, and there were a number of camouflaged oil storage tanks up in the hills. We drove down the coast towards Saudi Arabia to find a good place for snorkeling along the beach. Across the water were the towering cliffs

---

261   Some photos of the view may be seen on the web: http://www.jordanjubilee.com/visitjor/rum4.htm.

of Sinai, which looked like a desolate, forbidding place. Huge ships steamed out of the port either hugging the Israeli side of the water or the Jordanian side, depending upon which country they visited.

The snorkeling was just spectacular. Even Alex was dazzled by it. There are coral reefs hiding brilliantly colored fish. We saw fire coral, fan coral, branch coral, and brain coral. Fish everywhere: navy blue with gold stripes, blue green with yellow stripes, black with gold stripes, sea urchins, sea anemones, green fish, and yellow fish. It was gorgeous.

At noontime we had all acquired sunburns from swimming on the water surface. We left for the Ali Baba Restaurant in Aqaba for lunch. Bob asked the owner to show us his fish, a flat whitish variety called "zubaida." Three of us had the fish with a sauce of garlic, lemon juice, and butter. Before the fish was served, we had hummus, tabbouleh, and baba ganoujh. The fish was superb. We finished with tiny cups of very sweet Arab coffee flavored with cardamom.

It was a long drive back to Amman. The next day we did nothing much except laze around Bob's apartment. I baked brownies for a pot-luck supper hosted by one of the US embassy attachés. There were about thirty people there, a few British, a Cypriot, a Jordanian, and a German woman. We met most of the embassy staff, including the ambassador's secretary. Her previous post had been in Moscow, which she loved. The host served Jordanian wine made by Franciscan monks, a variety of dishes, and a cranberry-vodka punch. This group in Jordan was the kind of foreign community I expected when I first came to Saudi Arabia. We played charades afterwards, and it turned out to be great fun.

Before the potluck supper, Bob took us to Mount Nebo from which Moses is supposed to have first sighted the Promised Land. Inciden-tally, we could not see the Promised Land from Mount Nebo because of a sandstorm in the desert. A monastery marks the site. Repairs are underway at the site of the monastery chapel to restore the mosaics. We were shown where the monks were buried beneath the floor. If we had a flashlight, we could have seen the bones. Fortunately nobody had a flashlight. Then we visited a couple of other early churches where there were restored mosaics. All these churches date from about 300 AD. An old gold-toothed Bedouin woman guarded one of them, and she delighted in telling everyone how she used to bake bread in the middle of the mosaic before some archaeologists discovered them. Sure enough there were black scorch marks defacing the very center of the nine by twelve foot mosaic. Some Jordanians from Madaba had taken us in tow and translated her remarks. We were taken to the home of one of them and offered Arab coffee and sweets. Our Jordanian host was in the Royal Air Force and had been sent to England for training, so his English was quite good. He and his friends made us feel very welcome.

The last day in Jordan we went to the gold souk where I bought a gold bracelet and on the way back a kilo of baklava, a flaky honey and pistachio pastry, which I have eaten too much of already. We found two-pound canned hams, which we bought to bring back to Saudi Arabia. Food prices seemed about the same as back in Al-Khobar, but the merchants in Jordan pay big import duties on what they buy.

It was one of the best vacations we have had, and I really didn't expect to find much there. We went mainly to see Bob.

April 11, 1977

We have decided that this is our last year, despite the offer they made of twenty thousand dollars.[262] The funny thing is that if the college had originally offered us a new contract in February for that amount we would have stayed because all along we had intended to remain for one more year. But they offered us only 8 percent. Given the increasing conservatism of the university and the fact that we exhausted all the possibilities for creative development at least a year ago, we decided to pack it in. Once our thinking turned towards leaving, making us the offer we originally expected was no longer sufficient. Also Jack would become the highest paid department member, and this would be resented by everyone, not to mention those who already signed their 5 percent and 6 percent contracts in February.

Poor Ragnar Fossgaard, a Swede from the consulting firm overseeing Naarden. He went to Sweden and returned via Lufthansa with

262   By 2012 dollars, about $75,847.

a suitcase containing ten pounds of fresh pork. His luggage has been lost for two days now.

April 23, 1977

We started on packing yesterday, getting a few things together to get some idea how much we have to send back. It seems that we may need another box.

April 27, 1977

The Korean carpenters here have built me a box slightly larger than the trunk we already have. Mohammed put it in the back of his car and is taking it to our house now. Jack is probably sleeping. I told the carpenters to make it light because it would be for airfreight. But I don't know what they did. Usually Korean carpenters build things to survive typhoons and cosmic catastrophes.

Queen Juliana's birthday party is being held this Saturday night at the Naarden Recreation Center. We have been invited, but I don't know if Jack will go or not. He doesn't particularly enjoy these parties. The invitation said to wear red, white, and blue (I think they're the colors in the Dutch flag).[263] I have a long blue-and-white dress, but the red will take some thought. Maybe somebody has a red bracelet scarf or beads I can borrow. There are some Italian subcontracting people here who speak practically no English. Apparently they noticed Jack sitting glumly at the last party and inquired in Italian of an Englishman who spoke their language, "Does he speak English?"

Our car insurance expires this Friday. We hope to sell the car sometime in May anyway. One guy is interested, but the college won't loan him the money to buy it. They say it is too late in the year, implying if he skipped the country they'd be out his salary for two months, which is the amount they will loan you interest free.

---

263   The flag of the Netherlands has three horizontal strips of equal width, whose colors from top to bottom are red, white, and blue.

322

May 2, 1977

The king returned Saturday from his hospital stay in London, and rumor had it there would be a three-day holiday to celebrate. Then rumor had it there would be a one-day holiday. Then a notice from the rector reduced it to the following:

> It is with great pleasure that we announce the arrival of HIS MAJESTY King Khaled Bin Abdul Aziz on Saturday 30 April 1977 after having completely recovered from his recent medical treatment. On this joyous occasion the University will be appropriately decorated to suit this occasion. We appreciate your help in giving the campus the proper appearance.

But boy are they decorating! A green-and-white Saudi flag waves from every light pole. There are six, fifteen-foot, wooden arches just on the road from here to Al-Khobar, spanning the asphalt. At night they are illuminated and in some instances with neon tubes in red, green, and blue. The Arab inscriptions welcome the king back to Arabia. Green-and-white bunting and pennants are everywhere. Flags fly from the tops of the government buildings. The police station near our compound looks like a German beer garden at night. Nasser, the printer, tells me the government says everybody must put a portrait of the king in his car. The Al-Khobar water tower has strings of lights descending its column and colored lights ringing the top. It looks like it should have a revolving restaurant upstairs and rides for the kiddies at the bottom. They are giving cash bonuses to all government employees and letting prisoners out of jail.

Yesterday I tried to explain to Alex why the college was hanging flags and banners from the buildings. I said that the king was feeling better and this was to celebrate. "King Fizzle?" he asked. "No," I said, "King Khalid. King Fizzle is dead."

The first memo is from the Consulate School; the second is from UPM.

MEMO: TO ALL PARENTS

In recognition of the safe return of the King to the Kingdom and in participation with the celebration of our hosts, we will be setting one day aside for celebration. We will not have school on Wednesday, May 4, in order that you may participate in the host country celebration. This date has been chosen in order to cooperate with other companies in the area who are taking the same day.

Dr. Emory Giles,

Superintendent

The following one superseded this notice. Sounds like somebody's arm got twisted.

DHAHRAN ACADEMY
May 2, 1977

Parents and Students:
In honor of the safe and healthy return of HM King Khalid, we have been requested to close the school immediately. School will resume on Saturday, May 7.
Thank you for your cooperation.

Michael Hobbs

Dean of Administration

There is the most disgusting half-pound beetle crawling up the wall near my wastebasket. This country has the most awful bugs. It probably bites, too. Now he's heading for the closed door. Maybe if I open it he will exit.

The night before last, the Dutch people at Naarden had a party to celebrate Queen Juliana's birthday. Jeff, who gives private English lessons to several Dutch people, took me. Jack stayed at home and babysat. The Middle East manager gave a speech in English praising their queen. Then they played the Dutch national anthem, and everybody who knew the words sang along. It seemed to have as many verses as our national anthem, and the voices became thinner and thinner the farther along they went.

May 4, 1977

On Wednesday, when Jack taught his last class, his students had a surprise party for him. They had taken all the lecterns from the other classrooms and made a long banquet table for the cake and Pepsi. The class contributed to the purchase of several gifts including a clock for Alex and also a shirt and jeans for him. They gave Jack ivory worry beads and an ivory bracelet "for your daughter when you have her, sir." They also gave him a stainless steel Arab coffee pot and Aramis aftershave.

May 7, 1977

We are in the process of trying to sell our car. Jack is asking $2,400,[264] but he's had one offer for $2,150, one for $2,300, and one for $2,315. One guy here had a look at the car without our knowing about it and wrote Jack a note saying that he thought the asking price was too high but if Jack "really wanted to sell it" they could work out something. Jack was insulted and wrote back a note saying his price was not negotiable, and obviously this was not the car for him. Then the guy called yesterday and asked Jack if he could take it for a test drive; he had some banking to do. I thought this was a bit much. A test drive is one thing, but doing an errand is another. The guy was gone for an hour and a half at least, and Jack needed the car a half hour before he returned. Not only that, the insurance expired about ten days ago, and we haven't renewed because we are selling it this month. So our uninsured car was gone with a driver we hardly knew. When he finally came back, he offered Jack $2,315 for it. Jack didn't accept it.

A neighbor bought my typewriter. I bought it in 1969 with gift money from my college graduation. If anyone had told me I would be selling it eight years later in Saudi Arabia, I wouldn't have believed it. Now I am reduced to typing letters at work.

May 11, 1977

Just now a five-foot Yemeni covered in cement dust came into the office. He wore a dirty thobe with a gutra tied around his waist. In

---

264   By 2012 dollars, about $9,102.

his right hand he had a one-foot long, rusty iron spike. He complained that one of the Koreans had damaged the door of his car. Presumably he wanted satisfaction. The quantity surveyor's reaction was that Yemenis shouldn't have cars. My reaction was they should have disarmed him before letting him into the office. "Never argue with a Yemeni carrying a one-foot long iron spike," is my motto. I don't know what happened. I disappeared. One superintendent here said when he worked outside he had about six cases a day like that. Maybe it's some kind of local racket.

In one month and seven days, we will be out of here, presumably for good.

May 14, 1977

We managed to sell about $320 worth of stuff, or three-quarters of what we hauled out to the green at the yard sale on Thursday.[265] Alex made almost sixty dollars selling his toys. However we still have the television set and the car, which are the biggest items. Early on a group of Arab workmen and gardeners gathered around our blanket. A Yemeni gardener bought our two-foot plastic Christmas tree. Another bought the string of colored lights. I had a blanket, queen size acrylic; a very poor looking Arab bargained us down from fourteen dollars to eleven dollars for it. Dr. Hough had given me a plaid suitcase with a zippered flap. I had it priced at ten dollars. Some Arab handed me eight dollars. I agreed to the transaction. Then he wanted to know where was the key to the zipper. He couldn't get a suitcase in Khobar like that for under sixty dollars. However I am still wondering why the gardener wanted an artificial Christmas tree. Maybe he wanted something he didn't have to water.

May 18, 1977

Husein told Jack he wants our television set, so the only big item remaining to sell is the car. Jack and I are going to try to get our airfreight shipment together this weekend. It's difficult to know how much stuff we have to take back when we still have to live in the house

---

265   By 2012 dollar, $320 is about $1,214.

326

from day to day. I have a horror of discovering on the evening of June
15 (the day before we leave) that we have more things to go back than
shipping containers to hold them.

May 21, 1977

Yesterday Jack and I packed the trunk and the large plywood box
with our things. He thinks we have between 75 and 100 kilos.[266]
We still have the car to sell. Everything else is gone. Last night was terribly humid. After we went to bed, we could hear thunder in the distance. During the night there was a drenching rainstorm. Al-Khobar is
flooded. This is very unusual this time of year, because it's usually dust
storm season. It sure is nice having the car in this weather.

Tomorrow King Khalid is supposed to arrive at Dhahran Airport
for a visit to the Eastern Province. Arch building is now going on with
a vengeance. Apparently the custom is to build arches when one is
pleased about something. I used to think they just killed sheep. When
you are having an important guest and you really want to roll out the
red carpet, you kill a sheep for him. This is such a frequent activity
around here that the College Recreation Center had to make a rule
that stated, "The slaughtering of sheep and other animals at the beach
and surrounding areas is not permitted." I imagine my arrival at work
will be difficult. They usually put the troops out early to guard the
king's route.

I put up a sign at the Recreation Center advertising my job. Hopefully the salary will tempt somebody.

May 23, 1977

The king came to this area yesterday morning. I managed to get to
the airport office a couple hours before he was due to fly in.

I saw an odd Telex the other day. It seems the Riyadh office was
concerned about some insulating material they were airfreighting to
Dhahran. This shipment was to share the cargo hold with a consign-
ment of live chickens, so they bagged and double-bagged the insulat-

---

266 A kilogram is 2.2 pounds.

ing material to prevent the auditorium they are building from smelling like a chicken coop on damp days.

We finally sold the car yesterday. After our ad got posted at Aramco's Mail Center, two Indians appeared at the house that afternoon. One of them gave Jack a thirty-dollar deposit after negotiating the price down to $2,300 from our asking figure of $2,400. We decided we just wanted to sell the thing rather than leave it over the summer, baking in the compound, to be sold for our asking price in September when the new people arrive. So yesterday afternoon at half past four they reappeared with $2,270 in cash, but first they wanted to take the car for a test drive. Then they handed Jack the cash and signed all the necessary papers. When Jack heard the guy talk about buying a lock for the gas tank (high test is only twenty-five cents a gallon here)[267] and getting an extra set of keys, he remembered that the hatchback did not lock, since we had been tapped in the behind by a large truck. However, Jack never locked it in Saudi Arabia.

Twenty minutes after the two Indians drove off, they were back. It seems the speedometer needle didn't work. Jack took them out on the road, got the car up to 30 mph, and thumped the glass with his knuckles. The needle sprung into action. But this didn't satisfy the Indian, who accused Jack of selling him a defective car (it is second-hand, after all). Jack kept insisting it was not defective, that once in a while the needle stuck and a thump was all it needed to make it work again. Now Jack is living in fear that the guy is going to discover that the back doesn't lock. This morning at six he heard a familiar squeak of Volkswagen brakes and ran to the back door, expecting to find the Indian making his way through the yard. It wasn't for us. Anyway, if he does return, we are going to plead ignorance of the defective lock in the back. I think the thing to do is sell a car late on the fifteenth of June and depart forever early on the sixteenth.

Now we've sold everything there is to sell, and we're camping out in our own house. We still have the television set. Husein wants that and will wait until we are ready to leave before he collects it. My vacuum is gone, so I do a lot of sweeping instead. Jack says he is going to

---

267   In 2012 dollars, about 95¢ a gallon.

go crazy the last few weeks with no car and nothing to do. I am working up until the day before we leave the country so I am OK.

A woman answered my ad at the Recreation Center for a replacement. She is American, married to an Iranian PhD in physics, with four kids. I think they need the money. She's had eleven years' experience and will interview here on Wednesday. After they got here UPM told them they wouldn't pay tuition for the four kids at the Consulate School because they were Moslem. In September the tuition for four children will cost $18,000.[268] They couldn't afford it, so they enrolled them in the Saudi school system in Dammam. He said $18,000 is more than he earns. Last year they were in Meshed, Iran, where he taught in the university. The children went to Persian schools and learned Farsi. He found out that if he taught at UPM his children could go to the American Consulate School in Dhahran and he signed a contract here, so his kids would get an American education and the college would pay for it. After he got here, the college suddenly changed the rules. He says they never would have left Iran if they knew this would happen. This change in policy affected about thirty-five families and is very typical of the cavalier manner taken by the administration towards its faculty members. It constitutes breach of contract, but foreigners can't sue here.

The students just got a big raise. They now receive a salary of $350 a month from the government.[269] They had been getting approximately $100 a month. The problem with paying students is that some of them just don't make it academically, but hang around forever taking up space and not coming to class, so they can collect their monthly payments. Jack had his worst English student ever this year, nicknamed "My Teacher" because after allegedly having six years of English in secondary school, all he could do when Jack tried to explain something to him was to smile and say, "My Teacher." This student withdrew officially last winter and was back again six weeks later. Jack hasn't seen him in three months. Suddenly Jack was given a form to complete because My Teacher was withdrawing officially again. Jack

---

268   In 2012 dollars, about $68,262.

269   In 2012 dollars, about $1,327.

figures he was hanging on to collect his salary. Jack put on the form that he had an F in the class and 175 unexcused absences.

Things at work are becoming interesting. The administrator van der Waal, a horse's neck if there ever was one, is being canned. His good buddy van Hout, the assistant site manager who aspires to the site manager position, says that if van der Waal goes, he goes too and he's taking all the Koreans with him. Where this little entourage is going is another question. Now the top management in Riyadh is trying to sort that out. Van der Waal supposedly is up to his eyelashes in intrigue, kickbacks, and skim offs. I can't understand why van Hout supports him, unless he's up to his earlobes in the same rackets, or very naive, or whatever. About five people are going in June too. They are really cutting back on the staff here.

May 28, 1977

The American woman who is married to the Iranian physicist got my job and will start June 4. Mohammed, my driver, told me that her husband is a "very good Moslem." Although Mohammed has Saudi citizenship, his parents and his wife came from Iran. Mohammed speaks Farsi fluently. When he heard that the lady was coming out for an interview and was married to an Iranian, he hung around so he could speak Farsi with her husband.

May 30, 1977

There is a long-standing suspicion here at the college that the administration withholds the mail of departing faculty members they would like to keep. That is, the administration pulls any letters from firms in the US who might be trying to hire them. Many sane, rational, otherwise reasonable and intelligent faculty members are sure that their mail is being tampered with in the college mailroom. For example, I heard yesterday that the chairman of systems engineering, whom they have not been able to replace yet, is having his letters intercepted and opened before he gets them. Other department faculty members learned by phone calls that letters sent months ago never got through. If this were the case, it would appear the administration feels that if they remove someone's options, he will change his mind and remain. Fortunately we have no pressing financial commitments and have the option of leaving without any specific stateside position to go to.

The big excitement at work is that the Saudi Air Force cadets have been sneaking away from exercises or drill practice or whatever they have to do outside in the hot weather these days and taking a dip in the Korean swimming pool. The Dutch people were upset because apparently this has been going on for a while, but the Koreans did not complain. For a few weeks some cadets were hiding out in the new auditorium being built and watching drill practice from the window openings. The Saudi printer here, Nasser, went for a swim in the Korean pool last week and broke out in boils. There is no drain, no filter system, and probably no chlorination. I expect an epidemic any day.

We are going to practice pack our suitcases this weekend to see if we can get everything in. Lufthansa voted to strike today. I saw a flight leave as I was coming to work so maybe the international flights aren't affected, or maybe an agreement was reached.

I am anxious to get back to the States again, to get in touch with my roots. The last few summers back I have had the feeling that my timing was off, that my responses to situations were not appropriate, that I am an anachronism in my own country. I've missed too much. On the one hand, I can't imagine settling down forever in the US. It seems like death to me. But on the other hand, I am looking forward to being a citizen of my own country again, at least for a while.

May 31, 1977

I'm trying to use up kitchen supplies. It's very difficult. You run out of cooking oil, but have a recipe to make that will use up the flour, and you need one-half cup of oil. I ran out of chili powder halfway through a recipe and ended up blending cumin and cayenne and paprika for a reasonable facsimile. If I were very organized, I could plan menus for the next fourteen days or so and have nothing left over. However, I'm not. In fact, it's driving me crazy. The Arsenaults are coming for dinner Friday night.

June 8, 1977

We have a lot of packing to do this weekend. I got all my money, vacation pay, final salary check, prorated bonus, on Sunday. Jack has been doing, banking, trying to convert all our riyals into negotiable currency.

One of the employees here, Magnus Burgstede, had his bed collapse. He asked the site manager Mr. Foking for a new one. Mr. Foking told him NO, for economy reasons. Then Magnus swapped beds with somebody who was leaving. Mr. Foking learned of it and made him swap back. Magnus got so angry at that point that he took his bed to the site and assembled it in the site manager's parking space, a prime piece of real estate located in the shade directly in front of the office door. It remained there for four days while the site manager parked elsewhere and ignored the gesture. Finally two Korean laborers welded the bed together and delivered it to Magnus's house. Now Mr. Foking is being referred to as "Sleep-Comfort" (a local furniture company).

June 13, 1977

The college has informed Jack that they will give him a letter of no objection, so he will be free to return to Saudi Arabia in the future should he wish to.

The tax situation is becoming ridiculous. The IRS is taking Frank Jungers, chairman of the board for Aramco, Dr. Don Smith of UPM, and Aramco's chief tax lawyer to court for not correctly reporting their income. One chemistry professor at the college has four school-age kids. Since UPM pays for his kids' education, he has to declare their tuition as income. He said his tax would be more than he earned and asked the female IRS representative from the Teheran office what he was to do. She told him to take out a loan.

June 15, 1977 [Same letter as above]

I am on the plane now, three hours to Frankfurt. What a relief! We seem to have a lot of stuff to take back: four suitcases, three carry-on bags. I like to travel light. Oh well, it's back for the last time. I was also given a carved ivory camel to take back, a gift from the office staff at Naarden.

The Priests from next door are on this flight. She just had two double vodka martinis (it is 8:30 a.m.). I confess I had a small bottle of Mosel. The only way to survive these six-hour plane rides is sloshed. I visited Mrs. Priest last night and bought from her a twenty-one karat gold bracelet she could no longer get on her wrist. It is lovely. I have narrow hands and wrists. She gave me a very good price: seventy dollars.

When the Priests joined us in the departure lounge, Mrs. Priest inquired, "What did you leave out in the trash? The Yemeni crew stopped their garbage truck at your house and didn't go any farther the whole time we were there." We had disposed of Jack's pile of *Playboy* magazines before we left for the airport, not daring to get rid of them earlier. The Yemenis probably thought they had died and gone to heaven.

We went through the most agonizing ordeal getting through customs and immigration. The Saudis were so slow. Four lines were open, and we stood in them for one hour waiting to be cleared to the transit lounge. The officials checking passports would suddenly shut down their booths and disappear for a pit stop, a tea break, or prayer time. We picked the wrong line once. I was tearing my hair by the time we got to the transit lounge. Then we had to wait for the rest of the passengers for Lufthansa to clear, and we were one and a quarter hours late because of sloppy organization at Dhahran Airport. Mrs. Priest was the last through, which probably explains the double vodka martinis. But we're on our way home at last!

EPILOGUE

When I reread the boxes of letters I wrote over twenty years ago, they brought back a rush of memories. Memories of the dust, the heat, and the smells of Arabia. And especially the memories of the people, the frustrations, the humor, and the discoveries. These are experiences that I wouldn't have missed for the world.

As for what happened to the people in our lives there: Joe Fahey got his doctorate, married Mildred, and lived in the Far East. He never did come to the United States. Dr. Hough and Jeff Crossley died a few years ago. Alex, our son, grew up and became an electrical engineer. Over the years we lost touch with the Priests, the Andersons, and the Goodbouts. The Al-Sayids and Bob Asa live in California. Harv and Kerry Woolrich settled in Maine. Husein eventually married, worked for a company in Jubail, and saved enough to return to Egypt with his family. I don't know what happened to Mohammed, my Saudi driver, or any of the Dutch people. In the mid eighties Marcie Wildermann and her husband retired to Virginia. We talked often to catch up on news of the people we knew. She once said, "The whole time we lived at the college we thought we were marking time until we could return to the States. But those were the best years of our lives." And they were, despite all the inconveniences and aggravations. We had time for friends, for talking, for sharing common experiences as outsiders in an alien culture. Christmas has never been as real and meaningful as it was in a country where it was forbidden. Creating our own celebration brought all of us closer.

In June of 1977, we came home to New Hampshire. Our daughter, Kathryn, was born the following summer. Two years later, we were back in Saudi Arabia for six more years. Jack took a job with Northrop in a different part of the kingdom. But that is another story.

APPENDIX 1

Recipes Referred to in Letters

ELLIE'S OATMEAL BREAD (NO KNEAD)

2 cups boiling water
1 cup quick oatmeal
1/3 cup shortening
½ cup molasses
4 teaspoons salt
2 envelopes or tablespoon yeast
2 eggs (beaten)
5½ cups flour

Combine water, oats, shortening, molasses, and salt. Cool to luke-warm. Add yeast; mix well. Blend in eggs. Add flour; mix until dough is well blended. (This dough is softer than kneaded bread.) Place dough in a greased bowl and cover. Store in refrigerator or cold place at least 2 hours or until needed. (I have stored it up to two days and find that it rises some in the refrigerator.) On a well-floured board shape dough into two loaves. Place in greased loaf tins (9 by 4 by 3 inches) and cover. Let rise in warm place until double in bulk (2 hours). Bake at 375° for 1 hour. This recipe can also be made into rolls.

SHRIMP MARINADE

2 pounds large shrimp
3 cloves garlic
1 medium onion finely chopped
¼ cup chopped parsley
1 teaspoon dried mustard
1 teaspoon salt
½ cup olive oil
Juice of one lemon

Marinate shrimp in above ingredients at room temperature for several hours. Then broil 4 or 5 minutes each side in preheated oven broiler. Turn once.

OATMEAL CAKE

1 cup oatmeal
1½ cups almost boiling coffee
½ cup butter
½ cup brown sugar
2 beaten eggs
1 teaspoon vanilla
1 teaspoon baking powder
½ teaspoon baking soda
1 teaspoon salt
1½ cups flour
1 teaspoon cinnamon
½ teaspoon allspice

Soak oatmeal in coffee for 20 minutes. Add butter, sugar, eggs, vanilla to oatmeal. Beat well with electric mixer until completely blended. Add dry ingredients. Beat well and bake in greased 9 by 13 pan at 350° for 35 minutes. When cake is just warm, spread topping.

TOPPING

4 tablespoons butter
1 cup brown sugar
½ cup chopped walnuts
    or pecans
½ cup evaporated milk
1 cup flaked coconut
½ teaspoon vanilla

Put all ingredients in saucepan. Cook and stir until sugar is dissolved. Spread warm on cake.

MOM'S SUGAR COOKIES

½ cup margarine or butter
½ cup oil
1 cup sugar
1 egg
1 teaspoon vanilla
2½ cups flour
½ teaspoon baking soda
½ teaspoon salt

Cream butter or margarine, oil, and sugar. Add egg and vanilla. Stir in dry ingredients. Mix well. Roll dough in balls the size of a walnut and flatten on ungreased cookie sheet with glass bottom dipped in sugar. Bake in 350°F oven for 10 minutes or until edges are light brown.

GINGERSNAP COOKIES

¾ cup butter
¾ cup vegetable oil
2 cups sugar
½ cup molasses
2 eggs
4 cups all-purpose flour
2 teaspoons baking soda
2 teaspoons cinnamon
2 teaspoons ground cloves
2 teaspoons ginger
¼ teaspoon red pepper

Cream butter with oil and sugar. Add eggs and molasses: beat until blended. Sift together flour, soda, cinnamon, cloves, ginger, and red pepper; add to creamed mixture. Mix well, then cover, and chill several hours or overnight. Dough is very soft.

Shape pieces of dough in balls. Roll in ¼ cup sugar. Place on ungreased cookie sheet and flatten with the bottom of a glass. Bake 7 to 9 minutes at 350°F.

HUMMUS

1 cup dried chickpeas, soaked and cooked with liquid reserved or two cans (19 ounces a can) of cooked chickpeas
2 teaspoons salt
2 medium cloves garlic, peeled
¼ cup fresh lemon juice
¾ cup tahini (sesame seed puree, available at natural food stores and some supermarkets)
Chopped parsley
Olive oil

In a blender add ½ cup reserved liquid, salt, garlic, and lemon juice. Blend until garlic is in very small pieces. Add tahini and combine. Add chickpeas and more reserved liquid if needed to puree mixture into a smooth liquid.

OR

In a food processor: drop garlic through feed tube. Chop finely. Add salt, lemon juice, tahini. Process for 30 seconds. Add chickpeas and ½ cup reserved liquid to start. Process for 2 minutes. If mixture is like peanut butter, add more liquid to make it more the consistency of a dip.

Spread into shallow bowls. Drizzle olive oil over surface. Sprinkle with chopped parsley. Serve with Arab bread slightly warmed or toasted. Tear bread into pieces and use to scoop the hummus.

PECAN PIE

1 uncooked piecrust
1 cup light brown sugar
¾ cup light corn syrup
¼ cup dark corn syrup
3 eggs
¼ cup cream
2 tablespoons flour
1 tablespoon butter, melted
½ teaspoon salt
½ cup water (coffee may be used)
1½ cups pecans

Mix all ingredients except pecans in order given. Stir in pecans. Pour into piecrust. Bake at 350°F for 45 minutes. Can be made in blender or food processor. Makes one 9-inch pie.

Flaky Piecrust

1 cup vegetable shortening or lard
2½ to 2¾ cups flour
1 teaspoon salt
½ cup milk
1 tablespoon vinegar

Combine flour and salt. Cut in shortening or lard using pastry blender or two knives until the fat is the size of corn kernels. Combine milk and vinegar. Add to flour mixture and stir until just combined. Chill the dough. Roll out on floured surface. Makes two crusts.

TABBOULEH

1 cup burghul (cracked wheat)
½ cup onion, chopped
3 medium tomatoes, chopped
2 bunches parsley, stems removed,
and chopped
½ cup mint, chopped
½ teaspoon salt
1/3 cup fresh lemon juice
1/3 cup olive oil
Tomatoes
Romaine lettuce

Pour 2 cups boiling water over burghul. Soak for 30 minutes. Drain and squeeze out excess moisture. Add chopped onions, tomatoes, mint, and parsley. Mix well. Mix together olive oil, lemon juice, and salt. Add to chopped ingredients.

Decorate with tomato wedges. Use romaine lettuce leaves to scoop up tabbouleh.

BESSIE'S CORNBREAD

1 egg
1 cup milk
¼ cup vegetable oil
1 cup sugar
¼ cup yellow cornmeal
2 cups flour
½ teaspoon salt
¼ teaspoon soda
2 teaspoons baking powder

Preheat oven to 375°F. Combine egg, milk, oil, and sugar; mix well. Add dry ingredients and mix until just combined. Recipe can be made into muffins or baked in an 8 by 8 or 9 by 9 greased cake pan. Muffins take 15 minutes. Cake pans will require 25 to 30 minutes. Check after 20 minutes.

Recipe comes from the late Bessie Germaine of Marblehead, Massachusetts. She was a superb cook. This cornbread is sweet compared to most cornbread recipes. Less sugar can be used, and the ratio of cornmeal to flour adjusted. For example, ½ cup cornmeal to 1¾ cups flour for a stronger cornmeal flavor.

JOHN'S BATTER FOR TWO POUNDS OF FISH

Dry fish thoroughly

2 egg yolks
1/3 cup milk
1/3 cup water
1 tablespoon lemon juice
1 tablespoon melted butter
½ teaspoon salt
1 cup sifted flour
2 egg whites stiffly beaten

Combine egg yolks, milk, water, lemon juice, butter, salt, and flour. Fold in egg whites. Dip fish pieces in batter and fry in hot oil until golden.

John notes: "Over the years we've tried many fish batters—and this is the best."

BUTTERSCOTCH SAUCE

1½ cup packed brown sugar
½ cup light corn syrup
¼ cup butter
½ cup cream
1 teaspoon vanilla
¼ teaspoon vinegar (my addition)

Heat brown sugar, syrup, butter, and vinegar over low heat to boiling, stirring constantly. Remove from heat. Stir in cream and vanilla. Stir again just before serving.

TOMATO SOUP CAKE

2 cups all-purpose flour
1 cup sugar
2 teaspoons baking powder
1 teaspoon baking soda
½ teaspoon salt (my addition)
1 teaspoon cinnamon
1 teaspoon ground cloves
1 teaspoon nutmeg
1 can (10¾ ounces Campbell's Tomato Soup)
½ cup shortening
1 egg
1 cup raisins
1 cup chopped nuts

Preheat oven to 350°F. Generously grease and flour an 8-inch square pan. Measure dry ingredients into large bowl. Add soup and shortening. Beat at low to medium speed for 2 minutes (300 strokes with a spoon), scraping sides and bottom of bowl constantly. Add egg. Beat 2 minutes more, scraping bowl constantly. Stir in nuts and raisins. Pour into pan. Bake 1 hour. Let stand in pan 10 minutes. Remove. Cool and frost with a cream cheese frosting

Cream Cheese Frosting

1½ cups of confectioners' sugar
1 package cream cheese (3 ounces) room temperature
1 teaspoon vanilla
With electric mixer beat all three ingredients in a small bowl until smooth. Spread.

PINEAPPLE UPSIDE DOWN CAKE

½ cup butter
½ cup packed brown sugar
1 small can sliced pineapple
    juice removed
1½ cups all-purpose flour
½ cup sugar
2 teaspoons baking powder
½ teaspoon salt
½ cup each: soft margarine, milk
½ cup reserved pineapple juice
1 teaspoon vanilla
½ teaspoon lemon extract
1 egg

Heat oven to 350°. Melt ½ cup butter in 9-inch square pan. Sprinkle brown sugar evenly over melted butter. Arrange pineapple slices (and cherries if you want) in attractive pattern on the butter-sugar coating.

Combine all remaining ingredients except the egg; beat with mixer for 2 minutes, scraping sides and bottom of bowl constantly. Add the egg and beat 2 more minutes scraping bowl. Pour batter over fruit. Bake for 40 to 50 minutes, or until cake tests done.

Immediately turn cake upside down on serving plate. Leave pan over cake for a few minutes. Remove pan and serve cake warm with or without whipped cream.

PUMPKIN BREAD

2 cups sugar
1 cup salad oil
3 eggs
1 can (15 ounces) pumpkin
1 teaspoon salt
1 teaspoon nutmeg
½ teaspoon baking powder
1 teaspoon soda
1 teaspoon ground cloves
1 teaspoon cinnamon
3 cups flour
1 cup raisins
½ cup chopped walnuts (optional)

Preheat oven to 325°F. Grease two 9 by 12 by 2 or three 8 by 4 loaf pans. Mix sugar, oil, eggs, and pumpkin by hand or at medium speed. Blend well. Mix and sift dry ingredients and add to pumpkin mixture. Add raisins and nuts. Bake 60 minutes. Bread should spring back when done. Cool 15 minutes before removing from pans.

MULLED WINE

2½ cups sugar
1¼ cups water
4 dozen whole cloves
6 sticks cinnamon
3 crushed nutmegs
Strips of fresh lemon and orange zest

Make a syrup by boiling above ingredients for five minutes. Strain and add syrup to 4 cups hot lemon juice. Mix with four bottles of hot red wine. Serve hot with thin slices of lemon and oranges floating in mugs. A large Crock-Pot set on low makes an excellent server.

EASY MEATLOAF

8 ounce can tomato sauce
1¼ pounds lean ground beef
½ cup quick raw oats
1/3 cup grated Parmesan cheese
1 large egg
1 small onion (chopped)
¾ teaspoon salt
¼ teaspoon pepper
Sweet-sour sauce (below)

Pour a little tomato sauce into bottom of a 9 by 5 inch loaf pan. Spread evenly. Add rest of sauce to meat, oats, cheese, egg, onion, salt, and pepper. Mix well and press into loaf pan and bake 30 to 40 minutes at 350°F. Drain off any fat and pour sweet-sour sauce over meat loaf, return to oven, and bake 30 minutes longer or until done.

Sweet Sour Sauce

Mix an 8-ounce can tomato sauce, ¾ cup brown sugar, ½ cup red wine vinegar, and 2 teaspoons prepared mustard. Blend. Simmer 5 minutes.

WALNUT CHEESE BALL

16 ounces cream cheese (room temperature)
6 ounces Roquefort cheese
1 teaspoon finely chopped parsley
¼ teaspoon onion salt
1 teaspoon mayonnaise
¼ teaspoon pepper
¼ teaspoon paprika
1 cup finely chopped walnuts

Mix all ingredients except chopped nuts. Roll into ball. Roll ball in chopped walnuts until well covered. Refrigerate for 2 to 4 hours until firm. Serve with crackers.

SOFT HERMITS

1 cup sugar
½ cup shortening
2 eggs
½ cup molasses
1 teaspoon cinnamon
½ teaspoon nutmeg
½ teaspoon cloves
1/2 teaspoon salt
2 ½ cups flour
1 teaspoon baking powder
1 cup raisins
1/2 cup walnuts, chopped

Cream shortening and sugar. Add eggs. Sift dry ingredients and add alternately with molasses. Grease a cookie sheet with 1 inch edges. Spoon in batter and spread to edges. Bake at 375°F. for 20 minutes. Cut while warm

Optional: Orange Glaze

Zest of one orange, minced
1 cup confectioners' sugar
2 tablespoons plus, of orange juice

Combine ingredients mixing until smooth. Glaze should be soupy. Smooth over warm hermits.

CINNAMON YOGURT PANCAKES

1 cup yogurt
2 eggs
1 cup milk
2 tablespoons oil
1½ cups flour
2 teaspoons baking powder
½ teaspoon salt
1 teaspoon cinnamon

Beat together first 4 ingredients. Sift in dry ingredients. Stir until combined. Let batter stand 20 minutes before cooking on very hot, lightly greased griddle.

Variations: Add ½ cup cottage cheese and cook pancakes a little longer. Add 1 cup blueberries, fresh or frozen. Stir in 1 cup grated apple (not red or golden delicious)

APPENDIX 2

MY FAVORITE RECIPES FROM THE

AL HASA COOKBOOK

In 1974 women from Aramco, Northrop, Bechtel, El Ajou, and the University of Petroleum and Minerals formed a committee to gather and publish their favorite recipes. In 1976 the *Al Hasa Cookbook* (General Publishing and Binding, Iowa Falls, Iowa) was printed containing the recipes from 340 women representing a wide variety of nationalities. Although I have not tried all of the recipes in this unique cookbook, I especially like the recipes that follow. Some of these recipes were circulated long before they appeared in the *Al Hasa Cookbook*.

Note: Al Hasa is the old name for the area of the Eastern Province of the kingdom where the towns of Dammam and Al-Khobar are situated. It is also the location of the University of Petroleum and Minerals and the Aramco towns at Dhahran, Ras Tanura, and Abqaiq.

HOT MUSHROOM TURNOVERS

Lu McClaine, Aramco—Dhahran

3 (3 ounce) packages cream cheese (softened)
1 1/2 cups flour (sifted)
1/2 cup butter or margarine (softened)

In a large bowl, with electric mixer at medium speed, beat cream cheese, 1/2 cup butter, and 1 1/2 cups flour until soft dough forms. Wrap dough in waxed paper; refrigerate at least 1 hour.

3 tablespoons butter
1 large onion (minced)
1/2 pound mushrooms (minced)
1 teaspoon salt
1/4 teaspoon thyme leaves
2 tablespoons flour
1/4 cup sour cream
1 egg (beaten)

In a medium skillet over medium heat, in 3 tablespoons margarine, cook mushrooms and onion until tender, about 5 minutes. Stir in salt, thyme, and 2 tablespoons flour until blended. Stir in sour cream.

On a floured board, thinly roll out 1/2 of dough, cut into about 12 circles with a 2 3/4 inch cookie cutter. Roll dough scraps into a ball. Refrigerate.

On one-half of each circle, place a teaspoonful of mushroom mixture. Brush edges with egg. Fold edge over filling to meet bottom edge. With a fork, press edges together and prick tops in 3 places to let out steam.

Place on ungreased cookie sheets. Brush turnovers with egg. Bake at 450°F for 12 to 15 minutes or until golden. Makes 50.

These freeze very well before they are baked. I always make mine ahead and freeze them and bake then so they are served hot.

GALA PECAN SPREAD

Sylvia Bullard, Aramco—Dhahran

8 ounces cream cheese (soft)
2 tablespoons milk
1 (2 1/2 ounce) jar dried beef
  (sliced)
1/4 cup green peppers (finely chopped)
2 tablespoon dried onion flakes
1/8 teaspoon black pepper
1/2 cup sour cream
1/2 cup pecans (coarsely chopped)
2 tablespoons butter
1/2 teaspoon salt
1/2 teaspoon garlic salt

Combine cheese and milk. Stir in beef (which has been cut into small pieces), green pepper, onion flakes, and the rest of seasonings. Mix well. Fold in sour cream. Spoon into an 8-inch pie plate. Sauté pecans in melted butter. Salt lightly. Sprinkle nuts over cake mixture.

Heat in a 350°F oven for about 20 minutes. Serve warm with crackers, raw vegetables, or toasted Arab bread. This recipe can be made early in the day and heated just before serving.

HOMEMADE CEREAL

Erma Britton, UPM—Dhahran

4 cups rolled oats
1 cup sesame seeds
1 cup wheat germ
1 cup grated coconut
1 cup powdered milk
1 cup honey
1 cup salad oil
1 cup raisins
1/2 cup nuts (chopped)

Mix dry ingredients (except raisins and nuts) in a large bowl. Mix honey and oil and stirring together, toss this mixture with the dry ingredients. Spread in thin layers on cookie sheets. Bake in a slow oven (250°F) for 1 hour or until lightly browned. Add the raisins and nuts and cool. Makes a good snack as is or a cereal with milk. May also be an ingredient in cookie recipes.

Note: For variety I sometimes add a tablespoon of cinnamon and 1 cup of sunflower seeds.

MARINATED SLAW

Betty Gay, Aramco—Abqaiq

1 large cabbage
2 green sweet peppers
2 onions
2 cups sugar
4 teaspoons sugar
1 cup vinegar
3/4 cup salad oil
1 teaspoon dry mustard
1 teaspoon celery seed
1 tablespoon salt

Chop cabbage, pepper, and onion and mix together. Add 2 cups sugar. Mix the sugar, with the vinegar, salad oil, mustard, celery seed, and salt. Bring to a boil. Pour boiled mixture over cabbage mixture. Seal in an airtight container. Do not stir or uncover for at least 4 hours. This slaw will keep in the refrigerator for a week or more.

THREE BEAN SALAD

Ruth Edmondson, Aramco—Dhahran

1 (1 pound) can cut green beans
1 (1 pound) can cut wax beans
1 (15 ounce) can dark red kidney beans
1/2 cup green pepper (chopped)
1/2 cup sugar
2/3 cup vinegar
1/3 cup salad oil
1 teaspoon salt
1/4 teaspoon pepper

Drain all the beans and combine. Add green pepper. Combine sugar, vinegar, oil, salt, and pepper. Pour over beans and toss. Chill. Serves 6.

Note: Sometimes I add a small onion, chopped.

MACARONI-SHRIMP SALAD

Helen Crawford, Aramco—Ras Tanura

3/4 cup small macaroni shells (cooked 1 1/2 cups)
8 ounces cleaned shrimp (cooked and cut in half lengthwise)
1/3 cup celery (chopped)
2 tablespoons pimiento stuffed green olives (sliced)
1 tablespoon parsley (snipped)

Combine macaroni, shrimp, celery, olives, and parsley.

DRESSING

1/2 cup mayonnaise or salad dressing
2 tablespoons red wine vinegar
2 teaspoons lemon juice
1/4 teaspoon garlic salt
1/4 teaspoon dry mustard
1/4 teaspoon paprika

Blend together mayonnaise, vinegar, lemon juice, garlic salt, mustard, and paprika. Toss with shrimp mixture. Serves 4.

PARTY MASHED POTATOES

Lois Robertson, Aramco—Ras Tanura

8 to 10 medium-sized potatoes
1 (8 ounce) package cream cheese
1/4 cup dairy sour cream
Salt and pepper
2 tablespoons butter
Paprika

Boil potatoes. Drain. Beat softened cream cheese and sour cream at medium speed until well blended. Add hot potatoes gradually. Beat until fluffy. Season to taste with salt and pepper. Place in a buttered dish. Brush with melted butter and sprinkle with paprika. Will keep in a warm oven.

[*Note:* I fold in 1/4 cup snipped chives if I plan to serve immediately.]

SPINACH CASSEROLE

Aloma Gies, Aramco—Dhahran

1 (10 ounce) package frozen chopped spinach
1 tablespoon onion (minced)
2 tablespoons butter or margarine
1 cup milk
Paprika
3 hard cooked eggs, chopped
1/8 teaspoon nutmeg
1/2 teaspoon salt
1/8 teaspoon pepper
1/2 cup Cheddar cheese (grated)

Cook spinach according to directions on package. Drain. Cook onion in butter until transparent. Add flour and blend thoroughly. Add milk and cook until thickened, stirring constantly. Add spinach, chopped eggs, and seasoning. Pour into a 1½ quart buttered casserole. Top with cheese and crumbs. Sprinkle with paprika. Bake at 350°F for 20 to 30 minutes. Makes 4 servings.

HAMBURGER UPSIDE DOWN CASSEROLE

Patsy Whitley, Aramco—Dhahran

2 1/2 cups elbow macaroni
  (uncooked)
3 tablespoons margarine
1/2 cup onion (minced)
2 teaspoons garlic (minced)
1 pound ground chuck
1 (8 ounce) can tomato sauce
1 teaspoon salt
1/4 teaspoon pepper
1/4 teaspoon oregano
1 (8 ounce) package Cheddar cheese (grated)
3 eggs, beaten
3/4 cup milk

The day before: Cook macaroni in salted water until tender; drain. In a skillet, sauté in margarine the ground beef, onion, and garlic until meat is browned. Stir in tomato sauce and spices. Simmer a few minutes, then spread over bottom of a greased 2 quart casserole. Toss macaroni with cheese. Arrange on top of meat, pressing it down. Combine eggs and milk. Pour over casserole.

Cover and refrigerate until the next day.

Next day: take casserole out and let set for 15 minutes. Preheat oven to 350°F and bake for 1 1/2 hours or until macaroni is golden and custard is set.

BAKED STUFFED RED SNAPPER

Glenda Shepard, Aramco—Ras Tanura

1 (4 to 5 pound) red snapper (cleaned)
2 (6 ounce) cans crab meat
1 cup green onion (chopped)
1 cup onion (chopped)
1 cup celery (chopped)
1 cup bread cubes (toasted)
2 eggs
Salt (to taste)
1/2 teaspoon red pepper
1 teaspoon black pepper
1/4 teaspoon garlic powder
3 teaspoons lemon juice

Wash and dry fish; set aside. Preheat oven to 375°F. In a large bowl mix crabmeat, onions, celery, bread cubes, eggs, and seasonings. Rub fish with lemon juice and stuff mixture in cavity of fish; if any is left over, place around fish in pan. Cover with foil and bake for 1 1/2 to 2 hours. Serves 4.

BAKED SHRIMP OREGANO

Helen Crawford, Aramco—Ras Tanura

1 pound raw shrimp (shelled, deveined)
2 tablespoons lemon juice
1/4 cup butter or margarine
1/2 cup fine bread crumbs
  (or a little more)
2 cloves garlic (peeled and crushed)
2 tablespoons parsley (chopped)
2 tablespoons Parmesan cheese (grated)
1 teaspoon dried oregano leaves
Dash of cayenne
Parsley sprigs and lemon wedges

Preheat oven to 350°F. Wash shrimp; drain well. Arrange shrimp in a 9-inch pie plate. Sprinkle with lemon juice. In a medium bowl, combine melted butter, crumbs, garlic, chopped parsley, Parmesan cheese, oregano, and cayenne. (Should be somewhat crumbly. If too "gummy," add a few more crumbs.) Spoon over shrimp.

Bake, uncovered, 15 minutes. Then broil 5 inches from heat until crumbs are browned, about 3 minutes. Garnish with parsley sprigs and lemon wedges. Serve immediately. Makes 2 to 3 regular servings. Makes 6 appetizer servings.

LASAGNA

Rose Mowbray, Aramco—Ras Tanura

1 pound sweet hot Italian sausage
1/2 pound ground beef
1/2 cup onion (finely chopped)
2 cloves garlic (crushed)
2 tablespoons sugar
1 tablespoon salt
1 1/2 teaspoons dried basil
1/2 teaspoon fennel seed
1/4 teaspoon pepper
1/4 cup parsley (chopped)
4 cups canned tomatoes (undrained)
2 (6 ounce) cans tomato paste
1 tablespoon salt
12 curly lasagna noodles (3/4 of 1 pound package)
1 (15 ounce) container ricotta or cottage cheese (drained)
1 egg
1/2 teaspoon salt
3/4 pound mozzarella cheese (grated or thinly sliced)
3/4 cup Parmesan cheese (grated)

Remove sausage meat from outer casings; chop the meat. In a 5 quart Dutch oven, over medium heat, sauté sausage meat and beef. Break up beef with a wooden spoon. Add onion and garlic, stirring frequently, until well browned, about 20 minutes. Add sugar, 1 tablespoon salt, basil, fennel, pepper, and 1/2 the parsley; mix well. Add tomatoes, tomato paste, and 1/2 cup water, mashing tomatoes with a wooden spoon. Bring to boiling. Reduce heat. Simmer, cover, stir occasionally, until thick, 1 1/2 hours.

In an 8-quart kettle, bring 3 quarts of water to a boil. Add 1 tablespoon salt and lasagna, 2 or 3 at a time. Return to boiling. Boil, uncovered and stirring occasionally for 10 minutes or just until tender. Drain in colander. Rinse under cold water. Dry on paper towels. Preheat oven to 375°F.

In a medium bowl, combine ricotta, egg, remaining parsley, and salt; mix well. In the bottom of a 13 by 9 by 2 inch pan, spoon 1 1/2 cups sauce. Layer with 6 lasagna, lengthwise and overlapping, to cover. Spread with 1/2 of ricotta mixture; top with 1/3 of mozzarella. Spoon with 1 1/2 cups sauce over cheese. Sprinkle with Parmesan. Repeat and cover with last 6 lasagna noodles. Spread with remaining sauce, top with rest of mozzarella and Parmesan. Cover with foil, tucking around edge. Bake 25 minutes. Remove foil. Bake, uncovered, 25 minutes longer. Cool 15 minutes before serving. To serve: cut in squares with a sharp knife; remove with spatula to serve.

CARBONADE OF BEEF

Ann Dymock, Aramco—Dhahran

1 to 1 1/2 pounds stew beef
2 tablespoons cooking fat
2 onions
1 tablespoon flour
1 clove garlic (crushed)
1 cup stock
1 cup beer
1 teaspoon sugar

Cut meat into 1-inch cubes. Heat fat and brown meat on all sides over a high flame. Remove meat. Fry onions until they begin to color. Add the flour and garlic to onions and mix well. Remove from heat and add the beer and stock gradually. Return to heat and bring to boil, stirring all the time. Season, add sugar, and return meat to the pan. Cover and simmer for 2 hours. Serves 4.

ROAST BEEF DINNER IN TINFOIL

Kaye Abikhaled, Aramco—Dhahran

3 to 4 pounds roast beef
1 can cream of mushroom soup
2 medium bay leaves
2 tablespoons salt
1 tablespoon pepper
1 teaspoon garlic powder
l teaspoon paprika
4 tablespoons oil
1 soup can of water
3 small onions (sliced)
5 medium potatoes (peeled and quartered)
5 carrots (scraped and sliced diagonally)
1 (10 ounce) package frozen corn

Heat oil in a skillet large enough to hold roast. Sprinkle roast on all sides with salt, pepper, garlic powder, and paprika. Brown on all sides, making sure fatty parts and skin on outside of meat are cut through at intervals. Meanwhile, line a large broiler pan with heavy duty (or double thickness) tinfoil large enough to wrap roast and all vegetables. When meat is brown, remove to tinfoil, turn down heat, add cream of mushroom soup and water, and stir until blended. Pour over roast, top with bay leaves and sliced onions. Arrange potatoes in opposite corners of pan, then fill remaining corners with carrots and corn. Fold tinfoil over, doubling at top and sealing well. Fold sides in, sealing well. Place in a 275°F oven and bake for 3 1/2 hours to 4 hours.

Let stand 10 minutes, then roll tinfoil back around edges of pan, garnish with a few sprigs of parsley, and serve immediately with rolls and butter. Yields 6 to 8 servings.

NOTE: Any kind of beef can be successfully roasted with this method, even the toughest. It will get tender. Juices remain in the meal flavoring the vegetables. Add 1/2 cup of cooking wine for a special kind of gravy.

OVEN CHICKEN WITH CURRIED RICE

Lutfiya Qahwash, UPM—Dhahran

1 cup onion (chopped)
2 tablespoons butter
1 cup light raisins
8 cups long grain rice
  (cooked)
1 (3 1/2 ounce) can flaked coconut
1 tablespoon curry powder
1/2 teaspoon salt
2 cups chicken broth
1/2 cup butter (melted)
1 tablespoon salt
2 teaspoons paprika
1/2 teaspoon pepper
2 (2 1/2 to 3 pounds) chickens (cut up)
3/4 cup salted peanuts (chopped)

Cook onion in 2 tablespoons butter until tender. Add next five ingredients; toss to mix. Place in a 17 by 12 by 2 1/2 inch baking pan. Drizzle chicken broth over evenly, mixing lightly with a fork. Cover with foil.

Combine 1/2 cup melted butter with 1 tablespoon salt, paprika, and pepper. [*Note:* I use less.] Rub well into chicken pieces. Place skin side up in a 15 1/2 by 10 1/2 by 1 inch pan. Bake rice, covered, in a hot oven (400°F) for 30 to 45 minutes and chicken, uncovered, for 1 hour and 15 minutes. Remove foil from rice. Add peanuts. Fluff and mix with a fork. Transfer rice to serving platter, if desired. Top with chicken pieces. Spoon some of the pan drippings over. Makes 8 servings. Rice can be prepared a day ahead and refrigerated.

LEMON CHICKEN

Lois Robertson, Aramco—Ras Tanura

3 pound broiler-fryer (cut up)
2 tablespoons olive oil
1/2 teaspoon salt
1/8 teaspoon pepper
1/3 cup fresh lemon juice
2 cloves garlic (crushed in
  press)
1/4 cup fresh parsley (chop fine)
1/4 cup fresh green onion (chop fine)
1/8 teaspoon basil
1/8 teaspoon sage
1/8 teaspoon marjoram

Wash chicken; pat dry with paper towels. Arrange in a shallow roasting pan. Drizzle with olive oil. Sprinkle with salt and pepper. Broil at 350°F, turning, until brown on both sides. Sprinkle with onions and parsley. In a small bowl, combine lemon juice, garlic, basil, sage, and marjoram. Pour over chicken; cover, and bake 15 minutes longer or until tender.

To serve: Arrange chicken pieces on heated platter. Spoon pan drippings over them. Garnish with thin lemon slices and parsley sprigs, if desired. Makes 4 servings. Good served with rice.

CHICKEN TARRAGON

Stephanie McNicholas, Aramco—Dhahran

2 1/2 pounds chicken breasts
2/3 cup butter
2 teaspoons flour
2/3 cup hot water
2 teaspoons A-1 sauce
1 1/2 tablespoons lemon juice
1/4 teaspoon Tabasco sauce
2 teaspoons sugar
1 teaspoon salt
1/2 teaspoon MSG or Ac'cent
1 teaspoon tarragon
1/4 teaspoon garlic powder
3/4 teaspoon paprika

Melt butter and stir in flour until blended smoothly. Add remaining ingredients and cook for 2 or 3 minutes or until slightly thickened. Pour over chicken breasts and marinate 2 to 3 hours.

Broil chicken breasts until brown. Place breasts in a pan and pour the marinade over them. Bake about 30 to 40 minutes in a 350°F oven. Hot marinade can be taken to the table separately. Serves 4 to 6.

CHICKEN OR TURKEY A LA KING

Christy Salam, Betchel—Al-Khobar

1 (6 ounce) can sliced mushrooms (drained,
  reserve 1/4 cup liquid)
1/2 cup green pepper (diced)
1/2 cup butter or margarine
1/2 cup flour
1/2 cup salt
1/4 teaspoon black pepper
2 cups light cream
1 3/4 cups chicken broth
2 cups cooked chicken or turkey (cubed)
1 (4 ounce) jar pimiento chopped
Toast cups or patty shells or toasted slices of white bread (usually 2 per person)

In a large skillet, cook and stir mushroom and green peppers in butter or margarine for 5 minutes, medium heat. Blend in flour, salt, and pepper. Cook over low heat, stirring until mixture is bubbly. Remove from heat. Stir in light cream, chicken broth, and the reserved mushroom liquid. Heat to boiling, stirring constantly. Boil and stir 1 minute. Stir in cooked chicken or turkey and chopped pimiento. Heat and serve over hot toast cups, patty shells, or toasted slices of white bread. Serves 8.

NOTE: This recipe can be made ahead, can be frozen, and used any time you want.

SPANISH TORTILLA

Angela Rimmer, UPM—Dammam

3 medium potatoes, sliced
1 large onion, chopped
Salt, pepper, and garlic powder (to taste)
2 to 3 tablespoons olive oil
2 eggs

Heat oil in an omelet pan, add potatoes, onions and seasoning. Fry gently until soft; remove from pan. In a small bowl beat 2 eggs lightly; add potato and onion mixture and stir. Return mix to omelet pan and cook until underside is firm. Put under grill to cook the omelet from above, slide from pan to plate. Made with larger quantities and cut into squares make a delicious party hors d'oeuvres.

CHICKEN ADOBO (JAPANESE)

Jo Zaki Marar, El Ajou—Al-Khobar

1 whole frying chicken, cut up and rinsed
2 cloves garlic (crushed)
1 tsp. black ground pepper
2 1/2 tablespoons Kikkoman soy sauce
3 tablespoons cider vinegar
4 tablespoons butter
1 teaspoon Ajinomoto (MSG may omit)
Salt (to taste)

Put chicken pieces into six quart Dutch oven. Add remaining ingredients. Mix well, and never at any stage of the cooking add any water. Cook on high heat for the first 15 minutes or so. Stir and mix every few minutes and keep covered at all times after each stirring. Reduce heat and continue cooking until liquid is reduced and thickish, the butter in it clarifies, and the chicken is tender and thoroughly cooked. Correct seasoning. Salting, especially, must be completed while it is being cooked or right before you turn off the heat, as this makes a big difference. This is a delicious dish if you like spicy food and something very different. It keeps up to a week, tastes even better after a few days, and is so easy to prepare.

THANH XAO (BEEF SALAD) (VIETNAM)

Sandra Hardin, Aramco—Abqaiq

1 pound round steak
6 to 8 green onions (chopped)
1/2 cup soy sauce
2 medium heads lettuce
1/4 to 1/3 cup vinegar
2 medium onions (sliced)
2 garlic cloves (minced)

Slice steak in very thin pieces (I use an electric knife). Marinate in mixture of soy sauce, green onions, garlic, and black pepper to taste. Let stand about 30 minutes. Place skillet on high heat; cover bottom of pan with oil. When hot, stir in meat mixture and cook quickly. Turn to simmer; add vinegar and onion. Simmer 3 to 4 minutes. Turn off heat. Break up lettuce into large bowl, and pour hot meat mixture over lettuce. Serve.

MALAYSIAN SATAY

Sylvia Bullard, Aramco—Dhahran

1/2 cup soy sauce
1 teaspoon dark molasses
1 teaspoon hot red pepper
  (ground)
3/4 cup hot water
1/3 cup peanut butter
1/2 cup roasted peanuts (ground)
1 garlic clove (minced)
Juice of 1 lemon
3 pounds beef tenderloin (cut in 1 inch cubes)

Combine all ingredients except meat in a medium-sized pan and bring to a boil. Stir until smooth, then cool. Pour 1/2 of sauce over beef cubes. Mix well and let stand 1 hour. Reserve rest of marinade for hot sauce. Arrange beef cubes on small skewers and broil meat quickly on all sides using either broiler or a hibachi. Serve with hot sauce recipe found on the following page.

HOT SAUCE

Reserved marinade
1/2 cup tomato sauce
1/4 cup water
Juice of 1 lemon
1 tsp. Tabasco sauce

Combine all and bring to boil. Use as dip for skewered beef cubes. This recipe is excellent served with a rice pilaf and tossed salad or as an hors d'oeuvres. Serves 6.

MEXICAN CHEF'S SALAD

Adele P. Allen, Aramco—Abqaiq

1 onion
4 tomatoes
1 head lettuce
4 ounces cheese
8 ounces 1000 Island or French
  dressing
1 bag Doritos (fried tortilla chips)
1 pound ground beef
1 can kidney beans (drained)
Salt (to taste)
Avocado (if available)
Hot sauce (to taste)

Chop onions, tomatoes, 1 head lettuce. Toss with cheese, dressing, and hot sauce to taste. Crush and add chips. Slice and add avocado. Brown and drain beef. Add can of beans, salt. Brown for 10 minutes and mix into cold salad. Decorate with chips, avocado, and tomato slices. Serves 6 to 10.

MEXICAN WEDDING RING COOKIES

Sharon Wythe, Aramco—Ras Tanura

1 cup butter or margarine
1/2 cup powdered sugar
2 cups flour
1 teaspoon vanilla
1 cup nuts (chopped)

Cream shortening and sugar using a mixer. Add remaining ingredients and mix well. Do not use electric mixer. Make walnut size balls. Bake on greased cookie sheet in a 325°F oven for 30 minutes. Roll in powdered sugar while still hot. Makes approximately 2 dozen. This recipe may be doubled, tripled, etc. These freeze well.

QUICHE LORRAINE

Michèle Cleron, UPM—Dhahran

8 ounce puff pastry (frozen)
4 eggs
1/2 cup light cream
1 onion
1/4 pound ham
Salt and pepper
1 ounce Gruyere or Emmenthal cheese, grated

Roll out pastry and line pan. Beat eggs and cream together. Slice onion and put in 10-inch pie pan. Chop ham and put on top of onion. Pour over cream and egg mixture. Sprinkle with grated cheese. Bake at 500°F for 30 minutes until top is brown. Serves 4 as an appetizer.

SCANDINAVIAN TEA RING

Louise M. Tucker, Aramco—Dhahran

2 eggs
3/4 cup water (85 °F)
1 package yeast
1 teaspoon salt
4 cups all-purpose flour
  (sifted)
2 tablespoons sugar
1/2 cup butter (softened) (4 ounces)
1 cup butter (cut into small squares)

Have all ingredients at room temperature. Beat 2 eggs, add the 3/4 cup water, and then dissolve the yeast in this mixture. Let stand in the refrigerator for 15 minutes.

In the meantime, using a pastry blender, blend the 4 cups flour, salt, sugar, and 1/2 cup butter thoroughly. Make a well in this mixture and pour in the egg, water, and yeast. Using the dough hook or spoon, thoroughly blend until all dry ingredients are combined. Knead for 2 minutes until smooth. Let rest in a covered bowl in the refrigerator for 20 minutes.

Lightly roll out dough into a rectangle, about 3/4 inch thick and 18 inches long by 8 inches wide. Dot the squares of butter over 2/3 of this oblong and then fold, envelope fashion, so that the butter surface is covered by an unbuttered surface. The dough is now in 3 layers. Swing the layered dough a 1/4 turn—for example from east to south. Roll lightly again into an oblong and repeat the butter dotting over 2/3 of the dough. Roll, dot, and fold twice more. Then place the dough in a bowl, cover, and chill for at least 2 hours. Grease 2 large cookie sheets. Cut the dough in half, making sure to cut in same direction as the last butter fold. Roll each half into an oblong 18 inches long by about 6 to 8 inches wide and spread filling. See filling #1 and #2 below. Roll up tightly and bring both ends together to form a ring. Then place onto the lightly greased cookie sheet. Using a pair of floured scissors, cut gashes about 1 inch apart into the outer edges of the ring to within 1/2 to 3/4 inch of center. Turn each slice flat onto the cookie sheet.

Cover with a wet cloth and let rise to double. Bake at 375°F for 25 minutes or until done, time depends on filling, give or take 5 to 10 minutes.

FILLING #1

1/4 cup butter
1/2 cup confectioners' sugar
1/2 teaspoon vanilla
1/2 cup almonds (ground)
For one ring only. Cream butter; add icing sugar, vanilla, and almonds. Spread over ring before rolling.

FILLING #2

1/2 cup raisins (chopped)
2 tablespoons sugar
1 tablespoon cinnamon
2 tablespoons butter (softened)

Mix the raisins, sugar, and cinnamon together. Spread the softened butter over the rolled pastry. Shake and spread the raisin mixture over the butter. Then roll and cut as above.

For a sweeter taste you may drizzle frosting made with confectioners' sugar and hot water all over the rings while they are still warm.

JOAN'S HUNGARIAN PASTRIES

Rose Ann Elbert, Aramco—Dhahran

1 (3 ounce) package cream cheese
1/2 cup butter or margarine
1 cup flour (sifted)
2 tablespoons sugar
Fruit preserves

Cream butter and cream cheese until smooth. Combine flour and sugar. Add 1/2 of flour mixture to cheese mixture, blending well. Then add remaining flour. Mix thoroughly, divide dough into halves, and shape each into a ball. Wrap in plastic wrap and chill until dough is easily handled. Roll out dough into 1/8 inch thickness and cut into diamond shapes. Spoon fruit preserves onto diamonds and overlap two corners. Bake on ungreased baking sheets at 425°F about 10 to 12 minutes. Makes 18 pastries.

OKLAHOMA BARBECUE SAUCE

Milo Cumpston, Aramco—Abqaiq

3/4 cup fresh lemon juice
1/2 cup hot sauce (Tabasco)
1/3 cup tomato catsup
1/3 cup cider vinegar
1/2 cup water
1 1/2 tablespoons brown sugar
1 1/2 teaspoons salt
1 1/2 teaspoons powdered dry mustard
2 teaspoons paprika
3/4 teaspoon ground black pepper
3/4 teaspoon ground cayenne
1/4 cup margarine or butter

Combine all ingredients. Heat only to boiling point. Cool and bottle for future use. Use as a basting sauce for barbecuing of meats and poultry. Tasty for people who like it hot.

RING-OF-COCONUT FUDGE CAKE

Peggy Smith, Aramco—Dhahran

2 cups sugar (can be
  1/4 cup less)
1 cup cooking oil
2 eggs
3 cups all-purpose flour
3/4 cup unsweetened cocoa
2 teaspoons soda
3 teaspoons baking powder
1 1/2 teaspoons salt
1 cup hot coffee
1 cup buttermilk or sour milk
1 teaspoon vanilla
1/2 cup nuts (chopped)

FILLING

1 (8 ounce) package cream cheese
  (softened)
1 teaspoon vanilla
1/4 cup sugar
1 egg
1/2 cup flaked coconut
1/2 cup flaked semisweet or milk chocolate pieces

Preheat oven to 350°F. Bake in a 10-inch tube or bundt cake pan, greased and lightly floured. Prepare filling; set aside.

Filling: In a small bowl, beat cream cheese, sugar, vanilla, and egg until smooth. Stir in coconut and chocolate pieces.

Cake: In a large mixer bowl, combine sugar, oil, and eggs; beat 1 minute at high speed. Add remaining ingredients except filling and nuts;

beat 3 minutes at medium speed, scraping bowl occasionally. By hand, stir in nuts. Pour 1/2 of batter into prepared pan. Carefully spoon prepared filling over batter; top with remaining batter. Bake at 350°F for 70 to 75 minutes until top springs back when touched lightly in the center. Cool upright in pan for 15 minutes; remove from pan. Cool completely. If desired, drizzle with glaze made by combining 1 cup powdered sugar, 3 tablespoons cocoa, 2 tablespoons butter, 2 teaspoons vanilla, and 1 to 3 tablespoons hot water.

MEXICAN FUDGE CAKE

Kay Orrick, Aramco—Dhahran

1 cup sugar
1 cup shortening
4 eggs
1/2 teaspoon salt
1 cup flour
1 teaspoon vanilla
1 cup nuts
1 (1 pound) can Hershey chocolate syrup

Mix together all ingredients well. Bake in a greased and floured 2 by 9 by13 inch cake pan for 35 minutes at 350°F or until done. Frost with corn starch icing.

CORN STARCH ICING

1 cup sugar
4 teaspoons cocoa
2 tablespoons corn starch
1 cup water
1/4 stick butter (2 tablespoons)
1/2 cup pecans
1 teaspoon vanilla

For the first 4 ingredients in a saucepan and cook until thick, stirring constantly. Add butter, vanilla, and pecans. Cool slightly and frost cake.

CHEESECAKE—NEVER FAILS

Susan Beck, UPM—Dhahran

[Cut by 1/3 for layer cake pan size.]

CRUST

1 cup graham crackers, granola
or cookie crumbs (crushed)
4 tablespoons sugar
5 tablespoons butter (softened)

FILLING

3 (8 ounce) packages cream cheese
3/4 cups sugar (or less)
1/2 teaspoon lemon rind
3 tablespoons flour
1 teaspoon vanilla
5 or 6 eggs (whole)
1 cup cream or 1 can Danish cream

Place 1 cup crumbs in a 9-inch cake pan. Add sugar and butter. Mix and spread evenly. Bake for 10 minutes at 300°F until hardened. Let cool while making filling.

With mixer cream the cream cheese, sugar, lemon rind, flour, vanilla. Add eggs, one at a time, beating well between each addition. Add cream and beat for 3 minutes. Pour mixture into cooked piecrust and bake at 500°F for about 10 minutes until cake sets and turns slightly brown on top. Then reduce temperature to 200°F and bake an additional hour until firm.

APPLE CAKE

Beth Kaparich, Aramco—Dhahran

I
2 eggs (beaten)
2 cups sugar
2/3 cup Wesson oil
2 teaspoons vanilla
4 cups unpeeled apples (chopped)

II
3 cups flour
2 teaspoons soda
2 teaspoons cinnamon
1/2 teaspoon salt

III: TOPPING
1 cup brown sugar
1/2 cup flour
1 cup nuts (chopped)
1/2 cup butter (softened)

Mix ingredients #I. Sift and add #II. Put in a 9 by 13 inch greased pan. Mix #III together and spread on top of batter. Bake 1 hour at 325°F. An easy recipe to halve. It freezes beautifully.

CARROT CAKE

Claudean Simon, Aramco—Abqaiq

1 3/4 cups sugar
3 cups flour
2 teaspoons soda
1 teaspoon salt
1 1/2 cup salad oil
3 teaspoons cinnamon
2 cups carrots (grated)
1 flat can crushed pineapple
1/2 cup nuts (chopped)
2 teaspoons vanilla
3 eggs
Icing

Sift together flour, soda, cinnamon, and salt. Mix together salad oil and sugar. Add 1/2 of dry ingredients; mix well and beat in carrots, pineapple, and nuts. Add vanilla and rest of dry ingredients. Add eggs, one at a time. Beat until well blended after each addition. Bake in a greased 9 by 12 inch pan at 350°F for 60 minutes or until brown and a toothpick comes out clean when tested. Cool and remove from pan.

CREAM CHEESE ICING

1 (8 ounce) package cream
  cheese
1/2 stick margarine
1 box powdered sugar
1/2 teaspoon lemon extract
1 teaspoon vanilla

Melt margarine and blend in with sugar, cheese, and extract. Mix well. Ice cake when cool. Serves 20 to 24.

TENNESSEE JAM CAKE

Kathy Hamlyn, Aramco—Dhahran

1 cup margarine
1/2 cup sugar
1/2 cup brown sugar
5 eggs
3 cups flour (sifted)
1 tablespoon baking soda
2 teaspoons cinnamon
1 teaspoon nutmeg
1/2 teaspoon cloves
1/2 teaspoon ginger
1 cup buttermilk
3 cups jam
1 cup walnuts or pecans
1 teaspoon vanilla

Cream margarine and sugar. Beat in eggs, one at a time. Sift dry ingredients together and add alternatively with buttermilk. Combine jam, vanilla, and nuts. Fold gently into the batter.

Turn into 3 well-greased layer pans. Bake at 300°F for 15 minutes and then raise to 350°F and continue baking for another 45 minutes. Cool for 10 minutes before turning out only racks. Spread jam between layers of the cake and frost with Sour Cream Frosting (following page). Serves 16.

SOUR CREAM FROSTING

1 cup sugar
1 cup brown sugar
1 cup or 7 3/4 ounce can sour cream
1 teaspoon vanilla

Combine the 2 sugars and sour cream in a saucepan. Cook over medium heat, stirring frequently until soft ball (236°F is reached). Remove from heat and cool to lukewarm. Add vanilla and beat with mixer until it is spreading consistency. If necessary, thin by adding a few drops of milk.

PEANUT BUTTER ROUND UPS

Hendrika Chute, Aramco—Ras Tanura

1 cup shortening
1 cup white sugar
1 cup brown sugar
2 eggs
1 cup peanut butter
2 teaspoons baking soda
1 cup rolled oats
2 cups flour
1/2 teaspoon salt

Add eggs to beaten sugar and shortening. Blend peanut butter. Add remaining ingredients. Make round balls and flatten with a fork. Bake at 350°F on ungreased cookie sheets for about 12 minutes. Makes 6 dozen.

DREAM BARS

Millie Van Ballegooijen, Aramco—Dhahran

1 cup shortening
1 cup brown sugar
2 cups flour
2 cups brown sugar
6 tablespoons flour
1 teaspoon baking powder
1/2 teaspoon salt
4 eggs (slightly beaten)
2 teaspoons vanilla
2 cups coconut
2 cups nuts (chopped)

Cream the shortening and 1 cup brown sugar. Stir in 2 cups flour. Pat evenly into a 9 by 13 inch pan. Bake at 375°F for 10 minutes
Mix 2 cups brown sugar with the 6 tablespoons flour, baking powder, and salt. Beat in the eggs and vanilla. Stir in coconut and nuts. Pour over the first layer. Bake at 375ºF for 30 to 35 minutes.
NOTE: These are especially delicious when made with half dark brown and half light brown sugar. Good warm or cold.

DATE FILLED BARS

Laura Cagle, Northrop—Al-Khobar

2 cups pitted dates (chopped)
2/3 cup water
1 tablespoon lemon juice
1/2 cup nuts (chopped)
1/2 cup butter (soft)
1 cup flour (unsifted)
2/3 cup brown sugar (packed)
1 cup oats
1 teaspoon cinnamon
1/4 to 1/2 teaspoon nutmeg

In a saucepan combine dates, water, and lemon juice. Cook over medium heat until thickened, stirring occasionally. Add nuts. Cool. Cream butter and brown sugar in a mixing bowl. Blend in remaining ingredients until crumbly. Pat 2/3 of crumbs in a lightly greased 9-inch square pan. Spread date mixture over base. Sprinkle with remaining crumbs. Bake 35 to 40 minutes at 350°F. They should be golden brown. Cool and cut into small bars.

These are very sticky and sweet. The dates will solidify more if left open to the air.

FROSTED LEMON BARS

Karen Shepard, Aramco—Abqaiq

1 cup flour
1/4 cup powdered sugar
1/2 cup butter or margarine

FILLING

2 eggs (beaten)
1 cup sugar
2 tablespoon lemon juice
1 cup coconut
1/2 teaspoon salt
2 tablespoons flour
1/2 teaspoon baking powder

FROSTING

3/4 cup powdered sugar
1 1/2 teaspoons milk
1 tablespoon butter
Lemon juice (to taste)

Cream butter and sugar; blend in flour. Press evenly in a 9 by 9 inch pan and bake 10 to 15 minutes at 350°F. Combine eggs, sugar, lemon juice, coconut, salt flour, and baking powder. Spread over cooked crust. Bake an additional 25 minutes.

Combine powdered sugar, butter, milk, and lemon juice and spread over warm bars. Cut in squares when cool.

MINI PECAN PIES

Linda Kelsey, Aramco—Dhahran

1 stick margarine
3 ounces cream cheese
1 cup flour
3/4 cup sugar
1 teaspoon vanilla
1 egg
3/4 cup pecans (chopped)

Cut off 1 inch of margarine and save. Cream remaining margarine and cream cheese and gradually add flour. Divide and press into 24 individual small greased muffin tins.

Cream the inch of margarine, sugar, vanilla, egg, and pecans. Fill shells. Bake at 325°F for 40 minutes.

BLUEBERRY BUCKLE

Margaret Boyes, Aramco—Dhahran

1/4 cup butter
3/4 cup sugar
1 egg
2 cups flour
1 pint blueberries (fresh, frozen or tinned)
2 teaspoons baking powder (heaping)
1/2 teaspoon salt
1/2 cup milk
1 teaspoon vanilla

Cream butter and sugar; add egg and beat well. Add flour, baking powder, and salt alternately with milk and vanilla. Beat for 2 minutes at medium speed until smooth. Fold in blueberries. Pour into a greased and floured tube pan.

TOPPING

1/4 cup butter (soft)
1/2 cup sugar
1/3 cup flour
1/2 teaspoon cinnamon

Combine until crumbly and sprinkle on top of cake. Bake at 350°F for 40 to 45 minutes.

GLOSSARY A

PLACES MENTIONED IN THIS BOOK

(Alphabetical Order after Saudi Arabia)

Saudi Arabia: The official name is "Kingdom of Saudi Arabia." The kingdom is about one-third the size of the continental United States. It is the same distance north of the equator as Mexico. The kingdom is bordered on the north by Iraq, Jordan, and Kuwait, on the west by the Red Sea, the east by the Persian Gulf, and the south by Yemen and Oman. Capital is Riyadh. Government, absolute monarchy. Political parties, none. Religion is 100 percent Muslim, no other religions tolerated. By law all citizens must be Muslims. Language is officially Arabic. There is no personal tourism. Saudi Arabia has 25 percent of the proven oil reserves in the world. It is the only country in the world named after a family—the house of Saud.

The vast majority of the people are Sunnis, and most are Wahhabis, which is the official religion. The Shiites (Shi'as) are excluded from the government and from holding any government office or job of importance. Many Shiites keep their religious preference secret. The current population is approximately twenty-four million. There are now about six million resident foreigners, most from Egypt, followed by Yemen, Jordan, Syria, and Kuwait, and others. About 250,000 came from America and European countries.

The government does not allow women to drive. It is the only country in the world with this ban. Also women cannot get an education, travel, or work without permission from her male guardian. And it is forbidden for women to associate publicly with men or to appear in public without their abayas (long black cloaks) and headscarves.

Saudi Arabia has religious police, known as the Mutawa [Mutawa'een]. Their official name is the "Commission for the Promotion of Virtue and the Prevention of Vice." They patrol the streets making sure that stores are closed at prayer times, that women wear their abayas properly—letting not even a strand of hair escape from their head cloths, that men's hair is cut short, and so forth. They also seize goods that they deem immoral, such as Barbie dolls, magazines with photos of women showing bare legs. Infractions can result in a beating, imprisonment, and/or fine.

The government recognizes only two holidays: Eid al Fitr (which is the end of Ramadan) and Eid Al Adha (which ends the Haj). Following Wahhabi practice, the birth date of the Prophet Muhammad is not celebrated.

The descendants of the Al Saud family are about thirty thousand, but of these only five thousand or so are considered royal—that is princes.

King Faisal reigned from 1964 to 1975, when his nephew shot and killed him. He introduced several reforms, such as schools for girls, and allowed his people to have television. Many, including members of the royal family, opposed these reforms. When he died, Khalid became king, and the kingdom became more conservative. When King Khalid died in 1982, King Fahad succeeded him. Fahad died in 2005 and Crown Prince Abdullah became king.

Abqaiq: A small city located in the interior southwest of the Dhahran, Dammam, Khobar triangle. Aramco's employees populate most of the town. It is a two and a half hour drive from Dhahran.

Al-Khobar: Sometimes called just Khobar. A town on the Persian Gulf. The nearest city to Dhahran, which is to the west of it— six miles away.

Arabian Gulf: See Persian Gulf.

Aramco (Arabian American Oil Company): In 1980 the government of Saudi Arabia gained full control of Aramco. In 1988 it changed the name to Saudi Aramco (Saudi Arabian Oil Company). Its headquarters, which is virtually a city unto itself, is located in Dhahran. The Aramco compound is an enclosed area that has its own post office, shops, theater, gymnasium, swimming pool, houses, and apartments for its employees.

Bahrain: A small country located in the Persian Gulf, about sixteen miles off the eastern coast of Saudi Arabia. In 1986 a four-lane road (the King Fahad Causeway) was completed that connects Al Khobar to one of the smaller Bahrain islands and then continues to the main island. It cost 1.2 billion US dollars and was totally paid for by Saudi Arabia.

Dammam: A Saudi Arabian port city on the Persian Gulf. Ten miles from Dhahran.

Dhahran: Situated in the eastern providence of Saudi Arabia about six miles from the Persian Gulf. It is the headquarters of Aramco (Arabian American Oil Company, now called the Saudi Aramco). Outside of the Aramco compound is the American Consulate. It is also the site of the College of Petroleum and Minerals (CPM), later called the University of Petroleum and Minerals (UPM), and still later the King Fahad University of Petroleum and Minerals (KFUPM). Dhahran has an international airport. It's about nine and a half miles south of Dammam. The nearest town is Al-Khobar to the east—six miles away. Basically in the 1970s the town consisted of Aramco and the college. The compound where the foreign faculty of CPM lived in the 1970s was on the campus of the college.

The weather information for Dhahran is as follows (Temperature is in degrees F; rainfall in inches) [270]

Month	Mean Temperature		Mean Total Rain Fall	Mean Number of Rain Days
	Daily Low	Daily High		
Jan	50.4	69.4	0.69	11.0
Feb	52.7	72.1	0.59	09.7
Mar	58.5	78.1	1.38	16.2
Apr	67.5	90.3	014	07.6
May	76.3	101.7	0.05	02.2
Jun	81.5	107.1	0.00	00.1
Jul	84.0	109.9	0.00	00.1
Aug	83.7	108.3	0.00	00.0
Sep	78.1	104.5	0.00	00.1
Oct	71.6	96.1	0.01	00.6
Nov	62.8	84.0	0.73	04.9
Dec	54.3	73.8	0.62	00.2

Half Moon Bay: A beach on the Persian Gulf, about three miles south of Al-Khobar. In the 1970s it was just a beach. Now it is a busy recreational area, with a Holiday Inn as well as water skiing and boating.

Khamis Mushayt: A town near the north Yemen border.

Persian Gulf: Called Persian Gulf by most Western countries and Arabian Gulf by the Arab countries. The Persian Gulf is six hundred miles long and separates Iran from the eastern coast of Saudi Arabia. At its narrowest point, it is only thirty-four miles wide.

Ras Tanura: The name of a city on a point of land extending into the Persian Gulf. It is the site of the largest oil refinery in the world, owned and operated by Aramco. It is about thirty-five miles north of Dhahran.

---

270   From the World Weather Information Service, http://www.worldweather. org/079/c00696f.htm#climate.

GLOSSARY B

BASICS OF ISLAM

Eids, the: In Arabic "Eid" means festival, celebration. The two Eids are Eid al Adha and Eid al Fitr.

Eid al Adha (Eid ul Adha): The festival of sacrifice. The second festival of the Islamic year (the first is Eid al Fitr) and the most important. By tradition the Eid al Adha follows the period of the **Hajj** (eighth to the tenth) and starts on the tenth of the twelfth month of the Islamic calendar and lasts for four days. In Saudi Arabia the government observes the ten days from the fifth to the fifteenth of the twelfth month as a holiday, although many in the private sector observe only the traditional four days. Eid ul Adha commemorates Ibrahim's (Abraham) willingness to sacrifice his son Ishmael at Allah's command. It is traditional to sacrifice a sheep in remembrance of this event.

Eid al Fitr (Eid ul Fitr): The festival of breaking the fast. The first festival of the Islamic year. The second is Eid al Adha. The Eid al Fitr signifies the end of Ramadan, which means that it starts on the first day of the tenth month of the Islamic lunar calendar. In Saudi Arabia it is celebrated for ten days by the government, although in the private sector many observe it for the traditional three days. It is the closest Muslim holiday to Christmas in that it is a time to give alms to the poor and needy and a time to appreciate past and present blessings with family and friends.

Hajj (Haj): The Fifth Pillar of Faith. Each Muslim (unless physically unable) is required at least once in his lifetime to make a pilgrimage to Mecca where he will perform certain rituals. The Hajj is from the eighth to the tenth day of the twelfth month of the Islamic calendar; since this calendar is lunar, the Hajj sometimes occurs in summer, sometimes in winter. At the end of Hajj is Eid Al Adha (Festival of Sacrifice). About two million Muslims perform the Hajj every year; many arrive in Mecca a month or more before Hajj starts, and many stay several weeks or more after it ends.

Islam: The religion founded by Muhammad. There are about 1.3 billion Muslims in the world. All Muslims would accept the following **Five Articles of Faith** and **Five Pillars of Faith**. In some presentations of these Articles and Pillars, the number is greater than five, but those given below are essential.

The Five Articles of Faith are:
1. Allah is the only one true God and Muhammad is his Prophet.
2. Angels exist and do reveal themselves to humans.
3. The Books of God are: the Torah of Moses, the Psalms of David, Gospel of Jesus, and the Quran. Only the Quran contains Allah's unadulterated truth.
4. The six greatest prophets who have been messengers of Allah are: Adam, Noah, Abraham, Moses, Jesus, and Muhammad who is the greatest and last prophet.
5. The Last Day will be a day of resurrection and judgment. Those who have been faithful will go to Paradise; those who have not will go to Hell.

The Five Pillars of Faith are:
1. One must say, "There is no God but Allah, and Muhammad is his prophet.
2. One must pray five times a day: upon rising, noon, midafternoon, evening, and before sleeping.

3. One must give alms to the poor and needy, one-fortieth of one's income.
4. One must fast during Ramadan from sunrise to sunset.
5. In a Muslim's lifetime at least one pilgrimage must be made to Mecca.

In the West there is a clear distinction between a country's legal code and their religious practices and obligations. In the United States this is embodied in the First Amendment. In Muslim countries this distinction is almost totally absent, since the laws devised by their religious leaders are the laws that the people live by. Laws that do not have a religious source or the approval of religious leaders are regarded, at best, as no law at all, at worst, as sinful.

Islam has no absolute religious leader—no pope. There is no universally accepted religious hierarchy. A Muslim is free to have his own opinions regarding his religious creed as long as they do not exceed the "sacred limits." However, different sects define these limits differently.

Muhammad, the Prophet (c. 570–632 CE): The founder of Islam. Born in Mecca (Makkah). Had his first revelation from the Archangel Jibril (Gabriel) when he was forty. Other revelations followed for twenty-three years. These recorded revelations became the Quran (Qur'an, Koran), which expresses the will of God (Allah). Muhammad's purpose was to restore the worship of the one true God as it was taught by the Prophet Ibrahim (Abraham) and to formulate a moral, ethical, legal, and social system for all mankind. He did not claim to be divine.

Quran (Qur'an, Koran): The recorded word of Allah as revealed to Mohammad by the Archangel Gabriel. The Quran is the literal word of Allah and (so far) Allah's final word. It is the Holy Book of Islam. It contains 114 chapters and 6,236 verses (excluding 112 unnumbered verses). The chapters are not arranged in the order in which they were believed to be revealed, but in another order (from the longest chapter to the shortest), which too came from revelation.

Ramadan: The month of fasting for all Muslims. It is the Third Pillar of the Five Pillars of Islam, and hence it is a religious obligation—a form of worship. It is the ninth month of the Islamic lunar calendar (which starts anytime from early September to early November). Each day during the month of Ramadan, from sunrise to sunset, Muslims abstain from food, drink, smoking, and sex. It is usual to eat a small meal before sunrise and to eat dinner after sunset prayers. During the month of Ramadan, Muslims try to read (or listen to) as much of the Quran as they can—the whole book if possible. At the end of the month the celebration of Eid ul Fitr (Festival of Breaking the Fast) occurs—one of the two celebrations in Saudi Arabia, the other is Eid al Adha. There is no fasting on this day.

Shiites (Shi'as) and **Sunnis:** Roughly 90 percent of the Muslims in the world are Sunnis. The Shiites are predominate in Iraq and Iran, and large numbers are found in Syria, Lebanon, India, Pakistan, and parts of Central Asia, but in Saudi Arabia they are the minority (5 to 10 percent) and for the most part are excluded from the government. The official religion in Saudi Arabia is Wahhabism.

The difference between the Sunnis and Shiites is about the qualifications of the successors to the Prophet Muhammad. When Muhammad died his father-in-law, Abu Bakr, became the first caliph, and the Sunnis accept this succession. The Shiites, who believe that it was Muhammad's intent to appoint his son-in-law Ali ibn Abu Talib, reject Abu Bakr as first caliph. Shiites hold that only the descendants of Muhammad's daughter, Fatima, and her husband Ali have the right to claim succession. There are many other more subtle, doctrinal differences between these two groups.

Wahhabism: Wahhabi was a derogatory term used to refer to a Salafi. It is commonly used now and no longer has this connotation. The term comes from the founder of the movement, Muhammad ibn Abd al Wahhab (1703–1792), born in what is now Saudi Arabia, where it is the official religion. Those who are called Wahhabis believe in the way of "Salaf as-Salih," which means the "the correctness of the predecessors." The reasoning is that those who lived at the time when Muhammad had his revelations or soon after were more likely to correctly interpret them than succeeding generations. It is a reform movement, rejecting later interpretations of the Quran, especially those that attempt to alter social and family relationships to make them more acceptable to Western countries. They are monotheists and consider praying to any prophet, saint, or angel to be polytheistic. They regard Christians as polytheists, since Christians believe that Jesus is divine. They are against annual celebrations of dead saints, including the prophet's birthday. They oppose any change in the form of worship, ban pictures and photographs of humans, are against singing and dancing, and frown on loud laughter and weeping. It is a conservative, puritanical movement. The Wahhabis, loosely speaking, may be regarded as a two and a half century old purification movement of the Sunnis. The Wahhabis have little regard for the less conservative Sunnis, and many of them regard the Shiites as polytheists and thus non-Muslim.

ANNOTATED BIBLIOGRAPHY

There are many books about Saudi Arabia. Of those that I (the editor) have read, the ones below I have found to be most helpful in understanding the politics, religion, and culture of Saudi Arabia and its relationship to the United States.

Abukhalil, As`ad. *The Battle for Saudi Arabia: Royalty, Fundamentalism, and Global Power.* New York: Seven Stories Press, 2004.

As`ad Abukhalil was born in Lebanon. He has a PhD in comparative politics from Georgetown University and is a professor of political science at California State University, Stanislaus. The author examines the relationship between Saudi Arabia and the United States and gives more than adequate evidence to justify his criticism of both countries.

After the introduction, the chapter headings are:

> The Paradoxes of Saudi Arabia
> What is Saudi Arabia?
> Wahhabiyyah
> Founding and Evolution of State
> Saudi Evolution of Da`wa: After the
>   Oil Boom
> The Question of Women
> Opposition and Inhumane (Lack of) Rights
> US-Saudi Relations
> Conclusion

Well worthwhile reading. More critical than Bradley's book.

Bradley, John R. *Saudi Arabia Exposed: Inside a Kingdom in Crisis.* New York: Palgrave Macmillam, 2005.

John Bradley lived in Saudi Arabia for two years where he worked as a journalist. He speaks Arabic fluently.

Bradley writes with intimate knowledge of the restlessness of the middle class Saudi youth, of the regional divisions within the kingdom, and of the corruption of the Al-Saud royal family. He gives an in-depth look at the forces that are changing Saudi Arabia. It's a change that may come in the near future, suddenly, and with explosive impact.

Gray, Seymour. *Beyond the Veil: The Adventures of an American Doctor in Saudi Arabia*. New York: Harper & Row, 1983.

In 1975 Dr. Gray was appointed chairman of the Department of Medicine at King Faisal Specialist Hospital and Research Center in Riyadh. Here he treated members of the royal family, women as well as men, becoming close friends to several of them. These friendships gave him the unique opportunity to share certain aspects of their lives that would otherwise be barred to outsiders.

From the inside of the dustcover:

Almost every aspect of life is made vivid by stories about love and marriage; crime and punishment; unbelievable wealth and corruption; sex, Saudi Arabian style; religion; predestination; the Saudi concept of life and death; and of course, the struggle of Saudi Arabian women to gain independence and a certain degree of equality in a completely male-dominated country.

An interesting book that gives the reader a sense of the life and culture of Saudi Arabia.

Lippman, Thomas W. *Understanding Islam: An Introduction to the Muslim World*. Second revised edition. New York: A Meridian Book, 1995.

For information on the author see the next entry.

If you want to understand Islam and only have time to read one book on the topic—this is the one. This book covers the origin of Islam as well as its basic beliefs and practices. Also covered are the law and government of Islam, its expansion, its schisms, and the modern Islamic community. The differences between the various Islamic countries are explained, and sufficient detail is given throughout the book, so that the reader has an understanding of how a Muslim's religion pervades his life as well as his world outlook.

Lippman, Thomas W. *Inside the Mirage: America's Fragile Partnership with Saudi Arabia.* Boulder, CO: Westview Press, 2004.

Thomas Lippman is an Adjunct Scholar for the Public Policy Center. He has been a reporter and editor for the *Washington Post* and covered the Iraq war for the *Post* in 2003. He is a member of the Council on Foreign Relations and the author of several books on the Middle East.

A very readable book. Explains how certain American citizens won the favor of the Saudi king before the discovery of oil, which helped to develop a Saudi-American partnership. The history of this relationship is told in part by the Americans who brought the industries and technical know-how to the kingdom.

The author gives the details of the history of this partnership, up to 2004, in an engaging way, letting the pioneers of these nascent businesses tell their stories in their own words. Unlike many recent books on Saudi Arabia, the author avoids a judgmental tone.

Schwartz, Stephen. *The Two Faces of Islam: The House of Saud from Tradition to Terror.* New York: Doubleday, 2002.

From the inside of the dustcover:

Stephen Schwartz is an author and journalist who has been Washington bureau chief for the Jewish *Forward* and an editorial writer for the Voice of America. Prior to that he was an interfaith activist in Bosnia-Herzegovina and Kosovo.

The life of Muhammad and the birth of Islam are covered in the first few chapters. The bulk of the book covers the rise of Wahhabism, its doctrines, its differences from traditional Islamic beliefs, its relation to the Saud royal family, and its detrimental influence in the world today.

Clearly written. Contains information not readily available elsewhere.

Wells, Colin. *The Complete Idiot's Guide to Understanding Saudi Arabia.* New York: Alpha, a member of Penguin Group, 2003.

Despite the title, a good book for giving an overall understanding of the history, religion, legal system, politics, and culture of Saudi Arabia. Colin Wells has written several books on the Middle East as well as numerous articles on this area.

This book will give the reader the history of Saudi Arabia, which includes the rise of Islam and the Saud family. It explains the difference between the Sunnis and the Shiite and describes the principles and practice of Wahhabism. Covered as well is the discovery of oil and Saudi Arabia's relation to the United States. A chapter is devoted to the Persian Gulf War and a section to 9/11 and the terrorists. There is a chapter on royal family and one on vital statistics, which covers demographics, Saudi economy, and the foreign workers. Everyday life for the average Saudi is described (including business, marriage, divorce, and children) as well as their cultural attitudes.

There are four appendices:

A. FAQs About Saudi Arabia
B. An Arabian Timeline from Before the Birth of Islam to the Present
C. Magazines, Websites, and Books
D. Glossary

Made in the USA
Lexington, KY
13 December 2013